STEREO
VIEWS
An Illustrated History and Price Guide

STEREO VIEWS

AN ILLUSTRATED HISTORY
AND PRICE GUIDE

JOHN S. WALDSMITH

W·H WALLACE-HOMESTEAD BOOK COMPANY   *Radnor, Pennsylvania*

Published in Radnor, Pennsylvania 19089, by Wallace-Homestead,
a division of Chilton Book Company

Designed by Adrianne Onderdonk Dudden
Manufactured in the United States of America

Library of Congress Cataloging in Publication Data

Waldsmith, John S.
    Stereo views : a collector's guide with prices for vintage stereo
views, tru-vues, view-masters, and other 3-D visual collectibles /
by John S. Waldsmith.
        p.   cm.
      ISBN 0-87069-598-3 (hc)—ISBN 0-87069-578-9 (pb)
      1. Stereoscopic views—Catalogs.   I. Title.
    TR199.W26   1991
    778.4—dc20   90-50638
                                                              CIP

1 2 3 4 5 6 7 8 9 0   0 9 8 7 6 5 4 3 2 1

Dedicated in loving memory of my grandparents,
Walter T. and Bertha Poppenger
and Herbert and Gertrude Waldsmith

CONTENTS

PREFACE

I began collecting stereo views in 1971. At that time I did not know any other collectors and there was no national organization for me to contact and join. My collection filled a small wood box, which I quickly outgrew. My stereo views expanded into an inexpensive four-drawer cabinet. By 1973 I had outgrown this form of storage and had no real idea what I was doing. I collected everything I could find, and I was thrilled with my color lithograph of the moon and my "set" of the French Cook by Keystone View Company. In the spring of 1973, I made contact with six other collectors within a few months—a life-changing event. I obtained a copy of William Culp Darrah's *Stereo Views: A History of Stereographs in America and Their Collection* (which was privately printed in 1964). I suddenly discovered the meaning and value of my hobby, and I could not get enough. However, written information was limited to *Stereo Views* and a few articles in magazines.

In the summer of 1973, twenty-five other collectors and I received a letter from Richard and Francine Russack, asking us if we wanted to form a national collector's club. I had grown up in a collecting family. My grandfather Walter T. Poppenger had been a leading stamp collector who also had developed an outstanding collection of seashells after retiring to Florida. Collecting was in my blood—and it is something that does not go away.

I wrote back to the Russacks and stated that I was ready to be an enthusiastic member of the new club. My main interest was in the production of the proposed newsletter. I wanted an information publication with articles about stereo photographers and the events they documented. I became the managing editor of the National Stereoscopic Association's publication, *Stereo World*, and served in this position until 1981, when I became a full-time dealer.

Over the years I have met hundreds of interesting people who always were willing to share information about stereoscopy. Many of them have played a role in this book, and I thank all of them for their knowledge and encouragement.

Special thanks go to Sheldon Aronowitz, Walt Burton, C. Wesley Cowan, John Dennis, Mike Griffith, Andrew Griscom, Bill and Estelle Marder, Roger Nazeley, Harry Newman, Russell Norton, Dick and Pam Oestreicher, Peter Palmquist, Mary Ann and Wolfgang Sell, Walter Sigg, T. K. "Tex" Treadwell, Len and Jean Walle, and Jack and Pat Wilburn.

John Weiler kindly allowed me to examine his fine collection and select key illustrations for this book. He provided a great deal of constructive advice.

Gordon D. Hoffman, stereo collector extraordinaire, provided much information and advice and allowed me to look through his outstanding collection. He also answered many questions from his vast experience in the hobby. My thanks to Gordon and his wife, Betty.

Finally, this book would not be possible without the support of my parents, Bob and Lois Waldsmith. My father proofed the text and my mother compiled much of the data for the price guide. They always were there with helpful suggestions and encouragement.

STEREO
VIEWS
An Illustrated History and Price Guide

1

HISTORY OF STEREOGRAPHY

From the early 1850s to the late 1930s, millions of stereoscopic photographs (stereographs or stereo views) were made by commercial and amateur photographers. At the height of their popularity in the late 1890s, a stereoscope and a selection of views could be found in nearly every middle- and upper-income home in the United States. Looking into a stereoscope at a scene captured in detail and depth creates a special magic. It is as though you were there. The development of the stereoscope must have been a visual revelation to the Victorian gentry of the 1850s, and it is understandable how stereoscopes became a parlor entertainment craze. Suddenly one is transported to exotic lands featuring banyan trees, pyramids, or rugged mountain cliffs. A person in Illinois could look along a street in New York City and feel a part of the crowd on the sidewalk. After a trip to Florida, a tourist could show his neighbor in New Hampshire the palmettoes and palms along the Ocklawaha River south of St. Augustine. The stereoscope opened a new visual world to a public limited by woodcut illustrations in books and newspapers.

The principles of stereoscopy generally were known in the early 1800s, but no one had been able to invent a device to prove the theories of binocular vision. In 1838, thirty-six-year-old Sir Charles Wheatstone published "Contributions to the Physiology of Vision—on Some Remarkable, and Hitherto Unobserved, Phenomena of Binocular Vision," a paper presented to the British Royal Society. He demonstrated that the mind perceives an object in three dimensions because each eye receives a slightly different view. Wheatstone devised the word *stereograph,* from the Greek words *stereo* (solid) and *graph* (I look at), to define this phenomenon. He prepared drawings of single objects seen by each eye and devised a viewing instrument (stereoscope) of angled mirrors. (Wheatstone had begun his experiments into binocular vision in 1832, thus both the 1832 and 1838 dates are found in modern histories.) In 1839, soon after the introduction of Henry Fox Talbot's photographic process (Daguerre had introduced the daguerreotype in France the same year), a Mr. Collen and Talbot made stereoscopic Talbotypes for Wheatstone. Stereoscopy was born, although it would be more than ten years before a practical instrument for viewing the stereographs would be introduced.

The first major public introduction to stereoscopy occurred at the 1851 International Exhibition of London, England. The making

Stereo-Travel, #1, "Tugging at their ballast before start. Balloon Races, June 5, 1909, Indianapolis Motor Speedway." Note the stereo photographer at right foreground. Nearly every major event, personality and interesting scenic vista was stereo-photographed from the 1850s to the present. (Gordon D. Hoffman Collection)

of stereographs as daguerreotypes and calotypes (Talbotypes) had been accomplished on a limited basis, mostly as experiments of the new photographic processes introduced in 1839. But the London Exhibition held at the Crystal Palace was the first time large numbers of people had access to these miniature treasures. The reason for the interest was the ease of viewing provided by Sir David Brewster's newly invented "improved" binocular-type stereoscope. This device duplicated the normal $2\frac{1}{2}''$ separation between the eyes by placing a pair of lenses side by side in a small box with a lid at the top to admit light and a slot at the opposite end for inserting the mounted pair of stereoscopic images.

Thousands of Brewster-type binocular stereoscopes were sold, which created a demand for hundreds of thousands of views. The market already was well established in Europe when William and Frederick Langenheim introduced their stereo views to America in 1854.

Working from a studio in Philadelphia, the Langenheim Brothers stereo-photographed scenes of Niagara Falls, the Catskills, Philadelphia, Washington, D.C., and New York City.

By 1859 stereomania was in full blossom in the United States, with local photographers and major publishers making scenes for a hungry public. Collectors and amateur stereo photographers began to systematically assemble collections and maintain regular correspondence. Most collectors were professional men: doctors, lawyers, publishers, merchants, and others. They returned from their "grand tours" of Europe with groups of views of the great cities and impressive scenery. One of these men was Dr. Oliver Wendell Holmes.

Holmes was a noted physician, poet and essayist whose contributions were published regularly in the *Atlantic Monthly*. He was mystified with this new phenomenon and was eloquent in his praise of stereoscopy. In an 1861 *Atlantic Monthly* he described Edward Antho-

Langenheim Bros., Glass view of "Genesee Falls & Mills, Rochester, N.Y.," 1854.

Langenheim Bros., "Capitol at Washington, D.C.," 1856. Ivory mount with blindstamp along right margin. (Gordon D. Hoffman Collection)

ny's instantaneous (frozen action) stereographs of New York City's Broadway:

What a wonder it is, this snatch at the central life of a mighty city as it rushed by in all its multitudinous complexity of movement! Hundreds of objects in this picture could be identified in a court of law by the owners. There stands Car No. 33 of the Astor House and 27th Street Fourth Avenue line. The old woman would miss an apple from that pile which you see glistening on her stand. The young man whose back is to us could swear to the pattern of his shawl. . . . What a fearfully suggestive picture! It is a leaf torn from the book of God's recording angel. What if the sky is one great concave mirror which reflects the picture of all our doings, and photographs every act on which it looks upon dead and living surfaces, so that to celestial eyes the stones on which we tread are written with our deeds, and the leaves of the forest are but undeveloped negatives where our summers stand self-recorded for transfer into the imperishable record? And what a metaphysical puzzle we have here in this simple-looking paradox! Is motion but a succession of rests? All is still in this picture of universal movement. . . . Yet the hurried day's life of Broadway will have been made up of just such stillness. Motion is as rigid as marble, if you only take a wink's worth of it at a time.

Holmes was swept up in the stereo view excitement and saw a need for a stereoscope for the masses that was lighter and cheaper than the cumbersome and expensive Brewster models then being offered. Holmes made a crude "skeleton" stereoscope from scraps of wood and showed the design to various people in Boston. He found an interested party in Joseph L. Bates, who had a small business in the sale of stereoscopes and views. Bates refined the Holmes design by adding the familiar sliding focusing stage with wire holders for the view. The Holmes-Bates stereoscope was an immediate success, and the lower cost brought stereoscopy to the masses. Although inexpen-

E. & H. T. Anthony, #2975, "Down Broadway, from below Wall St.," from their instantaneous series of New York City. Note the buildings are decorated for Lincoln's funeral, dating this view as April 1865.

sive, the stereoscope was confined almost entirely to middle- and upper-income families until the 1880s, when further price reductions, competition, mail-order, and door-to-door sales began.

The stereoscope became a fixture in the home, much like television is today. Like television, stereoscopes and views were relatively expensive for the first few decades. Independent stereo photographers gave way to large publishers who sent teams of photographers into the field. The stereo views were visual souvenirs of major tourist attractions. Therefore, views of Niagara Falls, Watkins Glen, Boston Public Garden, New York City's Central Park, and Philadelphia's Fairmount Park were popular subjects made in huge quantities. Consequently, stereo views of small towns and remote areas generally are less common today.

The early stereoscopic photographers often referred to themselves as artists, and indeed, many of them were artistic in their approach to stereoscopy. Just recently the art community has begun to appreciate these miniature studies for something more than visual curiosities or historic records. In time the collector recognizes the aesthetic quality of stereo views. A number of collectors are interested only in views that are fine examples of the stereoscopic art form.

Many fine examples can be found and often at reasonable prices. It is strongly recommended that all views be seen in a stereoscope before purchase and appreciated for composition, print quality and what is called "presentation." This presentation factor was a deliberate marketing ploy in the nineteenth century and is reflected in the style and color of the mounts, frame designs on the fronts, and back labels or imprints. Some of these mount designs become familiar to collectors, making the photographers as recognized for the mount as the view itself.

Excellent stereo photography actually is quite difficult, and one must admire the stereographer who worked without the aid of light meters and quick, flexible films yet produced excellent results. Working in the field making landscape studies was often a backbreaking chore. Before the 1880s the glass plates had to be prepared, exposed, and processed at the scene. It was not uncommon to make only a dozen glass negatives a day. The printing was done on sunny days and all mounting, which had to be precise, was done on rainy or cloudy days. Remarkably, poor mounting of stereo pairs is the exception rather than the rule. A scratched or cracked negative could ruin the pair, destroying forever the captured moment.

Proper composition is crucial to a fine stereoscopic image. From the "deep" interiors of cathedrals by G. W. Wilson (1860s) to the blazing light effects in the View-Master "KISS" packet (1970), the three-dimensional effect was the hook that made stereoscopy unique. Expert print quality with rich, even tones was the signature of the best stereo photographers. Views by Francis Bedford, Charles Bierstadt, J. J. Reilly, Eadweard Muybridge, Carleton E. Watkins, John P. Soule, Charles Weitfle and others are small visual gems that draw the viewer into the scene. The magic is the unmistakable experience felt by those who have taken the time to look at these works of art in a stereoscope.

The wide range of subject matter in stereo

Charles A. Zimmerman, "Chippewa Indian Deer Hunt, on Snow Shoes," an artistically composed view taken outside in winter, ca. 1870.

Potter & Bro., Mansfield, Ohio, Untitled view of church in Mansfield, ca. 1878. Note the clouds were added to the negative later, using a special overlay negative. Slow speeds of emulsions made cloud photography very difficult, as a result most nineteenth-century photos have milky white skies.

views is amazing. Nearly every geographic location has been stereo-photographed. Most commonly found are views of large metropolitan areas, natural wonders and resorts. Least common are stereo views of small towns, remote areas, and less picturesque parts of cities (such as slums). The exceptions are the many small-town photographers, especially in New England, who produced stereo views. Views of Newburyport, Massachusetts, Concord, New Hampshire, and Providence, Rhode Island, are relatively common. Views of Fort Wayne, Indiana, Pittsburgh, Pennsylvania, and Kankakee, Illinois, are very uncommon, especially prior to 1890.

The views presented very real indications of social and especially racial stereotyping, most particularly when African-Americans were depicted in stereographs. They were portrayed as not very bright, unclean, loving watermelon and chicken and prone to petty theft. The comic captions even used dialects (described by Frederick Douglass as "the plantation manner of speech") to enhance the humorous situations. Blacks occasionally were shown outside the comic realm as cotton pickers toiling in the fields or as workers loading barrels of molasses or bales of cotton at the levee. Some stereographs even show white persons posed in black face, minstrel-style, in comic situations. By today's racially aware standards, these stereographs seem embarrassing and pathetic, but they do represent the social attitudes of the time.

Seldom do we encounter stereographs of white poverty. A few undaunted photographers stereo-photographed the unpopular subjects of child labor, the northern urban ghetto and the dreadful working conditions in many factories. Were these photographers acting as social historians, with the intention of showing these social abuses, or were these sel-

H. C. White, #5010, "Git on quick Rastus,—he done got it mos' eat up." Typical black subject of kids playing in comic situation with caption in dialect.

dom-encountered views taken merely by chance? Certainly they are recognized today as being socially significant. We may never know the motivations that generated these views.

Stereographs of various modes of transportation are popular with many collectors. The rule of thumb is the further west the subject, the more uncommon it is to find. Thus a stereo view of a passenger train stopped on a trestle in New Hampshire is far more common than the same subject in Colorado or Utah.

Famous personalities, including all United States presidents from Lincoln to Bush, have been stereo-photographed. Lincoln stereo views sold during his lifetime or shortly afterward are eagerly sought by collectors. Less common are views of presidents Hayes, Garfield, Arthur and Harrison, with Arthur among the rarest. It is believed that President James Buchanan was stereo-photographed, but an example has not been found. Also uncommon are views of presidents Truman and Eisenhower on standard view mounts. All of the more recent presidents (including Eisenhower and Truman) have been stereo-photographed on View-Master or by amateurs. The most common presidents in stereo views are McKinley and Theodore Roosevelt. According to the files of the Library of Congress, there may exist more than 800 different stereo views of Teddy Roosevelt taken between 1898 and 1912.

News events such as wars, natural disasters, fires, festivals, expositions and the like are found in stereo views. Rare are reliably identified views of the Crimean War, the Italian revolutions of the 1850s, the San Francisco earthquake of 1868, and the original London Crystal Palace of 1851. Common are views of World War I, the San Francisco earthquake of 1906 and the 1904–1905 Louisiana Purchase Exposition in St. Louis.

The financial crash of 1873 sent the stereo view business into a decline. The demand for stereo views dropped dramatically and many local photographers ceased production or even went out of business. From this decline grew a trade in "pirated" or "copy" views. The copyright laws in the early 1870s were weak and unenforceable. These publishers simply copied existing views and placed cheap-quality prints on a low-quality card stock. This type of view undercut the major producers and caused them to issue a lower grade of views to meet the competition. The copy publishers flourished at one point, even sending stereo photographers to make original negatives to fill out a series of copies. As a result, some examples of better print quality can be found on these copy views.

The stereo view business began to come back in the 1880s thanks to door-to-door stereoscope sales. Companies, most notably Underwood and Underwood, sent teams of college students into communities and systematically canvased neighborhoods. Once a stereoscope and a sample of views were sold, another more experienced salesman would call on the customer to sell larger amounts. In the early 1890s these publishers began selling the customers entire series. Up to that time views were sold in sets of a dozen or a half dozen. As a result, when we find an unpicked lot, it usually contains 24, 36 or maybe 144 views. Underwood

Typical pirated copy view. Note the original view, an English Classic comic, had domed or arched prints. Original ca. 1860; this copy ca. 1890.

Whiting View Co., #314, "East Corridor, Congressional Library, Washington, D.C.," 1905. Typical shot by a stereo photographer using a long corridor or hallway for enhanced 3-D effect.

and Underwood introduced their seventy-two-view "Tour Around the World" in a flip-top box in 1897. The success of the boxed set was immediate, and Underwood and Underwood expanded to boxed sets of individual countries. Around 1900 they introduced the "book box," which held one hundred views and broke with the tradition of selling in dozens. The book boxes were sold on the merit of simple storage among the family's permanent library of books. A "system" was sold that included guide books, often with maps, written by noted authorities. This mass production and selling method caused the demise of the small photographers and publishers.

By 1900 the stereo view market was dominated by six major producers: Underwood and Underwood, Keystone View Company, B. W. Kilburn, H. C. White, Griffith and Griffith and C. H. Graves's Universal Photo Art Company. Smaller companies such as International View Company; Universal View Company; Whiting View Company; Berry, Kelley and Chadwick; and Stereo-Travel Company typically existed less than a decade and eventually were absorbed by one of the larger companies. The competition was fierce. By 1921 Keystone View Company had emerged as the leader in the stereo view market, having purchased the negatives and remaining stocks of their competitors. Until the Great Depression began in 1929, Keystone View Company sold their stereo "system" in large numbers to schools, libraries, churches, and private individuals. Their main item was the "Tour of the World," which was sold primarily in a 600-view format and eventually was expanded to a 1200-view set that included a metal "Telebinocular" viewer. A deluxe version was offered with a lighted viewer on a metal stand.

The depression saw the decline of stereo views. Other popular markets, such as radio, motion pictures and pictorial magazines, had emerged. Keystone View Company concentrated on the educational aspects of stereo views, and even with a financial depression they

T. W. Ingersoll, #1387, "Characteristic Street Scene in Modern City of Luxor, Egypt," a typical color lithograph (printed view). There is very little collector interest in lithos—such views usually sell for less than a dollar each.

Keystone View Co., #17398, "Zeppelin ZR-3 Acquired by the United States from Germany." The United States Navy airship Los Angeles.

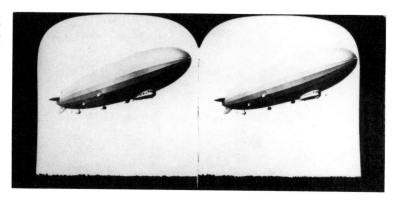

produced thousands of stereoscopes and possibly hundreds of thousands of stereo views in the 1930s. Keystone remained in business and made stereo views until 1964. They continued into the 1970s as a manufacturer of eye-testing equipment and eventually were purchased by Mast Industries of Davenport, Iowa. The huge collection of glass negatives sat in a dusty vault and eventually was donated, along with the collection of file prints, to the California Museum of Photography of the University of California at Riverside. In 1990 the Keystone-Mast Collection was moved into a new research facility in downtown Riverside, California.

Stereo view collecting has been pursued actively by enthusiastic individuals almost from the time the first commercial views reached the market in the 1850s. As previously mentioned, Dr. Oliver Wendell Holmes was an early promoter of stereoscopy and probably the first major collector in the United States. President Rutherford B. Hayes also had a fine collection. In the last century and the first third of this

century, stereo view collecting basically was confined to wealthy individuals who traveled and purchased views of personal interest.

After 1930 a new generation of collectors emerged who saw the vast historical importance of stereo views. Collectors such as Lorraine Dexter, William Culp Darrah, Earl Moore, Dr. Guy Howe, Paul Wing, T. K. Treadwell, Ron Lowden and Gordon D. Hoffman, to name a few, began a regular collecting relationship and shared their knowledge. William C. Darrah published *Stereo Views: A History of Stereographs in America and Their Collection* in 1964. The Darrah book set the stage for the next generation of collectors, including myself. In 1974 the National Stereoscopic Association (NSA) was founded, and for the first time collectors were united and could share information through the NSA magazine *Stereo World*. William C. Darrah's *The World of Stereographs* followed in 1977. Both Darrah books are now out of print and the printing plates have been destroyed.

Charles A. Zimmerman, "Scene at Indian Payment—Odanah, Wis.," ca. 1870s. Typical of the stereo view as a visual historic record. (Gordon D. Hoffman Collection)

Stereo view collecting has seen rapid growth since the early 1970s. Over time, stereo view collectors have developed techniques and terms that might seem a bit complicated to the newcomer. A glossary has been included in this guide and should be consulted often until one is familiar with terms used in this collecting field.

The following pages will show you how to start a stereo view collection, including where to obtain views and how to store, organize and enjoy them. Here you can see what is meant by a square-cornered mount, a copy view, a book-boxed set, curved mounts, flat mounts and lithos. Techniques also are explained.

Today, stereo views are a recognized collectible. New enthusiasts enter the hobby each day and the supply of stereo views has begun to dwindle. There are still "finds" to be made, and new information comes forth through communication and research among collectors. This guide will help answer the many questions of new collectors as well as provide a handy reference for the advanced collector.

2

COLLECTING STEREO VIEWS AND STEREOSCOPIC VIEWERS

COLLECTING STEREO VIEWS

Getting Started

Most collectors of stereo views usually come from other areas of collecting. Many have collected, or still collect, postcards, trade cards, photos, stamps and other visual items. For the postcard collector, stereo views take them back fifty years before postcards became popular, thus the backward progression in time is natural.

Collectors may obtain their first views from family or friends, purchase them with a stereoscope at an estate auction or make a purchase at an antique show. After obtaining a small collection, they realize the necessity of specialization. Millions of stereo views were produced from the 1850s to the late 1930s, but even with that fact in mind some collectors limit their collecting too much and eventually become discouraged.

I was contacted a few years ago by a collector who requested stereo views of famous western lawmen and outlaws. Such stereo views were made but are very rare and not generally offered for sale on a regular basis. I passed this information along to him. After several months of hunting, he had not been able to obtain any of the stereo views in this category. Therefore, it must be understood from the beginning that one may face limitations in collecting stereo views. The views are out there, but it will take time and persistence to build a specialized collection. That same collector could have expanded his interest to collect law enforcement views in general. In this broader category he would find views of prisons, policemen in major cities, local jails and even hangings.

I recommend that new collectors try to obtain views of subjects that relate to their own geographic area or occupation. A civil engineer has built a fine collection documenting bridge construction. There is a geologist with a fine collection of views of caves. A Florida collector has been collecting views of his state for a number of years. These and many other collectors have developed interesting and valuable collections by being persistent and always on the hunt.

The Hunt

Much of the fun of this hobby is the hunt. I have spent countless hours searching in antiques stores and flea markets and standing in the rain at estate auctions trying to keep the views I want from being ruined.

There are a number of areas to explore in your quest to enlarge and improve your collection. First, start at home. Ask older relatives and friends if they still have their family collections of views and stereoscopes. Check your local antiques and secondhand stores. Leave your name and check back frequently. I know one collector who visits monthly about twenty shops within one hundred miles of his home. By now the dealers all know he is an active and interested collector.

Watch your newspapers for antiques shows and flea markets in your area. These events are often good sources for contacting dealers outside your area.

The National Stereoscopic Association

Join the National Stereoscopic Association. The NSA is a nonprofit educational organization. They publish *Stereo World,* an excellent magazine, six times per year and also issue a membership directory. Check the "Events" section of *Stereo World* for shows featuring photographica. In the last few years most of these shows have concentrated on dealers who offer more modern photo equipment, but a number of dealers who specialize in photographic images, including stereo views, also appear at these shows.

Check the NSA Membership Directory for members with a *D* after their name. Many will offer stereo views by mail or inform you of auctions or direct mail listings.

Attend the NSA's annual convention and regional meetings. The location and date of the convention are publicized well in advance so that you can make plans. The convention is the "Super Bowl" of stereo view collecting, with more than one hundred tables filled with thousands of views for sale. Also visit the Oliver Wendell Holmes Stereoscopic Research Library in the Warner Library of Eastern College in St. Davids, Pennsylvania.

To contact the NSA write to

National Stereoscopic Association
P.O. Box 14801
Columbus, OH 43214

Send a self-addressed stamped envelope (S.A.S.E.) when requesting information.

Another organization, the View-Master and Tru-Vue Collectors Association, is new and publishes a newsletter. Their address is

View-Master and Tru-Vue Collectors Association
P.O. Box 47891
Minneapolis, MN 55447

Dealers

The following are people who have offered stereoscopic collectibles for sale in recent years. There are very few full-time dealers, as most are collectors who will offer a listing of duplicate or unwanted items on an irregular basis. All dealers listed are members of the National Stereoscopic Association and are believed to be reliable and fair.

Marvin A. Balick
5900 Kennett Pike
Centreville, DE 19807

Dealer in photographs and stereo views.

James G. Becker
4 Plains Dr.
Walden, NY 12586

Stereo views.

David Belcher
231 S. Main St.
Orange, MA 01364

Dealer in antique images, stereo views and literature.

Bennett Studio
215 Broadway
Box 145
Wisconsin Dells, WI 53965

They still sell original uncirculated Bennett stereo views.

David Berenson
32 Colwell Ave.
Brighton, MA 02135

Larry Berke
28 Marksman Ln.
Levittown, NY 11756

Stereo views, nineteenth- and twentieth-century photographica.

Edward J. Cohen
Box 211
Bristol, CT 06010

Dealer in nineteenth- and twentieth-century photographica and stereo views.

A. Verner Conover
10907 Orchard St.
Fairfax, VA 22030

Dealer of stereo views.

C. Wesley Cowan
2125 Sinton Ave.
Cincinnati, OH 45206

Stereo views and nineteenth-century images.

John S. Craig
Box 1637
Torrington, CT 06790

Full-time dealer in photographica, stereo views, View-Master and Tru-Vue and other items.

Howard C. Daitz
Box 530
Old Chelsea Station
New York, NY 10011

Dealer in pre-1880s stereo views, related books and photographica.

Robert G. Duncan
Box 382
Holyoke, MA 01041

Dealer of antique photo images and stereo views.

William G. Eloe
10401 Grosvenor Pl. #315
Rockville, MD 20852

Stereo views, nineteenth century, American West.

Michael G. Fairley
17430 Ballinger Way NE
Seattle, WA 98155

Dealer of stereo views, photos and postcards.

Bryan W. Ginns
152 E. 84th St.
New York, NY 10028

Stereo views, viewers, and cameras.

Larry Gottheim
33 Orton Ave.
Binghamton, NY 13905

Stereo views and other early images.

Michael W. Griffith
4316 Hale Dr.
Lilburn, GA 30247

Stereo views.

Theodore L. Hake
Hake's Americana and Collectibles
Box 1444
York, PA 17405

Mail/phone bid auctions often feature stereo views, Tru-Vue and View-Master items.

Paul M. Hertzmann
Box 40447
San Francisco, CA 94140

Nineteenth- and twentieth-century photos and stereo views.

Gordon D. Hoffman
918 East 4th St. Road #206
Fond Du Lac, WI 54935

Dealer of stereo views, Tru-Vue, View-Master and more.

Hollywood Stereo
Box 7331
Burbank, CA 91510

Supplier of reproduction stereo views in 35mm slide format.

Hilde and Leon Jacobson
Box 6128
Syracuse, NY 13217

Dealer of stereo views, viewers and other photographica.

Robert Joki
612 Lake Ave.
Saratoga Springs, NY 12866

Photographica and stereo views.

Lawrence T. Jones III
Box 2084
Austin, TX 78768

Nineteenth-century images, especially Civil War and old West stereo views.

George H. Kirkman
Box 24468
Los Angeles, CA 90024

Vintage stereo cameras and catalogs.

Krainik Gallery
P.O. Box 6206
Falls Church, VA 22046

Appraiser of stereo views and early photo images.

Robert F. Kroeger
The Raven Antiques
Box 433
Plymouth, NH 03264

Stereo views and stereoscopes plus other photo items.

Bill Lee
8658 S. Gladiator Way
Sandy, UT 84094

Stereo views.

Lewis Lehr
444 E. 86 St.
New York, NY 10028

Dealer, wants filled, collections purchased.

Frederick S. Lightfoot
Box A-F
Greenport, NY 11944

Stereo views.

Ronald D. Lowden, Jr.
314 Chestnut Ave.
Narberth, PA 19072

Stereo views.

David Margolis
Box 2042
Santa Fe, NM 87501

Stereo views, books, prints, photos and ephemera.

Chum Martin
47 Bishoplea Rd.
Claremont, Capetown 7700 South Africa
Dealer in modern Holmes-type stereoscopes.

Roger Alan May
Box 1271
Grass Valley, CA 95945
Publisher of 3-D comic art and anaglyph comic books.

Tim and Monica McIntyre
137 Nile St.
Stratford, Ontario, Canada N5A 4E1
Stereo views.

Andrew and Dalia Miller
P.O. Box 492
Corte Madera, CA 94925
View-Master and stereo views.

Larry Moskovitz
P.O. Box 13151
Oakland, CA 94661
Stereo views.

Lyman and Renee Moss
900 Bay Dr. #125
Miami Beach, FL 33141
Stereo views.

Roger T. Nazeley
4921 Castor Ave.
Philadelphia, PA 19124
View-Master.

Jack L. Nelson
1693 Robertson Ave.
Galesburg, IL 61401
Stereo views, antique photos and American Western books.

Harry L. Newman
48 Summit Rd.
Murray Hill, NJ 07974
Boxed sets of stereo views.

Russell Norton
Box 1070
New Haven, CT 06504
Stereo views and photographica. Storage sleeves.

Dick and Pam Oestreicher
4025 Saline Street
Pittsburgh, PA 15217
Stereo views and photographica.

Graham Pilecki
6910 Bristol Dr.
Berkeley, CA 94705
Stereo views and equipment.

Harry Poster
Box 1883
S. Hackensack, NJ 07606
Used 3-D cameras, viewers, projectors, accessories, Realist and View-Master formats.

Ken Prag
Box 531
Burlingame, CA 94011
Stereo views.

Al Raymond
14 Elm, Box 509
Richfield Springs, NY 13439
Stereo views.

Reel 3-D Enterprises, Inc.
Susan Pinsky and David Starkman
Box 2368
Culver City, CA 90231
Slide and print viewers, 3-D literature, slide mounts and storage systems.

Reels-West
21075 NW Quatama Rd.
Beaverton, OR 97006
View-Master reels.

Chuck Reincke
2141 Sweet Briar Rd.
Tustin, CA 92680
Stereo views.

John Saddy
Jefferson Stereoptics
50 Foxborough Grove
London, Ontario, Canada N6K 4A8

Mary Ann and Wolfgang Sell
3752 Broadview Dr.
Cincinnati, OH 45208
View-Master.

Walter Sigg 3-D Entertainment
P.O. Box 208
Swartswood, NJ 07877
View-Master.

Talisman Press
Box 455
Georgetown, CA 95634
Western U.S. stereo views.

Greg Taylor
Stereo Photography Unlimited
1005 Barkwood Ct.
Safety Harbor, FL 34695
Stereo equipment.

Taylor-Merchant Corp.
212 W. 35th St.
New York, NY 10001
Stereoscope and stereo view reproductions, folding 35mm slide viewers.

Don Ulrich
1625 South 23rd St.
Lincoln, NE 68502
Stereo views and photographica.

John Waldsmith
P.O. Box 191
Sycamore, OH 44882
Stereo views and photographica, View-Master and Tru-Vue.

Wantagh Rare Book Co.
Box 605
Neversink, NY 12765
Stereo views and books.

Allen Weiner
80 Central Park West
New York, NY 10023
Stereo views and photographica.

Dave Wheeler
Box 796
Stevenson, CT 06491
Stereo views, stereoscopes and photographica.

Laurance Wolfe
Box 62
North Sutton, NH 03260
Stereo views and stereographica.

Worldwide Slides
7427 Washburn Ave. So.
Minneapolis, MN 55423
View-Master reels and packets.

Harvey S. Zucker
A Photographer's Place
133 Mercer St.
New York, NY 10012
Photographica, photo books and stereo view reproductions.

Now that you know where to search, let us discuss how best to spend your time and money to find what you wish to collect.

Bidding in Mail/Phone Auctions

Several dealers conduct regular or periodic mail/phone auction offerings of views. These may be simple, one-page lists in *Stereo World* up to large, illustrated catalogs with hundreds of lots. Read carefully the terms of sale or rules. Each sale is different and will have rules and conditions that are the responsibility of the bidder to understand. Note the closing date for bidding. This is the last day bids will be received. After looking through the listings, check those lots of interest. For bidding by mail, type or print your bids clearly. Recheck your bids to make sure you are bidding on the lots you want to purchase. Make a copy for your records. Mail your bids and allow time for them to reach the person conducting the sale. A letter from Los Angeles to New York City can take from two days to a week to get there.

The greatest concern for new collectors is knowing how much to bid. Most dealers place an estimated value on each lot. This is not a minimum bid unless the seller has stated that he is noting MB (minimum bids) in his terms

of sale. Bid what you feel the view is worth to you and what you are prepared to pay. Putting very low bids in an auction may get you some bargains, but in most cases such bids will be too low—especially on highly sought items. Some dealers will readjust high bids down to some amount higher than the next highest bid. This will be noted in the terms or rules. Bidding at or near the estimate will be successful about 50 percent of the time.

Telephone bidding is for the collector who has a strong interest in an item. This gives him a better-than-average chance of obtaining the lots he desires. It is best to place moderate mail bids and then follow up with a call on the last night of the sale. In most cases the dealer will inform you of the current high bid. It is customary to bid 10 percent above the current bid if you decide to bid. Bidding terms usually are spelled out in the terms of sale. Some active bidders will call back two or more times to check their bids, assuring them of reasonable success.

Bidders should understand that they must honor their bids with a purchase when they are successful. Failure to complete the purchase denies another collector having an opportunity to purchase and is costly to the dealer who thought he had the item sold. However, you may return a view that is not as it was described. Most dealers are happy to make refunds or adjustments when they fail to give a proper description. Also, auctions are not an approval service. Views should not be returned if found to be duplicates. Check your collection or send for a photocopy if there is any question of duplication. Common courtesy is the best rule.

FREE-VIEWING

Stereo views were meant to be viewed in a stereoscope and should be seen with the full three-dimensional effect. Of lesser value to collectors are views that are "flat" or have no 3-D effect. When searching at flea markets, shops or shows, it is not practical to carry a stereoscope, and the seller often does not have one to use. There is no greater disappointment than returning home from a sale to find a view is "flat." This problem can be eliminated by learning to free-view. Most people can free-view stereo views, but it seldom comes easily.

Official logo for National Stereoscopic Association Convention where President Eisenhower was honored as our only president who was an active stereo photographer. The logo is excellent for practicing free-viewing.

It is much like learning to ride a bike. Once you have fine-tuned the proper eye muscles, it becomes simple.

Free-viewing is looking at a stereoscopic image and seeing it in 3-D without using a viewer. This method is common in various scientific professions where stereoscopy is used for imaging.

Use a view with good stereo effect in a format smaller than the standard 3½″ by 7″ when first learning to free-view. The view at the top of this page is suitable for practicing free-viewing.

The idea is to see three images; the middle one will be in 3-D. Once you have mastered free-viewing, the outside images will be ignored and your brain will concentrate on the middle image. To adjust your eyes, focus on a distant object. If you could see your eyes, you would notice that they turn outward slightly to adjust to the distance. This is the position you want for free-viewing; in other words, you want to look through the near object (the stereo view) and direct your eyes out into space. Hold the view (the illustrated example or any good, smaller stereo view) from 14″ to 18″ in front of your face. Look into the distance and keep your eyes focused far away. Now bring the view into your line of sight either from below or above. At first you will see three images, and then they will dissolve into one (the center one). For an instant you will see the middle image in 3-D. Practice a few minutes each day until your eyes are strong enough

to hold their position and see the middle image in 3-D. As noted, this takes practice. Some people cannot do it; others do it on the first try. It took me several weeks; one evening it just "popped in." Free-viewing will not harm your eyes—in fact, it strengthens your eye muscles.

STEREOSCOPIC VIEWERS

There are hundreds of different stereoscope designs and variations. The value guide is given as a basic reference. Values vary geographically in the United States. Regular Holmes-Bates hand viewers may vary as much as 20 to 30 percent as one moves west. In recent years stereoscopes generally have sold for more on the West Coast than in the east.

Collecting Hints

Condition is the key in determining price. Undamaged wooden hood models are scarce and demand a premium price in burled or bird's-eye maple. All original parts increase the value. Lots of engraving adds 20 percent on metal hood models. Often the focusing slides and/or handles are missing; if so, deduct 75 percent. Lenses held in place by metal are better than those shimmed in by wood. The stereoscope must have a proper "pair" of lenses. If a lens is missing, the pair must be replaced. Magnification varied in these viewers; therefore, replacing just one lens will cause distortion and improper viewing.

History

The first stereo viewers, based on a design by Sir David Brewster (Brewster viewers), were made in England and France starting in 1851. They are uncommon in the United States. The Brewster viewer is a box with paired lenses at one end; a slot at the other end for inserting glass, and later paper, views; and a small door on top with a mirror to admit light. Brewster viewers were also made with a pedestal stand, but these are rare. The familiar table viewer with an aluminum or wooden hood was the joint invention in 1859–1860 of Dr. Oliver Wendell Holmes and Joseph Bates, a Boston photographer. This type of viewer also was made in a much scarcer pedestal model.

In hand viewers (Holmes-Bates models), four companies—Keystone, Griffith and Griffith, Underwood and Underwood, and H. C. White—produced viewers in large quantities between 1892 and 1908. The total number of viewers made in this period is in the hundreds of thousands. Keystone View Company dominated the market after 1908 with their aluminum hood "Monarch" viewer and all-metal Telebinocular.

In the late 1850s, a combination stereo viewer and picture magnifier was developed in France and eventually made in England and the United States into the 1890s. The instrument was called a Graphascope. It usually consisted of three major pieces and was folded for storage. When set up it had two round lenses for stereo viewing; a large round magnifying lens to view larger photographs; and a slide, often with opaque glass, for viewing stereo glass transparencies. The height was adjustable. They were made in a variety of woods including some with inlay and carving.

A rotary or cabinet viewer was made from the late 1850s to about 1870. Alexander Becker is the best known maker. The standing floor models hold several hundred slides, the table models hold fifty to one hundred (back to back).

From the late 1860s to the 1880s there were hundreds of different viewer designs. Models had folding wire view holders, collapsible parts

(Corte-Scope), pivoting lenses to view postcards (Sears' Stereographascope) and telescoping card holders. The hoods also became ornate with silver, nickel and pearl trimmed in velvet and rosewood.

Corte-Scope (1914), folding aluminum or metal, came in box with views	40–50.00
Hand (Holmes-Bates), common maker	
Aluminum hood, folding handle	45–75.00
Bird's-eye maple hood, folding handle	60–90.00
Walnut, screw on handle, velvet hood	60–90.00
Wide hood for people who wear glasses, dark brown or green metal hood	65–95.00
Hand, scissor device to focus, groove and wire device to hold card	100–125.00
Pedestal	
Foreign, French or English, nickel plated with velvet hood	350–450.00
Keystone, school and library type, black crinkle metal finish with light	75–85.00
Sculptoscope (Whiting), countertop style, penny operated	400–600.00
Stand, Holmes-Bates, paper, wood or metal hood	125–175.00

Holmes-Bates stereoscope on a wood stand, ca. 1870s–1880s. $125–175.

Table models

  Graphascope

    E. & H. T. Anthony (Lewis model), burled wood with large magnifying lens, folds down into attractive box with handles, ca. 1875 ——————— 400–600.00

    Folds flat, black enameled with wood cut inlay, ca. 1880s, various sizes ————————— 250–350.00

  Rotary, Alexander Backer, two pairs of lenses, holds fifty glass or one hundred back-to-back cards — 200–300.00

  Telebinocular, all-metal, binocular style, pebble or crinkle finish, excellent optics, came in booklike box, often with Keystone tour sets ———— 35–45.00

Note: Values are given for viewers in excellent condition. Deduct for missing parts, wear and soil.

3

CARE, CONDITION AND DATES OF STEREO VIEWS

ORGANIZATION AND STORAGE

Most collectors prefer to store their collections in some type of file boxes or drawers. An over-size men's shoe box usually will work for small collections but is not practical for larger collections and may actually harm the views you are trying to preserve because of the acidity of the cardboard. Some office supply stores stock or can order a file box suitable for stereo views. A collector might consider buying the file drawers currently sold to house videocassette tapes. They often can be found in major discount stores at reduced prices. Sturdy and stackable, these files can be purchased as the collection grows. For larger collections one might use the files designed for IBM computer cards. Most of these files were sold off to discount office supply houses in the 1970s, but they still can be found. The drawers are ideal for standard-size stereo views but will not accommodate the taller cabinet-size views. A few file cabinet makers offer files with 5" by 8" drawers or 5" by 16" double drawers. These are hard to find used, and the new cabinets are fairly expensive.

Store your collection in a dry place. In humid areas of the country, use of a dehumidifier is recommended. I strongly recommend your views be stored in transparent sleeves. The best are the polypropylene or archival polyester sleeves, although Mylar also is recommended. The very best sleeve, and the one I recommend, is sold by Russell Norton, whose address is P.O. Box 1070, New Haven, CT 06504. He offers three sizes of sleeves: $3\frac{3}{4}$" by 7" (standard size), $4\frac{3}{8}$" by 7" (cabinet size), and 5" by 7" (oversize).

Wash and dry your hands thoroughly before handling your views because oil, dirt and moisture will damage them. Persons who smoke should be careful while around the views. Tobacco smoke breaks down the chemical structure of the photographic emulsion.

The arrangement of the collection is based on individual taste. Most collectors file their views by subject and photographer. Many keep the later curved-mount views separate from the earlier flat mounts. A geographic collection may be stored in alphabetical order by city or town. When collecting a major photographer or publisher who used negative numbers, views often are stored numerically. A sample checklist (page 19) is included in this guide. Many collectors carry these checklists to shows to avoid buying duplicates.

Some photographers listed their complete selection on the backs of their views. These

Photographer _____ **No.** _____ **to No.** _____

00	1 2 3 4 5 6 7 8 9	100	1 2 3 4 5 6 7 8 9	200	1 2 3 4 5 6 7 8 9
10	1 2 3 4 5 6 7 8 9	10	1 2 3 4 5 6 7 8 9	10	1 2 3 4 5 6 7 8 9
20	1 2 3 4 5 6 7 8 9	20	1 2 3 4 5 6 7 8 9	20	1 2 3 4 5 6 7 8 9
30	1 2 3 4 5 6 7 8 9	30	1 2 3 4 5 6 7 8 9	30	1 2 3 4 5 6 7 8 9
40	1 2 3 4 5 6 7 8 9	40	1 2 3 4 5 6 7 8 9	40	1 2 3 4 5 6 7 8 9
50	1 2 3 4 5 6 7 8 9	50	1 2 3 4 5 6 7 8 9	50	1 2 3 4 5 6 7 8 9
60	1 2 3 4 5 6 7 8 9	60	1 2 3 4 5 6 7 8 9	60	1 2 3 4 5 6 7 8 9
70	1 2 3 4 5 6 7 8 9	70	1 2 3 4 5 6 7 8 9	70	1 2 3 4 5 6 7 8 9
80	1 2 3 4 5 6 7 8 9	80	1 2 3 4 5 6 7 8 9	80	1 2 3 4 5 6 7 8 9
90	1 2 3 4 5 6 7 8 9	90	1 2 3 4 5 6 7 8 9	90	1 2 3 4 5 6 7 8 9

300	1 2 3 4 5 6 7 8 9	400	1 2 3 4 5 6 7 8 9	500	1 2 3 4 5 6 7 8 9
10	1 2 3 4 5 6 7 8 9	10	1 2 3 4 5 6 7 8 9	10	1 2 3 4 5 6 7 8 9
20	1 2 3 4 5 6 7 8 9	20	1 2 3 4 5 6 7 8 9	20	1 2 3 4 5 6 7 8 9
30	1 2 3 4 5 6 7 8 9	30	1 2 3 4 5 6 7 8 9	30	1 2 3 4 5 6 7 8 9
40	1 2 3 4 5 6 7 8 9	40	1 2 3 4 5 6 7 8 9	40	1 2 3 4 5 6 7 8 9
50	1 2 3 4 5 6 7 8 9	50	1 2 3 4 5 6 7 8 9	50	1 2 3 4 5 6 7 8 9
60	1 2 3 4 5 6 7 8 9	60	1 2 3 4 5 6 7 8 9	60	1 2 3 4 5 6 7 8 9
70	1 2 3 4 5 6 7 8 9	70	1 2 3 4 5 6 7 8 9	70	1 2 3 4 5 6 7 8 9
80	1 2 3 4 5 6 7 8 9	80	1 2 3 4 5 6 7 8 9	80	1 2 3 4 5 6 7 8 9
90	1 2 3 4 5 6 7 8 9	90	1 2 3 4 5 6 7 8 9	90	1 2 3 4 5 6 7 8 9

600	1 2 3 4 5 6 7 8 9	700	1 2 3 4 5 6 7 8 9	800	1 2 3 4 5 6 7 8 9
10	1 2 3 4 5 6 7 8 9	10	1 2 3 4 5 6 7 8 9	10	1 2 3 4 5 6 7 8 9
20	1 2 3 4 5 6 7 8 9	20	1 2 3 4 5 6 7 8 9	20	1 2 3 4 5 6 7 8 9
30	1 2 3 4 5 6 7 8 9	30	1 2 3 4 5 6 7 8 9	30	1 2 3 4 5 6 7 8 9
40	1 2 3 4 5 6 7 8 9	40	1 2 3 4 5 6 7 8 9	40	1 2 3 4 5 6 7 8 9
50	1 2 3 4 5 6 7 8 9	50	1 2 3 4 5 6 7 8 9	50	1 2 3 4 5 6 7 8 9
60	1 2 3 4 5 6 7 8 9	60	1 2 3 4 5 6 7 8 9	60	1 2 3 4 5 6 7 8 9
70	1 2 3 4 5 6 7 8 9	70	1 2 3 4 5 6 7 8 9	70	1 2 3 4 5 6 7 8 9
80	1 2 3 4 5 6 7 8 9	80	1 2 3 4 5 6 7 8 9	80	1 2 3 4 5 6 7 8 9
90	1 2 3 4 5 6 7 8 9	90	1 2 3 4 5 6 7 8 9	90	1 2 3 4 5 6 7 8 9

900	1 2 3 4 5 6 7 8 9
10	1 2 3 4 5 6 7 8 9
20	1 2 3 4 5 6 7 8 9
30	1 2 3 4 5 6 7 8 9
40	1 2 3 4 5 6 7 8 9
50	1 2 3 4 5 6 7 8 9
60	1 2 3 4 5 6 7 8 9
70	1 2 3 4 5 6 7 8 9
80	1 2 3 4 5 6 7 8 9
90	1 2 3 4 5 6 7 8 9

Series name

_____

Collection of:

_____

_____

_____

Sample checklist.

B. W. Kilburn, #14565, typical example of a variant negative. Kilburn made up to twenty variants of most negatives. These views, ''The last sad home coming. At the depot, Canton, O.'' were from the popular series of President McKinley's funeral in 1901.

''backlists'' give some idea of what was made and also can be used as a checklist. The NSA has published a loose-leaf book of all known backlists. They also offer reprints of catalogs issued by photographers and publishers.

CLEANING

Caution must be taken when attempting to clean stereo views. Pre-1890 albumen prints may be cleaned by using a clean cotton cloth moistened with a special solution. In a small bowl, mix approximately twenty parts of distilled water to one part of standard ammonia. Make the cloth just barely wet with solution (too much moisture will cause the print to break down or come away from the mount). Wipe surface dirt off the view using a single-direction motion. *Do not* rub back and forth. Soil should appear on the cloth. Rinse the cloth in the solution, wring it out and repeat the process. Another method is to use very fresh white bread. Peel the crust and make a ball of the bread in your fist. Then rub the dirt off, again in a single direction. Experiment on common or damaged views to decide the best method for your purposes. A number of collectors also use spit, which works fine but is unappealing to some people. Some art supply stores sell a cleaning eraser. Experiment with these, because some do not work and some will harm your views.

More caution should be taken with post-1890 curved-mount views. These use a gelatin silver emulsion and moisture will break down the surface gloss. Standard rubbing alcohol will clean some of these views, but experimentation is important to avoid damaging them.

The best course of action is no action at all! Much dust and surface grime can be wiped off with a clean cloth. This sometimes is all the cleaning that is necessary before placing a view in a sleeve. Once in the sleeve, you should not have to remove the view. *Do not* use adhesive tape of any type on the view or sleeve. Any markings on the mount back should be made with a No. 2 pencil. *Do not* use *any* type of ink.

CONDITION

The condition of a stereo view is of great importance to the collector. Surprisingly, many stereo views have survived more than one hundred years without any major change in appearance. Collectors seek these examples and strive to upgrade their collections to the best condition possible. Views that are badly damaged, soiled, stained, creased and faded have very little value to the collector. He may add these lesser views to his collection as a space filler until a better view is found or to obtain

some information from the view, such as a backlist. Also of importance to collectors is the "viewability" (3-D effect). Views that originally were mounted poorly or mismounted are shunned by collectors.

Over the years some standard terms regarding condition have been developed and are shared by most collectors/dealers. Each is described and illustrated.

EXCELLENT (ALSO FINE OR MINT): This is a view that has a clear and sharp image on a clean, undamaged mount.

VERY GOOD: This is a slightly less-than-perfect view. There will be no major defects in the view or the mount, but there will be signs of some usage.

GOOD: The view is in about average collectible condition. It may be slightly faded, and corners may be rubbed or the mount may be stained.

An example of a bent or creased corner. This is a black-and-white litho, but such conditions exist on all views and detract from the appearance (and thus the value).

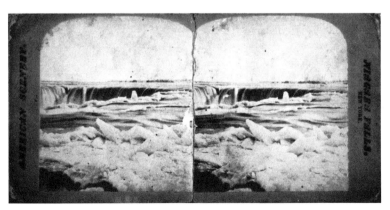

An example of a view that was folded or bent between the print pairs. It also was soiled with wear on the corners. Such a view would grade fair to good in condition.

George E. Curtis, #254, "Bridge to First Sister Island," Niagara. The upper-left corner is badly damaged with a heavy crease and tear vertically through the left image. Such a view has little or no collector value.

Early full-length portrait of a black servant girl, ca. 1860s. The left image is faded with water stains at the mount edges. A better subject in less than perfect condition would grade good and sell at $10 to $20. In excellent condition it would be valued five or six times more.

Close view of soiling and foxing in sky area of part of a view. Note that the black blotch near the bottom center is a flaw in the original negative.

Webster & Albee. A faded view with a soiled mount.

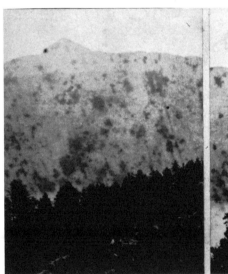

Close view of heavy foxing or mold spots on a view.

The brittle card mount of this view is chipped and worn. It has a reduced value, but is still collectible because of the subject—a resort hotel.

Close view of scratches and tears in an image. Also note the number scratched in the negative at the bottom center.

Close detail of light soiling, or foxing. Such minor soil is acceptable on desirable subjects, but it does lessen the value.

A typical example of a badly soiled view. It also is water stained at the ends. This view would grade poor.

A view with glue or emulsion streaks. Such views had this problem when the original adhesive was contaminated and a mold had formed.

Close view of water stains on a mount. The corner is also rubbed.

B. W. Kilburn, #3564, "Suspension, Bridge and New York City, from Brooklyn." This view has a light water stain visible toward the middle of the view. Otherwise, it is an excellent view that would be graded good to very good.

Close detail of a badly worn corner. Note also that it was water stained, which possibly caused the mount to soften and allowed the corners and edges to wear.

Keystone View Co., #2347, "After Marriage," 1896. An example of a view with near-excellent prints but a soiled and rubbed mount. Grading is a judgment call. The view would grade very good with mount soiling.

Alex Martin, #282, Railroad bridge in the Grand Canyon of the Arkansas, Colorado, ca. 1880. An example of a mount with rubbed and worn corners. The prints are sharp overall and clear with some soiling in the sky area at the top. This view would grade between good and very good.

FAIR (OR POOR): This view has major faults, including stains, heavy soiling, foxing (brown spots), bends and a damaged mount. Such views have very little value to most collectors.

Some dealers use a plus (+) or minus (−) designation in catalogs and sale lists. Usually this is followed by a clarification of condition such as "worn at corners" or "small stain in left image." Call or write a dealer when you are unclear about the condition of an advertised view.

MISMOUNTED VIEWS

A stereograph must be properly mounted to have the correct 3-D effect.

FLAT (no stereoscopic effect): A stereograph must have a left and right image. Just placing two photos side by side will not work. A stereoscopic camera has two lenses (left and right) that correspond to the left and right eyes. Once

the negative is exposed, the left and right halves must be transposed. The negative is then printed and mounted for viewing.

PSEUDOSCOPIC (reversed pairs, not properly transposed): Here the images were photographed in stereo, but in mounting the pairs were not transposed. One experiences a strange effect that makes the foreground part of the background.

MISALIGNMENT: For proper viewing, the stereo pairs must be level and the images must be on the same plane. An image that is higher or lower or rotated left or right will give a poor stereo effect or might not be viewed at all.

HYPERSTEREO: This is not a fault but in most cases is a plus in stereo viewing. In the 1850s many of the stereo photographers used a single-lens camera. After photographing the left image, the camera was shifted to the right and the second image was taken. As a result, any movement in the first image will appear differently in the second. A wagon or carriage

B. W. Kilburn, #14570, "Bearing the President's Body into the Court House, Canton, O.," 1901. An example of a pseudoscopic view where the left and right images are transposed.

Keystone View Co., #34115, "An Air View of Downtown Cleveland." An example of a hyperstereo taken from an airplane with a lens separation greater than 2½".

An example of a view made with a single-lens camera, one image being taken a few seconds after the other. Note the man's left arm has moved and the wagon in the street has moved farther away while another is blurred at the right. This is a view with no title or maker, ca. 1880. A very late example.

will appear to have moved down the street. If the separation between the lenses was greater than the standard 2½", then one gets a "hyperstereo" effect. The greater the distance, the greater the effect. The result is an appearance of miniaturization. Many European views from the 1850s are in hyperstereo. It is as though you were a giant looking at the scene or you were looking at a model of the scene. Hyperstereos are commonly used today in aerial stereo photography. Most of the NASA space photographs in books and magazines actually are halves of hyperstereos. Keystone made a number of hyperstereos in the 1930s—aerial views by the Fairchild Corporation—with outstanding views of major cities like Washington, Boston, New York, Cleveland and Pittsburgh. The view of Mount Hood, in my opinion, is the best. There are collectors who actively seek good hyperstereo examples.

DATING STEREO VIEWS

Stereo views can be dated to within about five years of actual production by examining the mount and print types. Many negatives were published for several years and often passed from one photographer to another. Thus a view negative made in 1870 still could be offered in 1895.

Card Mount (or Stock)

Pre-1860 mounts are usually on a thin stock in a variety of colors. Most common are ivory or off-white, but lavender, lilac and pink mounts are known. The European mounts are usually a dark buff or a creamy white.

From 1861 to about 1873, mounts in the United States were yellow, reddish orange, green, pink or lilac. Prior to about 1865, mounts were square cornered. After the Civil War, round-cornered mounts became the norm. Many of the mounts were enameled. Around 1870 photographers began using listings of titles (backlists) on the backs of the views. From 1864 to 1866 an excise tax was charged on photographs, and views with United States revenue stamps affixed can be dated to this period. Although interesting, the tax stamps have very little extra value. They add about 10 to 20 percent to the value of a view if the stamp is complete and has a cancel imprint that identifies the seller or gives a date.

Square-cornered mounts were used into the 1870s by European publishers, but by the late 1870s most mounts were round cornered.

After the depression of 1873, there was increased use of wood pulp in card stock. Mounts from this period often chip easily. Prior to 1873 mounts were the standard 3½" by 7" in size. Around 1874 a taller "artistic" or "cabinet" mount was introduced in the United States. Still 7" wide, these mounts were from 4" to 4½" tall, which permitted a larger print size. The cabinet mount never was popular in Europe and rarely was used by publishers outside the United States.

In 1882 B. W. Kilburn introduced the warped or curved mount on a thicker card stock. These were sold as an improvement in the stereo effect. By 1890 most publishers were using the curved mount, and thus 1890 becomes the cutoff date for the flat-mount views. Flat cabinet mounts were still in use by some local makers as late as 1905.

The curved mounts in the early 1890s usually were a light buff to a salmon buff color. An orange mount became popular in the late 1890s and was used by Keystone View Company, B. W. Kilburn and Whiting View Company. In 1901 Keystone switched to a gray color and Underwood and Underwood began offering a brownish gray mount. Until 1901 H. C. White mounts were a creamy, enameled card stock that became a dark, greenish brown. The black type on these mounts often is hard to read. C. H. Graves's Universal Photo Art Company used a light gray curved mount with platino (platinum prints) finish.

About 1902 H. C. White began offering a deluxe mount with gold lettering on a deep black stock. Keystone, not to be outdone, also offered a gold-lettered gray mount, but the printing was poor and today examples are found with the titles rubbed off.

4

LEADING PHOTOGRAPHERS AND PUBLISHERS

The following individuals and companies produced the majority of the stereo views encountered by collectors. It has been estimated that more than 10,000 photographers and publishers issued commercial views in the United States and Canada. This listing provides information concerning rarity and types of views issued to assist the collector both to identify his views and to determine their relative importance to the history of stereoscopy.

Adams, S. F.
New Bedford, Mass. (active 1866 to about 1873)

S. F. Adams was the successor to Bierstadt Brothers. He produced stereos from negatives made by the Bierstadts but without credit to them. Most notable is the rare series of approximately eighty views of the Colonel F. W. Lander Expedition of 1859 by Albert Bierstadt. Also among the Bierstadt negatives was the full moon by L. M. Rutherford taken in 1864.

Andrieu, J.
Paris, France (active mid-1860s to about 1877)

J. Andrieu was commonly identified as "JA of Paris." He was a large publisher who employed many photographers and published thousands of views. He is notable for French

tissues marked "JA." Early issues are known with full-name imprints, but most common are later "JA" issues. J. Andrieu had a trade list of more than 9000 titles covering Europe, Egypt, Algeria and the Near East. Of historical importance is the series of the destruction of Paris during the Paris Commune. Andrieu also published a scarce series of the celebration at the opening of the Suez Canal in November 1869 at sites in Port Said and Suez. This series includes the procession of vessels that made the first passage. Rarer yet is the series on tinted tissues. Also rarely found in JA tissues is the series on the Franco-Prussian War.

Anthony, Edward
New York City (active 1859 to 1862)

E. and H. T. Anthony and Company
(active 1863 to 1889)

E. and H. T. Anthony and Company was a major publisher that employed many photographers. Most of the early New York views were done by Edward Anthony, whose company produced thousands of views. Most notable is the Edward Anthony series of New York City begun in 1859, which numbers approximately 175 views, including a Fourth of July regatta in New York Harbor. These early views have square-cornered ivory mounts with paper labels on the reverse. (Early manuscript labels are known but are extremely rare.) In 1860, Anthony moved from 308 Broadway to 501 Broadway. In 1862, he joined with brother Henry to form E. and H. T. Anthony. From 1863 to 1874, E. and H. T. Anthony produced dozens of series, including

A Ramble Through the So. Tier on the route of the Erie Railroad
A Trip to Coney Island
Beauties of the Harlem River
Beauties of the Hudson
California Views
Camp Scenes (Civil War)
Camp Scenes, Feats of the Chivalry (Civil War)
Central Park Views
Delaware Water Gap
Egyptian Views
English Views
Fourth of July in and about New York
French Views
Fulton Street Prayer Meeting
Glens of the Catskills
Glimpses of the Great West
Greenwood Cemetery Views
Hills and Dales of New England
Instantaneous
Irish Views
King Solomon's Temple (views of model)
Miscellaneous
Niagara in Winter
Passaic Falls, N.J.
Photographic History—The War for the Union
Prominent Portraits
Public Buildings in N.Y. City and Brooklyn
Reception of the Japanese Embassy
Scenes in China
Sing Sing Views, Prison Views, and Croton Aqueduct
The Great Union Meeting, Union Square
The Majesty and Beauty of Niagara
The Picturesque on the Pennsylvania Central Railroad
Up and Down the Shrewsbury
Views in and About Saratoga Springs
Views in Cuba
Views in "El Ecuador" [The Andes]
Views in Venezuela
Views in Washington City
Views near Baltimore
Views in New Grenada
Views of the Great Metropolitan Fair
Views on the Line of the N.Y. and New Haven Railroad
West Point Views
White Mountain Views
Winter in the Catskills

After 1874, E. and H. T. Anthony and Company became a wholesale agent, and many of their views were sold without labels and blind-stamped at the bottom center with *EA* in a circle. The last stereo views published by E. and H. T. Anthony is a series of several dozen unnumbered views titled "Views of New York and Vicinity by the New Gelatine-Bromide Process." It was a series intended to demonstrate the qualities of the new dry plates being sold by Anthony. Many of the views are lacking in contrast and are not up to the quality of the 1860s and 1870s views.

Appleton, D.
New York City (active 1853 to 1866)

Appleton was the first large distributor of foreign stereo views in the United States in the early 1850s. In 1856 Appleton began issuing views in books or folders, which usually contained a dozen views. Subjects included Niagara Falls, Paris, and American scenery. These are early photomechanical prints on thick mounts. Starting in 1859, Appleton issued a series on New York, Boston and Washington, D.C., on ivory enameled mounts. Most notable is a small series of the American visit by the Prince of Wales in 1860. From 1860 to 1864 D. Appleton offered views as The New York Stereoscopic Company. These are usually on a dark buff mount with a fancy imprint back. More than 600 titles are known. Most notable are the series of Moscow, St. Petersburg and Constantinople. All are extremely rare.

Barker, George
Niagara Falls (active early 1860s to late 1890s)

Barker's studio at Niagara Falls produced a large variety of views of the falls. He also produced a number of non-Niagara series, including the Centennial Celebration of 1876 in Philadelphia (views were made outside the grounds because Edward Wilson's Centennial Photographic Company had exclusive rights); hunting views, including camps (1880s); Iroquois and Onandaga Indians of New York State (most common is a mother with a papoose); the Johnstown flood (1889) and scenes in Florida. In the mid-1880s Underwood and Underwood became the distributor of Barker's views and continued to sell his views, usually with proper credit, as late as 1908.

George Barker, "The Belle of Dark-town," 1890, a typical genre view of blacks.

The Belle of Darktown.   Copyright 1890, by Geo. Barker.

Barnard, George N.
(active early 1860s to late 1870s)

Barnard was a Civil War photographer first employed by Mathew Brady whose early views were published by Brady's Album Gallery and by Anthony without credit. Barnard left Brady in 1863 (along with other photographers) because of Brady's financial troubles. His privately issued Civil War views are extremely rare. From 1863 to 1866, views offered as "Incidents of the War" by Alexander Gardner gave credit to Barnard. His Civil War views include fortified Washington City, Centreville, Manassas, Yorktown and Hampton, Virginia. He was assigned to General Sherman and photographed the siege of Atlanta and the "March to the Sea." He eventually reached Charleston, South Carolina, where he remained after the war. He photographed the destruction in Charleston plus a series of blacks. He also made a series of the Chicago fire (1871).

Barnum, Delos
(active 1857 to 1875)

Barnum made early photographs of Boston (ca. 1857) on early ivory mounts with blind-stamped identification. Most notable is his "American Historical Series" (1859) of more than fifty views of Revolutionary War landmarks in and around Boston. These are on ivory mounts with ornate and fancy descriptive backs. He also did a fine series of Saratoga and Niagara Falls plus a series of Washington, D.C.

Beato, Felice (or Felix)
(active 1855 to 1862)

As Robinson and Beato, made a series of Cairo, Egypt (1858), "Views in China" (about 200

titles) and published by Negretti and Zambra. Made both tinted and untinted views on cream card mounts (1860s), which were sold by Joseph L. Bates in the United States.

Bedford, Francis
(active 1857 to 1869)

Bedford was a British photographer noted for high-quality scenic and architectural views. He produced more than 3000 numbers. Major series on yellow mounts include

Bristol Illustrated
Chester Illustrated
Clifton Illustrated
Devonshire Illustrated
Exeter Illustrated
Gloucester Illustrated
Herefordshire Illustrated
Ludlow Illustrated
Monmouthshire Illustrated
North Wales Illustrated
South Wales Illustrated
Warwickshire Illustrated
Welsh Costumes

Beer Brothers (Beer and Company)
(active early 1860s)

They made a rare series of views of New York City and Lake George, New York, and also published L. M. Rutherford's view of the moon (1862).

Behles, E.
(*See* Sommer and Behles in Chapter 4)

Bell, C. M. and F. A., Bell Brothers
Washington D.C. (active 1865 to 1875)

The Bells were noted Washington, D.C., photographers who made more than 1000 views of the city and vicinity, including many fine architectural studies (usually on yellow or pink

Bell & Bros., "Washington Monument," (under construction), ca. 1870.

mounts with paper labels). They made the best early series of Arlington National Cemetery.

Benecke, R.
St. Louis (active late 1860s to late 1870s)

Benecke published the rare Jenney and Newton Expedition to the Black Hills (1875) for the Interior Department plus sixty views by Dr. V. T. M. McGillycuddy. They also published a series of views of the Eads Bridge construction at St. Louis and the dedication ceremony (1869–1874).

Bennett, H. H.
Kilbourn City, Wisc. (active 1860s to late 1890s; studio still in business)

Bennett made many views of the Wisconsin Dells plus views of Winnebago Indians. He also produced "The Camera's Story of the Raftman's Life on the Wisconsin" and a scarce series titled "A Summer in Japan" with negatives by William H. Metcalf.

Bennett and Brown
W. Henry Brown, Santa Fe (active 1877 to 1883)

Bennett and Brown produced more than 550 titles. Their series include

Along the Line of the A.T. & S. Fe Railroad in New Mexico
Among the Ancient and Interesting Scenery of New Mexico
Atcheson, Topeka and Santa Fe Railroad Scenery
Trip from Trinidad, Colorado through New Mexico to Paso del Norto, Mexico
Santa Fe and Vicinity

Berry, Kelley and Chadwick
Chicago and other locations (active 1900 to 1914)

They made a wide variety of views, usually on dark gray mounts. Their work is of particular interest because they issued subjects and views of personalities not offered by their competitors. Views also were made under the imprint of E. W. Kelley.

H. H. Bennett, #481, "Among the Winnebago Indians—Ma-Bes-e-da-he-gah. (Bear that Digs a Hole)", ca. 1870. (Gordon D. Hoffman Collection)

Henry Brown, #196, "The Indian Pueblo of San Felipe," ca. 1880.

Bierstadt Brothers

New Bedford, Mass. (active 1860 to 1865)

Bierstadt Brothers published a series of eighty titles of Colonel F. W. Lander's Expedition (1859) with negatives by Albert Bierstadt. They also issued L. M. Rutherford's view of the moon (1862) plus at least twelve Civil War views (1861) that are rare. Of particular note is the fine series of New Bedford whaling made about 1865. The views were offered as paper prints or as glass transparencies. The negatives passed to S. F. Adams in 1866.

Bierstadt, Charles

Niagara Falls (active 1868 to 1890s)

Most common are Bierstadt's many views of Niagara Falls, including Iroquois and Tuscarora Indians at the falls and mother and papoose. He issued a series of Rogers's Groups (1868) and "skeleton leaves." He journeyed west in 1873 and made views in California, including fine scenes of the Sierra Madres and Yosemite Valley. He visited the Holy Land and North Africa and made approximately 250 negatives. He returned to the West in 1882 and made views of the Grinnell, Iowa, tornado damage and the new Iowa State Capitol Building in Des Moines. He also made a few views in Colorado. In the late 1880s, Underwood and Underwood became the distributor for Charles Bierstadt views and issued them until about 1900.

Bisson Brothers

France (active 1860s)

The Bisson Brothers made views known as "Collection Bisson" of France and Switzer-

land. They also made views of Syria, Damascus and Egypt, which were published by Leon and Levy. There is also a fine series of Alpine views, including photographs of climbers.

Black, J. W.

Boston, Mass. (active 1860s to early 1870s)

Black's views are scarce but he was an important early Boston photographer. He made a rare advertising view for the American Missionary Society of Fisk University Jubilee Singers, ca. 1872 (see Blacks in Chapter 5).

Blanchard, Valentine

London, England (active ca. 1860 to 1872)

Blanchard made fine architectural and scenic views. His early views were not credited and may be found with the Elliott imprint. After 1863, his name usually appears on the mount. A notable series is London (#140–240), and views of Ramsgate and Margate. He also made many fine instantaneous seascapes.

Bonine, R. K.

Tyrone, Pa. (active 1880s to early 1890s)

Bonine made scarce series of machine shops of the Pennsylvania Railroad at Altoona, Pennsylvania. He also made a series of the Johnstown flood (1889). He joined with Carlton H. Graves, L. M. Melander and Brother, W. M. Chase and Gates Brothers to form the Globe Photo Art Company in Bettsville, Ohio, which centralized printing and distribution. Their views sold for $2 per dozen, which was a competitive price in 1890. Bonine issued views either copied or obtained from other photographers, including lumbering views in California.

Brady, Mathew B.
New York City and Washington, D.C. (stereo activity 1860 to 1865)

Brady photographed the Japanese Embassy (1860), New York City and Washington, D.C. He formed Brady and Company in 1861 to cover the Civil War. Brady's views were published as "Brady's Album Gallery" and were also published by E. and H. T. Anthony (#2275–2522, #3030–3630). Brady hired teams of photographers to cover the Civil War. The most notable of these photographers were George N. Barnard, Alexander Gardner, James F. Gibson and Timothy H. O'Sullivan. In 1863 Gardner and most of the Brady photographers left Brady because of Brady's financial difficulties. Brady also made a series of West Point, New York (published by Anthony).

Braun, Adolph
Dornach, Switzerland (active 1856 to early 1870s)

Braun made rare early still lifes. Most of the Anthony European views were made by Braun; he was one of Europe's most prolific publishers, making thousands of views in the 1860s. He photographed the Upper Rhine and Germany, and also made Alpine views. By 1866 Braun offered more than 8500 titles. He also photographed Belgium, Holland and a "Costumes of Switzerland" series (1868, sixty views) as well as an excellent series of the Grindewald Glacier ice caves and views of Palestine and Egypt.

Brown, W. Henry
(*See* Bennett and Brown in Chapter 4)

Campbell, Alfred S.
Elizabeth, N.J. (active 1893 to 1904)

Campbell made a nice series of New York City and the New Jersey shore resorts. His views of street types—candy seller, ice cream vendor, organ grinder and monkey, etc.—are of special interest. He also made a small series of Long Island and the America's Cup, including most of the racing yachts—most notably *Defender*. Campbell made a series of Cleveland, Ohio, and vicinity (#418–460) during the winter of 1895–1896; some of the views had an ad on the reverse side for the American Tobacco Company.

Carbutt, John
Chicago, Ill. (active 1860s)

Carbutt made a classic series of Chicago on yellow mounts. In 1866 he offered views of the J. L. Fisk Expedition (to Montana; negatives by William H. Illingworth) on yellow mounts, #234–260. Most notable is his series "Union Pacific Railroad Excursion to the 100th Meridian, Oct. 1866" on yellow mounts (#198–233).

Carter, C. W.
Salt Lake City (active 1860s to 1880s)

Carter documented the construction of the Mormon Temple and Tabernacle. He made fine views of Shoshone Indians, mining, the Transcontinental Railroad construction and Mormons.

Centennial Photographic Company
Philadelphia (active 1876 to 1885)

This publishing firm was established to be the exclusive maker of 1876 Centennial Exhibition views. The partnership was formed by

C. W. Carter, "East Temple Street, West Side, Salt Lake City," ca. 1870.

Centennial Photographic Co., "Ohio State Building," 1876 Centennial Exhibition, Philadelphia.

William Notman, Edward L. Wilson, W. Irving Adams and J. A. Fraser. They issued more than 4000 views of the exhibition on cream cabinet mounts. Centennial received the exclusive for the Cotton International Exhibition in New Orleans, 1884–1885, and issued a series on nearly identical mounts (*see also* Edward L. Wilson in Chapter 4).

Chamberlain, W. G.
Denver (active 1861 to 1887)
Joined W. H. Jackson and Company in 1887 and eventually became partner (worked to 1890)

Chamberlain made approximately 750 views of Colorado including Denver, Gray's Peak, mining towns, Indians and Mrs. Maxwell's Rocky Mountain animals.

Chase, W. M.
Baltimore (active 1867 to 1890)

Chase was the official photographer for the United States Naval Academy in Annapolis with David Bachrach, Jr. (1868). He made a series of Baltimore starting in 1872 and also made views of Washington, D.C., and Niagara Falls. Chase issued pirated copies of a variety of subjects. A notable series is scenes on the "Line of B. & O. R. R." In the 1890s his views were distributed by Globe Photo Art Company.

Christmann, S. P.
Berlin, Germany (active 1868 to 1876)

Christmann made hand-tinted views of children and local types. He used elaborate staging, especially of occupations. His series in-

clude "Outdoor Work," "Housework Indoors," "In the Workshop," "Dreams" and fairy tales— "Cinderella," "Puss in Boots" and "Hansel and Gretel." Of particular note is his "Italie-Italien" (1870s).

Clark, D. R.
Indianapolis (active 1870s)

In 1874 Clark made twenty-one titles of Ceylon and transit of Venus in Siberia. His 1875 series included ten views of Vladivostok, Siberia. The quality of his views varies.

Climo, J. S.
St. John, New Brunswick, Canada (active 1870s)

Climo made an extensive series of St. John, New Brunswick. Notable are his views of the New Brunswick fire, June 1877.

Continent Stereoscopic Company
New York City (active in 1870s to 1880s)

Continent Stereoscopic's views were from original negatives and pirated copies, especially of western United States. Continent's subjects included Arizona, California, Colorado, Washington Territory, and Alaska. The quality of the views varies.

Cremer, James
Philadelphia (active 1870s)

Cremer produced many views of Philadelphia; his most common views are of Independence Hall and the Liberty Bell. He also made views of buildings and streets. A notable series is of the New Masonic Temple (1873). Cremer also published views of the Zoological Gardens by Schreiber and Sons. Cremer was a major distributor, and many non-Cremer views can be found with the Cremer label on the reverse.

Delamotte, P. H.
England (1850s)

Delamotte made English tissues and views of Oxford, England, in the 1850s. His most notable series is "The Art Treasures of the Manchester Exhibition," published by the London Stereoscopic Company on ornate gilded card mounts (1857).

Elliott, James
England (active 1855 to early 1860s)

Elliott made a variety of fine views, including tissues. He made a series of English architecture, but he is best known for elaborate studio-posed still lifes, comics and sentimentals, and historical recreations. Of special note is his "Mary Queen of Scots," "Sacking the Jews Home," "Little Red Riding Hood" and excellent "ghosts." Elliott also published "Picturesque Ramblings in Old England" by William N. Grundy. Most Elliott views were distributed by the London Stereoscopic Company and are usually hand colored and have the London Stereo blindstamp. Many Elliott views are unmarked, but those that are marked have a blindstamp or imprint on the reverse.

England, William
England (active late 1850s to early 1870s)

England was a prolific photographer who made English views, and a variety of special series, primarily for the London Stereoscopic Company. Of special note is the London Stereoscopic Company's "North American" series (1859), made along with other photographers. There is a similar series of Canada (1859–1860). England made a series of Ireland (1858), Paris (1860–1861) and Germany (1866). He also made a series of the Crystal Palace at Sydenham (1860) and a large series of the International Exhibition of 1862 (London) plus skeleton leaves and statuary (1872–1873). England made more than 500 views of Swiss scenery for the Alpine Club (1863–1868). These are on yellow mounts.

Fenton, Roger
England (1850s)

Fenton was an important photographer, but is rarely encountered. He made fine still lifes, including views of sculpture, Scotland (1857), England, and Wales. He also took photographs of posed actors in costume. Most of his views were published by the London Stereoscopic Company.

Ferrier, C. M. (Ferrier and Soulier)
Paris (active 1858 through 1870s)

Ferrier was a major publisher of glass transparencies. He also made card-mounted views, often without identification. More than 40,000 titles on glass were produced, including views of Europe, the Near East and North Africa. In the late 1860s his negatives were passed to Leon and Levy—the Ferrier name is sometimes blotted out or covered over with binding tape. Of special note are his fine views of Germany, Belgium and Egypt.

Fredericks, C. D.
New York City (active late 1850s to early 1860s)

Fredericks was an important, but scarce, maker. He photographed the Japanese Embassy (1860) and made a rare series of Cuba (ca. 1860s).

Freeman, J.
Nantucket, Mass. (active 1865 to 1885)

Freeman made an excellent series of Nantucket (more than 300 titles) and views of whaling (at least thirty).

Frith, Francis
England (active 1850s to 1860s)

Frith made an excellent series of Egypt and the Holy Land (1856–1857), which was published by Negretti and Zambra; it included approximately 500 titles. Frith established his own company in 1860; most of his views are signed in the negative. He also issued views on glass. Frith made a series of English scenery but they lack the print quality of competitors like Bedford.

Gardner, Alexander
Washington, D.C. (active 1861 to late 1860s)

Gardner is noted for his excellent Civil War views. He first worked for Mathew Brady but

Alexander Gardner, #226, "Dead Artillery Horse, Gettysburg, July 6, 1863."

left in 1863 to open a studio in Washington. He issued views that were published by Philp and Solomon and distributed by E. and H. T. Anthony. After the war he went to Kansas and made a series on Union Pacific Railroad eastern division (1867; 160 views). This latter series usually is on yellow mounts, sometimes without the series identification.

Gates, G. F.
Mauch Chunk, Pa. (active late 1860s through 1870s)

Gates made an extensive series of Mauch Chunk (now Jim Thorpe) and the area including Glen Onoko. He published a series of India, apparently from original negatives (late 1860s) and a small series taken outside the grounds of the Centennial Exhibition (1876).

Good, Frank M.
England (active 1860s)

Good made views of England, and his glass views were published by Leon and Levy. He also made a series of mosses and ferns plus views of Derby Day and Epsom Downs. Most notable is his "Eastern Series" of the Holy Lands and Egypt (1860s; about 250 titles).

Graves, Carlton H. (Universal Photo Art Company)
Philadelphia and Naperville, Ill. (active early 1880s to about 1910)

Graves became a major publisher after 1890 and offered more than 10,000 different views. In the late 1890s he began offering "Art Nouveau Stereographs" on light gray curved mounts. His trade list offered excellent views of hunting scenes, Jamaica, Japan, Java, New York City, Palestine, and others. To compete with low-priced lithos and copies, Graves offered his "Universal Series," or "Universal Views," on black mounts with no credit to himself. These have the number and title in the negative and were sold at a reduced price from the regular "Art Nouveau" issues. Graves also offered book-boxed sets but they were not sold in the quantities of Underwood and Underwood, Keystone and H. C. White.

Griffith and Griffith, George W.
Philadelphia (active 1896 to about 1908)

Griffith was a major publisher who began as a canvasser for Underwood and Underwood, which he left to form his own company. He became the publisher and distributor of views by H. L. Roberts (Roberts and Fellows), William H. Rau and M. H. Zahner (Niagara Falls). Griffith also added to the negative files. Eventually he made more than 10,000 titles, including mostly United States subjects, Japan, Palestine, Puerto Rico and the Spanish-American War. Griffith made boxed sets, but they are rare. To compete with the other major publishers, Griffith produced thousands of color lithos. He also issued a black-and-white set of the San Francisco earthquake both as lithographs and photo prints. The lithos are very common.

Gurney, Jeremiah, Gurney and Son
New York City (active 1860s)

Gurney made an extensive series of famous personalities, including literary portraits and noted theatrical performers. He also issued views

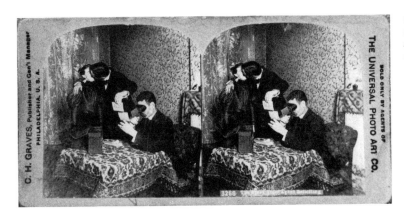

C. H. Graves (Universal Photo Art Co.), #3268, "The fresh view agent soliciting," the salesman kisses the wife as the husband looks at view.

of Rogers Groups and portraits of children and animals, sometimes in comic poses. Most notable are his views of the Japanese Embassy (1860) and Lincoln's funeral (1865).

Gurnsey, Byron H.
Pueblo and Colorado Springs, Colo. (active 1872 to 1880, views published into 1882)

Gurnsey made an extensive series of Colorado scenery as well as a series in New Mexico. His views are usually cabinet mounted.

Gutekunst, F.
Philadelphia (active 1860s to 1880s)

Gutekunst made extensive series of Philadelphia, including the New Masonic Temple. He made a few rare Civil War views. Most notable are his views of the Pennsylvania Railroad "Horseshoe Curve" (common) and scarce views of the railroad shops in Altoona, Pennsylvania.

Hart, Alfred A.
Sacramento, Calif. (active 1860s)

Hart was the official photographer for the Central Pacific Railroad (1865–1869); he made approximately 400 views, including excellent construction scenes in the Sierra Nevada Mountains. He made views of the Promontory Point "Joining of the Rails" (1869). Hart's negatives were purchased by C. E. Watkins in 1869 and were published by Watkins and Taber into the early 1880s, without credit to Hart.

Haynes, F. Jay
Moorhead, Minn., Fargo, Dakota Territory (active in Moorhead 1876 to 1879; in Fargo, 1879 to about 1911. Haynes's descendents still maintain concessions at Yellowstone)

Haynes was the official photographer of the Northern Pacific Railroad. He made an exten-

B. H. Gurnsey, #114, "Colorado Springs from the Cupola of the Public School Building, looking East," ca. 1875.

sive series of Yellowstone National Park of more than 4800 views. He made excellent views of the Dakota Territory, including farms, river steamboats, Fort Abraham Lincoln (1877), Deadwood during the mining boom (1877) and hunting parties. He also made views of Montana Territory (1887), Idaho (1884), including mining scenes, and a trip to Alaska and the northwest (1891).

Hayward and Muzzall
Santa Barbara, Calif. (1870s)

They made an excellent series of Santa Barbara, including the mission, Indians and the Chinese. Their views usually are on yellow mounts.

Hazeltine, M. M.
California (active late 1860s to mid-1870s)

Hazeltine made excellent views of California and the northwest. He made the John P. Soule "California" series (1870) without credit.

Henderson, Alexander
Montreal, Canada (1860s to 1870s)

Henderson was a leading photographer in Montreal, making large series of the city and vicinity.

Heywood, John
Boston (active 1860s)

Heywood made a variety of fine series published by either Hervey Friend or Frank Rowell. Later views were issued by "The American Stereoscopic Company" (not to be confused with earlier Langenheim and Loyd Company). His main series include

Cape Ann, #1–61, #210–245 and #310–333
Green Mountains, #138–187 and #419–429
Lake Winnipiseogee, #430–456
Miscellaneous, #521 (coral), #522–523 (wax cross), #524 (Book of Psalms), #527–528 (coral) and #530–546
Mount Desert Scenery, #704–754 or #1800–1849 (American Stereoscopic Company)
New York State (except Niagara), #582–661
Summer Views of Niagara, #662–690
White Mountains, #246–309 and #457–520
White River, #430–435
Winter Views of Niagara, #334–400

Hillers, Jack L.
Survey of Colorado River (active 1871 to 1875)

Hillers succeeded E. O. Beaman and James Fennemore (who together took more than 550 negatives) on the United States Geological Survey. His views were published as "U.S. Topographical and Geological Survey of the Colorado River of the West By J. W. Powell and A. H. Thompson" by James F. Jarvis on yellow cabinet mounts. Nearly 700 views were issued commercially, including scenics, Indians and members of the survey.

Hine, Thomas (assistant on Hayden Survey)
(active 1870 to 1878)

Hine was originally Brady's assistant during the Civil War. Hine made the series "Stereo Views of Colorado" (territory) in 1873, which was published by Copelin and Son (Chicago).

Jack L. Hillers, #169, "Pinnacles on the Kai-par-o-wits Plateau in southeastern Utah," 1875 Powell Survey of the territories.

Holmes, W. H.
New York City (active 1860s to 1870s)

Holmes made many fine views of New York City, which are much scarcer than the views by Anthony. He also issued a series of European and American authors and personalities.

Hook, W. E. (Hook View Company)
Manitou and Colorado Springs (active 1888 to 1897)

Hook made an extensive series of Colorado, including a notable series of Manitou Caverns.

Houseworth, T. and Company
San Francisco (active 1860 to 1868)
Lawrence and Houseworth and Thomas Houseworth and Company (active 1868 to 1886)

These two firms made a remarkable record of San Francisco as well as scenes in most areas of California and Nevada plus views of the Orient. Most notable is the series of the Sacramento flood (negatives by Charles Leander Weed) of January 1862 (at least twenty-nine

views). They also made views of Yosemite Valley, San Francisco, hydraulic mining in Yuba County, big trees in Calaveras County and Sacramento street scenes. Oriental scenery includes China and Japan with negatives by Weed (not credited). There is a scarce series of the Mechanics' Institute Fair of 1869 in San Francisco (#2001–2100) plus rare views of Niagara Falls (possibly more than twenty views).

Illingworth, W. H.
(also as Illingworth and McLeish)
St. Paul (active 1860s to 1870s)

Illingworth made a nice series of Minneapolis and St. Paul plus views of the Dakotas. Notable series include the Fisk Expedition (1866), published by Carbutt, and the Custer Expedition to the Black Hills (1874). Most of his views are on yellow mounts.

Ingersoll, T. W.
St. Paul (active 1880s to about 1910)

Ingersoll produced a large series of hunting scenes (more than 300 views), scenes of Yel-

Lawrence & Houseworth, #209, "Merchants' Exchange building, South side of California Street, bet. Leidesdorff and Montgomery, San Francisco," 1866.

Ingersoll View Co., #138, "Mamie, Kiss Your Honey Boy," ca. 1890s. The quality and values vary for Ingersoll views.

lowstone National Park and other western views (nearly 300). Unable to sustain the competition of the major publishers, he began issuing copy views and color lithos in about 1898. The most common group is the "American Cities/New Series" copied from views of local makers throughout the United States. In this series a few possibly are made from original negatives, but the quality of the prints is not up to the standards of Underwood and Underwood or Keystone. The color lithos were made in huge quantities, some were given as premium inserts in Quaker Oats products. There is little or no interest in these litho views among collectors.

Jackson, William Henry

Omaha, Nebraska as Jackson Brothers (active 1866 to 1870)
With Hayden Survey (active 1870 to 1878)

In Denver, Colo., as W. H. Jackson and Company (active 1880 to 1897)

Jackson made many western views (*see* Expeditions and Surveys in Chapter 5) of Omaha and vicinity; Colorado, including Denver, Mount of the Holy Cross, Leadville and other mining towns; Mexico; and a rare series of the Northwest Coast.

Jarvis, James F.

Washington, D.C. (active early 1870s to late 1890s)

Jarvis operated a large photo printing and publishing concern and printed many of the survey views, including the Powell Survey to the Colorado River region. He made an extensive series of Washington, D.C., recording major events, including parades and inaugurations. Jarvis made a fine series of White House

William Henry Jackson, #504, "Pikes Peak from the Garden of the Gods," ca. 1880.

James F. Jarvis (sold by Underwood & Underwood), "Inauguration of President Harrison, Washington, D.C." (Gordon D. Hoffman Collection)

Keystone View Co., #17404, "President and Mrs. Coolidge at Christening of Giant Zeppelin Los Angeles, Washington, D.C., Nov. 25, 1924." (Gordon D. Hoffman Collection)

interiors, some of which were tinted. Starting in the 1880s he had a working relationship with Underwood and Underwood, who purchased his business in 1897.

Kelley, E. W.
(*See* Berry, Kelley and Chadwick)

Keystone View Company
Meadville, Pa. (active 1892 to 1964)

Keystone was the largest publisher of stereo views in the United States. It dominated the market after purchasing Underwood and Underwood, H. C. White and others. Early views (1892–1894) are by B. L. Singley, who was the founder of the company. Beginning in 1895, Singley began purchasing negatives, and by 1897 he had begun hiring photographers. Keystone grew quickly, using thorough canvassing sales techniques. Seeing the success of the Underwood and Underwood boxed sets, Keystone developed an entire "system" using sets as visual aids in education. Nearly every country, major event and personality were stereo-photographed (*see* Chapter 6). Between 1912 and 1922, in various stages, the Underwood and Underwood; Kilburn; H. C. White; C. H. Graves; Berry, Kelley and Chadwick; and T. W. Ingersoll collections of negatives were obtained by Keystone. By the mid-1920s, Keystone had the stereo view business almost entirely to itself. Schools were key customers (the public school system of Pittsburgh bought 52 of the 600-view sets plus viewers in oak cabinets). The Keystone View Company views are the most commonly encountered photographic views (color lithos are the most common, because huge quantities were printed).

Kilburn Brothers
Littleton, N.H. (active 1865 to 1877)
B. W. Kilburn (active 1877 to 1909)

Beginning as a supplier of views of the White Mountains, Kilburn Brothers quickly ex-

Kilburn Brothers, #2025, "The Harbor, Plymouth, Mass.," ca. 1870.

panded, and by 1869 it had a 1200-view production in a large plant with an expanded title list. In 1877 Edward Kilburn retired and Benjamin West Kilburn took over full operations, including the photography. By 1909, when it ceased operations, the highest negative number was #17342 (New York Hudson-Fulton Celebration), but there were nearly 100,000 glass negatives. This is because many variants exist for most negatives. For example #8055, "Pennsylvania State Building at Columbian Exposition," has twenty versions, or nineteen variants. James M. Davis became associated with B. W. Kilburn in the early 1880s and was in charge of distribution. He also acted as a photographer. Davis took over most of the operations after 1901. B. W. Kilburn never issued boxed sets, which may have been a reason for the company's decline. Many of the post-1900 views are excellent and cover subjects not available by the competition.

Kimball, W. G. C.
Concord, N.H. (active 1870s)

Kimball was a very fine stereo photographer who made many views of his part of the country. Some notable series include the following

Concord and Vicinity (thirty-one views)
Hopkinton, N.H. (twenty-two views)
Orphan's Home and Webster Place Scenery, Franklin, N.H. (seven views)
Proctor House and Vicinity (eight views)
Shaker Village, Canterbury, N.H. (1878; fifty-eight views)

Kleckner, M. A.
Allentown and Mauch Chunk, Pa. (active 1865 to 1876; Kleckner moved to Kansas in 1877 and operated as Conklin and Kleckner until 1883)

Kleckner made many fine views, including the series "On the Line of the Lehigh Valley R.R." The views usually are of high quality and are on yellow mounts. Some notable series include

Glen Onoko
Lehigh Valley
Mauch Chunk, The Switzerland of America and a
Trip around the Switchback Railroad

Lamy, E.
Paris, France (active 1860s to 1870s)

Lamy made many nice tissues, blindstamped *E.L.* He made views of France, Belgium, Holland, the Rhine and Italy.

Langenheim, Frederick and William
Philadelphia (active 1854 to 1864)

The first American commercial stereo photographers and publishers were Frederick and William Langenheim. Their early issues are on either glass or card-mounted paper prints with gold borders and the date and manuscript titles. They also distributed views, mostly supplied by Negretti and Zambra and by European photographers. Early issues from late 1855 to 1858 are blindstamped. Starting in 1858 the views have small paper labels on the reverse that say, "The American Stereoscopic Co., Langenheim, Loyd & Co." Notable series include

Baltimore
Beauties of the Hudson River
Mount Vernon
Niagara Falls (also in Winter)
Philadelphia and Environs
Pittsburgh
The City of Washington
The White Mountains

The glass views are often beautifully hand-tinted and are highly prized by collectors, especially in excellent condition.

Lawrence and Houseworth
(*See* Thomas Houseworth and Company)

Paper label affixed to Langenheim stereo views, 1858–1860.

Leon and Levy ("LL")
France (active 1867 to 1880s)

Leon and Levy issued tissues, paper prints and views on glass. They were the exclusive photographers of the Paris International Exhibition (1867) and later that year obtained the Ferrier negatives making them the largest distributor of glass views in the world. They published high-quality views for several photographers. Leon and Levy photographed the Vienna International Exhibition (1873) and made several fine series of non-European views, including the Bisson series of Damascus, Egypt and Syria as well as "Grece & Turquie" (Greece and Turkey).

Levy
(*See* Leon and Levy in Chapter 4)

Lewis, T.
Cambridgeport, Mass. (active 1870s)

Lewis made an extensive series covering the celebration of the centennial of the American Revolution. He also made fine views of the Massachusetts area plus an important series of the Waltham Watch Manufactory. Notable series include

Concord [Mass.], April 19, 1875
Gardner and South Gardner
June 17th, 1875—Bunker Hill Centennial, Charlestown, Mass.
Leominster, Mass.
Lexington [Mass.], Apr. 19, 1875
Mt. Wachusett, Mass.
Narragansett Beach
Norwood, Mass.
Palmer and Westboro
Philadelphia Centennial (1876)
3rd of July Centennial Celebration of Washington's taking command of the American Army (1875)
Waltham Watch Manufactory (forty-four views)
Winchendon, Mass.

Lilienthal, T.
New Orleans (active 1860s to 1870s)

Lilienthal was a major New Orleans photographer. Most of his views are on yellow mounts. His Civil War era views are rare.

Linde, E. and Company
Berlin, Germany (active ca. 1862 to 1895)

Linde was the major publisher of several photographers, including Sophus Williams. He sold views of J. F. Stiehm and L. Gothe as well. Linde had a huge production, possibly equal to Anthony's output. He published a series of London and vicinity (with titles in English and German) and views of Italy, including "Florence and Its Edifices" and the Vienna International Exhibition (1873; negatives by Williams).

Littleton View Company
Littleton, N.H. (active 1880s to 1897)

Littleton obtained F. G. Weller's negatives, which for a short time had been published by G. H. Aldrich. Underwood and Underwood became the exclusive distributor in late 1880s and eventually published the Littleton/Weller negatives in the 1890s. Littleton made several personality flower-framed portraits. They also issued views from copy negatives (for example, blacks picking cotton).

Loeffler, J.
Tompkinsville, N.Y. (Staten Island) (active late 1860s through 1870s)

Loeffler made more than 150 views of Catskill Mountain scenery in several series. He also made the series "Scenery of Lake Mohonk & Vicinity" (more than 50 views). The quality varies, but overall both series are notable.

London Stereoscopic Company
London, England (had a location in New York City in 1860s) (active 1855 to 1890s)

One of the major publishers and distributors of stereo views in the early years was the London Stereoscopic Company. They offered more than 100,000 titles. The majority of the views were blindstamped but not all blindstamped views were published by the London Stereoscopic Company. They acted as the distributor for many European photographers and issued views by J. Elliott, many of which were from Grundy negatives. These are often called English Classics by collectors. Tinting is common on the staged comic and historical views. They published an early series of Italy (1855–1857) and in 1859 sent chief photographer William England to make a North American series in the United States and Canada. In addition to the England negatives, London Stereoscopic Company purchased negatives from local makers. The North American series was issued in 1860 and included more than 400 titles on ivory mounts; the mounts had a fancy back that featured an eagle with wings spread above a descriptive text. A similar series of 150 views was issued in Canada with a back featuring the royal coat of arms instead of the eagle. William England made a series of Ireland (1858) and an extensive series of the International Exhibition in London (1862).

Lord, R. E.
Boston (active 1870s)

Lord made an extensive series of Boston plus Harvard University (1874). His views usually are on orange cabinet mounts.

Lovejoy and Foster
Chicago (active 1870s)

Lovejoy and Foster made an extensive series of the Chicago fire plus a series of the city in recovery after the fire (1871). "Rebuilt Chicago, 1872" shows the downtown nearly completely rebuilt and a beehive of activity. This series also includes some fine interiors of businesses. They issued a series of the Interstate Industrial Expositions in 1873 and 1874 including a view of their booth selling views. Lovejoy and Foster were a major distributor of views, especially by midwestern photographers, and their label appears on many views they did not publish. They did offer non-Chicago subjects, including an especially fine series of Yellowstone National Park.

Luckhardt, F.
Austria (active 1867 to 1870s)

Luckhardt was noted for portraits of females wearing attractive clothes and often hats; these were called "Luckhardt's Heads" (about 200 views). He also made a series of Austria, which is rare.

Luke and Wheeler
Leadville, Colo. (active 1879 to 1881)

Luke and Wheeler made some outstanding mining views in the San Juan Mountains of southwest Colorado. They also made several nice interiors and exteriors of businesses in Leadville during the mining boom.

Marshall, W. I.
Fitchburg, Mass. (active 1870s)

Marshall made a fine series of 120 views of Yellowstone National Park. His views usually are high-quality prints on red mounts with descriptive backs.

Martin, Alexander
Boulder, Central City and Denver, Colo. (active 1874 to 1901)

Martin made many fine views of Colorado, including mining towns, studio portraits of Indians, business interiors and scenery of the Rocky Mountains.

Mather, J. A.
Titusville, Pa. (active 1862 to 1895)

Mather documented the Pennsylvania oil boom of the 1860s at Petroleum Center, Pithole and so forth. He continued to photograph from a floating studio on Oil Creek in the 1870s and 1880s. The quality of his 1890 views does not match the early albumen prints for richness of tone.

McClees, J. E.
(also McClees and Germon)
Philadelphia (active 1855 to 1860)

McClees made a rare series of Philadelphia, Wissahickon Creek and "Washington City" (1859). Some of his views are tinted. He was making views in 1853 and 1854, but did not issue them commercially.

McClure, James
St. John, New Brunswick, Canada (active 1870s to 1880s)

McClure made excellent views of New Brunswick. Notable is his "Great Fire of 1877."

McIntosh, R. M.
Northfield, Vt. (1870s to 1880s)

McIntosh issued high-quality views on cabinet mounts, including the "Gems of Vermont Scenery." He made views of the Northfield quarries, Cavendish, Mt. Mansfield and others. One notable series is the "Ausable Chasm" (more than forty-five views).

McIntyre, A. C.
Alexandria Bay, Thousand Islands, N.Y. (1870s to 1880s)

McIntyre is known for his excellent coverage and high-quality views of the Thousand Islands. His views include Alexandria Bay, Westminster Park, Thousand Island Park and various islands. He made many nice views of groups at picnics, posed at boat docks and in front of hotels.

McLeish
(*See* W. H. Illingworth in Chapter 4)

McPherson, J.
Niagara Falls (1850s)

McPherson made many nice glass views of the falls and area. His glass views tend to be scarcer than those by Platt Babbitt, his chief competitor.

Meinerth, C.
Newburyport, Mass. (active 1860s to early 1870s)

Meinerth's views often were blindstamped for identification. His views are not common, but usually are of high quality. He also made still life scenes of shells, plants, and so forth.

Melander, L. M., and Brothers
Chicago (active 1860s to 1880s)

Melander made a number of fine series of views. Most notable are "Stereoscopic Groups and Portraits" (studio-posed groups, often with children; more than forty views, 1874–1875), "New Mexico and the Great South West" and "Views in the Black Hills" (including mining, Indians and towns; 1879). They also offered more than one hundred titles of Chicago plus a rare series of Mexico (1875). Most of the views before 1890 were distributed by Lovejoy and Foster. After 1890 they joined a co-op, The Globe Photo Art Company, which included Graves, Chase and others.

Moran, John
Philadelphia (active 1860s to 1870s)

Moran made a scarce series of Philadelphia. Most notable is "Sanitary Fair" in Philadelphia (1863). He also made a nice series of Delaware Water Gap (1865). In 1871 he joined Commander T. O. Selfridge's expedition to the Isthmus of Darien. That series was distributed by E. and H. T. Anthony. In 1872 Moran issued some Darien views, usually without credit and

John Moran, #167, "Water Birch, Catawissa Island, Catawissa Creek," near Philadelphia, ca. 1859.

Typical John Moran paper label affixed to backs of views.

limited manuscript titles. He is also noted for his beautifully hand-tinted views; his "Autumn Studies" are like miniature paintings.

Morgan, Rufus
Morganton, N.C. (active 1870s)

Morgan was a leading North Carolina stereo photographer. His notable series include

In and Around Raleigh, N.C.
Morganton, N.C. and Vicinity
Wilmington, N.C.

Morrow, S. J.
Yankton, Dakota Territory (active 1870s–1880s)

Morrow was an important western photographer, who made excellent (but rare) studio portraits of Indians. He also made views of Yankton and the Dakotas. His most notable series is "Gen. Crook's Expedition and the Black Hills" (1876) in pursuit of Sioux (thirty-one views plus eight additional views of Deadwood, Crook City and Custer City). Morrow was also the photographer on the General D. S. Stanley Yellowstone Expedition (1873).

Moulton, J. W. and J. S.
Salem, Mass. (active 1870s)

The Moultons offered a large and varied number of views in more than thirty series. The majority appear to be from original negatives, but not all were taken by the Moultons. Further study is needed of this publisher. They must have had wide distribution and a large output, because their views are encountered in nearly every large collection gathered in or from the 1870s. Their notable series include

Cape Ann, Mass. and Vicinity
Cape Ann Scenery
Central Park Scenery, New York
Colored Landscape Series
Gems of American Scenery
Groups of Statuary
Hopkinton and Westerly [R. I.]
Hudson River Scenery
Mauch Chunk, Pa., The Switzerland of America
New York City and Vicinity
New York State Scenery
Philadelphia, Pa. and Vicinity
Prospect Park, Brooklyn, N.Y.
Ruins of the Great Fire in Boston, Nov. 9th & 10th, 1872
Salem [Mass.] in 1876
1775—Centennial Series—1875, Views of Boston, Mass. and Vicinity

Views of Baltimore, Md. and Vicinity
Views of Boston, Mass. and Vicinity
Views of Lynn, Mass. and Vicinity
Views of Portland, Me. and Vicinity
Views of Salem, Mass. and Vicinity
Views of Washington, D.C.
White Mountains and Vicinity
Worcester, Mass. and Vicinity
Yosemite Valley, California

Muybridge, Eadweard J.
San Francisco (active 1867 to late 1870s, making stereo views as "helios")

Muybridge made more than one hundred views of Yosemite plus excellent views of railroads, the Mammoth Trees, San Francisco (and the earthquake of 1868) and the Modoc War (1872). Most of his views were published by Bradley and Rulofson of San Francisco. Many of the views are signed in the negative "helios."

Negretti and Zambra
London (active 1850s to 1860s)

Negretti and Zambra was a major early publisher. Most notable is a large series of the Crystal Palace and views of London and the British Isles, including Ireland. The company also issued Frith's series of Egypt and acted as a major distributor of paper and glass views for a number of photographers, many of whom go unnamed.

Nickerson, G. H.
Provincetown, Mass. (active 1860s to 1870s)

Nickerson is important for his many fine maritime views, including excellent scenes of ships and the whaling industry. He made an extensive series of the town of Provincetown, Cape Cod. He also made a view of the effects of ice on the fishing industry (winter of 1875) plus outstanding deck views. Nickerson made a small series of Truro, including the lighthouse and Kennebago, Maine.

Notman, William
Montreal, Canada, plus other locations in Canada and the United States (active 1856 to 1885)

Notman was a major photographer and publisher in Canada. He made views of the building of the St. Lawrence (Victoria) Bridge (1857), which are rare. In addition to views of Montreal and scenic studies, he made excellent stu-

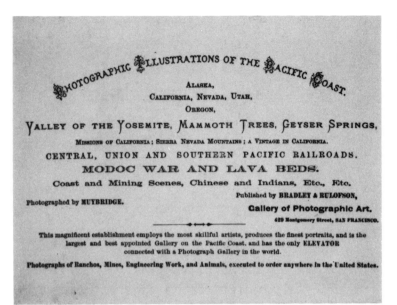

dio-posed "types," which include Indians, native costumes and special effects like falling snow. He opened branch galleries in various cities, including Albany, New York. He was involved with Edward L. Wilson in the Centennial Photographic Company (1876).

O'Sullivan, Timothy H.
(active 1859 to 1880)

O'Sullivan was a major Civil War and survey photographer. He originally was hired to work in Brady's Washington, D.C., studio with Alexander Gardner (1859). When the war started (1861), he was sent into the field with teams to make documentary coverage. He left Brady in 1863 and joined up with Gardner and others. He accompanied King's Fortieth Parallel Survey (1867) and photographed the Snake River and Shoshone Falls. O'Sullivan also made views of the Salt Lake area. The King Survey ended in 1869 and in 1870 O'Sullivan joined the Selfridge Expedition to the Isthmus of Darien. He joined the Wheeler Survey in 1871 and continued with his survey photography into 1879. He became an employee of the United States Treasury Department in 1880.

Timothy H. O'Sullivan, Wheeler Survey, expedition of 1873, "Ruins of Canon de Cheele. [sic]" (John Weiler Collection)

G. W. Pach, portrait of President Grant with his wife and son, posed before their cottage in Long Branch, N.J., 1872.

Pach, G. W.
(active 1862 to 1904, made few stereos after 1881)

Pach made views of New York City but is noted more for his views of Long Branch and Asbury Park, New Jersey, resort areas. He opened a branch gallery in Long Branch in 1867 and made views of groups posed on the beach as well as views of cottages. He made a nice series of Wesley Lake and Ocean Grove. Most of his views are on red mounts, sometimes without titles.

Parks, J. G.
Montreal, Canada (active 1860s to 1880s)

Parks made excellent views of Montreal and the surrounding area. He had a branch studio in Ottawa. Of particular note are Parks's views of crowded wharfs with tall ships. Most of his views are on red mounts.

Pollock, Charles
Boston (active 1860s to 1870s)

Pollock was a major photo printer in Boston and made views for a number of New England photographers. He also issued series with and without credit. Most notable are his views of Boston and vicinity (1872–1876); the Boston Fire (1872); Bristol, Rhode Island; Jamaica Plain, Massachusetts; and the White House (1870s; tinted). He also was the printer of the "Florida Club" series of St. Augustine. This was a co-op formed by George Pierron, Charles Seaver, the Ober Brothers and others to produce a uniform product for the tourist trade. Their views first went on sale in the winter of 1868. Pollock also produced the extensive series made by Seaver (*see* his listing). Most views appear without credit to Pollock. The majority of views are on yellow mounts with back lists of titles.

Charles Pollock, interior view of the "World's Peace Jubilee," Boston, 1872. (John Weiler Collection)

Proctor Brothers
Gloucester, Mass. (active 1870s)

The Proctor Brothers made an extensive series of Cape Ann scenery and the surrounding area. Their views usually are of high quality.

Purviance, W. T.
Philadelphia (active about 1867 to late 1870s)

Purviance made many views in the series "The Scenery of the Pennsylvania Central Rail Road." It is believed he was the official photographer. He made excellent views of the entire route, including bridges (Pittsburgh, Sharpsburg and others) and the railroad shops (Altoona). Most of his views are on yellow mounts. Purviance also made numerous scenic studies.

Rau, William H.
Philadelphia (active 1874 to 1905)

Rau was the assistant to John Moran on the Transit of Venus expedition to Tasmania (1874).

He also photographed the Rockies and Yellowstone Park and worked as a photographer for E. L. Wilson of the Centennial Photographic Company (1876). Rau accompanied E. L. Wilson to Egypt in 1881, making the "Scenes in the Orient," which was published by Wilson without credit to Rau. In the 1890s Rau was a prolific maker of stereo views, which were published by Griffith and Griffith, and in the late 1890s to 1905 he published by himself as Universal View Company. Notable views are of the Boer War, the Spanish-American War, United States Navy vessels and the St. Louis Fair (Louisiana Purchase Exposition, 1904).

Russell, A. J., and Company
New York City (active 1860s to 1870s)

Russell worked as a Civil War photographer for the United States Military Construction Corporation. He made the extensive series

The Ohio River at Cincinnati.

(Top) William H. Rau (sold by Griffith and Griffith), #7880, The busy levee in Cincinnati, an 1872 negative published about 1890 and (bottom) the same view as a color lithograph published about 1905.

"Union Pacific R.R. Stereoscopic Views," photographing railway construction from Cheyenne, Wyoming Territory, to Promontory Point (1868–1869). He made the "Joining of the Rails" series (1869). In 1870 he continued coverage of Union Pacific Railroad as far as California. In 1868 Russell began publishing the series "Pacific R.R. Views Across the Continent West from Omaha." The views are found without credit to Russell, but rather credit went to O. C. Smith, who obtained the negatives in about 1875 and issued them until the late 1870s. Notable series include

Platte Series
Black Hills Series
Uintah Series
Echo Kanyon [*sic*] Series
Echo City Series
Weber Kanyon [*sic*] Series
Devil's Gate Series
Salt Lake Valley Series
California Series
Groups & Indians Series

Savage, Charles R.
Salt Lake City (active 1863 to 1870 as Savage and Ottinger and remained into the 1880s)

Savage made a remarkably complete record of the Mormon settlement of Utah, including Salt Lake. He photographed the "Joining of the Rails" at Promontory Point (1869) plus made a number of fine railroad views. He made many scenic studies. Most of Savage's views are on green standard-size mounts or orange cabinet mounts.

Seaver, Charles
Boston (1860s to 1870s)

Seaver was a prolific photographer who made series of views throughout the eastern United States. Unfortunately, most of his views are without credit. Charles Pollock printed the views usually on yellow mounts with backlists of titles. Along with George Pierron and others, he formed the "Florida Club," a co-op of stereo photographers that issued views to tourists at St. Augustine. The Seaver "Tropical Series" documented Seaver's trip on the Ocklawaha River from Silver Springs, Florida. Other views were made at Macon, Georgia, and Cincinnati, Ohio. The views are characterized by high-quality prints. His notable series include

Ashaway and Vicinity
Boston and Vicinity
California [possibly purchased negatives]
Gems of American Scenery [selections from various series, including Niagara Falls, White Mountains, New York City, etc.]
Hopkinton and Westerly
Mill Creek Flood
Mount Auburn Cemetery, Cambridge, Mass.
Newport, R.I.
New York City
Providence, R.I.
St. Louis, Mo. [part of Ohio and Mississippi River series, which included Cincinnati]
Tropical Series [Florida]
Worcester, Mass.

Soulier
(See C. M. Ferrier in Chapter 4)

Sommer and Behles, G. Sommer
Naples and Behles, Rome, Italy (active 1860s to 1874)

Their views are on thin off-white mounts with gold borders boxing in the prints and titles. The print quality generally is very high and the subject matter is varied. Their series include Pompeii, Sicily, Naples and antiquities. Sommer and Behles also issued views separately. Sommer issued views into the 1870s.

Soule, John P.
Boston (active 1860 to 1872)

Soule was a prolific maker of views in the 1860s and 1870s; his views usually are of high quality. The early issues are on ivory mounts and include the White Mountains (1861). He made a nice series of Niagara beginning in 1862, including scenes of the suspension bridge. This was followed by marine studies at Cape Ann (1863). Most public buildings, parks, gardens and streets in Boston were documented by Soule. He photographed the Portland, Maine, fire (1866) and the Boston fire (1872). He issued a series of more than 250 views of California in 1870 from negatives obtained from M. M. Hazeltine (without credit). These views are on yellow mounts and include excellent scenes of lumbering and the Yosemite Valley. Soule made a series of Washington, D.C. Of interest is a series of about 30 views of "skeleton leaves" designed by Mrs. I. L. Rogers (1870). Notable is the unique vignetted kittens

Fancy back imprint used by A. F. Styles, ca. 1866.

series of at least 50 views using kittens in playful poses (1869–1872).

Styles, Adin F.
Burlington, Vt. (active 1860 to 1868, in Vermont; 1869–1870 in Florida).

Styles thoroughly covered Vermont, making views of most of the towns and scenic areas of the Green Mountains. His views were sold by Ward of Boston, sometimes without credit. Styles made a series of the White Mountains; the Adirondacks; Fort Ticonderoga; Greenwood Cemetery, New York; James River, Virginia; and Florida. He was an excellent landscape photographer and taught many photographers who established New England galleries in the following twenty years. Most notably he taught William H. Jackson to be a landscape photographer (*see* Jackson). Styles used an attractive "fancy" imprint on many of his Green Mountain views.

Sweeny, Thomas T.
Cleveland, Ohio (active 1860 to 1889)

Sweeny was one of the better Midwest photographers. He made more than 500 views of Cleveland and vicinity, including architecture, streets, canal boats, and shipping. He also photographed the Chicago fire ruins (1871; 112 views); Sandusky Bay, Ohio; Nashville, Tennessee; St. Louis, Missouri, and Detroit, Michigan. He also made a series of advertising views for the Cleveland Bridge and Car Works, which included scenes of bridges completed by the company in Ohio, and Indiana. His most notable views are of the National Photographer's Association Convention of 1870 in Cleveland.

Thurlow, James
Manitou, Colo. (active 1874 to 1878)

Although active only a short time, Thurlow made a fine series of views of Colorado, especially around Manitou Springs: "Manitou and Vicinity." Mrs. Thurlow sold the collection of negatives to Charles Weitfle in 1879. These were published for the next four years without credit to Thurlow. In addition to Manitou Springs, Thurlow made a large series of the Garden of the Gods rock formations, Pike's Peak, the Grand Canyon of the Arkansas, Twin Lakes and Leadville. The views usually are on light gray cabinet mounts with thin paper labels at the lower left front of the mount.

Underwood and Underwood, Bert and Elmer
New York and many other locations worldwide (active about 1882 to 1921, and continued afterward as a news service)

At one time, Underwood and Underwood was the largest publisher of stereo views in the world, producing 10 million views a year. The brothers developed a selling system of thorough canvassing using college students. They became the sole distributors of views by Charles Bierstadt, James F. Jarvis and the Littleton View Company in the mid-1880s. By 1900 they had added the George Barker views and were producing views under their own imprint. They outgrew their original office in Ottawa, Kansas, by 1887 and their headquarters were moved to New York City; offices were also opened in Canada and Europe. They purchased the photoprinting works of Strohmeyer and Wyman,

Underwood & Underwood, "Prince Henry, Chief Wilkie, Asst. Gen. Passgr. Agt. Boyd and Engineer Gilchrist—on the Western Tour," 1902.

Underwood & Underwood, privately issued view of Elmer Underwood and his family, 1908. (Gordon D. Hoffman Collection)

and by 1901 they were producing 25,000 views a day and 300,000 stereoscopes a year. They hired James Ricalton to make a series in the Orient and India and Albert K. Hibbard (later to make Corte-Scope views) to make occupational scenes in the United States and, later, in Europe, including World War I views. Bert Underwood learned photography in 1891 and eventually made diverse views in Arizona, Italy, Greece and many of the comic scenes. Henry Strohmeyer made the animal views and many of the Spanish-American War views, Prince Henry's visit and United States naval ships. The firm could not keep up with the tremendous competition of Keystone View Company and ceased production in late 1920. The negatives passed to Keystone, which issued them with a *V* prefix.

Universal Photo Art Company.

(*See* Carlton H. Graves in Chapter 4)

Universal View Company

(*See* William H. Rau in Chapter 4)

Vallee, L. P.

Quebec City, Canada (active 1860s to 1880s)

Vallee made a fine series of Quebec and vicinity. Notable are his busy market scenes and views of people.

Waldack, Charles

Cincinnati, Ohio (active 1857 to 1873)

Waldack was one of Cincinnati's most important photographers. He made many excellent views of buildings, streets, the steamboat landing and the suspension bridge. Most notable is his "Magnesium Light Views in Mammoth Cave," made during a thirty-five-hour expedition into the cave in 1866. These were the first successful photographs made by artificial light in a cave. A forty-two-view series was published by E. and H. T. Anthony and remained on their trade list until 1873.

Wasson, C. L., International View Company

Decatur, Ill. (active about 1900 to 1908)

Little is known of Wasson or his company and further study is needed. He produced a num-

Charles Waldack, "Incline, Cincinnati," ca. 1870.

ber of excellent views, including more than 200 titles of the Spanish-American War, a fine series of McKinley's funeral in Canton, Ohio (1901), and many comic and sentimental views.

Watkins, Carleton E.

San Francisco (active as a stereo photographer 1860 to 1891).

Watkins was one of the west's most famous photographers. He made several series of Yosemite, beginning in 1860. The first issue is on glass and paper prints with manuscript titles and are signed (thus they are called "signed Watkins" by collectors). He made a series of Mariposa Grove, Big Trees, New Almaden mines and Mendocino as "Watkins' Pacific Coast." He obtained A. A. Hart's Central Pacific Railroad negatives in 1869 and published them without credit to Hart. Watkins greatly expanded his stereo view business in the 1870s, including views of Mt. Shasta and additional San Francisco views. In 1873 he published

Modoc War views from negatives by Louis Heller. In the same year, he photographed in Utah. Nevada's Comstock Lode was documented in 1875, but the economic slump caused Watkins to lose his gallery in 1876 to I. W. Taber, who issued Watkins's views without credit. Watkins rephotographed California and produced the "New Series," beginning in 1875. In 1880 Watkins photographed in Arizona, including mining scenes. He photographed the northwest (Puget Sound) in 1882. Although Watkins suffered numerous setbacks, he produced some of the best stereo views of the far west.

Webster and Albee

Rochester, New York (active 1880s to 1890s)

Webster and Albee were a major publisher of pirated copies of views. Much of the activity in printing copy views was centered in Rochester (Union View Company, C. W. Woodward and Webster and Albee issued huge

C. E. Watkins, #1091, "Tutocanula Pass, Yosemite Valley," 1867.

quantities). Confusion exists because Webster and Albee also issued views from original negatives, but often the quality is low. They issued a series of about 200 views of the Spanish-American War (*see also* C. W. Woodward in Chapter 4).

Weitfle, Charles
Central City, Colo. (active 1878 to 1883)

Weitfle was a major Colorado photographic entrepreneur who arrived in Colorado at the height of the mining boom. He purchased the stereo negatives of James Thurlow, F. D. Storm, Ben Hawkins and some of the William Chamberlain views. Weitfle added his own negatives over the following five years to become a major producer. He contracted with Barkalow Brothers Railroad News Agents, who sold Weitfle's views in newsstands throughout the west. In addition to scenic Colorado, there are excellent mining and railroad views plus scenes of the boom towns of Leadville, Central City, Idaho and Blackhawk. The negative numbers from #401 to 478 are of scenes in Utah and Wyoming, including the Union Pacific Railroad construction and Salt Lake City. Views are on light gray, yellow or buff cabinet mounts with a fancy back showing medals won by Weitfle.

Weller, F. G.
Littleton, N.H. (active 1867 to 1877)

Weller was best known for his series "Stereoscopic Treasures," which features nice studio-posed views depicting family strife, children and ghosts. Notable is the "Night before Christmas" series based on the famous poem. He also issued White Mountain scenery. Many of Weller's views were tinted. The negatives passed to G. H. Aldrich and soon after (about 1879) were obtained by Littleton View Company, which gave credit to Weller. Eventually the views were sold by Underwood and Underwood, thus making them available from the 1870s into the 1890s.

White, H. C.
North Bennington, Vt. (active 1899 to about 1912)

White was a major publisher of high-quality views. He offered more than 12,000 views of nearly every worldwide subject. The views are on deep greenish brown or black mounts. The black lettering is often difficult to read on the mounts. They also issued an attractive series with gold lettering. The first issues are on buff mounts. Although the gold lettering is stunning, they are rarely offered today at a premium price. White issued book-boxed sets, but they are much scarcer than those issued by Keystone View Company or Underwood and Underwood. Hawley C. White, the owner and namesake of the company, coined the name "Perfec-Stereographs" to describe his views. The negatives passed to Keystone View Company in 1915. Notable series or sets include

Animals, #6201–6220
Baltimore Fire (1904), #10381–10395
Coney Island, #490–513
General Slocum Disaster (1904), #8298–8299 and
    #8400–8405

Charles Weitfle #182, "Georgetown [Colorado], Looking North," ca. 1879.

Inauguration of Theodore Roosevelt, Washington, March 4, 1905, #9911–9928

India, #14001–14100

Martinique Disaster, (1902), #8201–8218

President Roosevelt's Hunting Trip in Colorado, #9929–9947

Prince Henry's Visit to the United States (1902), #8155–8192

San Francisco Disaster (1906), #8701–8733

Whiting View Company

Cincinnati, Ohio [active 1900 (although some negatives date earlier) to 1943. Regular card-mounted views were published to 1908]

The Whiting Brothers (Richard R. and William A.) were Keystone salesmen up to 1899. Richard Ross Whiting had made many of the 1897–1899 Keystone negatives. They published card-mounted views (some beautifully hand colored) up to 1908. Later they reorganized as the American Novelty Company (1913) and began manufacturing Whiting's "Sculptoscope," a metal drumlike penny arcade viewer. The views were trimmed and notched photographs or lithographs (supplied by Ingersoll). Although business declined after 1929, they remained active to 1943. The card-mounted views of the "Twentieth Century Series" are on buff, orange or dark gray mounts and span a variety of subjects. Most notable are their excellent views of the Louisiana Purchase Exposition in St. Louis (1904–1905).

Whitney, J. E., Whitney and Zimmerman

St. Paul, Minn. (active 1860s to 1870s)

Whitney made many fine early views of Minnesota, especially of Minneapolis and St. Paul,

Whiting View Co., #614, "Air Ship Station, World's Fair Grounds, St. Louis, Mo., 1904." (Gordon D. Hoffman Collection)

Whiting View Co., photographic views trimmed and notched for their penny arcade Sculptoscope viewer, ca. 1912. Note the misspelling of stereographs. They also issued color lithos, which are very common.

Fort Snelling and scenic areas. The most common is the large series of Minne-ha-ha Falls, which was photographed in summer and winter, vignetted and seen from all angles. There are even some beautifully hand-colored views of the falls. Of note are the fine Indian views, mostly of Sioux and Winnebagos; many of the Indians are posed in front of their teepees. Whitney made historic series of refugees fleeing from the Indian massacre in Minnesota (1862). Most of the Whitney views are on yellow or cream mounts, imprinted with "Gems of Minnesota Scenery"; they often have copyright dates.

Wilson, Edward L.
(active 1870s to 1890s)

E. L. Wilson, noted as publisher of *The Philadelphia Photographer*, ventured into the stereo business in 1876 by forming the Centennial Photographic Company along with Notman and others. Wilson hired Rau to be his chief photographer. Most notable is "Scenes in the Orient," which was published in 1882. Wilson was a very influential person in the promotion of stereo photography in the 1870s and 1880s (*see also* Centennial Photographic Company and William H. Rau).

Wilson, George Washington
Aberdeen, Scotland (active 1850s to 1870s)

G. W. Wilson was one of the early masters of stereo photography. He was noted for beautiful compositions and the use of light to enhance his subjects. His views are found on bright yellow mounts with paper labels (usually blue or green) on the reverse. He made many fine views in Scotland, especially of Edinburgh, ships and Greenwich. Wilson is also noted for his pioneer work in making "instantaneous" views in the days when wet-plate photography was so slow in exposure that any motion was blurred. Wilson also made a series in Ireland (Giant's Causeway).

Wilson, J. N.
Savannah, Ga. (active 1860s to 1870s)

J. N. Wilson was a leading photographer in Savannah. He made many views of the city and waterfront. He also stereo-photographed the loading of cotton at wharves, ships and so forth. His most common views are the many views of Bonaventure, showing moss-covered trees, palmettoes and the cemetery. Although popular in the 1870s, these views are of little interest to collectors. In contrast, the waterfront views by Wilson are eagerly sought by collectors. Wilson took a partner in the late 1870s (O. P. Havens) and operated as Wilson and Havens. Havens eventually took over the business.

Wittick, George Benjamin
(also as Wittick and Russell)
Albuquerque, N.M. (active 1880s)

Wittick was a prolific photographer, but examples of his work are scarce. He made excellent views of Indians and the territories, the most notable are his views at Walpi Mesa in the late 1880s. Most of his views are on orange cabinet mounts.

Woodward, C. W.
(also as Woodward View Company)
Rochester, N.Y. (active 1870s to 1880s)

Confusion exists because Woodward issued a variety of views in several qualities. It is known

George Washington Wilson, #186, "Princess Street, Edinburgh—Looking East," ca. 1859. An early "instantaneous" street scene.

that Woodward supplied the trade with low-cost views, offering copies at $1–2 per dozen for views from "original" negatives (June 1876 catalog). He also offered "seconds" in 1000-view lots at reduced prices. In the 1870s Union View Company also offered cheap copies. These apparently were made by Woodward. Webster and Albee, also located in Rochester, offered copy views, but those views appear to be different from the Woodward/Union View Company views. Major series include

Central Park, New York City and Greenwood Cemetery

Fairmount Park, Philadelphia
Genesee Falls, Rochester and Vicinity
Groups [copies]
Holyland and Egypt [copies]
Mount Hope Cemetery, Rochester
Niagara Falls, N.Y.
Philadelphia and Vicinity
Switzerland [copies]
(*see also* Webster and Albee).

Zimmerman
(*See* J. E. Whitney)

5

EVALUATING STEREO VIEWS

Many factors must be considered in the evaluation of stereo views. As noted, condition is very important. The photographer or publisher, the subject and the vintage of issue are the other factors. All taken together, the value then must be considered in terms of the location of the eventual sale. A stereo view of the Alaska Gold Rush of 1898 may sell for more in Alaska than in other parts of the United States. A view of California may sell for less in Ohio than in California.

The basic rule of thumb is that a view tends to increase in value as the subject moves west in the United States. In other words, a view of a railroad locomotive in New Hampshire will sell for less than the same subject in Illinois, and a premium is paid for a locomotive view in the west. Pre-1890 flat-mount views are of greater value than post-1890 curved-mount views. There are exceptions, of course. There is very little collector value for views copied from an original source (pirated copies) or for printed views (lithographs). Views that have damaged mounts, heavy soiling, stains, bends, tears, fading or other flaws sell for far less than the same view in excellent, near-new condition.

Rarity has very little to do with the value of stereo views. Some views by local makers were made in very small quantities. Unlike coins and stamps, where the only known existing example of an item may have great value, a one-of-a-kind stereo view will have little premium value unless the subject is highly collectible.

Values in this price guide were based on more than nine years of mail/phone auction sales I have conducted. I also consulted sales conducted by more than a dozen other dealers in addition to the National Stereoscopic Association's annual Spotlight Auction. A comparison of all of these sales shows some very interesting patterns.

ARE STEREO VIEWS A GOOD INVESTMENT?

The answer is yes and no. Some views that sold for $2 in 1981 are still selling for $2 in 1990. At the current rates of inflation, one must conclude that the value of such a view has fallen. Other views that sold for $20 in 1981 sell for $200 or more today. The views that have appreciated the most are classic western United States subjects such as the 1869 Transcontinental Railroad views, busy street

Keystone View Co., #38554, "President Eisenhower." This view has advanced to nearly $250 in excellent condition, about four times its value in 1981. (Gordon D. Hoffman Collection)

scenes, mining views and views by noted photographers.

Pre-1890 views in general have advanced, but some have failed to keep up with inflation. Strong categories include famous people, transportation (especially railroads), occupationals and expositions. Slow growth has been experienced in views of such cities as Boston and Chicago, but there has been strong growth in views of western cities such as San Francisco and Denver.

Post-1890 views have had mixed sales. Good street scenes, occupationals, historic events (other than World War I), aviation and famous people views have all advanced. Mass-produced "tour" views and World War I views have not kept pace with inflation.

Since 1981, there has been tremendous growth in the modern-era material, which includes views produced by View-Master and Tru-Vue. Most of this material was made in large quantities and should begin to level out in the next few years.

FACTORS IN PRICING

Prices given are for very good condition (i.e., some wear and very slight soiling). For excellent condition add 25 percent. Deduct 25 percent for good condition (i.e., moderate soiling with some damage to the mount, minor streaking of prints, some foxing/brown spots). Deduct 75 percent for poor condition (i.e., folded mount, very dirty, damage to tone, faded). Where applicable, a price range is given. Regional factors should be considered when evaluating stereo views. All views listed are

card-mounted real photos unless noted otherwise. Lithographic views (printed on the cards) have very little collector value.

VIEWS AND THEIR PRICES

Advertising
(See also Corte-Scope views in Chapter 6)

Early on, enterprising individuals and companies saw the value of using stereo views to sell products and services. Advertising views fall into three basic categories. First are views where the advertising on the mount front or reverse relates directly to the stereo view subject. An example is an interior of a store with a full advertisement on the reverse for the store's wares. Second are views that indirectly advertise the product without any special descriptive imprint. An example is a scene of a hotel with the name and location of the hotel imprinted on the reverse along with the name of the proprietor. Third are views where the advertising does not relate to the subject depicted. An example is a view of Paris with ads on the reverse for stores in Portland, Maine. This third type of advertising view can be found in a variety of mount and print qualities.

Bridge—Wrought Iron Bridge Co., Canton, Ohio, Iron bridge across Allegheny River at Kittany, Pa. _____ 8.00
Hair Dressing Parlor—Interior of Clough & Co., Providence, R.I., 1882, Label on reverse _____ 45.00
Railroad Co.—L. McLean view of Beaver Brook Station, Clear Creek, Colo., with train in distance, ad on reverse for railroad and the benefits of this stop _____ 35.00

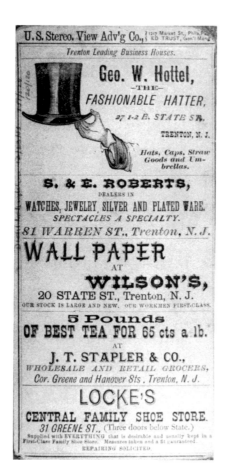

Example of multiple ads sold on views by U.S. Stereo View Advertising Co. The view on the front does not relate to the ads; ca. 1870s. $2–4 each.

Real estate—J. Wing view of Dr. H. E. Bennett, Rockport property for sale _____ 45.00
Stereo view manufacturing—H. C. White, #8272–8290, Views of factory and operations _____ 75.00–150.00
Stereo view sales—Keystone View Co., Scene showing use of 600-view World Tour in home _____ 45.00
Store—Interior of J. W. Hutchinson & Son's Books, Music and Jewelry Store, Appleton, Wisc., 1870s _____ 20.00
Tailoring—Interior of E. N. Winslow's Establishment, Lawrence, Mass., 1870s, ad for store on reverse _____ 15.00
Tools, machine—J. R. Brown & Sharpe Co., Providence, R.I., Complete technical description on reverse _____ 50.00
Yosemite Valley—Scene with ad on reverse for Boston 99¢ store, 1870s _____ 2.00

Africa

(See also Egypt *in Chapters 5 and 6 and* Near East *in* Chapter 6*)*

The Dark Continent was being fully explored when stereo views first came into vogue. Pre-1890 views showing areas other than Egypt and the Barbary Coast countries such as Tunis and Morocco are very uncommon. The interior of Central Africa was not fully documented until about 1898. A few photographers, most notably G. Burger of Berlin, made views of South Africa (Cape Colony) prior to 1900, but these are very rare. The Boer War (1899–1901) was covered in detail by Kilburn, Underwood and Underwood, Keystone View Company and H. C. White. These views of what was called the "South African War" are listed under Wars.

G. Burger, Cape of Good Hope scenes, ca. 1872 _____ 35–50.00
E. Burmester, Cape Town, ca. 1867 ___ 25–35.00

Special unnumbered Keystone View Co. view used by salesmen to show the 600-view world tour set in use in a typical home. Note the boxes in the view are the earlier flip-top book boxes. $45 (Gordon D. Hoffman Collection)

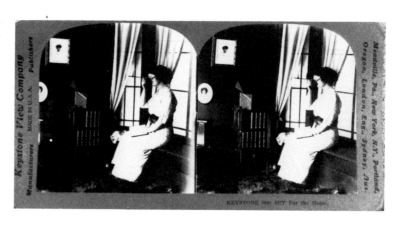

Richebourg, Algiers, blindstamped, ca.
1856 _____ 50–75.00
Keystone, #961, Tangier _____ 5.00
Keystone, #8659, An Oasis Town in
the Sahara _____ 2.00
Keystone, #V17095, Ivory and rubber
ready for shipment (Underwood &
Underwood negative) _____ 3.00
Keystone, #33382, An Arab woman
in street costume _____ 3.00
Underwood & Underwood, #(29),
Cape Town with Table Mountain in
the distance _____ 6.00
Universal Photo Art, #7393–7399,
Views of Algiers _____ 3–6.00
    #7393, In the Native Quarter
    #7394, A Street in the European
    Quarter
    #7395, The Entrance to a Mosque
    #7396, A Writer of the Koran
    #7397, Algerian Children
    #7398, Algerian Women and Babies
    #7399, A Street in the Arab Quarter
H. C. White, #3101–3161, Views of
South Africa _____ 3–6.00
H. C. White, #16401–16433, Views of
Algeria _____ 3–6.00
H. C. White, #16502–16511, Views of
Tunis _____ 4–8.00

Alaska (Gold Rush)

Very few stereo views were taken in Alaska before the Gold Rush of 1898. The exception is the remarkable, but rare, series by Eadweard Muybridge of San Francisco, published in 1868. The Muybridge views may possibly be the earliest stereo views of Alaska. There may have been a Russian photographer operating in the area, but no examples of views have surfaced. The views of Sitka by Muybridge are eagerly sought by collectors. Another photographer visited Sitka in the late 1870s, and this series was published by Continent Stereoscopic Company about 1878. T. W. Ingersoll made a series in the late 1880s that was published until about 1905. These vary in quality and often are faded. A few views were taken by photographers from Washington and Oregon in the 1890s and are generally uncommon outside their area. Fred G. L. Hunt of Skagway, Alaska, made a series around 1900 that includes views of local Indian natives and the fishing industry. Mention also should be made of the rare series made in 1891 by F. Jay Haynes of Dakota. The series includes outstanding scenes of Juneau and Sitka plus the Taku Glacier.

Few Americans knew much about Alaska until the Great Klondike Gold Rush, which began in 1898. The purchase of the vast territory by Secretary of State Seward for two cents an acre during the Civil War had been greeted with scorn by citizens taxed with the financial burden of the war effort. This was all forgotten as the area often called "Icebergia" yielded riches beyond imagination. Along with the many miners, supply outfitters and prostitutes came the stereo photographers ready to record the excitement. As a result, the stereo record gives a remarkable glimpse of this time in our history. Nearly every major publisher, plus a few lesser-known publishers, offered extensive series showing the mining camps, claims and harsh weather conditions. In addition, look for views of outfitters and ships being loaded at Seattle.

Berry, Kelley, & Chadwick (negatives by William H. Rau)
    Dawson City and Yukon River,
    1900 _____ 6.00
    Miners working claim _____ 18.00

Whiting View Co., #1352, "Uckalook, a Cobuck Indian, Alaska." $18.

Keystone View Co., #9288, "An Alaskan Deity, Wrangel, Alaska," 1898. $10.

F. J. Haynes, Juneau and Sitka
scenes _____ 50–100.00
Fred G. L. Hunt, Native fishermen's
children _____ 20.00
T. W. Ingersoll
   Totem poles at Kiang-Kwan _____ 4.00
   Old Greek cemetery, Sitka _____ 3.00
Keystone View Co.
   Gold Rush series _____ 5–10.00
   President Harding's trip to Alaska,
   #18514–18597 and #28002 _____ 15–30.00

In the summer of 1923, President Warren G. Harding made a special trip to Alaska. He traveled by train and was the first United States president to visit the territory. On the return home, President Harding died suddenly in San Francisco. Keystone rushed the views of the trip onto the market in a special boxed set. Shortly afterward, the Harding administration was racked with scandal and Harding quickly became unpopular. Keystone broke up the unsold sets and the remainder was sold off. (*See also* Personalities in Chapter 5.)

B. W. Kilburn
   #12726, "Bound for the Klondyke
   [*sic*]" _____ 5.00
   #12734, Supply camp at base of Chil-
   koot Pass _____ 6.00
   #13106, "Mine Exchange and Post Office, Dawson" _____ 20.00
   #13109, "Street Scene, Dawson
   City" _____ 20.00
   #13115, Sternwheel steamer on Yukon
   River _____ 15.00
   #13132, "Newcomers selling out to go
   home" _____ 20.00
Eadweard Muybridge (1868), published
by Bradley & Rulofson of San Francisco _____ 75–125.00
Underwood & Underwood
   Mine where a single pan of gravel
   yielded $400 _____ 15.00
   Curious totem poles at Wrangel, 1902 ___ 6.00
   #4710, "The Fantastic Potlatch Dancers, Indian Village of Klinkwan." _____ 20.00
   #4714, "A Native Home, with its totem
   poles and Laundry Pool." _____ 15.00
   #4852, Gold miners at Sluice, Klondike, Yukon _____ 15.00
   #10655, "Miners on the Rim of the
   'glory hole' at the Treadwell Mine." ____ 10.00

R. Y. Young (American Stereoscopic Co.) "Getting the drop on him—Barroom scene in the Klondike," 1901. This is tinted tissue format. The view can also be found as regular prints on buff card mount. Dramatically staged scene of gamblers about to get into a gunfight. Note black man seated at right. $20.

Universal Photo Art Co. (C. H.
Graves) ————————————————— 8–15.00
Universal View Co. (negatives by William
H. Rau, also sold by Griffith & Griffith,
and Berry, Kelley & Chadwick)
   Claim 23, above Hunker, the Klon-
   dike ————————————————— 15.00
   The Gorge of Miles Canon [*sic*], the
   Klondike ———————————————— 9.00
   #2766, The Klondike, crowd at Steam-
   boat Landing, Dawson ——————— 15.00
   #3220, Working #4, Bonanza ———— 20.00
   #3229, Mining gold in the Klondike —— 15.00
   #3238, Working #6, Eldorado ———— 20.00
Whiting View Co. ————————————— 2–8.00
R. Y. Young (American Stereoscopic Co.;
also available as tissues)
   "A Baloon [*sic*] Ascension in Dawson,
   Y.T., 1900." ——————————————— 40.00
      (Same view as a tissue) ————— 80.00
   "Getting the drop on him," Barroom
   scene in the Klondike, 1901 (staged
   scene) ————————————————— 10.00
      (Same view as a tissue) ————— 20.00
   Police station, Dawson, Yukon Territory,
   1900 —————————————————— 15.00
      (Same view as a tissue) ————— 30.00

Amateur Views

Soon after the Langenheim Brothers introduced their views in the United States, amateurs were purchasing equipment to make their
own views. Most of the early activity was centered in the Philadelphia area, New York City
and upstate New York.

   The major supplier of equipment was Edward Anthony and his brother, Henry, who
was an avid stereo amateur. A correspondence
and friendship was struck with F. F. Thompson of New York City. Thompson had written
to some other amateurs and proposed the formation of a club that eventually became the

Amateur Photographic Exchange Club. Two
leading members were Professor John Towler
of Geneva, New York, and Coleman Sellers of
Philadelphia. Each member of the club (which
eventually included more than twenty members) exchanged a stereo view of their own
making with every other member six times a
year. F. F. Thompson acted as secretary and
issued a newsletter. The first exchange was
made in 1861. Dr. Oliver Wendell Holmes was
an honorary member but never made an exchange. The Amateur Photographic Exchange
Club only lasted three years and was finally
disbanded when supplies became scarce due
to the Civil War. In addition, some members
had joined the war effort and were unable to
complete their exchanges. Thompson and
Towler continued an unofficial correspondence in the 1870s, and a few of their views
surface in old collections.

   After the Civil War, cameras and supplies
became available and many amateurs made
views. Quality varies on these views. Many
amateurs failed to wash their prints properly
to remove all latent light-sensitive chemicals,
and thus many existing views today are found
badly faded or streaked. Mounting also was a
problem, and flat or pseudoscopic images were
made by uninformed amateurs. Unfortunately, many amateur stereo views were unmarked and unlabeled.

   Several societies were organized to band together amateurs. The oldest is the Stereoscopic
Society, which was founded in England in 1893
and continues today. Members exchange information and mail folios to a route list. Each
member prepares a stereo view. When the fo-
lio box arrives, it includes a view made by each

Amateur view of a steamer on Lake Yellowstone. Most amateur views are uninteresting or of poor quality. Occasionally one is found like this with an interesting subject and above-average print quality. $15. (Gordon D. Hoffman Collection)

Scarce view by an accomplished amateur of construction of the Williamsburgh Bridge, New York City. Often an amateur took the only known views of a subject, but the views often are inferior in quality. This is an exception. $15.

Charles Lindbergh seated in Navy biplane during his visit to the Naval Air Station, Pensacola, Fla., Oct. 9, 1928 by amateur photographer L. E. Goodnight, a member of the Stereoscopic Society. $100.

member of the society. Each view is in a special envelope large enough for members to write on their comments. The recipient removes his view and replaces it with a new view, makes his comments on the others, and sends the box on to the next name on the route list in no more than five days. Today, the Stereoscopic Society has expanded to North America and Australia. In 1990 the Stereoscopic Society, American Branch (of which I am member #712), became the Stereoscopic Society of America. The National Stereoscopic Association will celebrate the society's centennial in 1993. Placing values on amateur views is difficult. Quality and subject matter are the main factors.

Amateur Photographic Exchange Club
(1861–1864) ——————————— 20–50.00

Animals
(See also Cats, Children and Hunting and Fishing in Chapter 5)

In the early years of stereo photography, views of animals were of mounted specimens. These often were placed in natural-looking tableaux or even photographed outdoors. The slow speed of the glass plates (negatives) made it difficult to photograph animals in the wild.

The earliest significant attempt at live-animal studies was made by Frank Haes at the London Zoological Gardens. First made in 1864, this series was published by McLean and Haes and is very rare in the United States. More common are the London Zoo views made by F. York in the 1870s. Schreiber and Sons made a fine series of the Philadelphia Zoological Gardens plus a series of trotting horses. Of particular interest are the finely hand-colored views of very natural-looking mounted specimens by James A. Hurst made in 1870. Called "Stereoscopic Studies of Natural History," the series is on yellow mounts with fully detailed labels on the reverse. B. W. Kilburn obtained the Hurst series negatives about 1880 and continued to publish them but with new numbers and without the high quality and tinting of the originals.

Kilburn, Keystone, Underwood and Underwood, H. C. White and others made many animal views. Faster dry-plate photography of the post-1895 period permitted the manufacture of some outstanding, detailed views of animals in the wild and captive in zoos.

Birds
Hurst, Natural History series _____ 4–6.00
H. C. White, #6275–6282 _____ 3–5.00
Bison
Keystone, #10692, Herd on plain, British Columbia _____ 3.00
Cattle
Keystone, #21561, White-faced beef cattle _____ 2.00
Dogs
Kilburn, #1644, Home protection, close-up _____ 6.00
Underwood & Underwood, "The Puppies Singing School." _____ 4.00
Universal Photo Art, #3231, A scramble for refreshments, typical view _____ 4–5.00
Farmyard
Kilburn, #739, Sheep and cows, 1870s _____ 4.00
Fox (live)
Keystone, #P7814 _____ 2.00
Fox (mounted in tableau)
C. Bierstadt (sold by Underwood & Underwood) "The Christmas Dinner." _____ 3.00
Horses
Schreiber & Sons, "Jarvis," and Sulky, 1870s _____ 18.00
Kangaroos
Keystone, #15902, in Australian zoo _____ 2.00
Lions (caged)
Keystone, #P-16533, Close-up in zoo _____ 5.00
Mrs. Maxwell's (mounted Rocky Mountain animals)
Centennial Photo Co., exhibit at 1876 Exposition _____ 10.00
Colorado Museum interiors by local photographer _____ 20.00

Copy (pirated from one of the above) _____ 1.00
Moth
H. C. White, #6279, Cecropia moth _____ 6.00
Mules
Underwood & Underwood, "When Shall We Three Meet Again?" _____ 2.00
Skunks
Keystone, #V34461, A family at feeding _____ 5.00
Walrus
Keystone, #V21232, In Bronx Zoo _____ 3.00
Wolf (Prairie)
Hurst, Natural History series, 1870, tinted _____ 6.00
Zoos
London Stereoscopic Co., London Zoo _____ 8–10.00
McLean & Haes, London Zoo, 1860s _____ 20–35.00
C. Muhrman, Cincinnati Zoo, 1880s _____ 6–10.00
Schreiber & Sons, Philadelphia Zoo __ 6–10.00
F. York, London Zoo _____ 5–8.00

Astronomy

Stereo views of the moon were taken as early as 1858, but the first recognized commercial views were made by L. M. Rutherford in 1862. Several publishers offered the Rutherford view, including Beer Brothers, Bierstadt Brothers (later Charles Bierstadt and even later Underwood and Underwood) and E. and H. T. Anthony. This view was followed by another in 1864 and proved a very popular subject. Many pirated copies exist. J. W. Draper made a series of the various phases of the moon in the late 1860s, which were offered by Charles Bierstadt.

In the nineteenth century several attempts were made to photograph solar and lunar eclipses. The transit of Venus in 1874 was pho-

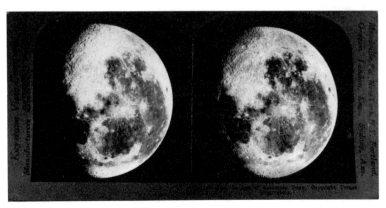

Keystone View Co., #16646, "Moon at Age of Seventeen Days." Note the 595 at top center indicates this view was from the 600-View "Tour of the World" book-boxed set. $4. (John Weiler Collection)

tographed by John Moran (in Tasmania) and D. R. Clark (in Siberia).

Keystone offered a nice series of heavenly bodies photographed at the Yerkes Observatory. They are often found as the last few numbers in the 600-View "Tour of the World" book-boxed set.

Many observatories and telescopes have been stereo-photographed. Many colleges and universities had observatories that were photographed by local makers.

Comet
Keystone, #16645, Morehouse
Comet _____ 9.00
Expeditions
The transit of Venus, Moran _____ 15–30.00
The transit of Venus, D. R. Clark
View of party or equipment _____ 15–30.00
Topographical views (local landscapes) _____ 5–10.00
Mars
Keystone, #16767 _____ 6.00
Meteor
Keystone, #16647, In constellation of Orion, 1904 _____ 3.00
Moon
S. F. Adams (by Rutherford) _____ 15.00
Bierstadt Bros. (by Rutherford) _____ 18.00
Charles Bierstadt (sold by Underwood & Underwood) _____ 3.00
Keystone _____ 4.00
Kilburn, #2630, full moon _____ 6.00
Rutherford, Beer Bros., blindstamp, 1866 _____ 15.00
John P. Soule, #602, last quarter _____ 8.00
Underwood & Underwood _____ 3.00
H. C. White, #8292–8294 _____ 5.00
#8292, First quarter
#8293, Full moon
#8294, Last quarter
Observatories
Pre-1900 by local photographers in the United States _____ 10–12.00

Underwood & Underwood, Lick Observatory, Calif. _____ 10.00
Underwood & Underwood, #9226, Observatory at San Domingo Convent, Lima, Peru _____ 5.00
Planetarium
Keystone, #32688, Adler's, Chicago _____ 10.00
Saturn
Keystone, #16767 _____ 6.00

Aviation

The history of flight is documented in detail in stereo views. Views of early balloon ascensions and famous aeronauts can be found, but the collector must be very persistent and prepared to pay top dollar for quality examples of pre-1885 views. The most famous aeronaut was Thaddeus S. C. Lowe who made his first flight in 1857. Lowe attempted a transatlantic flight by balloon in his *Great Western.* There are four known views of this failed attempt by an unknown photographer. The Civil War ended Lowe's attempts to cross the Atlantic but gave him the opportunity to display the military value of his balloons. E. and H. T. Anthony published several views of Lowe's flights including scenes at the Battle of Fair Oaks, Virginia.

A sensation of the 1867 Paris Exposition was Henry Giffard's huge captive balloon. Giffard's as well as other French balloons are seen in stereo views of the late 1860s into the 1870s. Professor King's *Buffalo,* flown in Ohio, New York and Tennessee in 1875 and 1876 drew huge crowds and was the subject of several fine views. Balloon stereo views are seen in series of exposition views including a number at the Louisiana Purchase Exposition in St. Louis (1904). The Boer War (South Africa)

Underwood & Underwood view of balloon used by Lord Roberts during advance on Pretoria, Boer War, South Africa, 1900. $25.

and Russo-Japanese War both used balloons for observation and these were stereo-photographed.

Lighter-than-air flight history is covered in detail from Baldwin's *California Arrow* airship to the great zeppelins. Amazingly, there is no view of the ill-fated *Hindenburg*. Keystone #33371 is often mistakenly identified as the *Hindenburg*, but it is actually the *Graf Zeppelin*. A rare series of one hundred views of the construction of the United States Navy airship *Macon* at Akron, Ohio, was made by Lynn Skeels. There are no known complete sets.

The Wright brothers and their *Flyer* changed the world forever. The first flight was not stereo-photographed, but a local amateur made a series in Dayton, Ohio, in the summer of 1904. Keystone #16644 may be the earliest commercial view of the Wright plane. Underwood and Underwood and Keystone made several views of the Wright demonstration for the army at Fort Myer, Virginia. Keystone was the primary maker of aviation views after 1912, making outstanding views of historic flights and noted aviators including Charles Lindbergh, Wiley Post and Major James H. Doolittle.

Keystone made a series "Air Travel," which features the exterior and interior of an American Airlines Stratoliner in the 1930s.

Air Mail

Keystone, #29446, United States air mail plane at Cleveland, Ohio _____ 25.00
Keystone, #32372, Inaugural flight, Ford trimotor New York to Los Angeles air-rail service, 1929 _____ 20.00

Aviators

Keystone, #26408, Six men who first circled earth _____ 15.00
Keystone, #28031, The flying major, James H. Doolittle _____ 40.00

Keystone, #32062, Colonel Charles Lindbergh with *Spirit of St. Louis* _____ 20.00
Keystone, #32762, Harold Gatty with Wiley Post, Chicago, Ill., 1931 _____ 35.00
Keystone, #34170, Amelia Earhart and others, Newark _____ 45.00

Balloons

Anthony, #2348, Professor Lowe observing the battle of Fair Oaks, Va. (seen standing in basket) _____ 100.00
Anthony, #2349, Professor Lowe replenishing the balloon from the balloon *Constitution* _____ 75.00
Anthony, #2350, Professor Lowe inflating his balloon on Gaine's Hill, Va. _____ 75.00
Anthony, #4114, Professor Lowe's flight from Sixth Avenue, in New York City _____ 100.00
Berry, Kelley, & Chadwick (negative by Rau), Ascension, Dawson City, Klondike _____ 40.00
H. R. Farr, Ascension at Minneapolis, 1882 _____ 65.00
Keystone, #12149 (negative by Underwood & Underwood), Army Signal Corp balloon ready to ascend _____ 30.00
Keystone, #15149, Balloon at St. Louis Exposition, 1904 _____ 65.00
Keystone, #26306, *Goodyear*, winner of elimination contest, starting great 1100-mile flight, 1924 _____ 20.00
Kilburn, #16512, Military balloons ascending, Liao Yang, Manchuria, Russo-Japanese War _____ 35.00
Kilburn, #16543, Military balloon, Manchuria, 1905 _____ 35.00
W. C. North, Cleveland, Ohio, *Buffalo* ascension, July 4, 1875, at least three known versions _____ 100.00
C. L. Pond, *Buffalo* in flight, 1875 _____ 50.00
W. G. Preston, Balloon ascending over Boston Coliseum, 1872 Peace Jubilee _____ 15.00
Underwood & Underwood (Jarvis negative), Balloon aloft over burn-

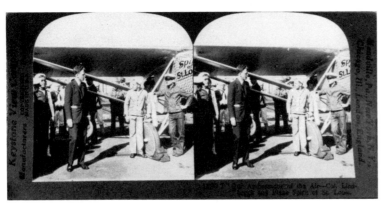

Keystone View Co., #32062, "Our Ambassador of the Air—Col. Lindbergh and Plane Spirit of St. Louis." $20.

C. L. Pond of Buffalo, N.Y., vignetted view of Professor King's balloon Buffalo *in flight, 1875. $50.*

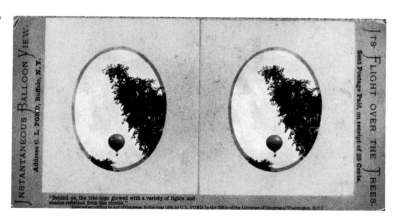

ing building, Russo-Japanese War, 1904 _____ 85.00

Underwood & Underwood, Lord Roberts's army advancing toward Johannesburg, 84th Battery and Balloon Corp., 1900 _____ 25.00

Underwood & Underwood, Lord Roberts's infantry crossing Zand River, balloon in background, Boer War, 1900 _____ 20.00

Underwood & Underwood, "Rival Airships, ready for race, Fair, St. Louis, 1904." _____ 50.00

Unknown maker
    Pre-1890 identifiable view _____ 50–100.00
    Post-1890 identifiable view _____ 25–50.00
    Unidentified view _____ 15–25.00

Whiting, #234 Great balloon race, St. Louis Fair _____ 50.00

Dirigibles and Zeppelins
  Keystone
    #11776, Early dirigible above crowd, Asbury Park, N.J., aviation meet, 1910 _____ 65.00
    #15168, Baldwin's *California Arrow*, St. Louis _____ 30.00
    #17397, *Los Angeles* at Lakehurst, N.J. _____ 45–50.00
    #17398, The *Los Angeles* _____ 45.00
    #18000, Flying over German Town, World War I _____ 5.00
    #18077, Troops holding down large observation balloon, officers in distance entering, World War I _____ 8.00
    #18632, French officers inspecting wrecked zeppelin after it crashed and burned, World War I _____ 10.00
    #18736, Attaching observation balloon to wench for towing into position, post-World War I _____ 5.00
    #18758, French soldiers hauling down observation balloon, World War I _____ 10.00
    #V19216, British R-34 at Mineola, N.J. _____ 10.00
    #32277, *Graf Zeppelin* in hangar, Lakehurst, N.J. _____ 35.00
    #32738, Close interior of framework, *Akron* _____ 50.00
      Same view marked *1* at top center, nonstereo, used for comparison by salesmen _____ 25.00
      The pair, marked *1* and *2* at top center _____ 75.00
    #32739, Nose of framework, ZRS-4 USS *Akron* _____ 65.00
    #32740, Inside framework, ZRS-4 USS *Akron* _____ 65.00
    #32744, Bow of *Akron* seen in airdock _____ 75.00
    #32745, Bow view of *Akron* during construction _____ 50.00
    #32763, *Akron* nearing completion _____ 100.00
    #32771, Maiden flight of *Akron*, September 23, 1931 _____ 75.00
    #33072, Goodyear blimp flying over Century of Progress Exposition, Chicago, 1933 _____ 50.00
    #33371, Tail of *Graf Zeppelin* showing swastika hovering above ground at Friedrichshafen _____ 75.00
    #W33864, Francois's airship starting on flight _____ 75.00

  Lynn Skeels, Ravenna, Ohio, USS *Macon* under construction at Akron, Ohio, series of one hundred views, 1931 _____ Each 75–100.00

  Underwood & Underwood
    "Starting for the skies in a 20th century airship—Jamestown Expo, VA.," 1907 _____ 75.00
    #11775, Baldwin dirigible ready to ascend, Aero Carnival, Arlington, N.J. _____ 75.00

General Plane Views
  N. A. Forsyth, Cromwell Dixon at Montana State Fair in his plane, 1911 _____ 75.00

Keystone

#16654, C. P. Rodgers ready for flight, Meadville, Pa., first coast-to-coast flight, 1911 _____ 75.00

#V18021, World War I double-seated biplane fighter _____ 25.00

#18080, French troops look up as scout plane flies over, France, World War I _____ 8.00

#V18891, Body of dead German aviator in wrecked plane back of French lines, World War I _____ 8.00

#18920, Michelin bomber, World War I _____ 15.00

#19049, Nieuport plane, World War I _____ 9.00

#28029, Lindbergh in plane with wife _____ 45.00

#32269, *Spirit of St. Louis* guarded by naval personnel in Washington, D.C. _____ 30.00

#32372, Ford trimotor in Columbus, Ohio, first air-rail, New York to Los Angeles trip, 1929 _____ 15.00

#32683, Navy seaplane type S-C-2 in flight _____ 30.00

#32689, Autogyro ready to take off _____ 40.00

#32765, the *Winnie May* in Chicago, 1931 _____ 45.00

#32770, The *Great Dornier* DO-X in New York Harbor, 1931 _____ 50.00

#32785, Five biplanes fly over Chicago _____ 10.00

#34173, American clipper in Florida _____ 50.00

#37247, Air travel—loading airliner with gasoline _____ 35.00

#37254, Air travel—Stratoliner warming engines _____ 35.00

#37257, Air travel—passengers entering sleeper _____ 35.00

#38018, B-36 bombers at home base, Ft. Worth, Tex. _____ 75.00

Underwood & Underwood

#12310, Machine gunner in nose of World War I plane _____ 20.00

#14195, The *Sunbeam,* ready for transatlantic flight, Bayonne, N.J. _____ 40.00

Wright Brothers

Amateur views _____ 50–75.00

Keystone View Co., #38018, B-36 bombers at home base, Fort Worth, Tex. Scarce later Keystone view taken in 1940s. $75. (Gordon D. Hoffman Collection).

Keystone View Co., #16643, Wright brothers' airplane starting on flight at Dayton, Ohio, 1910. $45.

Keystone View Co. (from Underwood & Underwood negative), #V26102, ''The Wright Airplane in Flight, Fort Meyer [sic], Va.,'' note the photographers at work in foreground. $45.

Keystone
    #11773, Ready for flight, Ft.
    Myers, Va. _____ 70.00
    #16643, Starting on flight, Day-
    ton, 1910 _____ 45.00
    #16644, Flying at Dayton,
    Ohio _____ 35.00
    #V26102, In flight, Fort Myer,
    Va., photographers in fore-
    ground by catapult _____ 45.00
    #V26103, In flight at Fort Myer,
    Va. _____ 85.00
Underwood & Underwood
    #11002, ''Flying through sunset
    sky.'' _____ 45.00

Beach Scenes

There are many fine views of turn-of-the-century life at the seashore. Bathing costumes, people in the surf and vendors at places like Atlantic City and Coney Island give us a glimpse of customs and vacation fun of a past era.

Kilburn, #4780, ''Life in the Ocean Waves,'' 1888, a typical example of this genre _____ 6.00

Bicycles

Most views of both high-wheel and standard safety bikes are incidental to the main subject. Search busy street scenes, people in parks and crowded market scenes for bicycles. Close-up views are very uncommon and are usually found in comic situations.

Local maker, High-wheel bikes on street _____ 25.00
Post-1890 views, Safety bikes in comic scene _____ 4–10.00

Blacks

We receive an interesting and often disturbing look at the life and times of African-Americans by looking at the variety of published stereo views. Pre-1865 views are rare and usually show freed men incidental to the main subject. There are some Civil War views of black troops and scenes of the slave pens at the close of the conflict. After the war, blacks were something of a curiosity to view purchasers from major metropolitan areas. There are several fine series by southern photographers of plantation life, most notable are those by J. N. Wilson and O. Pierre Havens of Savannah, Georgia, and J. A. Palmer of Aiken, South Carolina. George Barnard made a small series of street urchins in his studio. He posed young boys behind a wall, bare chested in angelic poses or as chimney sweeps. Many of the scenes were derisive and showed blacks as lazy, shiftless and dishonest. This stereotyping was carried into the comic views of the post-1890 period. Stereo views most certainly contributed to the misconception and prejudice that eventually lead to the civil rights movement. We see the boss system in the cotton fields with white overseers on horseback in the background as men, women and children bend to the task under the hot sun. There are excellent views by J. N. Wilson and others of the cotton presses and ginning mills. Cotton-picking views are the most common. The humor of the comic views today is offensive, but was not limited to blacks as there exist derisive views of Irishmen and Jews, but not in the quantity of the black views. There are some excellent documentary views, especially those by Underwood & Underwood, of the Tuskegee Institute and Booker T. Washington. In the 1870s the Fisk University Jubilee Singers made tours to large United States cities and were

Keystone View Co., #12323, "I'm sure Massa Brown will prefer my apple pies, And I'll not git fired fo' makin' goo goo eyes." The last view in the twelve-view "New French Cook" series, 1903. Alone this view is of interest to collectors of views of blacks but is part of a set of otherwise nonblack subjects. $6. as a lone view or $60. for the set of twelve.

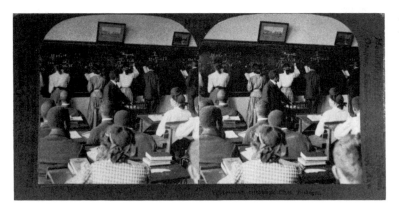

Keystone View Co., #V26144, "An Arithmetic Class, Tuskegee," Ala., ca. 1900. $20. (John Weiler Collection)

photographed by several local photographers. Blacks were a major attraction at the Cotton States Exposition in Atlanta in 1895. So-called Africans seen in the large B. W. Kilburn series were actually unemployed Georgia African-Americans hired to display their cultural heritage. There are also views of whites in black-face, usually in comic situations.

G. N. Barnard
   "Laborers Returning from Picking Cotton at Sunset on Alex Knox Plantation, near Charleston, 1874." _____ 75.00
   The chimney sweeps—boys posed in studio _____ 45.00
J. W. Black, Fisk University Jubilee Singers, 1872 _____ 50.00
English Classic, no maker, "High Life Below Stairs," man in blackface opens wine bottle under stairway, 1872, tinted _____ 20.00
O. Pierre Havens, Savannah, Ga., "Chimney Sweeps," studio pose of four boys, 1880s _____ 50.00
Keystone _____ Each 6–12.00
Kilburn _____ 3–15.00

A. C. McIntyre, Jubilee Singers posed on lawn, Thousand Islands, N.Y., 1870s _____ 20–40.00
Rufus Morgan, N.C., "Gossiping on the Way." _____ 20.00
J. Mullen, Ky., plantation scenes, 1866 _____ 25–35.00
J. A. Palmer, "Aunt Betsy's Cabin," 1870s, typical genre scene _____ 10–20.00
Underwood & Underwood
   Children picking cotton (negative by Jarvis), 1892 _____ 10.00
   Cotton is king, picking _____ 5.00
   "How de Debble does dey make a Bicycle," boy and parts _____ 5.00
   Cheating at cards, stealing melons, infidelity, etc.—wide variety of derisive subjects _____ 10–15.00
Universal Photo Art (C. H. Graves) #4540, "All coons look alike to me," typical _____ 5–10.00
C. L. Wasson (International Stereo. Co.) #4412, position #12 from "French Cook" series, new black cook in kitchen _____ 6.00
H. C. White _____ 5–10.00
Whiting View Co. _____ 8–10.00

Bridges

Stereo views give an excellent glimpse at the civil engineering of the nineteenth century. Iron and massive suspension cable bridges served heavy traffic of loaded wagons and the emerging railroad industry. The construction of the Transcontinental Railroad from Omaha, Nebraska, to the Pacific coast is documented in detail in stereo views by official and unofficial photographers, including A. A. Hart, A. J. Russell, William H. Jackson and C. R. Savage, to name the major makers. Railroad bridges were built over most large rivers during this period. Collectors seek out construction scenes and close views of the spans. The most photographed bridges were the great suspension bridges of John Roebling. The bridge at Niagara Falls was photographed by dozens of stereo photographers. Roebling's greatest triumph was the Brooklyn Bridge in New York City, which was completed by his son, Washington A. Roebling, after the elder Roebling died at the age of sixty-three from injuries resulting from a freak accident. The Brooklyn Bridge was photographed in documentary style by numerous stereo photographers. Collectors seek out construction views. Other Roebling suspension bridges at Cincinnati and Pittsburgh were stereo-photographed, but in fewer numbers—the Pittsburgh bridge views are the least common.

Covered bridges, especially in the New England states, were photographed by many regional and local photographers. The most common is the pair of covered bridges at Bellows Falls, Vermont. Excellent views of this bridge were made by P. W. Taft.

The London Bridge is the most famous bridge in Europe. Now removed to a site in Arizona, the London Bridge was photographed by both American and English photographers.

Brooklyn Suspension (East River)
Construction scenes _____ 15–30.00
    Anthony, #11166 and 11169,
    footbridge and towers
    Hall Brothers of Brooklyn, "spiders" being put in Kilburn,
    #3168, looking down from pier
Completed scenes _____ 5–8.00
    Griffith & Griffith (negative by
    Zahner) overview
    Keystone, #2499, Cable road
    Purviance, Scene on roadway
    Roberts & Fellows, Side view,
    ships in foreground
    Universal Photo Art (C. H.
    Graves), #4274, Elevated railroad
    bridge in background
Cincinnati Suspension
Local makers (Muhrman, Waldack,
etc.) _____ 8–12.00
Anthony _____ 6–10.00
Post-1890 views (Kilburn, Whiting,
etc.) _____ 4–6.00
Eastern United States
L. E. Walker, #802, Reflection view
of Portage railroad bridge in New
York State _____ 15.00
Underwood & Underwood, #11166,
high bridge across Hudson River
near Poughkeepsie _____ 6–8.00
Midwestern United States
Copelin & Son, #34, Minneapolis &
St. Paul railroad bridge near Kilbourn Dales, Wisconsin _____ 12.00
Keystone, White, Underwood & Underwood, etc., Ead's Bridge, St.
Louis, Mo. _____ 4–6.00
Niagara Suspension
Pre-1880 by local makers (Barker,
Curtis, etc.) _____ 5–10.00

E. & H. T. Anthony, #7552, "The Cincinnati and Covington Suspension Bridge," 1873. $10.

New Jersey Stereoscopic View Co. issue of E. & H. T. Anthony view #11182, "West from East River Bridge Tower," the Brooklyn Bridge under construction. $30.

Underwood & Underwood, "Brooklyn Bridge," early 1890s issue. $8.

Post-1880 by most major publishers	3–5.00
Pittsburgh Suspension (Purviance and others)	15–20.00
Western Railroad	
W. H. Jackson, #81, Devil's Gate, Union Pacific Railroad	10.00
C. R. Savage, Gold run, Secrettown Trestle, Central Pacific Railroad	50.00
European Bridges	
Keystone, #2101, London Bridge, busy	2.00
Local makers in England, France, Germany, etc.	4–6.00

Canada

Like the United States, Canada has been stereo-photographed in detail. Views of the western provinces are scarce. The most common are views of Montreal, Quebec City and St. John, New Brunswick. William Notman was the leading photographer from the late 1850s into the 1880s. Of particular interest are his views of the construction of the Victoria Bridge (1857–1858) and portraits of native types in the studio with painted backdrops. Alex Henderson was Montreal's leading photographer and made many views of the city. Most common are the monuments and the French Cathedral. Other important photographers who made large numbers of views were L. P. Vallee, J. G. Parks, James Esson and J. S. Climo. All of the major makers made fine series after 1890. In 1907, Kilburn made an outstanding series at Sault Ste. Marie, Ontario, showing the ironworks and steelworks (#17078–17092) but these are very uncommon today, coming at the end of Kilburn's business operations.

Anthony, Monument erected for Victoria Bridge	2.00
Charles Bierstadt, #1472, Ice Palace, Montreal	2.00
J. S. Climo, Scenic view of falls on Salmon River	4.00
Alex Henderson	
French Cathedral	3–5.00
Street scenes, business buildings	6–10.00

Keystone
#10656, Crowd waiting for unveiling of Victoria Statue, Ottawa, 1901 _____ 2.00
#13837, Overview of western terminus of Central Pacific Railroad _____ 4.00
#13987, Overview of Quebec _____ 2.00
#16317, Fisherman's quarters, St. John's, Nfld. _____ 3.00
#16318, Man with Eskimo dog team, Labrador _____ 4.00
#27310, Banff Springs Hotel in winter, Alta. _____ 2.00
#31069, Buchart's Sunken Gardens, Victoria, B.C. _____ 5.00
#31087, Lake Louise, Mt. Victoria in distance _____ 2.00
Kilburn
#9833, Alexander Bay, Thousand Islands _____ 2.00
#12799, Soldiers marching to Church, Halifax _____ 4.00
#17078, Algoma Steel Co.'s boat unloading ore, Sault Ste. Marie _____ 8.00
#17111, Below Bala Falls, Muskoka, Ont. _____ 4.00
#17128, Corner of Victoria Street and Simpson Avenue, Fort William, Ont., 1907 _____ 10.00
William Notman
Construction of Victoria Bridge, 1857 _____ 20–40.00
Indian squaws, studio posed, 1857 _____ 50.00
Montreal street scene, 1870s _____ 10–20.00
Scenic landscapes _____ 5–10.00
J. G. Parks
Ice Palace, Montreal Winter Carnival _____ 2–6.00
Busy wharf with tall ships _____ 10–20.00
Underwood & Underwood
Children at play in Rockies, Morley, Alta. _____ 2.00
Government buildings, Ottawa, 1890s _____ 4.00
Interior of Laliberte's fur market, Que. _____ 2.00

Lover's walk on government grounds, Ottawa _____ 3.00
Man fishing at Bala Falls, Muskoka _____ 2.00
People by fountain in Ottawa Park, Ottawa _____ 2.00
#(55), Men unloading steamer loaded with wheat _____ 4.00
#4780, Gannet ledges on St. Lawrence River _____ 3.00
L. P. Vallee
Nuns working in Hotel Dieu Hospital, Que. _____ 25.00
Views of Quebec City _____ 5–10.00
Views of Quebec Province scenery _____ 3–5.00

Caribbean and Cuba

Pre-1890 views are very uncommon except the fine early series published by Anthony called "Views in Cuba" (1862). W. Watson in Port au Prince, Haiti, A. Duperly and Sons and P. Sarthou of Jamaica made some early views of the area. The Spanish-American War brought public interest to the area and a demand for scenes of local natives and scenery as well as the war views. Many fine views of Puerto Rico were made by several major publishers including Underwood & Underwood, Keystone and H. C. White after the American occupation in 1898. Although not a part of the Caribbean, Bermuda will be mentioned here. A large series was offered by J. B. Heyl of Hamilton (1870s), who may have been the photographer for a nice series published by B. W. Kilburn (1875). Both of these series appear on similar yellow mounts.

Bermuda
J. B. Heyl, Scenes _____ 6–8.00
B. W. Kilburn, Scenes _____ 3–4.00

E. Anthony, #39, Spanish troops marching in column on busy street returning from Mass, Cuba, ca. 1860. $12.

Cuba
(*See* Wars, Spanish-American in
Chapter 5)

Anthony, "Views in Cuba" series
#1, 146, and 147, The Plaza de
Armes, Havana _____ 8.00
#39, A street view from the Domin-
ica, a company of Spanish troops returning from Mass _____ 12.00
#44, Instantaneous view of dashing
spray, Moro Castle in background,
Havana Habor _____ 6.00
#99 and 103, Instantaneous, a
schooner in the harbor _____ 15.00
Keystone
#9072, Reconcentrado farming
scene _____ 4.00
#9093, Reconcentrados going to
work _____ 5.00
Underwood & Underwood
#6519, Officials at birth of Cuban
Republic _____ 4.00
#6545, Ladies in courtyard _____ 4.00
#6587, Hauling loads of sugarcane
with oxen _____ 4.00
Haiti and Jamaica
Pre-1890 views _____ 5–10.00
Post-1890 views _____ 3–6.00
Puerto Rico
Pre-1890 views _____ 10–25.00
Post-1890 views _____ 4–10.00
West Indies
Pre-1890 views _____ 8–15.00
Post-1890 views _____ 1–4.00

Cats, Domestic

(See also *Children in Chapter 5*)

A popular topic for collectors are views of cats. Feline mischief is the usual subject, with cats or kittens climbing, at play with children or getting a squirt of milk from a farmer as he milks the family cow. Cats also were dressed as humans (usually grandma) and propped up for portraits.

Cats also appear as main subjects and in-cidental parts of comic views. The best series is John P. Soule's views of kittens made in the early 1870s. These are unnumbered, but there may be as many as 200 in the series. The most common—but possibly one of the best—cat views is Underwood and Underwood's "Tired of Play." There are many versions of this title showing a little girl asleep next to her cat. There is one version that features a large doll as well.

N. S. Bennett of Medford, Oreg., man milking cow, squirting milk into cat's mouth; scarce maker _____ 12.00

Griffith, #14884 "An Entre [*sic*] of
kittens," six kittens posed on a plate _____ 12.00
Kilburn
#789, "A Happy Family," cat and
kittens, 1870 _____ 4.00
#4812, Marguerite's kittens, baby
with kittens _____ 5.00
#6073, Little grandma, little girl
with cat _____ 6.00
Parmelee of Windsor Lock, Conn.,
"Rosa's Kittens." _____ 10.00
John P. Soule (1870s)
Kittens in playful poses _____ 8–15.00
Kittens posed with cameras _____ 20–50.00
Same series on Kilburn mounts,
1880s issue _____ 6–12.00
Underwood & Underwood
"Don't Shoot Please," cat jumps on
man asleep in bed _____ 4.00
"Tired of Play." _____ 3.00
Farmer squirts milk into cat's
mouth _____ 2.00
Universal Photo Art (C. H. Graves)
#3225, "Tabby as Grandma," cat in
dress _____ 6.00
Wasson (International View Co.)
#720, "Tabby Tabby," monkey with
arm around cat _____ 7.00
F. G. Weller #327, "Strangers," tinted
view of dog and cat on back step of
house _____ 4.00

Caves

The first photographs made in a cave were stereo photographs by Charles Waldack, a leading photographer from Cincinnati, Ohio. Financed by local businessmen, Waldack made a series by magnesium light flares inside Mammoth Cave, Kentucky, in 1866. The forty-two view series was published by E. and H. T. Anthony as "Magnesium Light Views in Mammoth Cave," first on yellow mounts and in the early 1870s on red-orange mounts. At least nineteen views in the series were sold by Waldack with manuscript titles. These are extremely rare. Large numbers of the Anthony views were sold, but complete sets are uncommon.

Nearly every major cave was eventually photographed in stereo. Ben Hains of New Albany, Indiana, returned to Mammoth Cave in the 1880s and made an extensive series by magnesium light. C. H. James made a fine series of Luray Caverns, Virginia. A. Veeder photographed Howe's Cave by calcium light.

Keystone offered a number of nice cave views. The group of Carlsbad Caverns, New Mexico,

A. Veeder, Rocky Mountains rock formation in Howe's Cave by calcium light. $8.

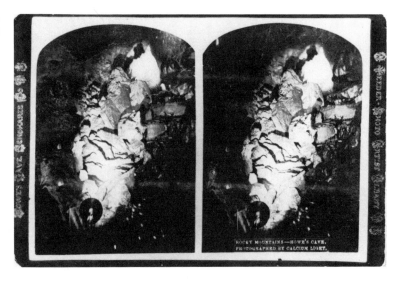

made in the early 1930s are extremely fine examples of cave photography.

Ben Hains, Mammoth Cave, 1880s,
cabinet mounts _____ 6–8.00
C. H. James, Luray Caverns _____ 5–8.00
Keystone
    #9586, Man in front of Great
    Oregon Caves _____ 6.00
    #24350, "Fairy Grotto," New
    South Wales, Australia _____ 3.00
    #24662, Natural Pit in Macorha
    Caves, Moravia, Czechoslovakia ____ 5.00
    #33516, Crystal Springs Dome,
    Carlsbad Caverns, N.M. _____ 5.00
Charles Waldack, "Magnesium
Light Views in Mammoth Cave,"
1866 (published by E. & H. T.
Anthony)
    #4, "Out for the Last Time,"
    crew with stereo camera and
    magnesium flare reflectors _____ 200–300.00
    #8, "Column of Hercules," typi-
    cal interior view _____ 10–15.00

Cemeteries

Stereo photography lends itself to the forms and shapes found in cemeteries. In the mid-1800s, there was a move away from the local churchyard burial places to planned garden settings with stately monuments placed among flower beds, ponds with waterfowl and playing fountains. Green-Wood Cemetery in New York City and Spring Grove in Cincinnati along with dozens of other cemeteries of this genre were photographed by local photographers. Local photographers made views of headstones of prominent citizens, which must have

been good sellers considering the number found today. Gravesites of notable Americans were also popular, for example, George Washington's tomb at Mount Vernon, Virginia, and Arlington Cemetery on the old Lee homestead overlooking Washington, D.C. A large series was made of Mount Auburn in Cambridge (Boston area), Massachusetts, by Charles Seaver. These are found on yellow mounts without credit to Seaver and usually with a list of titles on the back label.

Anthony
    #1592, Monument of Henry Ruggles,
    Green-Wood, N.Y. _____ 4.00
    #5300, Calvary Cemetery, Omera's
    Monument _____ 2.00
Keystone, #6299, Sleepy Hollow, N.Y. ____ 1.00
Thomas of Racine, Wis., Monument for
James Dekoven _____ 3.00
Charles Waldack, Cincinnati, Spring
Grove Cemetery _____ 3–5.00

Children

Most of the pre-1875 views of children were made in the studio with settings to look like home parlors, schoolrooms and even backyards with trees and fences. Many fine hand-tinted views were made in England, published by the London Stereoscopic Company and imported by E. and H. T. Anthony and D. Appleton of New York. These views were very popular in the 1860s up to about 1873 when similar views were being offered at lower prices by United States makers. These English Classics show kids in various situations, usually involving some mischief. Tinting often varies from superb to sloppy. Finely tinted examples in excellent condition are sought by collectors of this genre.

Kilburn Brothers and F. G. Weller were the most commonly encountered early United States makers. Kilburn posed the children outside with toys and at play. In the 1880s, Kilburn offered a large series of studio-posed views with children in comic situations. Weller made a series he called "Stereoscopic Treasures," which proved to be extremely popular. "A Stitch in Time," showing a little girl repairing her doll, is often encountered and is known in several versions, tinted and untinted. Other fine series were offered by E. and H. T. Anthony, J. A. French and M. M. Griswold. Griswold's "Compositions" can be found beautifully tinted on yellow mounts with paper title labels.

Thousands of new titles were added by the major publishers in the 1890s. Many of the same situations may be found on 1860s through 1890s views by different makers. After 1905, fewer views of children were made. The later Keystone views show children in noncomic situations often helping mother, working in the garden or playing with toys. A rare series of schoolchildren was made by Keystone in the mid-1930s. These were made on location at schools in Cleveland and Columbus, Ohio, and are often found in the "Primary" boxed sets with the *P* prefix. Other Primary views from this set are more common and show children in domestic situations.

Anthony, #44, Two week's ironing, two girls iron doll clothes, early black doll in view, ca. 1868 _____ 9.00
English Classics (published by London Stereoscopic Co.)
   Tinted view of little girl (by A. Silvester, blindstamped) _____ 6.00
   "The Bird Nest," child and nest _____ 2.00

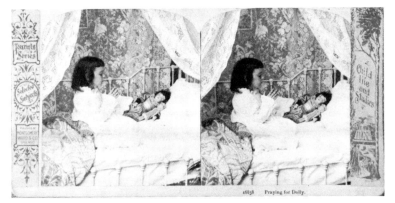

William H. Rau, #16838, "Praying for Dolly," (sold by Montgomery Ward & Co.). $8.

French of Lawrence, Kansas, #1, "The May Pole Dance" from a set of twelve called "Eight Little Maidens," featuring remarkably staged dolls at play. $8. each, set of twelve, $100.

"Just as Papa Does." _____ 1.00
"Neglected Genius." _____ 12.00

(*Note:* add $3 if tax stamp is affixed to back.)

J. A. French, mother and little girl, doll
pushes a toy stroller, tinted _____ 7.00
Gates of Chicago, #584, Goat cart with
kids, Lincoln Park, Chicago, tinted _____ 6.00
Graves (Universal Photo Art) _____ 4–8.00
Griffith & Griffith
  #2065, "Playmates," kids in toy
  wagon _____ 4.00
  #4879, (negative by Rau) "Writing
  to Papa," girls seated at desk _____ 6.00
M. M. Griswold _____ 3–7.00
J. Gurney & Son, child on chamber
pot _____ 4.00
T. W. Ingersoll _____ 2–4.00
  #28, "I don't want to go to sleep,"
  girl in bed
  #44, "Snow Birds," kids posed in snow
Keystone
  #7, "This little pig stayed at home,"
  girl counts toes _____ 3.00
  #2314, "Look at yourself, Pussy,"
  little girl and cat before a mirror _____ 5.00
  #2316, "Awful cold, but lots of fun,"
  little girls in sleigh _____ 5.00
  #8095, "No, 'oo tan't det down,
  pussy," girl talks to cat on table _____ 2.00
  #9026, "The interrupted meal," baby
  cries as cat eats from her dish _____ 4.00
  #9477, "Undergoing Repairs," little
  girl mending _____ 3.00
  #P-9715, Arabian children at school _____ 3.00
  #10479, "The Wedding March," girls
  lead march _____ 3.00
  #10567, "Look out Johnny, you'll
  break the eggs." _____ 2.00
  #11404, "June Carnival—Dancing
  around the Daisy Pole," girls in field _____ 3.00
  #11407, "Serving refreshments at
  Baby's Expense." _____ 2.00
  #11416, "Child's Prayer," girl kneel-
  ing in prayer _____ 2.00
  #11422, "Isn't our stock looking
  fine," boy and girl with rabbits and puppies _____ 3.00
  #11432, "Cherries Ripe, Cherries
  Red," girl in cherry tree _____ 7.00
  #11448, "Five minute stop for
  lunch," girl sits on hog _____ 3.00
  #11498, "Where do you think they
  are going?" boy and girl climb fence _____ 2.00
  #34400, "Playing Train," school kids
  in classroom _____ 7.00
  #34597, Five girls having tea party
  at table _____ 7.00
Keystone of New England, unidentified
kids _____ 3–6.00
Keystone, Cleveland, Ohio, Kids at
home and at school, most unidentified,
1930s _____ 6–12.00

Kilburn
  #3896, "Gentle Annie," girl with
  dog _____ 3.00
  #4596, "Dollies friends," girl on
  pony, another girl in wicker buggy
  with dog and boy _____ 7.00
  #4665, "Little Wanderers," two kids
  in snowy woods _____ 5.00
  #5954, "The Whole Family," little
  girls with baby, doll and dog _____ 5.00
  #6516, "God and Our Flag," group
  before large flag, baby in wicker
  pram, 1891 _____ 10.00
  #7330, "Sweet as honey," baby in
  basket, 1892 _____ 2.00
  #11608, "Children must be seen—
  not heard," kids beside piano with
  dog and doll _____ 5.00
R. B. Lewis "Morning Glories," twelve
babies all kept still, posed in carriages
and prams, 1874 _____ 10.00
Littleton (published by Underwood &
Underwood)
  #349B, "Trials of the Day are over,"
  girl asleep with cat, 1889 _____ 2.00
  #1534, "A spanking good time,"
  mother spanks kid as husband
  watches _____ 2.00
Melander, #151, "Grandma's Surprise," two children _____ 3.00
Sterro-Photo, #226, "The Happy Fam-
ily," baby outdoors with cat and dog _____ 6.00
L. G. Strand, "The Bird Trap," kids and
bird (pirate) _____ 2.00
Underwood & Underwood
  "Comrades," little girl between two
  donkeys, 1894 _____ 2.00
  "Going to Market," girls with baskets, 1889 _____ 3.00
  "Good Night," four girls wearing
  nightgowns, one holds puppy _____ 2.00
  "Little Mischief," baby with coal in
  front of stove, 1896 _____ 6.00
  "Nellie's first painting," girl behind
  frame _____ 5.00
  "Preaching his first sermon," baby
  with arm outstretched _____ 3.00
  "Room for one more," five kids on
  donkey, Colorado _____ 3.00
Webster & Albee, little girls putting on
stockings _____ 2.00
F. G. Weller, "Stereoscopic Treasures,"
1870s
  #314, "The Tea Party," girls and
  dolls _____ 8.00
  #317, "What shall I write to
  Grandpa," girl with tablet _____ 7.00
H. C. White _____ 4–7.00
Whiting View Co., #2728, "Papa's
Dear Girls," two girls with dog outside _____ 7.00
R. Y. Young (American Stereoscopic
Co.), "The Battle of the Pillows," girls'
pillow fight _____ 3.00

Underwood & Underwood, "The watchful Guardian," 1902. $6.

China

(See Wars, Boxer Rebellion in Chapter 5)

The earliest published views of China were taken by Felix Beato and published in England by Negretti and Zambra. These were sold in the United States, but are scarce. Beato's "Views in China" were probably made in 1859 or 1860 and include outstanding portraits showing native costumes. In 1862 E. and H. T. Anthony offered "Views in China and Japan" from negatives by M. Miller. Thomas Houseworth offered the series "Views in China and Japan" in 1869; these views are very uncommon. The studio portraits from this series are an outstanding part of the group of sixty views.

The Boxer Rebellion, which began in 1899, put China in the news and created a demand for this exotic area of the world. James Ricalton was sent by Underwood and Underwood to cover the rebellion, which was characterized by brutal beheadings and ghastly murders. The Ricalton views show the horrible executions, but the series by an unknown photographer for B. W. Kilburn is more complete in its coverage. This series includes views of an executioner holding up a severed head above a pile of six other heads (#14356).

C. H. Graves (Universal Photo Art) offered an outstanding series in about 1900, which includes scenes in Chee-foo, Peking, Tientsin (Boxer Rebellion), Hong Kong, Macao, Canton and Shanghai. Less common are a number of the H. C. White views made at the same time. This series shows many of the local natives and street life. Keystone views are fairly common, but are not as interesting.

Anthony, "Views in China and Japan."	30–40.00
Felix Beato (sold by Negretti Zambra, London)	50–75.00
Thomas Houseworth & Co., "Views in China," ca. 1869	40–75.00
Keystone	
#12052, Hong Kong, busy Queens Road	2.00
#12076, Nanking, men with stone roller on street	2.00
#V23927, Passing life in the land of Confucius, street scene in Canton	4.00
Universal Photo Art (C. H. Graves)	
#8601, On the Yellow Sea	3.00
#8609, A portion of Tientsin and the Pei-ho River	3.00
#8622, Arrival of a train at the Peking railway	6.00
#8648, Washing vegetables in one of the filthy streams of Peking	5.00
#8649, A Manchurian archer (Boxer Rebellion)	8.00
#8689, The Great Wall of China	4.00
#8690, On the way to the tombs of the Ming dynasty	3.00
#8730, Grotesque figures formed from plants, Honam Temple gardens	2.00
#8731, A canal in Honam	4.00
#8759, Courtyard of the Temple of Ancestors	3.00
#8760, The Temple of the Five Hundred Genii	3.00
Underwood & Underwood	
View on Shameen Canal, Canton, small crafts	3.00
Women just emerging from rice field, Honam	4.00
H. C. White	
#3703, On the Praya (waterfront), harbor of Hong Kong	4.00
#3780, Dragon Stairway of the Imperial Palace, Forbidden City	3.00
#3782, In the court of the Imperial	

Palace, Forbidden City	3.00
#3755, A group of camels, China's beast of burden	4.00
#3761, Where the Chinaman seeks his paradise—an opium joint, Peking	12.00

Christmas

Many views were made depicting the Christmas season. The most popular with collectors are scenes with Santa Claus. These views often show the jolly gentleman with early toys and decorated trees. F. G. Weller offered a nice series based on Moore's classic "Night before Christmas" in the 1870s. This poem along with Thomas Nast's drawings set the image of Santa Claus:

Universal Photo Art, #4679, Brownies and Santa	15–20.00
Griffith, #16833, "Children's Christmas dinner."	12–17.00
Santa Claus	
Keystone	10–20.00
#987, Santa in front of fireplace	
#9445, Santa loaded with toys, 1898	
#11434, Santa coming down chimney with toys	
Underwood & Underwood, "O Ho! Another Stocking to Fill."	10–15.00
H. C. White, #5219, "Are you Santa Claus?"	10–15.00
F. G. Weller, "Night before Christmas."	10–20.00

Circus

Views of circuses are very uncommon. Small circuses, carnivals and freak shows traveled throughout the United States in the nineteenth century. Often a local photographer made a view of the parade on the main street or the tent at the local fairgrounds. Close views of performers or acts are rare. Some views of Christian revival tents are mistakenly thought to be circus tents. Webster and Albee made a small series, in about 1890, of a circus parade in downtown Rochester. Although fairly distant, one can clearly see the finely carved wagons in the parade. John P. Soule offered a view of an elephant of Costello's Circus in Sacramento, California, 1870 (#1119). Views of freaks and midgets were also made, the most notable being the studio portraits of Tom Thumb plus views of the "Fairy Wedding Party." P. T.

Barnum was photographed while visiting Yosemite in the 1870s and a close portrait exists, but the example examined is flat (nonstereo). The various World's Fairs had sideshow attractions that were photographed in detail, especially in St. Louis (1904–1905). Lynn Skeels of Washington, D.C., made a rare series of "The Greatest Show on Earth" in about 1940 when the show visited the nation's capital. On Keystone-like gray mounts, the views show rare interior views of the big top.

Animals	
Soule, #1119, "The Educated Elephant, Costello's Circus, Sacramento, California," 1870	50–75.00
Midgets and Dwarfs	
Anthony (from Brady negative), "Fairy Wedding."	75–100.00
Holmquist Photo Co., #97, Portrait of midget woman seated on full-sized husband's lap	15–25.00
Underwood & Underwood, reprint of "Fairy Wedding." ca. 1890s	30–40.00
Parades	
Webster & Albee, Rochester, N.Y., ca. 1890	10–15.00
Views by local photographers, 1870–1880s	30–50.00
Performers	
Whiting, #74, Bostock Wild Animal Show, tamer with his lions	20–30.00
Sideshows	
Lynn Skeels, ca. 1940	35–50.00
"The Greatest Show on Earth" and P. T. Barnum	
Barnum and Party in Yosemite, 1870s	50–100.00
Lynn Skeels, Circus in Washington, D.C., ca. 1940	35–75.00

Civil War
(See *Wars in Chapter 5*)

Comics and Sentimentals
(See also *Children in Chapter 5*)

Stereo views give us a good look at the morals and humor of the Victorian era. The early examples, mostly made in England and France in the 1860s, show great care in design of studio sets to create realism and good stereo effect. Views by Elliott, Silvester and Phiz are sought by collectors in excellent condition with fine tinting. London Stereoscopic Company published the vast majority of these views and the views often have a London Stereoscopic blindstamp. Many of these were pirated and sold at reduced prices. The tinting on these copies often is sloppy. The London Stereoscopic Company comic and sentimental views are collectively called "English Classics," a descriptive name coined by the late Earl Moore, an early collector of these gems. After 1870, several American photographers began offering series, many patterned on the English views. The leading maker and the most common from this period is the series by F. G. Weller (*see* Children in Chapter 5), who used less elaborate set designs but made views of more homely scenes. Subjects include law breaking ("The Bicycle Bum"), drinking and temperance, marriage humor, infidelity, romance, rumors, sentimentality and weddings. Nearly every major publisher after 1890 offered these types of views. The Spanish-American War brought a new genre of sentimental view showing the soldier off to fight, his lonely sweetheart waiting his return, his battle wounds and his triumphant return. This sequence was repeated with the Boer War.

The wedding was a popular series and is presented as individual views and in small sets. There are many versions of a view variously titled "Alone at Last!" showing the newlyweds in their honeymoon bedroom. Some versions show them kissing; others, just holding hands. Another version shows them fully dressed, another, in nightclothes. "Last one in bed blows out the light" was another title with many versions showing the couple in bed. Although a bit silly by today's standards, some of these views were considered risqué in 1900.

Bicycle Bum
    Graves (Universal Photo Art), #4551–4558, "Weary Willie," four-view set _____ 20.00
Drinking
    American Stereoscopic Co., Woman drinking, 1901. _____ 16.00
    Kilburn, #7348, "Brown just in from the club." _____ 3.00
    Underwood & Underwood, Man sneaks in after drinking, two-view set, 1897, typical of this genre _____ 6–8.00
English Classic (sometimes found with London Stereoscopic Co. blindstamp)
    "Affectionate Husband," signed "A. Silvester," tinted _____ 15.00
    "Bite-Apple," people playing parlor game _____ 6.00
    "Domestic Bliss," tinted, husband complaining _____ 3.00

"Now Ma'rm, Say When," men help woman into omnibus _____ 6.00
"Picnic," early 1860s _____ 7.00
"Strawberries & Cream," lady at table, 1860s _____ 2.00
"The Anxious Mother," tinted, shows dolls _____ 8.00
"The Belle of the Ball," lady in ball gown, tinted _____ 5.00
"The Attack," boy carves roast, tinted _____ 4.00
"The Lost Ring," people at wedding looking at floor _____ 3.00
"The Thief Captured," young man holds hand of maid _____ 12.00
"Too Hot," little girl eating soup at table _____ 4.00
French Classic
    "Petite Scene," maid combing hair of lady _____ 2.00
Humor
    American Stereoscopic Co., "Biddy and the Rat," women stand on chairs _____ 1.00
    Keystone, #2346–2347, Before and after marriage, set of two, couple under umbrellas _____ 7.00
    Kilburn, #7444, "Where in Thunder is the towel?" dripping husband with hands extended implores wife who appears unconcerned _____ 5.00
    Underwood & Underwood, 1904, "Four queens and a jack," four girls and a jackass _____ 4.00
    Universal Photo Art (Graves), #3193, "Don't swear, dear." _____ 5.00
    H. C. White, #5422, "How Biddy served the tomatoes undressed," typical _____ 3–4.00
Infidelity
    Foolin' around, Husband fools around with his secretary, set of twelve, offered by several publishers, 1910 _____ 45.00
    Keystone, #12312–12322, The French Cook, set _____ 35–45.00
    Underwood & Underwood
        Sneaking in, Caught by wife, 1897 _____ 6.00
        The French Cook, ten-view set _____ 45.00
    Universal Photo Art (Graves), Mr. & Mrs. Honeymoon's French Cook, twelve views _____ 45.00
    H. C. White, Flirtation series, #5442–5445, four-view set _____ 25.00
Romance
    Underwood & Underwood, "Going with Stream," hugging couple _____ 6.00
    Weller, #353, "Unexpected," necking _____ 4.00
Rumors
    H. C. White, #5576–5578, Quickest way to spread news: "Tell a graph, tell a phone, tell a woman," set of three, shows early wall telephone _____ 20.00

Sentimental
American Stereoscopic Co.,
#2001–2012, He goes to war, is
wounded, returns, is reunited, etc.,
twelve-view set _____ 50.00
Wedding Set
H. C. White, #5510–5519, typical
of this genre, many different sets
made by most publishers _____ 40.00

Coral and Shells

A number of photographers and publishers offered "Gems of the Sea." These were displayed on tables in various arrangements. These views displayed for the viewer the depth of the stereoscopic effect. Although not particularly popular with collectors, these views are fine examples of stereoscopic still life photography, especially the pre-1865 hand-tinted versions.

Anthony, several different numbers,
1860s _____ 3–4.00
J. G. Parks, Five types of coral, typical of
1870s local maker. _____ 2–3.00
Underwood & Underwood, Typical later
view of coral, 1890s. _____ 1.00

Costumes

The stereo photographers of the nineteenth century made a remarkable record of native costumes from all parts of the world. Many were offered beautifully hand tinted, both as individual views and in sets.

Francis Bedford made a delightful series of Welsh women in native tall hats and long dresses, titled "Welsh Costumes," on yellow mounts (1860s). William Notman, in Canada, offered studio-posed portraits of native types of his country in the late 1850s. Fritz Luckhardt made a series of about 200 close portraits ("Heads") of attractive women in Victorian clothes. The beautifully hand-tinted series by S. P. Christmann on orange mounts is probably the best of the early 1870s costume views. Little is known of this photographer, other than he operated from Berlin until the mid-1870s. The views have titles in French, English and German, and the tinting, most of the time, is flawless.

The post-1890 publishers offered many fine costumes, both tinted and untinted. Keystone assembled a hundred-view boxed set from their extensive worldwide inventory and offered them with expert tinting. These often were sold to schools and libraries and as a result had excessive use. Examples from this series in excellent condition are scarce.

Francis Bedford, "Welsh Costumes." __ 20–30.00
S. P. Christmann, hand tinted, orange
mounts _____ 8–15.00
J. A. French, typical United States
maker of local types _____ 8–15.00
Graves (Universal Photo Art)
#8483, Japanese belles in sunny
weather dress _____ 3–6.00
#8598, Pretty Japanese girls in a
jinkriksha _____ 2–5.00
Griffith
#1811, Ladies in a Wisteria Pavilion, Japan _____ 5.00
#8729, Group of Buddhist priests,
Tientsin, China _____ 5.00
Ladies in rowboat, Stronsholm
Canal, Sweden _____ 5.00
Keystone
#12510, Costumed Hindu dancers,
Tanjore, India _____ 3.00
#13895, Woman in native dress,
Nova Scotia, Canada _____ 2.00
Tinted view with C-prefixed numbers at top center, from "Costumes"
boxed set _____ Each 4–6.00
Underwood & Underwood, Kids in
schoolyard playing, Japan _____ 4.00

Cowboys

Pre-1890 views of western-range cowboys are rare. A few views were made in Montana by L. A. Huffman in the late 1870s and early 1880s. Kilburn offered some distant views of a cattle roundup in Colorado. There are a few known views taken in New Mexico and Arizona in the 1880s but these are very uncommon.

Underwood and Underwood made some excellent views on the Sierra Bonita Ranch in Arizona (1890s). Keystone offered views of cowboys at work on ranches in North Dakota and Montana and on the Paloduro Ranch in Texas.

The rodeo at the Century of Progress was published by Keystone in 1933. There are some great views of trick riders and roping events in this small series on standard gray mounts and the smaller "Junior" unmounted prints. There is a scarce fifty-view boxed set of cowboys published in the early 1930s by Keystone.

L. A. Huffman, Miles City, Mont.,
cowboy on horse _____ 50–100.00
Keystone
#13641, Montana cowboy on
horseback, Yellowstone _____ 4.00

Ingersoll View Co., #X16, "The Mess Wagon Cook," a better cowboy view, ca. 1900. $15. (John Weiler Collection)

#13756, Texas cowboy making drive, Paloduro Ranch _____ 2.00

#33455, Trick roper at Century of Progress, 1933 _____ 20–25.00

#33471, Two cowboys on horseback, N. Dak. _____ 6.00

Kilburn, #2947, Distant view of cattle roundup, Colo. _____ 6.00

Underwood & Underwood
Cowboy on horseback, Wilderness, Ariz. _____ 7.00

#6155, Herd being moved on Sierra Bonita Ranch, Ariz. _____ 3.00

#6156, Cowboys on horseback roping yearling, Ariz. _____ 5.00

Cuba

(See Caribbean and Cuba in Chapter 5)

Daredevils and Wire Walkers

The most often encountered views of wire walkers are those showing crossings at Niagara Falls. The most famous was Blondin who made several spectacular walks over Niagara in 1859 and 1860. Several photographers made views of these events. Madam Spelterini was the first woman to cross Niagara (1872). Every major stereo photographer working in Niagara made views of this walk. Many of these are found mislabeled as "Blondin" showing the popularity of his feat twelve years earlier. Eventually ten daredevils would cross Niagara and the only one to die was Stephen Peer (often misnamed *Pierre*). His attempt in 1887 did not faze Samuel John Dixon of Toronto, who used the same wire to cross in 1890. This event was stereo-photographed by George Barker and published for several years by Underwood and

Underwood. Other wire walkers at Niagara were Belleni and Calvaly, who is seen sitting on a straight chair on the wire in Whiting View Company #816 in 1904.

Charles Bierstadt issued a view in the 1870s showing Peer falling from the wire. This view is actually a trick; the figure of the tumbling man was drawn into the negative.

Other wire walkers traveled about the United States in the 1870s and 1880s. These adventurers would get a local sponsor to put up a purse, and a wire was strung across the main street. Local stereo photographers often covered these events.

Daredevils appeared at the World's Fairs but only a few were photographed. Whiting View Company made at least two views of the daring "Miss Lizette," who would "leap the gap" on a bicycle after riding down a steep incline. "Kilpatrick," a one-legged daredevil, rode a bicycle down steep "steps" on the pike at St. Louis in 1904.

George Barker (later published by Underwood & Underwood)
#375, Belleni at Niagara _____ 15.00

Blondin at Niagara, scarce facing view on wire issued ca. 1865 _____ 70.00

Dixon at Niagara, 1890 _____ 15.00

#378, Peer, mistitled "Pierre crossing Niagara on rope," 1887 _____ 15–20.00

Charles Bierstadt, Peer falling from rope _____ 6.00

Curtis, Niagara Falls, Madam Spelterini on wire _____ 15.00

London Stereoscopic Co., Blondin on wire, 1860 _____ 45–65.00

Underwood & Underwood, #5409, "Dixon crossing Niagara on a rope below great cantilever bridge." _____ 15.00

Whiting View Co.
#616, "Kirkpatrick," the one-legged
daredevil riding a bicycle down the
steps, World's Fair, 1904 ———————— 20.00
#617, Miss Lizette "Leaping the
Gap" on her bicycle at the World's
Fair, St. Louis, 1904 ———————— 20.00
#816, Calvaly performing over Ni-
agara Falls ———————————————— 20.00
Wide variety of local makers,
1870s–1880s, wire walkers entertain-
ing crowd on Main Street ————— 35–45.00

Disasters

*(See also *Railroads* and *Ships and Maritime*
Views)

Nearly every major fire, flood, volcanic eruption, earthquake, tornado and tidal wave has
been photographed in stereo since the early
1860s. Thousands of views have been published ranging from the burning of a local business block to the devastation of the Galveston
tidal wave and flood.

The first great city to burn was Portland,
Maine, in 1866. An excellent series by John
P. Soule shows the ruins in the burned districts
plus the refugee camps. Other great fires include Chicago (1871), Boston (1872), Baltimore (1904) and San Francisco (1906). All
were covered in detail by numerous photographers and publishers of stereo views. The
great floods were the Mill Creek in Massachusetts (1874); Worcester, Massachusetts
(1876); Johnstown, Pennsylvania (1889); and
Galveston, Texas (1900). Like the fires, these
were shown in large series that sold for many
years after the event. Johnstown and Galveston are of particular interest in the way the
photographers made their views. To bring home
the horror of the tragic force of the water, they

posed "dead" bodies among the ruins for added
realism.

Several major publishers sent photographers to record the ruins of the volcanic eruption at St. Pierre on the island of Martinique.
More than 40,000 lives were lost after Mount
Pelée exploded making the city a fiery waste-
land. This was the worst disaster in modern
times but the San Francisco earthquake and
fire is the most popular with collectors. Dozens
of series were made by both the major publishers and local area photographers.

Appomattox River Flood (Great
Freshet), Va., 1865
E. & H. T. Anthony, part of "War
Views." ———————————————— 4–6.00
Baltimore Fire (1904)
Underwood & Underwood, Views of
ruins ———————————————————— 8–12.00
H. C. White, 10381–10395 ————— 9–15.00
Boston Fire, 1872
John P. Soule, Views of ruins ——— 8–10.00
Brattleboro, Vt., Fire (late 1860s)
C. L. Howe ———————————————— 5–8.00
Chicago Fire (1871)
Lovejoy & Foster, Views of ruins ——— 8–10.00
P. B. Greene, Views of ruins ———— 8–10.00
J. A. Pierce & Co., "Place where the
fire originated. The cow that kicked
over the lamp!" ——————————— 10–12.00
Fulton, N.Y., Fire, (ca. late 1870s)
"Fulton after the Fire," burned-out
buildings ———————————————— 1–2.00
Galveston, Tex., Tidal Wave and Flood
(1900)
Keystone ———————————————— 4–6.00
#10985, Galveston in ruins
#10986, Power House, Galveston
City Railway
#10987, Rear view of Opera
House after the storm
#10988, Sacred Heart Church, ruins
#16577, Sea wall at Galveston
after it was built following recovery from the flood

R. Grobe, Fremont, Ohio, "Sandusky
Ave.," after flood of 1881. A typical
example of a local disaster usually done
as a series documenting the event. $6.

Underwood & Underwood, Scenes
of ruins _____ 7–9.00
Universal Photo Art _____ 8–12.00
    #5441, Commissary Department
    #5442, Elevator and grain cars
    #5443, Among the wreckage
    #5444, Jesuit Church where 400 perished
C. L. Wasson (International View
Co.), #624-C, Wreck, ruin and
death in sad Galveston _____ 10.00
R. Y. Young (American Stereoscopic
Co.), Burning bodies of the dead _____ 9.00
M. H. Zahner (sold by Griffith &
Griffith) _____ 8–12.00
    Houses turned over by storm, Avenue M
    Interior, St. Patrick's Church
Grinnell, Iowa, Tornado (1882)
    Charles Bierstadt _____ 6–10.00
Huntington, W.V., Ohio Valley Flood,
1884
    George W. Kirk views of flood _____ 6–10.00
    Other makers _____ 4–8.00
Johnstown, Pa., Flood (1889)
    George Barker, Views on orange
    cabinet mounts _____ 9.00
    R. K. Bonine (Complete set of
    twenty-five views: 95.00) _____ 3–7.00
    B. W. Kilburn _____ 4–6.00
        #5237, Rubble at bridge of death
        #5247, Iron piled like straw
        #5248, Iron piled with tree stumps
        #5249, Overview of railyard, box cars, etc.
        #5250, City of canvas showing tent camp
    William H. Rau (published by Grif-
    fith & Griffith) _____ 4–9.00
        #6293, Main Street in ruins
        #6390, Tree through house
    Underwood & Underwood, 1890s
    issues of Barker negatives, buff
    mounts _____ 4–7.00
Kansas City Flood (1903)
    Underwood & Underwood, gray
    mounts _____ 5–7.00

Messina, Italy, Earthquake (1909)
    Underwood & Underwood _____ 5–7.00
Mill Creek Flood (1874), series made
by various local Massachusetts pho-
tographers
    C. Seaver (published by Pollack),
    #2, Wreckage, typical view _____ 3.00
    Other makers, Typical house ruins _____ 4.00
Portland, Maine, Fire (1866)
    Soule, #469, Typical view of ruins __ 8–12.00
Richmond, Va., Fire at Gallego Mills
(1873)
    George O. Ennis, View of ruins _____ 8–12.00
St. Louis, Mo., and East St. Louis, Ill.,
Cyclone (1896)
    Keystone _____ 4–9.00
        #2214, Ead's Bridge
        #2219, Lafayette Park Presbyterian Church
        #2241, Transfer boat *Henry Sackman*, East St.
        Louis, Ill.
        #2255, St. Louis Transfer Co., East St. Louis,
        Ill.
St. Pierre, Martinique, French West
Indies, Volcanic Eruption (1902)
    Kilburn, #14941, Typical ruins _____ 3.00
    Keystone _____ 6–8.00
        #14366, Refugees escaping Mount
        Pelée's fury
        #14367, Natives fleeing
    Underwood & Underwood, Typical
    ruins _____ 4–6.00
San Francisco Earthquake and Fire
(1906)
    Berry, Kelley & Chadwick, View of
    ruins _____ 20–28.00
    Keystone, #13264, Market Street,
    typical ruins _____ 8–12.00
    Kilburn, #16891, Typical ruins,
    Merchant's Exchange _____ 12–15.00
    Underwood & Underwood _____ 12–15.00
        #8180, California Street ruins
        #8195, Wrecked domes of St. Dominick's
        Church

George Barker, ''The Johnstown Calamity, A slightly damaged house,'' 1889, Barker's tongue-in-cheek title was unusual for people at that time who took such disasters very seriously. $9.

H. C. White, #8720, Market Street in ruins, San Francisco earthquake and fire, 1906. $10.

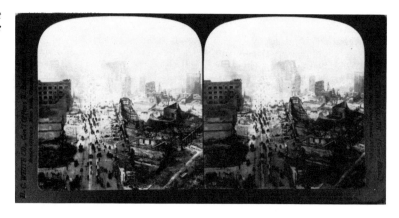

H. C. White, #8729, Twisted Valencia Street, typical	6–10.00
Wisconsin, Clintonville Flood, 1880	
C. A. Spicer, typical ruins	12–15.00
Worcester, Mass., flood, 1876	
Various makers, typical ruins	4–6.00
Yankton, South Dakota, flood, 1881	
Various local makers	15–20.00

Dolls
(See *Children* and *Christmas*)

Down Under (Australia, New Zealand, and Surrounding Areas)

Pre-1890 views of Australia, New Zealand, and other South Seas areas are extremely rare. A series of unknown quantity was made in the early 1870s marked simply "Australian Scenery." Views of Hobart, Tasmania, are known, which were published by G. Cherry. Only a few early views of New Zealand have been seen. Collectors should look for the fine series by George Rose of Windsor, Victoria, Australia. Rose Stereograph Company was formed in 1880 and may still be in business. (Rose Company was still making postcards in 1978.) Rose made an outstanding series of the visit of the American "Great White" fleet to Australia in 1908. It is estimated that Rose published about 9000 different views. The views are very uncommon in the United States though.

All of the major publishers offered a limited number of views of the area. Keystone views from the various world tour boxed sets are very common.

Pre-1890 views, Interesting subject	20–30.00
Pre-1890 views, Rocks, trees, ferns, etc.	5–10.00
George Rose (Rose Stereograph Co.), 1880–1908	
Scenic views	2–6.00
Duke of York Celebrations, Hobart	6–8.00
The Delhi Durbar (India)	20–30.00
Victoria, Australia views	8–10.00
Visit of the United States fleet	10–15.00
Keystone	
#15978, Pastoral scene, Auckland	1.00
#24352, Derwent, Tasmania	2.00

Eastern United States
Cities and Towns

Connecticut	
Webster, Norwich, view of residence, typical	8–10.00
Delaware	
Joseph A. Maybin, People on small footbridge, Wilmington, 1875, typical type	5–8.00
Maine	
Henry Bailey, Residence at Augusta, typical	12–15.00
Maryland	
E. Anthony, #254, "Views in Baltimore," shows water with building, ca. 1860	25–30.00
E. & H. T. Anthony, "Views in Baltimore," ca. 1870	15–20.00
W. M. Chase, Views of buildings in Baltimore	10–20.00
Town views other than Baltimore, pre-1880	10–20.00
Massachusetts	
Boston	
D. Appleton, close-up of apple seller on Common, nice 1860s people view	15–20.00

D. Barnum, Dedication of Webster Statue, large crowd, 1860s _____ 6–10.00
Harbor scene, sailing ships, 1870s _____ 12–15.00
Public Garden, 1860s–1880s _____ 3–6.00
Keystone, #22655, Horse-drawn delivery wagon in front of building, site of Franklin's birthplace _____ 15–20.00
John P. Soule, State House, 1870s _____ 3–5.00
H. C. White, Public Garden, 1900 _____ 1–3.00

Cambridge
Mt. Auburn Cemetery, various makers _____ 1–3.00
Underwood & Underwood and others, Bunker Hill Monument _____ 1–3.00

Concord
J. S. Moulton, #1, Rustic bridge with girl, 1880 _____ 1–3.00

Fitchburg
J. C. Moulton, Fitchburg jail, typical _____ 1–3.00

Nantucket
J. Freeman, Town views _____ 8–15.00

Provincetown
Cape Cod Pilot whales beached, unusual subject _____ 15–20.00
G. H. Nickerson, Views of town _____ 10–15.00

Salem
J. W. & J. S. Moulton, Scenes of town _____ 4–8.00
Views of towns in eastern part of state _____ 3–8.00
Views of towns in western part of state _____ 5–12.00

New Hampshire
Concord
B. Carr, Clough & Kimball, C. M. Couch, E. Gould, W. G. C. Kimball, H. P. Moore and others, Town scenes, buildings, homes, etc. _____ 4–8.00

Lebanon
E. T. Bagley, W. W. Culver and others, Town views _____ 6–10.00

Manchester
C. K. Burns, L. W. Colby, J. G. Ellinwood, D. O. Furnald and others, Town views _____ 5–10.00

Nashua
E. J. Copp, E. Glenton, Hamilton and others, Town views _____ 8–12.00

New London
H. J. Currier and others, Town views _____ 8–12.00

New Market
O. H. Copeland, Town views _____ 8–12.00

North Conway
N. W. Pease, Town views _____ 5–10.00

Peterborough, Jaffrey and area
G. H. Scripture, Town views _____ 3–8.00

Shaker Villages, Canterberry, and so forth
H. A. Kimball, #7, Church family houses, typical _____ 30–60.00
H. A. Kimball, Views showing Shakers _____ 75–100.00
Various Towns by Kilburn Brothers, 1860s–1870s _____ 5–8.00

Warren
A. H. Clough and others, Town and residences _____ 5–10.00

New Jersey
Asbury Park
S. Shear, Pach and others, 1870s, Buildings _____ 8–12.00
Campbell, Underwood & Underwood, Post-1890s views _____ 4–8.00

Atlantic City
S. R. Morse _____ 10–15.00
Kilburn, #6756, Family posed, typical _____ 1–2.00
Post-1890s makers, Mostly of beach area _____ 1–3.00

Cape May, Vineland and southern Part, Resort Hotels and Residences
O. H. Willard and others _____ 10–16.00
Long Branch, Pach and others _____ 8–12.00

Newark
T. Gubelman, Very scarce _____ 10–15.00
Keystone _____ 1–3.00

E. & H. T. Anthony, #3695, Junction of Chatham and Centre Streets, New York City, ca. 1860s. $15.

Paterson
  J. Reid and others, Scarce _____ 10–15.00
Red Bank
  C. Lane, Pach and others, Views
  of buildings _____ 8–12.00
Trenton
  E. E. Seeler and others, Town
  views, factories _____ 15–20.00
  Keystone _____ 1–3.00
Various Other Towns, Pre-1880 _____ 8–12.00
Various Makers, Industries in
State, and so on, 1890–1920 _____ 1–3.00
New York City
(*See also* Bridges, Brooklyn Sus-
pension in Chapter 5)
  Anthony, 1859–1870s
    #304, Fifth Avenue Hotel and
    Worth Monument _____ 15–20.00
    #3694–3697, Junction of
    Chatham and Centre Streets _____ 15–20.00
    #5077, Broadway from
    Broome Street _____ 15.00
    #5290, Entrance to Green-
    Wood, south side _____ 2–4.00
    #6608, Stock Market, large
    crowd in street _____ 45.00
    #7640, Vault in Green-Wood
    Cemetery _____ 1–3.00
    #8643, City Hall, 1870s _____ 8–10.00
    #11173, Overview, ships at
    docks _____ 6–8.00
    #11176, Overview of city,
    tall-masted ships _____ 8–12.00
  A. J. Fisher, "Looking north—
  showing new Post Office Building and Broadway," instantaneous panoramic _____ 5–10.00
  Keystone
    #1009, Wall Street _____ 2–4.00
    #9370, General Grant's Tomb,
    Riverside _____ 1–3.00
    #V26894, Horse-drawn street-
    car, Metropolitan Belt Line on
    Broadway, elevated station _____ 30–40.00

Kilburn, #4055, Three-masted
ship as seen from under the
Brooklyn Bridge, typical _____ 6–10.00
London Stereoscopic Co.
(1859–1862), North American
Series
  Tinted view of High Bridge,
  Harlem, typical _____ 20–25.00
  Parade for Japanese Embassy,
  Broadway, rare _____ 50–75.00
G. W. Pach (active 1866–1900;
sold by G. W. Thorne)
  Views of the city _____ 15–20.00
  #423, Close-up of five male
  skaters in Central Park, better
  subject with people, 1870s _____ 15–25.00
  Views of Central Park without
  people _____ 8–12.00
Henry Ropes & Co. (active as
distributor of views made for
him, 1865–1880)
  #12, Grand Central Depot,
  typical _____ 10–15.00
  Central Park views _____ 3–8.00
George Stacy (1859–1864), usually on yellow mounts without
credit, marked "American Sce-
nery/New York City" on the front
with number less than 400 printed
below right image or manuscript
on the reverse at one end
  #341, A. T. Stewart's Store,
  Broadway, Brady studio seen
  at right _____ 30–40.00
  Central Park _____ 6–12.00
  Green-Wood Cemetery _____ 3–8.00
  Japanese procession _____ 30–40.00
  Various views of buildings in
  city _____ 12–20.00
Stereo-Travel
  Jewish Fish Markets, 1909 _____ 15–20.00
  Polo Grounds baseball field _____ 25–30.00
  Various views of city
  buildings _____ 6–8.00

Stereo-Travel Co., #89, "View on Harlem River," New York City, 1914. Photographed by Lynn Skeels. $15. (Gordon D. Hoffman Collection)

George W. Thorne (distributor
and publisher), Views usually
blindstamped "G. W. Thorne 62
Nassau St."
Views of Central Park, 1870s _____ 5–8.00
Views of city, buildings, etc. _____ 6–10.00
Underwood & Underwood
(Strohmeyer & Wyman)
Central Park views _____ 2–4.00
Views of city _____ 3–6.00
Submarine, Brooklyn Navy
Yard, 1898 _____ 20–30.00
Universal Photo Art (C. H. Graves)
#2823, Post Office Park Row
and World Buildings _____ 4–6.00
#4408, Nassau Street _____ 5–8.00
Peter F. Weil (often marked
"P.F.W.-N.Y."), manuscript titles
on reverse (active 1865–1878)
Views of Central Park _____ 4–8.00
Views of streets and buildings _____ 6–9.00
H. C. White
#1, America's great thorough-
fare, Broadway _____ 2–4.00
#9, The famous Bowery,
north from Grand Street _____ 3–5.00
#29, Busy harbor of New
York, Brooklyn Bridge _____ 4–6.00
#31, Hippopotamuses, Central
Park Zoo _____ 2–3.00
#49, Photographer working
250 feet above ground _____ 30–50.00
#50, Immigrants on deck of
SS Amerika [*sic*] _____ 15–25.00
#60, New York Herald
Building _____ 5–6.00
#61, The Cactus garden, Pros-
pect Park, Brooklyn _____ 2–3.00
#70, Watching election re-
turns, crowd before the Times
Building and Astor Hotel,
1907 _____ 8–12.00
#490, Happy youngsters, Co-
ney Island _____ 5–8.00

#500, View in Luna Park, Co-
ney Island _____ 12–15.00
#501, Trained bears riding on
merry-go-round pulled by a
pony, circus, Coney Island _____ 15–20.00
#513, The ballroom at night,
Dreamland, Coney Island _____ 12–15.00
Whiting View Co.
#407, Broadway, wagons and
trolley _____ 8–10.00
#422, Brooklyn Bridge show-
ing tugs, East River _____ 10–12.00
New York State
(*See also* Niagara Falls in Chapter 5)
Albany
William Notman, Capitol build-
ing interior _____ 3–5.00
A. Veeder, Views of city _____ 5–8.00
Brooklyn (*See* Eastern United States,
New York City in Chapter 5)
Buffalo
C. L. Pond, Views of the city,
1870s _____ 8–12.00
A. W. Simon, Views of the city,
1880s _____ 6–10.00
Lake George
S. R. Stoddard
Close view of stagecoach at
Fort William Henry Hotel _____ 15–25.00
Views of hotels, buildings _____ 10–15.00
Rochester
C. W. Woodward, "Rochester
and Vicinity"
#1–6, Powers' Building, in-
cluding interiors _____ 4–6.00
#8–18, Panoramas from Pow-
ers' Block Tower _____ 5–8.00
Various views of buildings,
streets _____ 6–10.00
Saratoga Springs
Baker & Record
#26, Crowded Veranda of
Grand Union Hotel, typical
hotel view _____ 3–5.00

Irving of Troy, N.Y., "Shaker Village, Mount Lebanon, N.Y." Mount Lebanon and the Shakers were extensively documented by Irving. $50.

Views of the Spring houses _____ 2–4.00
Various Small Towns by Local
Photographers _____ 6–8.00
Pennsylvania
Allentown and Bethlehem Area
M. A. Kleckner, Views of
buildings _____ 6–8.00
Chambersburg
Bishop, Views of buildings _____ 8–10.00
Bradford (Oil Regions)
Detlor & Waddell, Street scenes
and buildings _____ 10–15.00
Lancaster
W. L. Gill, Views of residences
and streets _____ 8–10.00
Mauch Chunk (now called Jim
Thorpe)
Gates, Views of town _____ 3–5.00
Kilburn, #2464, Canal lock and
town _____ 8–12.00
Zelner, #10, View of town and
Bear Mountain _____ 1–3.00
New Brighton
Noss, Views of town _____ 8–10.00
Philadelphia
James Cremer
Fairmount Park _____ 3–5.00
Independence Hall, exteriors
and interiors _____ 2–5.00
Masonic Temple _____ 5–8.00
Street scenes _____ 8–12.00
Langenheim (1855–1860) _____ 50–90.00
Roberts & Fellows _____ 3–6.00
Post-1890 views, numerous
makers _____ 3–6.00
Pittsburgh
Purviance, Suspension bridge,
1870s _____ 10–20.00
Purviance and other local mak-
ers, Streets and buildings _____ 20–30.00
Views of the Incline Plane, pre-
1890 _____ 25–35.00
Plymouth
E. W. Beckwith, Views of town _____ 8–12.00
Pottsville
A. M. Allen, Views of town _____ 8–12.00
Reading
J. M. Bertolet and other local
makers _____ 6–12.00
C. W. Woodward, views of
Canal _____ 4–10.00
Various Small Towns by Local
Makers _____ 6–12.00
Vermont
Bellows Falls
P. W. Taft, #138, Interior of
hotel lobby _____ 15–25.00
Views of the town, streets _____ 4–8.00
Brandon
A. F. Styles, #385, Simonds
Block, typical _____ 3–5.00
Burlington
A. F. Styles, #177, College
Street, 1860s _____ 4–6.00

Montpelier
C. H. Freeman, State Capitol
Building _____ 4–8.00
Kilburn, Styles and others, State
Capitol _____ 3–5.00
Views of the town, pre-1885 _____ 12–15.00
St. Albans
T. G. Richardson, Views of town,
1870s _____ 5–8.00
Waterbury
E. R. Ober, Town views _____ 4–6.00

Eastern United States
Landscapes and Scenic Views

Connecticut
Bundy & Williams, Scenes in New
Haven area, typical of 1860s–1880s
scenics _____ 4–6.00
Delaware
T. E. Sexton, Scenic study, Wil-
mington area, typical _____ 8–10.00
Maine
J. O. Durgan, Views of Old Orchard
Beach, typical scenes on coast _____ 8–10.00
M. F. King, Scenic studies in Port-
land area _____ 8–12.00
Maryland
E. M. Recker, Scenes on Western
Maryland Railroad, scenery at Penn
Mar., 1880s _____ 12–15.00
Massachusetts
Cape Cod
Views by numerous makers,
1860s–1880s _____ 4–6.00
Provincetown
G. H. Nickerson and others,
Coastal area _____ 4–6.00
Salem
J. W. & J. S. Moulton and others _____ 3–5.00
Truro Scenes
Nickerson, Highland Clay Cliffs _____ 4–5.00
New Hampshire
Belknap Mountains
Heywood, #450, Seen from
Wolfborough, typical better scenic
photography, 1860s _____ 4–6.00
Franconia Notch
Kilburn and many others,
1860s–1890s _____ 2–5.00
Milford and Vicinity
S. R. Hanaford (published by E.
Lovejoy), ''Middle Falls and
Bridge,'' typical _____ 3–5.00
Waterville
E. J. Young, #1, Welch Moun-
tain, from Davis' Hill, typical _____ 2–5.00
White Mountains
Kilburn Brothers, Cascades, the
notches, etc., 1860s–1870s, yel-
low mounts _____ 4–6.00
N. W. Pease, North Conway area,
yellow mounts _____ 3–5.00

John P. Soule, #527, Crystal Cascade, Pinkham Notch, 1860s, typical example ___ 3–5.00

Various makers, post-1885 views ___ 1–3.00

New Jersey
Series by Moore, Trenton Fall, 1870s ___ 2–5.00

New York State
(*See also* Niagara Falls in Chapter 5)

Adirondack Mountains
S. R. Stoddard and others, 1860s–1880s ___ 4–8.00

Ausable Chasm
Baldwin, McIntosh, Styles and many others, 1860s–1890s ___ 2–5.00

Catskill Mountains
Anthony, 1860s–1870s, yellow mounts ___ 3–6.00
J. Loeffler, 1870s–1880s ___ 4–8.00

Cayuga Lake Scenery
C. W. Woodward, #1322, Cascade above the falls, 1870s, typical view ___ 2–3.00

Glens Falls
G. W. Conkey and others, 1870s ___ 5–8.00

Havana Glen
C. M. Marsh and others, 1860s–1880s ___ 3–5.00

Hudson River
Anthony "Beauties of the Hudson." ___ 3–8.00
#337, View near Cold Spring
#349, View from Fort Putnam
#1348, View from West Point
#4117, The mouth of the Moodna
Pirated copies of Anthony views ___ 1.00

Portage Falls
L. E. Walker, C. W. Woodward and others, 1860s–1880s ___ 3–8.00

Seneca Lake (*See* Watkins Glen below)

Thousand Islands
A. C. McIntyre, 1870s, red mounts ___ 8–15.00

Kilburn, #9839, St. Lawrence River, 1894 ___ 1–2.00

Underwood & Underwood, #4749, Man and two women in boat ___ 2–4.00

Watkins Glen
R. D. Crum, #2, Entrance stairs, typical ___ 2–4.00
G. F. Gates, #26, Looking out over entrance gorge, 1870s, typical, red mount. ___ 1–3.00
Keystone, #26508, Rainbow Falls ___ 1.00
Universal Photo Art, #5530, Cavern Cascade and Jacob's Ladder, typical example ___ 1–2.00
H. C. White, #376, Shadow Gorge, typical ___ 1–3.00

Pennsylvania
Beaver Valley, near New Brighton
H. Noss, More than one hundred views ___ 3–5.00

Catawissa
Langenheim, 1856 ___ 20–30.00
John Moran, 1860 ___ 15–25.00
C. W. Woodward, 1870s ___ 2–3.00

Delaware Water Gap
Jesse A. Graves, #11, Sawkill, Forest Fall, typical example ___ 4–6.00
C. W. Woodward, #1256, View at Rebecca's bath, 1870s–1880s, typical example ___ 1–3.00

Mauch Chunk
G. F. Gates, #27, Flag Staff Ledge—South Mountain, typical example, cabinet mount ___ 1–3.00
M. A. Kleckner, #108, Bear Mountain ___ 2–5.00
Purviance, Scenics, yellow cabinet mounts ___ 2–4.00

Wissahickon Creek
C. W. Woodward, #1059, Falls on creek, typical example, 1870s–1880s, red mount ___ 1–3.00
Pirated copies ___ 1.00

Frank M. Good, Eastern Series, #104, "Tombs of the Mamelukes, showing the Citadel, Cairo, Egypt." $6.

Egypt

The ancient lands of the East were first stereo-photographed about 1855. The best series was by Francis Frith who saw the shapes and forms with artistic flare. These are now considered classics and are sought by collectors. The views are usually identified by Frith's signature and the number scratched in the negative. Negretti and Zambra first published the series on cards and on glass in 1857. After 1861, the series was published by Frith and stayed available into the 1880s. They were pirated, and poor-quality copies were still being sold in 1900.

Another fine series was produced by Frank Good in the 1860s. Called the "Eastern Series," the fine-quality print on yellow mounts with a special label on the reverse are highly prized by collectors. J. Andrieu (J. A.) offered a small series of tinted tissues of the Suez Canal dedication, 1869.

W. Hammerschmidt made a series similar to the Good "Eastern Series," but is not as extensive. Kilburn Brothers issued several dozen views in 1875 and in the 1890s made an outstanding series, which includes native and street life.

William H. Rau was the photographer on an expedition led by Edward Wilson of the photo publication *The Philadelphia Photographer* in the winter of 1881–1882. Published as "Scenes in the Orient" on cabinet mounts, the series has more than 650 titles; not all of the views are of Egypt. Another fine series was published by Charles Bierstadt on orange cabinet mounts. These were reissued by Underwood and Underwood and later by Keystone View Company.

All of the major publishers offered Egypt views, mainly confined to the ancient wonders of the pyramids and the great ruins at Karnak. Underwood and Underwood and Keystone both offered interior views of the Cairo Museum, including views of mummies.

Anthony, 1860s _____ 8–12.00
  #1407, The court of Sheshouk at
  Karnac [*sic*] showing column
  #1408, The Pyramids and Sphinx
  #1409, The Cross of the Scriptures
  #1569, The Obelisk and Temple of
  Karnak, at Thebes
  #1571, Rock Temple, Nubia
Charles Bierstadt, #59, Ruins of the
Temple and Sphinx in background ____ 4–6.00
Francis Frith, #376, Two largest pyramids at Geezech [*sic*], 1858 _____ 10–20.00

C. H. Graves (Universal Photo Art) _____ 3–5.00
  #9301, Pompey's Pillar, Alexandria
  #9306, Sultan Hassan Mosque and
  Cairo from the citadel
  #9337, Crossing great Nile Bridge
  #9355, Avenue of Sphinxes and
  Great Pylon, Karnak
  #9370, The Banks of the Nile near
  Luxor
  #9382, Great Nile dam at Assouan
  [*sic*]
  #9383, Nile flowing through eight
  gates of the great dam at Assouan
  [*sic*]
  #9398, The lemonade vendor
Frank Good, "Eastern Series" _____ 5–8.00
Griffith, #57, "Pyramids of Gizeh
[*sic*]," 1900 _____ 3–5.00
W. Hammerschmidt, yellow mounts _____ 5–8.00
Keystone, 1890s _____ 1–4.00
  #6233, Native boys spinning cotton
  #6242, Overview of Assuan [*sic*] Dam
  #8613, Arab Grocery Store, Cairo
  #9707, Lake of Karnak, women
  with oxen
  #9737, Ruins of Karnak
  #9741, Sunset on Nile (tinted), 1899
Kilburn
  Scenes of ancient ruins and Cairo,
  1875, on yellow mounts _____ 3–5.00
  Scenes, especially of street life plus
  the ancient ruins, 1890s, buff
  mounts _____ 4–6.00
Underwood & Underwood, Overview
of Cairo, 1897, typical _____ 1–2.00
H. C. White, #1012, Obelisk at Heli-
opolis, 1901, typical example _____ 2–4.00
Edward L. Wilson "Scenes in the Orient," 1882 _____ 5–10.00

England
(See *Europe in Chapter 5*)

Entertainers
(See *Personalities in Chapter 5*)

Europe

Belgium
  Keystone, #518, Public Fountain,
  Brussels _____ 1–2.00
  J. Queval, 1870s _____ 2–4.00
  F. Tessaro, Scenes of Brussels,
  1860s _____ 3–5.00
  Universal Photo Art, #7701, Place
  de Brouckere, 1890s, typical view ____ 1–2.00
  H. C. White, #6701, Van Dyck
  Quay and Steen Museum,
  Antwerp _____ 2–3.00
Czechoslovakia
  F. Fridrich, Lachman, M. Klempfner,
  etc., Prague, 1860s–1870s _____ 4–8.00
  Keystone
    #15634, Overview of Prague _____ 2.00
    #24648, Overview of Gablonz,

Francis Bedford, North Wales Illustrated, #651, "Conway Castle, General View and Shore." $6. (John Weiler Collection)

Bohemia _____ 3.00
#24653, Women weaving Oriental rugs _____ 4.00
#24710, Children in Trilnak _____ 4.00
Denmark
Fabrik Fangel, Vilhelm Tryder, etc., Scenes of Copenhagen 1860–1880s _____ 4–8.00
Keystone, #27829, Dining hall of Fredericsborg Castle, Copenhagen ____ 2–4.00
Underwood & Underwood, Interior of Rosenborg Palace, Copenhagen ____ 1–3.00
H. C. White, #4914, Castle of Kronborg, Elsinore _____ 1–3.00
England
Francis Bedford, 1857–1863 (*see also* Costumes in Chapter 5), More than 3000 classic views _____ 4–6.00
   Major series, mostly on yellow mounts
      Bristol Illustrated
      Chester Illustrated
      Clifton Illustrated
      Devonshire Illustrated
      Exeter Illustrated
      Gloucester Illustrated
      Herefordshire Illustrated
      Ludlow Illustrated
      Monmouthshire Illustrated
      North Wales Illustrated
      South Wales Illustrated
      Warwickshire Illustrated
      Welsh Costumes
Valentine Blanchard, 1860s–1870s ____ 4–6.00
Francis Frith, 1850s–1860s, usually light gray card mounts, signed in negatives _____ 6–12.00
Keystone
   #3015, Overview of York _____ 3.00
   #3023, Village of Symond's Yat _____ 2.00
   #13120, Lake Grasmere, man on bench _____ 2.00
   #28161, Old Clock Tower, Hampton Court, London _____ 2.00
   #V28166, Stoke Poges, Country Churchyard _____ 2.00
   #W28198, Ruins, Banquet Hall,

Kenilworth _____ 2.00
   #28246, Interior of Queen Anne's bedroom _____ 3.00
   #28355, Interior of Chester Cathedral _____ 3.00
Kilburn, #6068, Windsor Castle with royal entrance, typical example _____ 1–3.00
Ogle and Edge, Rustic scenes, 1857–1866, tinted and untinted (*OE* in the negative) _____ 10–12.00
H. Petschler, 1858–1865 (Manchester Photograph Co., 1866–1875), Manchester, Wales, etc. _____ 5–10.00
Sedgfield, 1855–1870, usually with paper strip labels, number in lower right corner or with *Sedgfield* signed in negative _____ 12–15.00
Seeley of Richmond, View of Hampton Court, typical view by local maker _____ 3–5.00
H. C. White, #2566, Salisbury Cathedral, 1902 _____ 4–6.00
France
J. Andrieu (J. A.), Views of Paris _____ 2–4.00
Anthony, #2237, "Place de la Bourse," 1860s, tinted, typical example. _____ 3–5.00
A. Braun, #1791, Bassin de Latone, Garden of Versailles, typical example _____ 1–3.00
N. C. of Paris, Overview of city _____ 1–3.00
William England, Often without credit, titles printed in French below right image, yellow mounts "Vue Instantanee," street scene _____ 3–5.00
Hautecoeur (A. H.) of Paris, "Maison Martinet," Rue de Rivoli, typical example _____ 3–5.00
Keystone
   #1601, Busy Bourse, Paris, 1895 _____ 3.00
   #1603, Grand Opera, Paris, many wagons and automobiles _____ 3.00
   #1619, Arch de Triumph, Paris _____ 3.00
   #1641, The Champs Elysees, Paris _____ 2.00
   #11724, Overview of Seine River, Paris _____ 3.00

#11741, Eiffel Tower and ferris wheel, 1900 _____ 5.00

#11750, Overview of Monte Carlo, 1900 _____ 2.00

#11754, Overview of Monaco, prince's castle _____ 2.00

#11765, Interior of Winter Garden in Casino Principal, Nice _____ 2.00

#11766, Nice, women washing clothes _____ 2.00

#24817, Notre Dame Cathedral, Paris _____ 2.00

Kilburn, #1545, Overview of Paris from Tuileries, typical example _____ 3–5.00

Neurdein, Aquarium at Le Havre, Normandy, typical example, ca. 1870, orange mount _____ 4–6.00

Underwood & Underwood, #9583, Men working in vineyard, Ay, 1907, typical example, gray mount _____ 1–3.00

J. Valecki "Vues de France/Views of France," late 1860s, usually on yellow mounts _____ 2–4.00

Vues Nouvelles/Paris, #2814, Church of St. Germain, ca. 1870, yellow mount _____ 1–3.00

H. C. White, #2036, Gallery of Francis I, Palace of Fontainebleau, typical example _____ 2–4.00

Germany

A. Braun, 1860s, ivory mounts with gold trim _____ 4–6.00

Keystone, #10304, Throne Room, Royal Palace, Berlin, typical example _____ 1–3.00

E. Linde, 1870s–1880s (earlier negatives by Sophus Williams) _____ 3–5.00

Underwood & Underwood, #1324, Ship canal and bridge at Kiel, typical example _____ 1–3.00

H. C. White

#2236, Ehrenfels Castle at Nahe and Rhine rivers _____ 1–3.00

"Artisque Coleur" series, #2259, Hohenschwangau and the Alpsee, Bavarian Highlands (beautifully hand colored, gold lettering on

mount) _____ 6–8.00

Sophus Williams, 1860s–1870s _____ 4–6.00

Greece

(*See also* Wars, Greco-Turkish in Chapter 5)

Keystone, #7170, Men threshing grain, primitive style, typical example _____ 1–3.00

H. C. White, #4128, Overview of Athens, typical _____ 2–3.00

Views by Greek photographers, scarce _____ 6–10.00

Holland

A. Jager, Leon & Levy, etc. pre-1890 views _____ 4–6.00

Keystone, Underwood & Underwood, White, etc. post-1890 views _____ 1–3.00

Pirated copies, *B* series, etc. _____ <1.00

Ireland

(*See also* Expositions and Fairs, Dublin International Exposition in Chapter 5)

E. & H. T. Anthony, "Irish Views," 1860s _____ 3–5.00

Douglas, "Irish Scenery." _____ 4–6.00

Hudson, "Stereoscopic Gems of Irish Scenery." _____ 4–6.00

London Stereoscopic Co., (negatives by William England)

1858–1860 issues, greenish, flat-toned mount, band of gold surrounding stereo pair, label on reverse. _____ 8–12.00

1860s, flat mount with brownish color, label on the reverse, often with blindstamp. _____ 8–10.00

London Stereoscopic Co. name printed on yellow mounts, ca. 1870 _____ 6–10.00

H. Petschler & Co. Country scenes, 1858–1865. _____ 5–8.00

G. W. Wilson, Giant's Causeway, 1857–1862 _____ 3–5.00

Keystone and Underwood & Underwood, Various post-1890 views. _____ 1–3.00

Italy

G. Brogi, 1860s–1880s _____ 2–4.00

C. Naya, Venice, 1860s–1870s _____ 2–4.00

B. W. Kilburn, #11778, "The Neva River in winter, St. Petersburg, Russia," 1897. The men are cutting ice. $16.

Sommer & Behles (or Sommer and Behles alone), thin white mounts with gold borders

Views of Naples _____ 3–5.00
Views of Pompeii _____ 4–6.00
Views of Rome _____ 3–5.00
Views of Sicily, Messina, etc. _____ 4–6.00
Various statuary, antiquities _____ 1–3.00

Keystone, Underwood & Underwood, Stereo-Travel, etc. (numerous makers), post-1890 views _____ 1–2.00
Pirated copies _____ 1.00
Color lithos _____ 0.25–0.50

Russia and Eastern Europe
(*See also* Wars, Russo-Japanese in Chapter 5)

Elliott, At least forty views, ca. 1860. _____ 20–30.00
Keystone, gray mounts _____ 4–6.00
B. W. Kilburn, many good views of people, occupations, etc., 1897 series. _____ 12–18.00
Langenheim Bros. About twenty views, 1857–1859. _____ 45–60.00
E. Linde, "Ansichten von St. Petersburg," about 200 views _____ 15–25.00
"Russie (Voyage en Russie)," unknown maker, probably published in France, late 1850s _____ 25–35.00

Underwood & Underwood
The Fair at Nijni-Novgorod (from Russia boxed set) _____ 6–8.00
Other views _____ 3–6.00
H. C. White
#4701–4705, Finland _____ 4–6.00
#4706–4796 _____ 3–6.00
#4797, The market in the Jewish quarters, Warsaw, Poland _____ 8–12.00
#4798–4800, Warsaw, Poland _____ 6–8.00

Scandinavian Countries
Pre-1890 views _____ 6–8.00
Keystone, Underwood & Underwood, and White, post-1890 views. _____ 3–5.00

Scotland
G. W. Wilson, yellow mounts, paper labels
#12, Balmoral Castle, in distance, 1860s, typical scene _____ 3–8.00
#186, Princes Street, Edinburgh, typical street scene _____ 8–15.00
Other makers, pre-1890 _____ 3–6.00
Pirated copies, usually simply marked "Scotland" _____ 1.00
Various makers, post-1890
Keystone, Underwood & Underwood _____ 1–3.00
Stereo-Travel, H. C. White,

G. W. Wilson, #16, The Clamshell Cave, Staffa, ca. late 1860s, a typical Scottish landscape study by Wilson. $6.

The Fine-Art Photographer's Publishing Co. (Keystone View Co. in England), #10708, "Guide Cutting Steps, Upper Glacier, Grindelwald, Switzerland," 1900. $4.

others		2–4.00
Color lithos		0.25–0.50
Switzerland		
Alpine Club, William England, #115, View of Interlaken, 1860s, yellow mounts, typical		2–4.00
Graves (Universal Photo Art), #2352, Houses on Lake Lucerne, typical post-1890 view		1–2.00

Expeditions and Surveys

The importance of stereo photography in the history of the United States is best seen in the use of this form of photography in the United States Geological and Topographical Surveys of the American west. The stereo views made by Albert Bierstadt on Colonel F. W. Lander's Expedition in 1859 are the first and possibly most prized by collectors. About eighty views were made and first issued by the Bierstadt Brothers of New Bedford, Massachusetts (Edward and Charles Bierstadt). The studio was sold by the brothers in 1866 to S. F. Adams who continued to publish the views into the early 1870s.

The next great survey was the Captain J. L. Fisk Expedition to Montana in 1866. Photographers on the expedition were William H. Illingworth and George Bill. Illingworth published the views with manuscript titles, but examples often lack contrast. John Carbutt obtained a portion of the Fisk Expedition negatives in 1866 and published a beautifully printed series on yellow mounts (#234–260).

B. H. Gurnsey also published Fisk views in the 1870s.

Lieutenant George M. Wheeler and Clarence King both led expeditions in the early 1870s. The chief photographer on the King Survey of the Fortieth Parallel was Timothy H. O'Sullivan who had gained fame as a Civil War photographer. The King series of views was probably not produced for commercial sale and examples outside government files are rare. With the King Survey completed, O'Sullivan joined the Wheeler Survey in 1871. He worked with that survey from 1871 to 1875, except for the summer of 1872 when William Bell took his place. The views were published by James F. Jarvis and E. and H. T. Anthony on special yellow cabinet mounts with paper labels on the reverse.

The Hayden Survey of the territories explored the area of the northern Rockies and the geological features of Yellowstone. The chief photographer was William H. Jackson, who was hired by Hayden in Omaha in 1870. Jackson worked with the Hayden Survey until 1878 and made more than 2000 negatives in stereo. Hayden had the views published by E. and H. T. Anthony on yellow cabinet mounts. Influential members of Congress and other public officials were given special presentation sets of the views. This helped Hayden gain funds for his survey plus allowed officials in the United States government to see the unusual scenic wonders of the west. The Hayden Survey views

Jack L. Hillers, portrait of Indian woman on the Powell Survey, 1875. One of many Indian views from this series. $40–60.

had a direct influence on lawmakers to create Yellowstone National Park.

The Powell Survey of the Colorado River was photographed by E. O. Beaman, Jack Hillers and James Fennemore. Although the survey began in 1869, the first stereo photographs were not taken until the second survey/expedition (1871–1872) with E. O. Beaman as chief photographer. He found the backbreaking work of climbing canyons and the hazards of the trip too much and he withdrew after taking less than 400 negatives. James Fennemore, Beaman's replacement, also found the work unbearable and taught Jack Hillers the basics of wet-plate photography and quickly left the survey. Hillers proved to be the right man for the job, and he went on to produce nearly 1000 negatives. More than 600 of the Powell Survey negatives were offered commercially by James F. Jarvis on yellow cabinet mounts.

Less common and highly prized survey series include General D. S. Stanley's Yellowstone Expedition (1873; S. J. Morrow, photographer), General Custer's reconnaisance to the Black Hills (1874; Illingworth, photographer), General Crook's pursuit of the Sioux on the Little Big Horn (1876; S. J. Morrow, photographer) and the Interior Department's Geological Survey to the Black Hills led by W. P. Jenney and Henry Newton (1875; Dr. V. T. M. McGillycuddy, photographer; published by R. Benecke, St. Louis).

Numerous expeditions were stereo-photographed throughout the world. The most sought after is the Commodore T. O. Selfridge Expedition and Survey of the Isthmus of Darien in Panama. The Darien Expedition was photographed by Timothy H. O'Sullivan in 1870 and John Moran in 1871. Confusion exists as to who took what views. The series was published in part by E. and H. T. Anthony and in part by John Moran. T. C. Roche published a rare series of about eighty views of the Kane Expedition to the Arctic region in 1860, with views copyrighted by Dr. I. I. Hayes. These are believed to be the first stereo views of icebergs and were used by the noted American oil painter Frederick Church in the creation of his "Iceberg" series. Other polar explorations include the Peary Expedition to the North Pole (Underwood and Underwood, 1909), the Nansen Expedition (Underwood and Underwood,

published in 1897), the Roald Amundsen Arctic and *Belgica* Expeditions (Keystone, 1912) and the Robert F. Scott-Schackelton Expedition to Antarctica, 1908 (Underwood and Underwood). Kilburn, #9622, shows A. W. Greely as a modeled figure with his equipment. Although it looks very realistic, it is not Greely.

Belgica Antarctic Expedition (1897–1899)	
Keystone, #13326, Men hauling snow for water supply, typical	6–10.00
Crook Expedition (1876) S. J. Morrow (thirty-two views), wounded troops	75–90.00
Custer Expedition to the Black Hills (1874)	
W. H. Illingworth	
Close view of expedition, wagons, men on horseback, etc.	200–300.00
#846, "Permanent Camp in Agnes Park," typical distant view of expedition	75–90.00
Landscape studies of Black Hills	20–30.00
Darien Expedition (1870–1871)	
E. and H. T. Anthony, yellow mounts	20–30.00
Jarvis, "Tropical Series."	15–25.00
Moran (no identification), manuscript *Darien* on reverse of cream mounts, 1870s issue	30–40.00
Photographer (Moran) with camera	200–300.00
Fisk Expedition (1866)	
Illingworth with manuscript titles	35–50.00
John Carbutt, #234–260, yellow mounts	30–40.00
B. H. Gurnsey	20–30.00
Hayden Survey (1870–1878)	
Anthony, credit to Jackson #186 (#708 is scratched in the negative), View north in the Elk Mountains, typical example	15–20.00
J. F. Jarvis (credit to Jackson) Scenic	15–20.00
Close view of expedition members	30–50.00
"Photographing in High Places." Jackson at work	125–200.00
Jenney Black Hills Expedition (1875)	
R. Benecke, Fifty-six views #9, "Indian Chieves [*sic*] & Interpreters."	75–100.00
#20, "Miner's camp on Castle Creek."	50–75.00
#24, "Surveying party at breakfast on Harneys Peak."	50–75.00
#44, "Dr. V. T. McGilliscuddy [*sic*]."	65–85.00

William Henry Jackson, #186, "View North in the Elk Mountains," Hayden Survey. $20.

#47, "Devils Rock," typical
scenic _____ 20–30.00
Colonel F. W. Lander Expedition
(1859)
  Bierstadt Bros. _____ 40–60.00
  S. F. Adams _____ 20–30.00
Peary and other Arctic Expeditions
(1897–1909)
  Underwood & Underwood _____ 6–12.00
Powell Survey (1871–1875)
  E. O. Beaman, #61, "Echo Park,"
  Green River, typical example _____ 10–15.00
  James Fennemore, "Water Pocket
  in a Glen," typical example _____ 12–20.00
  Jack K. Hillers
    #24, "Ashley Falls, letting
    down with lines," three men
    letting themselves down on
    rope, example of Survey party
    at work _____ 25–35.00
    #39, Powell seated with Indi-
    ans of the Colorado Valley "In
    Council." _____ 50–60.00
    "Driftwood—Cataract Canon,"
    typical scene _____ 12–20.00
    Group of Indian women,
    typical _____ 40–60.00
Stanley Yellowstone Expedition
(1873)
  S. J. Morrow _____ 50–75.00
Wheeler Survey (1871–1875)
  William Bell (1872), most
  scenes _____ 20–30.00
  Timothy H. O'Sullivan, most
  scenes (1871–1875) _____ 20–30.00
    "The Start from Camp, Ari-
    zona, Sept. 1871." _____ 50–60.00
    "Canyon de Chelly," 1873 _____ 25–30.00
    Most scenes with people, Indi-
    ans, etc. _____ 30–50.00
    Most scenic landscape studies ___ 15–25.00

Expositions and Fairs

The London International Exhibition (Crystal Palace), started in 1851, was the first great exposition and the stereo photographers were on hand. For most people, this was their first introduction to stereo photography, which was exhibited by Sir David Brewster and his new binocular stereoscope. The views of the Crystal Palace were a sensation. The Crystal Palace building was disassembled and reconstructed in a large park at Sydenham. Most stereo views encountered by collectors are of the Sydenham Crystal Palace (1853–1860s). Negretti and Zambra published a large number of views in the 1850s on a dark buff mount. The prints are often rounded at the corners. William England made an extensive series at Sydenham; these are found on canary yellow mounts and are sometimes beautifully hand tinted.

The Crystal Palace set the standards for all future expositions. Not to be outdone, Paris had an international exhibition in 1855 and London returned with an even larger event in 1862. Again, William England made a large series on yellow mounts. Other European fairs and expositions were Dublin (1865), Paris (1867), Vienna (1873), Paris (1878), London (1886), Paris (1889) and again in Paris (1900). All were stereo-photographed.

The celebration of our nation's first century was marked by the Centennial International Exhibition in Philadelphia (1876). Edward L. Wilson, William Notman and others received an exclusive contract to make and sell stereo views of the exhibition. The Centennial Photographic Company was formed and had a building on the grounds. More than 4000 different views were made of nearly every exhibit and event. James Cremer, George Barker and L. E. Walker made Centennial Exhibition views but these were taken outside the main grounds. Barker made some nice views of the encampment of the United States Military Academy cadets at Fairmount Park on the edge of the grounds. Kilburn offered views pirated from Centennial Photographic Company prints.

Many pirated copies were made and sold. Most are on poor-quality red or yellow mounts simply marked "Centennial" or the like. A few Philadelphia photographers including Gutekunst and Cremer were able to get into the grounds before the exclusive contract was signed. These rare views show the buildings under construction and exhibits still in shipping crates. A series of the Philadelphia Zoological Gardens at Fairmount Park are found on Centennial mounts, but it was not part of the official exhibition.

The next great exposition was at New Orleans in 1884 to 1885. After the success of the Centennial, Edward L. Wilson obtained exclusive rights and made a fine series. The cream cabinet mounts look almost identical to the Centennial mounts except for the markings.

Late in the 1880s, officials in Chicago began plans for a World Columbian Exposition to celebrate the 400th anniversary of the discovery of America. Set for 1892 on Chicago's lake shore, the fair was planned as the ultimate event up to that time. Leading architects designed the buildings and parklike grounds. The Great Ferris Wheel was brought from Paris and nearly every nation in the world was represented by displays. The depression of 1891–1892 caused the fair to be opened a year late (in 1893), but it lived up to all of the pre-event publicity hype, becoming the most visited fair of its time. Seeing the success of Wilson in 1876 and 1884, B. W. Kilburn was able to obtain an exclusive for the sale of stereo views of the World Columbian Exposition. More than 27.5 million people visited the fair and it seems probable that many bought Kilburn's views. The views are found on a gray mount with official logo (Columbus's head in a circle) on the reverse. These were the views sold on the grounds. The general issue sold door-to-door or through distributors was on the standard Kilburn buff mount. They sold for $2 per dozen. In anticipation of hard use of the negatives back at the factory in Littleton, New Hampshire, Kilburn made up to twenty-four of some negatives. As a result, collectors will find several variants of more than 95 percent of the views. Some are not obvious, but views of people are easily identified as variants. An examination of the original ledger of the Kilburn Company at the California Museum of Photography in Riverside, shows the number of negatives made of each number. In my listing, I have indicated these with a number in parentheses after the title. I do not have room to list every title but I will list a cross section to give readers some idea of the diversity.

B. W. Kilburn, #14619, "A Marvel of Human Genius, the Great Electric Tower by night, Pan American Exposition." 1901. $6.

Kohl & Tyler, Cincinnati Industrial Exposition, 1870, "Gold Medal Furniture," typical local exposition. $20.

The Columbian Exposition was followed in 1894 by the California Midwinter International Exposition in San Francisco, also exclusively offered by Kilburn. Kilburn made the exclusive series of the Cotton States International Exhibition in Atlanta (1895). This series has some outstanding views of African-Americans (blacks).

Buffalo hosted the Pan American Exposition in 1901. Kilburn again received exclusive rights, but made a modest series compared to his earlier efforts. Most of the negatives are believed to be by James M. Davis, who had become chief distributor of Kilburn views. The Pan American would probably have been overshadowed by the next great fair in St. Louis, except for the tragic assassination of President William McKinley. The president visited the fair in Buffalo and made speeches to large crowds. This was photographed by the Kilburn photographer. Large crowds are seen waiting in line to see McKinley outside the Temple of Music, the site of the attack. There is a detailed group of views leading up to the assassination.

There are no views or photographs of any kind of McKinley's assassination. The only other related views are of the operating room, the ambulance and the place of the event. There are views of the mourners in Buffalo and the return of the body to Washington. Either the photographers were unlucky or they deliberately did not photograph the immediate aftermath of the attack, which must have been chaotic. Possibly the photographers felt a sense of responsibility to shield the public from the horrible sights. If so, it is a dramatic contrast to photojournalism of the present time.

The Louisiana Purchase Exposition in St. Louis in 1904 was up to the standards set in Chicago. Several photographers attempted to gain exclusive rights. William H. Rau was named official photographer but failed to gain an exclusive for making stereo views. The fair officials granted rights to make stereo views to nine companies—C. H. Graves (Universal Photo Art), Griffith & Griffith, Kilburn (James M. Davis), Keystone View Company, William H. Rau (Universal View Company), Underwood and Underwood, H. C. White, C. L. Wasson (International View Company) and Whiting View Company. Each paid a fee of $300 to ply their trade. The coverage of the St. Louis Fair is remarkable, including outstanding views of the Observation (Ferris) Wheel and the many industrial exhibits.

The Panama-California International Exposition (San Diego) and Panama-Pacific International Exposition (San Francisco) were both in 1915 and were stereo-photographed by Keystone View Company. Keystone made a few views of the Philadelphia exhibition in 1926 and more than one hundred views of the Century of Progress Exposition in Chicago (1933). The Century of Progress was offered in the smaller format Keystone "Junior" size unmounted prints with a folding viewer in either red or black metal. Views on the standard mounts are uncommon.

Many lesser fairs were stereo-photographed. Those of particular interest are the Philadelphia Sanitary Fair, 1864; the Mechanics' Institute Fair, 1869; the Cincinnati Industrial Exposition, 1870; the Interstate Industrial Exposition, Chicago, 1873; the International Cotton Exposition, Atlanta, 1881; and the Baltimore & Ohio Railroad Centenary, 1926.

There are many local fairs and exhibitions such as the World Peace Jubilee, Boston, 1872; the Lewis and Clark Centennial, Portland, Oregon, 1905; the Jamestown Exposition, 1907; and the West Michigan State Fair, 1908, all photographed in stereo.

1851, London International Exhibition
    Marked examples are very rare ____ 50–100.00
1853, London International Exhibition, Sydenham
    Negretti & Zambra _____ 30–50.00
    William England, yellow mounts ____ 15–25.00
1855, Paris, marked examples are rare, suspect views are probably 1867 _____ 40–80.00
1862, London International Exhibition
    William England (London Stereoscopic Co.) on yellow mounts, tinted and untinted
        Interior exhibits _____ 15–20.00
        Machinery, industrial views _____ 20–25.00
        Statuary, sculpture _____ 3–5.00
        The exterior showing building ____ 10–15.00
        Tinted _____ add 50 percent
        Views of plants, ferns, horticultural _____ 4–6.00
1864, Sanitary Fairs
    New York, Anthony, #1689–2864, Views of fountains or statuary (major exhibits are double value) ____ 12–18.00
    New York, J. Gurney, "Interior of Building," typical example _____ 15–20.00
    Philadelphia, James Cremer, "Atrophy Exhibit," typical _____ 12–20.00
1865, Dublin International Exhibition
    London Stereoscopic Co.
        Views of exhibits, machinery, etc. _____ 15–25.00
        Views of sculpture and statuary ____ 3–5.00
1867, Paris International Exhibition
    Leon & Levy (official photographers), some with *L. L.* identification _____ 6–10.00
1869, Mechanics' Institute Fair, San Francisco
    Thomas Houseworth & Co. (#2001–2100), #2021, J. Mallon, Glass cutter, 14 Beal Street, typical example _____ 30–50.00
1870, Cincinnati Industrial Exposition
    Kohl & Tyler, #137, "Gold Medal Furniture," typical example _____ 10–20.00
1872, World Peace Jubilee, Boston
    Charles Pollock, Interior of Coliseum _____ 6–10.00
    William G. Preston, Tinted interior _____ 2–6.00
1873, Interstate Industrial Exposition, Chicago
    Copelin & Son "Grand Inter-State Exposition," cabinet mounts _____ 6–10.00
    Lovejoy & Foster
        "Lovejoy & Foster's Booth," showing stereoscopes _____ 75–100.00
        Exposition building exterior, 1874 _____ 5–8.00
    Woodward Stereoscopic Co., Interior _____ 5–8.00
1873, Vienna International Exhibition
    Leon & Levy, Sophus Williams and Vienna Photographic Association, More than 450 views _____ 6–12.00
1875, Bunker Hill Centennial
    T. Lewis, #2, Bunker Hill _____ 2–4.00
1876, Centennial International Exhibition
    Centennial Photographic Co. (official)
        Grounds and building exteriors ____ 4–10.00
        Corliss engine _____ 12.00
        Monorail _____ 65.00
        Statue of Liberty arm and torch _____ 85.00
        #412, Hawaiian Island exhibit, typical _____ 10–12.00
    George Barker, Outside grounds ____ 4–10.00
    L. E. Walker, Cabinet mounts similar to Centennial Photographic Co.'s _____ 6–10.00
1878, Chicago Exposition
    Gates, Exposition building, typical ____ 4–6.00

B. W. Kilburn, #8483, "The Pride of Midway Plaisance, World's Fair, Chicago," 1893, published 1894. $15.

B. W. Kilburn, #8561, "Esquimau Homes, World's Columbian Exposition," copyright 1894. $10.

1878, Paris International Exhibition _____ 6–10.00
1878–1900, Copy views of exposi-
tions, usually on poor-quality
mounts without identification to
photographer _____ 1.00
1881, International Cotton Exposition, Atlanta
  J. G. Evans _____ 10–15.00
  Stoddard & Co. _____ 10–15.00
1884, New Orleans Cotton Exhibition
  Centennial Photographic Co.
  (official) _____ 10–15.00
1886, London Exhibition _____ 6–10.00
1889, Paris International Exhibition
  Views of Eiffel Tower _____ 15–25.00
  Views of exhibits and buildings _____ 7–10.00
1893, World's Columbian Exposi-
tion, Chicago
  B. W. Kilburn (official), add 25
  percent for official gray mounts,
  deduct 50 percent for faded prints
    Ferris Wheel, #9151, "Looking,
    moving Heavenward" (12), typi-
    cal example _____ 10–15.00
    Various buildings and exhibits _____ 4–7.00
      #7554—7565, Prefair opening
      #7833–7955, Openings of
      buildings, fair

#7956–9178, Interiors and
exteriors
#7554, World's Fair from the
Tower, early construction
scene (7)
#7929, "Surging Sea of Hu-
manity at the Opening" (40),
most common view
#7954, "Electric Button
pressed by President Cleveland
to unfurl flags and start machinery, opening" (4)
#8228, "This train made the
quickest time on record," Locomotive 999 (11)
#8232, "Burning of the Cold
Storage Building" (5, two different positions of camera)
#8851, "Santa Claus has
come again" (8)
#8866, "Largest Telescope in
the World, Liberal Arts Building" (6), typical
George Barker, "The *Santa Maria*
Flag Ship of Columbus," identified
as the Columbian Exposition but
probably taken at Hampton Roads,
Va. _____ 3–5.00

Keystone View Co., #11708, "La Porte Monumentale—Chief Entrance to the Exposition, Paris, 1900." $12.

H. H. Bennett, yellow mounts
Views taken from outside
grounds _____ 10–15.00
#1350 and 1351, The Ferris
Wheel _____ each 40.00
L. M. Melander & Bro., Views of
the grounds after it closed, 1894. ____ 6–10.00
Underwood & Underwood _____ 6–10.00
Ingersoll, Keystone, Webster & Al-
bee, etc. _____ 3–5.00
1894, California Mid-Winter Exposition, San Francisco
B. W. Kilburn
Urns and statuary, often found
tinted _____ 8–12.00
#9513, The camels awaiting ri-
ders, typical better subject _____ 15–25.00
1895, Cotton States International Exposition, Atlanta, Georgia
B. W. Kilburn
Blooded stock cattle exhibit,
most common _____ 3–5.00
Blacks (African Exhibits) _____ 12–15.00
Interiors and exteriors _____ 6–12.00
1900, Paris International Exposition
Keystone
#11708, "La Porte Monumen-
tale—Chief Entrance," photographer at work on ladder _____ 10–12.00
#11713, "Old Paris"—reproduc-
tion of city of Charles VII,
typical _____ 4–6.00
Kilburn
#13960, View of Great En-
trance, typical _____ 2–4.00
Underwood & Underwood, Build-
ings and exhibits _____ 2–4.00
H. C. White, #10250–10340
#10282, Small Palace of Fine
Arts, typical example _____ 3–5.00
1901, Pan American Exposition, Buffalo
(*See also* Personalities, McKinley,
William in Chapter 5)
Kilburn, #14450–14681 and 14848
Most views _____ 4–6.00
#14450, The romantic and pic-
turesque (4), typical example
President McKinley _____ 7–9.00
#14539, The last words of
President McKinley's address
(4), typical
1904, Louisiana Purchase Exposition,
St. Louis
Keystone, #15002, Napoleon Bo-
naparte statue and Festival Hall,
typical _____ 5–7.00
Kilburn, #16206, Festival Hall and
fountains at night, typical _____ 5–7.00
Universal Photo Art, Underwood &
Underwood, most views _____ 4–8.00
Whiting, #620, Missouri Fruit
Exhibit, typical example, often
tinted _____ 8–12.00
Color litho, Ingersoll and others _____ 1.00
1905, Lewis & Clark Centennial,

Portland, Oregon
Watson Fine Art, #34, Buildings ____ 8–12.00
1907, Jamestown Exposition, Virginia
Keystone, #14219, Lifesaving
demonstration _____ 4–6.00
1908, West Michigan State Fair
Keystone, #21507, Typical _____ 6–10.00
1915, Panama-California Interna-
tional Exposition, San Diego
Keystone, Views of buildings _____ 6–10.00
1915, Panama-Pacific International
Exposition, San Francisco
Keystone, #17772, Race cars for
Baby Vanderbilt Cup race _____ 6–10.00
1926, Sesquicentennial Exposition,
Philadelphia
Keystone, View of Liberty Bell,
scarce _____ 10–15.00
1926, Baltimore & Ohio Railroad
Centenary
(*See* Railroads in Chapter 5)
1933, Century of Progress Exposi-
tion, Chicago
Keystone, #32993, Lief Ericksen
Drive, typical example _____ 12–20.00
Keystone "Junior" (smaller
format) _____ 6–10.00
(*See also* Tru-Vue Filmstrip Price
Guide in Chapter 7)

Famous People
(See *Personalities* in Chapter 5)

Far East
(See *China; India, Burma and Ceylon; Japan;*
and *Philippine Islands* in Chapter 5)

Farming

Nearly all aspects of agriculture are portrayed
in stereo views. Views of planting, harvesting
and processing various products were popular
subjects. Many local photographers in the 1870s
and 1880s made views showing early horse-
drawn machinery, wagons in fields, barns and
farm homesteads. F. Jay Haynes made an outstanding series of farming in the Red River
Valley north of Fargo, Dakota Territory, in the
late 1870s.

Hundreds of views were made by the major
publishers after 1890. Many were made in huge
quantities and are relatively easy to find. Also
look for good views of agricultural displays at
the various expositions.

Pre-1890 views
F. Jay Haynes, Ready to start toward
the horizon with harrows (horse-
drawn) of the Grandin farm, Red River
Valley, typical scene with teams lined
to horizon _____ 30–40.00
D. Filson, Steubenville, Ohio, men

C. H. Graves (Universal Photo Art Co.), #5302, "Modern Steam Thresher, with self-feeder, stacker, and bagging attachment," 1905. $15. (John Weiler Collection)

D. Filson, Steubenville, Ohio, "Harvesting Cabbage," ca. 1882. $15.

harvesting cabbage, shows wagons, etc., typical 1880s example _____ 12–18.00

Kilburn, Hops growing, 1870s–1880s _____ 6–10.00

Post-1890 views

Apple orchard, Keystone, #16754, Men spraying trees, Hilton, N.Y. _____ 1–2.00

Combining wheat, Keystone, #20215, Steam harvester in Calif. field _____ 3–5.00

Cotton, Keystone, #9508, Loaded wagons in Greenville, Tex., gin _____ 2–4.00

Cutting hay, Keystone, #10376, Men and women in hayfield, Bavaria _____ 1–3.00

Cutting wheat, Underwood & Underwood, Man with horse-drawn harvester in field, Manitoba _____ 4–6.00

Harrowing, Keystone, #16734, Man driving Case tractor with double disks and harrows, S. Dak. _____ 2–4.00

Harvesting
  Barley, Keystone, #13719, Man driving harvester near Ft. Collins, Colo. _____ 1–3.00
  Vegetables, Keystone, #6712, Gathering eggplant near Buffalo, N.Y. _____ 2–4.00
  Wheat
    Keystone, #11624, Horse-drawn harvester in Washington field _____ 2–4.00

Keystone, #16740, Steam thresher in N. Dak. _____ 3–5.00

Underwood & Underwood, #6226, thirty-three-horse team pulling combine, Walla Walla, Washington _____ 2–4.00

Hogs, Keystone, #16715, Agricultural Experimental Station, Ames, Iowa _____ 1–2.00

Melons, Keystone, #6708, Loading cantaloupes in wagon near Buffalo, N.Y. _____ 2–4.00

Milking cows (dairy), Keystone, #16749, Men milking in modern dairy _____ 2–4.00

Oranges, Underwood & Underwood, #5958, Picking, Riverside, Calif. _____ 3–5.00

Peaches, Keystone, #6952, Men gathering, Del. _____ 1–2.00

Plowing, Keystone, #16733, Man driving Case tractor in S. Dak. _____ 2–4.00

Pumpkins, Keystone, #16755, Men in field, Indiana _____ 1–3.00

Threshing, Keystone, #7170, Men at work in Greece _____ 1–3.00

Ferris Wheels

(See Expositions and Fairs in Chapter 5)

Thomas T. Sweeney, "Engine Co. No. 2," Cleveland, Ohio, ca. 1867. $150.

Stereo-Travel Co., #53, "New York Firemen in Action," 1914. $45.

Fire Fighting and Fire Equipment
(See also *Disasters in Chapter 5*)

Highly sought by collectors are views of early horse-drawn and steam-pumping equipment. A view of a steam pumper as the main subject with or without the fire crew is the hardest to find. There are views of equipage as an incidental part of other subjects, for example, as seen in the distance at a parade or in a fire view. The most common are views by New England photographers, but even these can command substantial prices if they're in fine condition and are close-ups of the subject.

Pre-1890 views
    Steam fire engine, at a fire in New
    Britain, Conn., fairly distant,
    1885 _____ 10–15.00
    Steam pumper, close portrait
    with crew, T. T. Sweeny, Cleve-
    land, Ohio, 1870 _____ 100–150.00
Post-1890
    Steam pumper at a Baltimore fire,
    Underwood & Underwood _____ 15–25.00

Fishing
(See *Hunting and Fishing in Chapter 5*)

Flowers and Fruit

Stereo views of flowers and plants were very popular in the nineteenth century. Nearly every photographer offered these, either as tabletop arrangements, memorial decorations or in the field. Some are beautifully hand tinted. These once-popular views are not very popular with today's collectors. Most flower collectors are looking for excellent examples, usually with fine detailed tinting and good stereo effect (depth). The most sought after are early cactus views; some of the best were made by noted western photographers such as C. E. Watkins. Cactus views made after 1890 are in less demand.

Pre-1890 views
    Allen, Boston, Basket of lilies,
    1870s _____ 1–3.00
    Amateur, still life of cut watermelon,
    peaches, etc., finely tinted, 1870 _____ 5–7.00
    Anthony, #5745, Study in skeleton
    leaves _____ 1–3.00
    Anthony, #7158, "The wreath,"
    skeleton leaves, 1860s _____ 1–3.00
    F. Arnold, Greenwich, N.Y., "Flow-
    ers used in Nellie Brown's Casket,

1878." _____ 1–2.00
D. Barnum, Floral wreath, tinted _____ 2–4.00
William England, "A thing of
beauty is a joy forever," floral
arrangement _____ 1–3.00
Kilburn, #4547, Night-blooming
cereus _____ 1–3.00
Watkins, #1326, Cactus, Calif. ____ 20–25.00
F. G. Weller, #98, Tinted arrange-
ment _____ 1–3.00
Post-1890 views
Gates, Chicago, #2880, Floral
Globe, Park _____ 1–2.00
Keystone
    #8225, Witch-hazel in blossom,
    wildflower _____ 3–5.00
    #9405, Close view of Night-
    blooming cereus _____ 2–4.00
    #9601, Flowers in greenhouse ____ 1–3.00
    #10169, Cactus plants, girl posed
    to show size _____ 3–5.00
    #20566, Breadfruit tree, Hawaii ___ 2–4.00
H. C. White, #6401, "Lilies," 1904 ___ 1–3.00

Glass Stereo Views

In the early development of collodion wet-plate photography, it was discovered that glass made a superb base. It was transparent, nonporous and would take the chemical coating evenly. The fine clarity and detail in a quality glass stereo view is remarkable. It is easy to see why they were popular when introduced to the United States by the Langenheim Brothers of Philadelphia in 1854. Of course, the major drawback is that they are breakable. Also, they were more expensive than paper-print stereo views. In 1861, E. Anthony offered glass views of Niagara Falls at $15 per dozen and the same subjects in paper at $4 per dozen. The Civil War essentially ended the popularity of glass views in the United States. Bierstadt Brothers offered a few glass views of their Civil War scenes taken in 1861. Glass stereo views continued to be made in Europe. The largest maker was Ferrier and Soulier. They may have made more than 10,000 different subjects on glass up into the late 1870s.

The most sought after by collectors are the fine tinted examples by Langenheim. These were made from 1854 to 1860. They often carry an 1850 copyright, which is a patent for "heliographic" printing on glass secured by Langenheim soon after his return from Europe in 1850. The earliest views were made in early spring of 1854 and show the snow still on the ground at Niagara Falls. Most are scenes of the falls and snow-covered trees. Langenheim made glass views, usually beautifully tinted, of Philadelphia; the Mine Hill Gap area of Pennsyl-

vania; Washington, D.C.; Mount Vernon; New York City; Catawissa; Baltimore; the White Mountains; and "Beauties of the Hudson River." There also was a small series of prominent persons, including Washington Irving and General Winfield Scott.

Niagara Falls was the most popular subject in the United States. Probably the best of the local makers was Platt D. Babbitt who had a photographic stand at the edge of the falls. This stand, sometimes showing the camera, appears in a number of Niagara views. Franklin White and Bierstadt Brothers made a fine group of views on glass, mainly in the White Mountains. As mentioned, Bierstadt Brothers made a few rare Civil War views on glass. Anthony offered glass views of Niagara, "American Scenery," "Snow Effects" and New York City but these are rare. There are at least two different glass views of the interior of E. Anthony's "Stereoscopic Emporium" in New York City. Anthony also sold glass views by others and imported the Ferrier and Soulier series. The foreign views sold for an astounding $36 a dozen in 1861.

Western United States views on glass are extremely uncommon. Langenheim advertised views of Pittsburgh but none are known to exist. An important series is the one made by C. E. Watkins during his first trip to Yosemite in 1861. One hundred glass negatives were secured on the difficult trip and apparently all were made as glass transparencies. Examples examined are magnificent. Ferrier and Soulier offered a series of Yosemite in about 1870 by an unknown photographer. These usually have titles in the negatives in French.

Condition is very important in evaluating glass stereo views. Views that are cracked or faded are only valued at a fraction of a superbly hand-tinted example in near-new condition.

Platt D. Babbitt, Niagara Falls
    Close-up of old Tower, Niagara,
    typical _____ 15–25.00
    Tightrope-walker (Blondin) over
    falls _____ 35–45.00
Bierstadt Brothers, Franklin White
and others _____ 30–45.00
Ferrier & Soulier
    #10284, Yosemite, "Three Broth-
    ers," typical _____ 40–50.00
    Various European subjects _____ 10–20.00
Langenheim
    Niagara, dated 1854, manuscript
    titles and date _____ 150–300.00
    Niagara Falls, 1855–1860, tinted __ 75–150.00

Town of Reading, Pa., showing covered bridge, 1854, tinted, typical example _____ 500–700.00
Washington Irving at Irvington, N.Y. _____ 600–800.00
Winfield Scott, seated, tinted ____ 700–800.00

Ghosts (Double-Exposures, Trick Photography)

Sometime in the early days of photography, a surprised daguerreotypist must have discovered, probably by accident, he could make a double-exposure on his plate. Thus was created "ghost" photography. In the late 1850s, the classic English photographers began offering these most unusual stereo views. They must have appeared as magic images to the viewers who saw them for the first time. The most common version is the "Guardian Angel" sold for many years in dozens of versions. It usually shows a sleeping child with an angel (as ghost image) standing by the bed or crib or hovering over the sleeping child.

Pre-1880 views
English Classic from Dicken's "Christmas Carol," Scrooge facing seated ghost, 1858 _____ 15–20.00
Post-1880 views
Keystone
#619, "Her Guardian Angel," most common _____ 1–3.00
#9463, "The Empty Crib," mother kneels by crib _____ 3–5.00

Haiti
(See Caribbean and Cuba in Chapter 5)

Hawaii

Pre-1893 views are very uncommon. Most views examined illustrate the geological landmarks (volcanoes and lava flows) and unusual plant life (bananas and breadfruit). The earlier photographers made some nice views of the missionary influence in the islands. Many of these views were made to be sold to missionary societies in major United States cities. Rare are views of local natives before 1893, when the Hawaiian Islands were annexed by the United States. The leading local photographers were H. L. Chase, M. Dickson, J. W. King and Montano. After 1898, the major publishers made a variety of views. Underwood and Underwood made a nice series in about 1908, which shows busy street scenes in Honolulu. In the 1920s, Keystone made a series that included many of the major buildings including the Kamehameha School. The Keystone pho-

tographer returned in the 1930s and made a scarce series of a tranquil island life soon to be changed by World War II. Other than a few Underwood and Underwood views, views of Oriental-Hawaiians are rare.

Pre-1893 views
H. L. Chase, Honolulu, House with family posed, 1870s, typical _____ 10–15.00
M. Dickson and J. W. King, 1870s __ 20–30.00
Montano, Honolulu "Photographs Illustrating the Hawaiian Islands," late 1870s–1880s
Volcanic geology _____ 6–12.00
Palms and plant life _____ 5–10.00
People and buildings _____ 10–20.00
Post-1893
Graves (Universal Photo Art) _____ 1–3.00
Keystone _____ 1–5.00
Underwood & Underwood
View in a row of bananas, plantation _____ 1–2.00
#10686, Busy Fort Street, Honolulu, streetcar _____ 10–12.00
#10694, Oriental woman and girl pose by palms, typical people view _____ 3–5.00
H. C. White, #3669, The paddy or rice fields, Waipahu, typical plant view _____ 1–3.00

Holy Lands
(See Near East in Chapter 5)

Hunting and Fishing

The collector of hunting and fishing views is most interested in the equipment such as rifles, early fishing tackle and so on. Kilburn made a large series in New England starting in the 1860s and added to it until about 1902. These were made before the days of major game laws, and we see hunters with piles of killed deer or long strings of trout. To make the views look more realistic, the photographers often posed mounted specimens of foxes, deer and bears being shot by hunters. Early examples were done in the studio with elaborate sets and later in the outdoors, often in snowy scenes. Shooting prairie chickens (Keystone, #11625) is one of the best of this genre. Such views must have taken great care to set up and make. The effect is dramatic. Also there are nice views of camps and cabins showing all types of gear, including snowshoes, skis and hunting garb.

Western hunting views are very uncommon. A few views were made in the Dakotas and Montana by Underwood and Underwood after 1895. Some views of this period may state they are in a western area but are probably made in the east or in a studio. A fine western

B. W. Kilburn, #14263, "The cele-brated field trial winner 'Prime Min-ister,' U.S. Field Trials." Notice the black trainer. $10.

series of hunting was made by F. Jay Haynes in the late 1870s. These show hunting parties in the Dakota Territory. Major rifle manufac-turers such as Remington and Winchester sponsored excursions to the territories, invit-ing wealthy patrons from Boston, New York and other cities. The patrons were taken by train, usually in deluxe Palace cars, to the rail depot in Fargo and they went by wagon into the frontier. Game was abundant and the hunters had little trouble shooting more than they could carry. Haynes documented this ac-tivity and these views are highly prized by col-lectors.

Big-game hunting was a popular subject after 1895, especially among wealthy hunters look-ing for more exotic game. There are excellent views of hunting in Africa, especially the slaughter of hippopotamuses and elephants.

Hunting
  Deer
    Keystone, #26396, Hunters and
    kill _____ 4.00
    Kilburn, #2198, "Discussing the
    shot," hunters with killed game,
    1876, typical _____ 2–4.00
    H. C. White, #6115, Hunter in
    camp, deer hangs from tree,
    typical _____ 4–5.00
  Moose, Keystone, #9451 and 9452,
  Hunters, big-game kill, typical _____ 4–6.00
  Staged scenes, Keystone, #11625,
  Shooting prairie chickens, typical ___ 1–3.00
  Western excursions, F. Jay Haynes __ 25–35.00
  Wildcat, Keystone, #12264, Man
  shoots sleeping wildcat _____ 5–7.00
Fishing
(*See also* Occupationals, Commercial
Fishing in Chapter 5)
  Bass, Ingersoll, #3159, String _____ 5–6.00
  Trout, Kilburn, #115, A day's catch,
  1870s. _____ 5.00

Various makers, Men with rods and
reels _____ 6–8.00

India, Burma and Ceylon

Negretti and Zambra probably published the earliest stereo views of the area in about 1858, called "Our India Empire," and imported them to the United States through D. Appleton in New York. They are rarely seen. More likely to be encountered are F. York's "Views in In-dia" and Anthony's "Views in India." These are both from the same negatives. The An-thony series is better known to United States collectors and was sold as late as 1868. York offered the series in London into the 1870s. A cheap series of pirated copies exist, simply marked *India* on yellow or cream mounts. Samuel Bourne was the major India local pho-tographer, publishing his series under the im-print of Bourne and Shepherd. These are gen-erally uncommon in the United States.

G. F. Gates of Watkins, New York issued a series that appears to be from original nega-tives. These may have been obtained from Bourne or were brought back to the United States by a missionary.

George Rose (*See* Down Under in Chapter 5) made a nice series of the Delhi Durbar. Other fine Delhi Durbar views were made by Underwood and Underwood's James Rical-ton.

Most of the major publishers offered views including an excellent series by H. C. White.

Burma and Ceylon (Sri Lanka) were also stereo-photographed. The tea industry in Cey-lon and elephants moving logs in Burma are the most common subjects. Least common are views of local natives, showing their homes

E. & H. T. Anthony, "Views in India" series, ca. 1870. Congregation of natives at a fair by the Dhul Lake, Sreenuggur. $12.

or lifestyles. There are a number of views showing British subjects and the influence of Western culture. Keystone offered an outstanding view of Gandhi (*see* Personalities in Chapter 5).

Pre-1890 views
   Anthony or York "Views in India." _____ 10–15.00
   Bourne _____ 15–25.00
   Gates _____ 8–12.00
   Negretti & Zambra, "Our India Empire." _____ 25–35.00
Post-1890
   George Rose, #455, Feeding the poor, Delhi Durbar, typical _____ 20–30.00
   Keystone, #12102, Ox cart on Colombo Street, Ceylon, typical _____ 1–3.00
   Underwood & Underwood and others _____ 1–3.00
   H. C. White, #14101, A Hindu boat on the Ganges River, typical _____ 2–4.00

Indians (Native Americans)

Collecting of American Indian views is very popular, although good, early examples in excellent condition are hard to find. In these views we catch a glimpse of native American cultures, changing dress and their eventual defeat by the white man's western expansion. Nearly every Indian culture was stereo-photographed, and the views show the dramatic changes. Not all Indian stereo views are rare, many fine views were made in large quantities but demand has kept many of the best at the high end of the market. Some of the more common are the California "Diggers." Views of Utes and Paiutes were also made in large quantities. There are a number of fine studio portraits by Carter and C. R. Savage (Salt Lake City) plus one can find scenes of camp life.

Even more common are the Indians of upstate New York, which were photographed by George Barker and others at Niagara Falls in the 1870s. Some excellent views were made of the Chippewa, Winnebagos (especially by H. H. Bennett) and Sioux. Early Plains Indians are popular with collectors, especially Cheyenne, Crow and Blackfoot. Some of the best are S. J. Morrow's portraits of Sioux warriors.

Hillers (*see* Expeditions and Surveys in Chapter 5) mostly photographed Paiutes and Utes in the Colorado River area. E. O. Beaman made some fine views of Pueblos. Wittick in Arizona and Brown of Santa Fe made many Indian views in their areas.

The Modoc War in California (1873) was photographed by Eadweard Muybridge and a series was offered by C. E. Watkins. Only a few of these show the Indians up close, but the ones known are often spectacular.

The post-1890 period saw many fine Indian views made to satisfy public demand. There are several nice views taken at Wild West Shows as well as some of native crafts such as weaving and pottery making. A group of black-and-white lithograph views on white card were made in about 1900. These are head and shoulder portraits and often were printed back-to-back. Although interesting, they have very little collector value.

Charles Bierstadt, #1221, "Digger Indian huts, Ca.", two people posed with pots, typical _____ 45–50.00
J. C. Burge, Apaches bathing _____ 75–125.00
J. H. Choate, Carlisle, Pa., Indian school, dozens in native costumes in front of building _____ 20–30.00
Continent Stereo Co., Close view of Pueblo in New Mexico _____ 25–35.00

Powell Survey, portrait of young Indian woman. $65.

Brubaker & Whitesides, Marquette, Mich., #79, "Chippewa Chief's Grave," ca. 1870s. $10.

Fisk Expedition, Chief of the Gros Ventres in costume, 1866. _____ 60–70.00

Griffith, #11873, "Esquimau" at St. Louis Fair _____ 8.00

Haynes, F. Jay
   #865, Crow burial grounds _____ 17–25.00
   #1742, Sioux _____ 40–60.00

Hillers, #43, "No-Nu-Shi-Unt," the Dreamer, Colorado River Valley, in brush hut, 1874. _____ 65–75.00

Ingersoll, #496, Color litho of Gray Eagle, typical printed litho view _____ 1.00

William H. Jackson, #202, Otoe, with bow _____ 90–125.00

Keystone
   #13882, Women weaving baskets, P.E.I., Canada _____ 4.00
   #23095, Chief Black Hawk _____ 8.00
   #23118, Indian girl, common view _____ 2–4.00
   #V23181 Blackfeet _____ 8.00

Littleton View Co., #1326, Kickapoo Chief _____ 5–7.00

Montgomery Ward, squaws _____ 8.00

Alex Martin, Denver, Studio portrait of three Indians fully dressed in native costume _____ 35–45.00

S. J. Morrow, Yankton, Dakota Territory
   #123, Red River carts made without iron, tires of rawhide, five Indians in view _____ 35–40.00
   #175, Group of Teton Sioux in council _____ 45–60.00

Eadweard Muybridge, #1618, Modoc War, The stronghold after its capture, men on rocks, typical _____ 30–35.00

F. A. Nims (Colo.), Tesuque Pueblo, on horseback, winter _____ 25–30.00

H. T. Payne, Los Angeles, #145, Close-up of cornstalk hut _____ 10–15.00

Pierron/Florida Club, large group of prisoners at Fort Marion, Fla. _____ 25–35.00

John P. Soule, Indian camp at Franconia, N.H., tents and Indians, 1861. _____ 15–25.00

Will Soule, #1312, Paiute squaw _____ 50–60.00

Charles A. Zimmerman, #131, "Domestic Life among the Chippewa Indians." $45.

Underwood & Underwood
  "Little War Eagle," boy in head-
  dress, Wild West Show, 1889 _____ 10–15.00
  Hopi or Wolpi, usually in villages _____ 9.00
C. E. Watkins
  #2503, Modoc War, Headquarters
  on Tule Lake _____ 80–90.00
  #2507, Modoc War, Close view
  "Group of Warm Springs In-
  dians." _____ 200–250.00
H. C. White, #12279, Pueblo _____ 10–15.00
Whitney, Sioux Massacre, "Old Bets
[sic], A Sioux Squaw, 105 years old,"
1862 _____ 25–35.00
Wittick & Russell, Studio portrait of
Albuquerque Indian School faculty,
1880s _____ 70–75.00
C. W. Woodward, #1909, Four
squaws and child before loom weav-
ing blankets, typical _____ 10–15.00
Charles Zimmerman, Minn., #112,
Studio pose of chief of Gull Lake
Chippewa _____ 45–60.00

Interiors

Early stereo views were taken with available light without the aid of flash. Even with the limitations of the slow photographic plate, many fine interior views were made from the late 1850s to the 1930s. We see the changes in furniture and lifestyles plus we can take a look inside mercantile establishments, hotel dining rooms and familiar places like the White House and George Washington's home at Mt. Vernon, Virginia. The most sought after interior views are store interiors, especially those before 1890 that are identified. House interiors are fairly common and a nice collection could be assembled quickly with a little effort. Eastern hotel interiors are common; the most common are those at Saratoga Springs, the White Mountains and St. Augustine (after 1890). Hotel

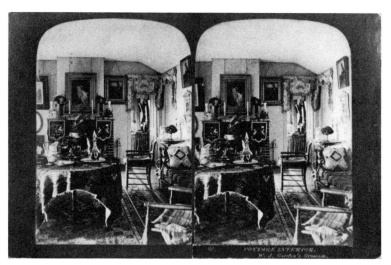

Horace D. Udall, Garrettsville, Ohio, #61, "Cottage Interior, W. J. Gordon's Grounds," Rocky River, Ohio, typical interior view, ca. 1880. $20.

interiors are relatively scarce from the Midwest and west. Staged interiors (in a studio) are popular if they show popular collectibles (stereoscopes, rocking horses, Belter-style carved furniture, and so forth).

Clothing Store, Barre, Vt., Mrs. A. C. Bradford's Millinery & Small Ware Store, Opening Day, 1878. ———————— 50–60.00
House, H. D. Udall, Cleveland, #61, "Cottage Interior, W. J. Gordon's Grounds," Rocky River, 1880s ———— 15–20.00
Hotel, Hotel Astor, N.Y., Underwood & Underwood, #10036, The Palatial dining hall, ca. 1905, typical ————— 5–7.00
Parlor scene, staged, Keystone, #11917, "Still there's no place like home," looking at stereo views ———— 15–20.00

Italy
(See Europe in Chapter 5)

Jamaica
(See Caribbean and Cuba in Chapter 5)

Japan
(See also Wars, Russo-Japanese War in Chapter 5)

The Japanese were a real curiosity to Americans in the late 1850s, when Japan established their embassy to the United States. Their arrival in New York set off a Japanese-mania and a demand for stereo views of members of the embassy in their colorful costumes plus their exotic land.

The same early photographers that covered China also went to Japan. Anthony offered a series of twenty-four views of the reception of the Japanese Embassy in New York (1860) plus sold views of Japan; the negatives prob-

ably were by Beato. Houseworth (*see* China in Chapter 5) offered a scarce series titled "Oriental Scenery" (#61–153) in about 1869.

H. H. Bennett published the fine series "A Summer in Japan," photographed by William H. Metcalf. These are on yellow mounts (1870s).

Views by Japanese photographers are rare. The most common (still very uncommon in the United States) is the series by Naito of Tokyo. It is believed that Naito was active from about 1890 to 1905. Some of the views may be from earlier negatives that he purchased from other photographers.

The post-1890 publishers made some of the best Japanese people views. Kilburn offered many nice studio portraits of young women in native geisha costumes, some beautifully tinted. Underwood and Underwood (James Ricalton), H. C. White, Graves (Universal Photo Art) and Keystone, among others, made some excellent views. Many of these are found tinted.

Anthony, Reception of the Japanese Embassy in New York, #14, Crowd in front of hotel, New York, 1860, a typical scene ——————————————— 15–25.00
H. H. Bennett (negatives by Metcalf), #361, English Hospital Grounds, Yokohama, typical scene, yellow mounts ——————————————— 10–20.00
Thomas Houseworth & Co., "Oriental Scenery—Japan," #100, The official quarters, Yedo, typical ————— 40–75.00
Keystone
    #14016, Taking a spin, woman being pulled in a ricksha by man, Nara, 1901, typical ——————— 3–5.00
    #14058, Japanese shoe shop, common ——————————————— 1–2.00
    #14739, Country girl in fields, very common ——————————————— 1–2.00

B. W. Kilburn, #13983, "The cooling Mountain Stream, Japan," 1901. $6.

Keystone View Co., #14016, "Taking a Spin through the Park at Nara in the Jinrikisha—The 'Pull-Man-Car' of Japan," 1901. $5.

Kilburn
> #13983, "The Cooling Mountain
> Stream," typical outdoor scene _____ 5–7.00
> Studio-posed portraits _____ 8–12.00

Naito, black mounts _____ 12–20.00

Underwood & Underwood
> #3965, People in Tokyo Park under
> cherry blossom, tinted _____ 8–12.00
> Regular views, not tinted, streets,
> people _____ 4–6.00

Universal Photo Art (#8401–8600)
> Agriculture, #8428, A field of rad-
> ishes, typical _____ 2–4.00
> Cloisonne manufacture,
> #8440–8449 _____ 5–10.00
> Geisha Girls, #8481, Pretty wait-
> resses, Fujiya Hotel, Miyanoshita,
> typical _____ 3–5.00
> Home Life, #8490, Very pretty
> geisha girl, at home, typical _____ 3–5.00
> Kyoto, #8494, Celebrated dwarf
> tree, 150 years old, four feet high,
> typical _____ 2–4.00
> Religion, #8495, Sacred deer of
> Nara Park, typical _____ 2–4.00
> Silk manufacture, #8532, Sorting
> silkworms, typical _____ 2–4.00

H. C. White, #3841, Ascending steep
slopes of Mt. Fujiyama, typical _____ 2–4.00

Logging and Lumbering

There is enough special interest in this category to separate it from the occupationals. The logging industry developed in the United States in the nineteenth century. The stereo photographers were on hand to make outstanding views of lumberjacks felling trees, hauling logs to the river or rails and moving the logs on to the mills. There are fine interior views showing saws, machinery and finishing. Also not to be overlooked are the views of lumberships being loaded in the northwest.

One of the best early series is James A. Jenney's "Gems in the Pineries of Michigan" (1870s). Mounts are yellow or green cabinet size, usually with paper labels on the reverse listing the titles. The sixteen-view series shows the operations of the L. B. Curtis and Company's camp in Midland County. Jenney also published a twelve-view set titled "Scenes taken at Gebhart & Estabrook's Camp, Midland Co. . . ." In this set, he reused some of the Curtis and Company negatives to fill out the set. The Goodridge Brothers of East Saginaw, Michigan, also made "Pineries" views but they are not as dramatic.

H. H. Bennett made a series titled "The Camera's Story of Raftman's Life on the Wisconsin" (#1400–1440). It is one of the best groups that show the use of log rafts to move the lumber to the mill. Two similar views were made by Copelin and Son of Chicago (#26 and 27), which were simply titled "Rafting" as part of their Kilbourn, Wisconsin, series. The Bennett views are on yellow cabinet mounts.

Other series were done by Upton (Minnesota) and S. S. Vose (Maine) in the 1870s and 1880s.

California logging was documented by a number of stereo photographers. The series by Hazeltine was published in part by John P. Soule, without credit to Hazeltine, in 1870 as part of his "California" series. These are on yellow mounts. The series by Underwood and Underwood shows redwood lumbering with outstanding scenes of blasting in the Converse Basin.

The best lumbering views in the Northwest were made by Darius Kinsey of Sedro-Woolley, Washington, in the late 1890s to about 1906. The later views are on gray mounts with Kinsey's Seattle address. Sold locally, the Kinsey views are not common outside Washington State. The major publishers including Keystone, Underwood and Underwood and H. C. White made many logging and lumbering views.

H. H. Bennett "The Camera's Story of Raftman's Life on the Wisconsin," yellow cabinet mounts ———————— 35–40.00
R. K. Bonine, #114, "Logging in Northern California." ———————— 12–18.00
Copelin & Son, Chicago, #26 and 27, "Rafting" (Wisconsin River), 1870s ——— 15–20.00
James A. Jenney, "Gems in the Pineries of Michigan," #16, "High Bank Rollway on Cass River," typical ——— 12–18.00
Darius Kinsey, Washington, #328, (#154 in negative), "Roadhouse on Skagit River," typical ———————— 20–30.00
John P. Soule (negatives by Hazeltine), "California," 1870
  #1146, Logging on Big River, Mendocino County ———————— 20–25.00
  #1148, Log Raft on Big River, Mendocino County ———————— 10–15.00
  #1159, Casper Mills, Mendocino County ———————— 20–25.00
Underwood & Underwood
  #5987, Blasting "Giant Tree," Converse ———————— 12–15.00
Log Raft on Columbia River, later published by Keystone, common view ———————— 2–5.00
Upton, Vose and other local makers, 1870s–1880s ———————— 8–15.00

Mexico

Pre-1870 views of Mexico are uncommon. A number of local makers made views of their areas. The most notable are Lagrange and Hermano in Monterey (1860s) and Juleo Michaud in Mexico City (1860s–1870s). The most commonly encountered early series is the group of views (more than 150 titles) published by Kilburn Brothers beginning in 1873. These are usually on yellow or cream mounts with the copyright date and the Kilburn monogram logo on the reverse. It is believed the views were photographed by Edward Kilburn. There are a number of fine views in the series including many of people.

A much scarcer series was published in 1875 by L. M. Melander. There are about one hundred views, usually on cream mounts.

W. H. Jackson made a fine group of views in the mid-1880s. These are usually found on

cream cabinet mounts. After 1890, a number of photographers traveled to Mexico. There are excellent views of Mexico City, Vera Cruz and ancient ruins. Some of the best are by Underwood and Underwood and Stereo-Travel. Keystone offered more than 200 different views of Mexico; many appeared in their book-box sets.

Pre-1890 views
  Local makers, 1860s–1880s ———————— 10–15.00
  Kilburn Brothers, 1873 ———————— 3–5.00
  L. M. Melander, 1875 ———————— 8–12.00
  W. H. Jackson (Denver) ———————— 10–15.00
Post-1890 views, numerous makers
(*See* Chapter 6) ———————— 2–4.00

Midwestern United States

Illinois
  Chicago
  (*See also* Disasters, and Expositions and Fairs in Chapter 5)
    Pre-1871 (pre-fire)
      John Carbutt, #140, Chamber of Commerce, typical view, yellow mount ———————— 15–20.00
      Other local makers ———————— 10–15.00
    1871–1890
      Copelin & Melander, #45, Washington Street from Wells Street, typical, usually yellow mount ———————— 8–12.00
      Gates
        Looking down on parade for Grant's funeral ———————— 8–12.00
        Views of parks ———————— 2–3.00
      Lovejoy & Foster, La Salle Street, carriages in street, typical scene ———————— 6–8.00
      P. B. Greene
        Window of Schweitzer & Beers, importers of toys and fancy goods, better ———————— 15–20.00
        Views of streets ———————— 10–15.00
    1890–1930s
      E. M. Brown (New York Stereo Co.), #748–B, Fern House, Lincoln Park ———————— 1–3.00
      Keystone, #2337, State Street, typical ———————— 1–3.00
      Kilburn, #7606, View from Auditorium Tower, typical ——— 2–4.00
      Universal Photo Art, #4365, Great Union Stock Yards, typical ———————— 1–3.00
      H. C. White, #201, State Street north from Madison, Masonic Temple in distance, typical ——— 3–4.00
  Non-Chicago
    Pre-1890 ———————— 10–15.00
    Post-1890 ———————— 5–10.00
Indiana
  Indianapolis

W. H. Salter, Views of city,
1870s _____ 10–12.00
H. Miller, late 1870s, views of
city _____ 8–12.00
Keystone, ca. 1915, Soldier's
Monument _____ 1–3.00
Pre-1890, Non-Indianapolis
Town views _____ 15–20.00
Scenery, rocks, trees, Wabash
River, and so on _____ 3–5.00
Iowa
(*See also* Disasters and Farming in
Chapter 5)
Des Moines
Charles Bierstadt, Views of State
Capitol Building, 1870s _____ 5–8.00
Pre-1890
Town views _____ 10–15.00
Scenery, Burt's Cave, etc. _____ 5–8.00
Michigan
(*See* Occupationals, Auto Industry in
Chapter 5)
Detroit
Jess Bardwell, 1860s–1870s _____ 15–20.00
Others, Pre-1895 _____ 6–10.00
East Saginaw
Goodridge Bros., 1860s–1870s _____ 8–12.00
Grand Rapids
S. C. Baldwin, 1870s _____ 8–12.00
Kalamazoo
W. S. White, 1870s _____ 8–10.00
Marquette
Brubaker, B. F. Childs, etc.
Lake Superior scenery _____ 5–8.00
Town views _____ 10–15.00
Other, pre-1895, Ann Arbor, etc. _____ 10–15.00
Other, pre-1895, Scenics, Lake
coastline, etc. _____ 4–8.00
Post-1895, Underwood & Under-
wood and others _____ 2–4.00
Minnesota
Falls of St. Anthony, Minne-ha-ha
Anthony, #325, Minne-ha-ha,
down glen, typical _____ 3–5.00
Whitney, Falls of St. Anthony _____ 3–5.00
Post-1890, Keystone and others _____ 1–2.00

Minneapolis
M. Nowak, ca. 1870s–1880s, city
views _____ 10–12.00
Post-1890 views, Keystone and
others _____ 2–4.00
Mississippi River, Fort Snelling
Whitney, Whitney & Zimmerman,
1860s _____ 5–8.00
Others _____ 4–6.00
Various pirated copies, 1870s _____ 1.00
Rochester
Park Bros., 1870s _____ 4–6.00
St. Paul
Illingworth, 1860s–early 1870s _____ 15–20.00
Nowak, others, 1870s–1880s,
cabinet mounts _____ 8–12.00
Missouri
St. Louis
(*See also* Bridges, and Expositions
and Fairs in Chapter 5)
Shaws Botanical Gardens
Boehl & Koenig, usually tinted,
1870s _____ 2–5.00
Keystone, #9529–9534
#9534, Conservatory and
Flower beds, typical _____ 1–3.00
Universal Photo Art, #5451
and 5452 _____ 1–3.00
Most others, cheap copies _____ 1.00
Views of the city
R. Benecke, 1870s _____ 12–15.00
Boehl & Koenig, Other than
Shaws Garden _____ 8–12.00
Post-1890, Keystone, others _____ 2–4.00
Pre-1890, Town views _____ 20–25.00
Post-1890, Town views _____ 8–10.00
Scenic studies _____ 4–6.00
Ohio
Akron
(*See* Occupationals, Rubber Industry)
George J. Snook, "Stereoscopic
Gems," more than one hundred
views, red cabinet mounts _____ 3–12.00
Cincinnati
(*See* Bridges, and Expositions and
Fairs in Chapter 5)

Gates (of Chicago), #42, "The Fountain, Cin[cinnati], O.," ca. 1880s.
Condition varies on Gates's "Picturesque America" series, usually on yellow or orange mounts, which vary and
are often brittle. Images also tend to
be faded. As shown, $5.

Kohl & Tyler, "In and Around
Our City." _____ 10–15.00
C. H. Muhrman, "Walnut St.
looking S. from Fourth," typical,
cabinet mounts _____ 8–12.00
Charles Waldack, "View of In-
clined Plane." _____ 10–20.00
J. W. Winder "Court House,"
typical _____ 10–15.00
E. & H. T. Anthony, #7576,
"Custom House and Post Office,"
ca. 1873, typical, red mounts _____ 8–12.00
Others _____ 4–8.00
Cleveland, pre-1890
Liebich, Residence on Euclid
Avenue _____ 5–7.00
Liebich, Ryder, others, Ship-
yards _____ 50–60.00
James F. Ryder, 2nd Presbyterian
Church, typical, red or yellow
cabinet mounts _____ 4–8.00
Thos. T. Sweeny, #102, Cuyah-
oga County Jail, 1860s, typical _____ 10–15.00
Columbus

Kelton, Kelton & Gates, William
Oldroyd, others
Ohio Penitentiary _____ 10–15.00
Hospital for insane, other state
buildings _____ 8–12.00
Ohio State House _____ 6–10.00
Busy streets, pre-1920 _____ 12–20.00
Conneaut
Keystone, Shipping, loading ore _____ 2–3.00
Dayton
National Soldiers Home
Bunker, Oldroyd and others,
1866–1872 _____ 8–12.00
Mote Bros. of Richmond, Ind.,
More than one hundred views,
1872–1880 _____ 4–8.00
Kilburn, Gates and others,
1880–1892 _____ 3–5.00
Post-1890, Keystone and
others _____ 1–2.00
Street views, buildings _____ 10–12.00
Oberlin
H. M. Potter, Smith & Co., others,
Views of college and town, 1870s,

H. A. Potter, Warren, Ohio, A bridge being rebuilt. $20.

Copelin & Son (Chicago), #11, "South End of Steamboat Rock," from a series "Views at Kilbourn Dalles, Wisconsin." A better scenic study from the late 1870s, typically $4–6 each.

1880s	10–12.00
Put-in-Bay	
Benedict, 1860s–early 1870s	10–12.00
A. C. Platt, 1870s–1880s	8–15.00
Toledo	
North & Oswald, others, 1870s, 1880s	8–15.00
Pre-1890, Scenery, Nelson Ledges, etc.	4–6.00
Pre-1890, Town views	10–20.00
Post-1890, Views	1–3.00

Wisconsin

Dalles of Wisconsin River, Kilbourn City

H. H. Bennett, yellow mounts	4–8.00

Madison

E. R. Curtiss and others

State Capitol Building	6–8.00
City views, buildings	8–12.00

Milwaukee

H. H. Bennett, 1870s	15–25.00
W. H. Sherman and others, 1870s–1880s	10–20.00
Cheap copies simply marked "Milwaukee"	1.00
Other Pre-1890, Scenic views	6–8.00
Other Pre-1890, Town views	15–20.00
Post-1890, Views	2–4.00

Mining

(See also Alaska, Gold Rush in Chapter 5)

All types of mining operations have been documented by stereo photographers. There are views of precious metal mining (gold and silver), open pit mines (copper) and below ground mining (coal). The early mining in the American west is the most popular. Less popular, but still highly collectible, is coal mining, primarily in Pennsylvania.

Anthony sold a series by F. B. Gage in the 1860s of the gold fields in Vermont. This group of views pales when compared to the gold mining views sold by Houseworth and Watkins of California and Nevada. In addition to the mine operation, there are excellent views of the town during the various booms.

Like the far western views, the Colorado mining booms of the late 1860s and the mid- to late 1870s are documented by more than a dozen series. The views by Jackson, Chamberlain and Weitfle are dramatic records of the brief period in Colorado's history.

Coal mining in Pennsylvania is covered in detail by Kleckner with views of mine entrances and breakers. Below-ground coal mining views were made by Keystone, Underwood and Underwood, H. C. White and others.

They show shovel and pick mining through to the use of heavy machinery in the 1920s.

N. A. Forsyth made an excellent series of the Butte, Montana, underground mining operations. These are some of the best underground stereos ever made by a commercial photographer.

Arizona

Underwood & Underwood, #6144, Inclines to copper mines, typical

Underwood & Underwood, #6144, Inclines to copper mines, typical	5–8.00

California

Birchville, Nevada County, Houseworth, #1402, hydraulic mining, the Kennebec claim	35–45.00
Columbia Gulch, Tuolumne County, Houseworth, #1015, Placer mining, "The Whim," close view of mining apparatus, buildings, etc.	300–350.00
Dutch Flat, Halsey & Coffin, "Hydraulic Mining."	20–30.00
Gold Hill, Houseworth, #743, Overview of city	70–100.00
Gold Run, Watkins, #61, Hydraulic mining, huge hoses	25–30.00

Hydraulic Gold Mining, no location

Houseworth, #797, The sluice	50–70.00
A. J. Russell, Miners at work	35–45.00

Placer Mining, no location

Charles Bierstadt, #1219, by Chinamen	125–175.00
Sutro, Sutterly Bros., Sutro Tunnel Building, many men posed in view	125–175.00
Virginia City, Houseworth, #713, C Street	70–100.00
Yuba, Houseworth, #799, Hydraulic mining, at Timbuctoo	65–85.00

Colorado

Alma, T. C. Miller, mining operation, 1881	60–75.00

Blackhawk

Kilburn, #5582, Mining camp	15–20.00
C. Weitfle, #15, Black Hawk Mills, 1878	65–75.00
Brownsville, Charles Bierstadt, #16, Mining camp	10–15.00
Buena Vista, C. Weitfle, #208, Silverbricks	45–65.00
Central City (Chases Gulch), William G. Chamberlain, View of three smelters	75–100.00

Idaho

C. Weitfle, Hydraulic mining	50–75.00

Leadville

W. H. Jackson, #1120, Little Pittsburgh Mine	50–60.00
C. Weitfle, #37, Town from rear of smelter	40–50.00
Oaura, C. W. Talbot "Coal Banks," men in camp	30–40.00

Ouray
　　Keystone, #8080, Stamp mill
　　and gold concentrater ——————— 2–4.00
　　Kilburn, #5507, "In town for
　　supplies," men and burros
　　heavily loaded ——————— 4–6.00
Silverton, Kilburn, #5525,
　　Miners loading supplies ——————— 6–8.00
Twin Peaks, McKirahan & Whit-
　　tier, Miner with pick ——————— 20–40.00
Post-1895, Views showing
　　mining operations ——————— 4–8.00
Michigan
　　Childs, Brubaker, Brubaker &
　　Whitesides and others, Views of
　　iron mines, 1870s ——————— 15–25.00
　　Underwood & Underwood,
　　#7973, Men posed by railcar
　　loaded with copper bars and
　　plate, Calumet and Hecla Mines,
　　1906, typical ——————— 6–8.00
Minnesota
　　Underwood & Underwood, #7954,
　　Digging with steam shovel, open
　　pit iron mine, Hibbing, typical ——————— 4–6.00
Montana
　　N. A. Forsyth, Views of miners in
　　mines, drilling, etc., Butte ——————— 35–45.00
　　Thomas H. Rutter, Men and wa-
　　gon near smelter ——————— 25–35.00
Nevada
　　Virginia City
　　　　Houseworth, #713, Street
　　　　scene ——————— 70–100.00
　　　　Noe, Consolidated Virginia
　　　　Mine ——————— 40–60.00
　　　　Watkins, "New Series." ——————— 80–125.00
　　Washoe City, Carson City, 1870s,
　　scarce ——————— 100–125.00
Pennsylvania (coal mining)
　　Keystone, #7057, Miners by
　　loaded cage ——————— 2–4.00
　　Kleckner, Men at mine opening,
　　1870s ——————— 10–15.00
　　Underwood & Underwood, Men
　　at work in shaft ——————— 3–5.00
　　H. C. White, #13220, Miners
　　pushing an "empty," typical ——————— 4–6.00

Music

(See also Blacks *and* Personalities *in Chapter 5)*

There are many collectors interested in brass bands and their development in the nineteenth century. One of the better sources of how these bands were dressed and the types of brass instruments used is shown in the stereo views. Pre-1870 views are usually studio posed and have a comic theme. Views of local bands as the main subject are fairly uncommon. More common are views of bands in parades or seen at a distance performing in a park.

There is less interest in stringed instruments; the exception is banjos. There are many views

of banjo players, or the banjo is seen leaning against a piece of furniture as part of a comic view. Collectors also are interested in views of pianos, organs, accordians and concertinas. Views of music machines such as Regina and other brands are rare.

F. G. Weller made a popular view of the country choir. It is very common and exists in many different versions. Less common are views of actual singing groups and actual performances. There are many views of opera singers (portraits).

Brass Bands
　　Griffith, #2873, Sousa's Band, 1900
　　Paris exposition, typical of noted
　　band ——————— 15–20.00
　　Kilburn, #133, Band in boat by
　　shore, Echo Lake, N.H., 1870s, yel-
　　low mount ——————— 25–35.00
　　Various makers, Children playing
　　band, usually toy instruments,
　　1870–1890 ——————— 5–8.00
　　Various makers, Local brass bands
　　as main subject, identified group ——— 25–35.00
　　Various makers, Local band at a dis-
　　tance or in a parade ——————— 10–15.00
String instruments
　　Banjo, Keystone, Underwood & Un-
　　derwood and others, Couple kissing
　　on love seat, banjo at side ——————— 3–6.00
　　Others, Child seated at piano, does
　　not want to practice, 1880–1900. ——— 2–4.00
Singing
　　Weller, "Country Choir," 1870s ——— 1–3.00

National Parks

(See also Expeditions and Surveys *in Chapter 5)*

Thousands of views have been made of our national scenic wonders. Yellowstone, Yosemite and Grand Teton National Parks all owe their existence to the power of stereo views to make a visual impact on the lawmakers who created the National Park Service and these wonderful parks. Yosemite is by far the most popular with collectors. The views by C. E. Watkins, J. J. Reilly, Houseworth and John P. Soule (Hazeltine) are highly prized for their detail and variety. Many of the major publishers such as Underwood and Underwood and H. C. White made a number of Yosemite views.

Yellowstone is documented in a large series by F. Jay Haynes. Early views of the Yellowstone area were taken by William Henry Jackson. Most popular with these early photographers were views of the geysers and the Grand Canyon of the Yellowstone. Least common today are views of hotels and public conveniences (*see* Western United States in Chapter 5).

Death Valley
  Keystone, #32666, Pool _____ 9.00
Garden of the Gods
(*See* Western United States, Colorado in Chapter 5)
Grand Teton
  William H. Jackson, #503, typical
  view, noted photographer _____ 15–25.00
Yellowstone
  F. Jay Haynes, View of geysers,
  typical _____ 8–12.00
  Keystone, Underwood & Underwood, etc., Geysers, Yellowstone
  Falls, typical _____ 1–3.00
  William H. Jackson, #422, Typical
  scene _____ 12–18.00
  Universal Photo Art, Stereo-Travel,
  Geyser view, typical _____ 3–5.00
Yosemite
  E. Anthony (negatives by Weed),
  early 1860, issued to 1862, ivory
  mounts _____ 15–20.00
  E. & H. T. Anthony, late 1860s–1870s
    #110, Hutchings' Hotel cottage, man
    on porch, typical building view __ 15–20.00
    "Glories of the Yosemite," scene ____ 5–8.00
  Griffith, #10238, Clouds Rest,
  typical _____ 3–5.00
  Thomas Housewortdh (*See* Lawrence & Houseworth below for earlier issues), #1121, Nevada Falls, typical
  scene _____ 12–15.00
  Keystone, #4001, Nevada Falls,
  typical _____ 2–5.00
  Kilburn, #9284, Bridal Veil Falls _____ 4–5.00
  Lawrence & Houseworth (1863–1870), #264, Three Brothers, Reflection, typical view, yellow mount ___ 15–20.00
  William H. Rau (Universal View
  Co.), View of El Capitan, typical _____ 2–4.00

J. J. Reilly, Reilly & Spooner, #415,
North Dome, typical scene _____ 9–10.00
John P. Soule (negatives by Hazeltine, without credit), 1870, yellow
mounts
  #1260, Close view of Hutchings'
  Hotel with people (Indians), better subject _____ 30–40.00
  Scenic studies, falls, etc. _____ 8–12.00
Underwood & Underwood
  J. F. Jarvis negatives, Man on the
  Glacier Point, 1890s, typical _____ 3–5.00
  1900–1904 negatives, gray
  mounts _____ 2–5.00
C. E. Watkins, #28, Bridal Veil
Falls, 1867 _____ 20–25.00
Woodward Stereo Co., #578, Nevada Falls _____ 1–3.00
R. Y. Young (American Stereoscopic
Co.), Man on Glacier Point _____ 4–6.00
Pirated copies, most simply marked
"Yosemite," various mounts _____ 1.00

Near East
(See also *Egypt in Chapter 5*)

In recent years there has been renewed interest in this part of the world. There are excellent views available of the areas we often call the Holy Lands. The early photographers concentrated on the ancient ruins, Moslem mosques and places visited by Christ. Palestine, Syria and Turkey changed in the nineteenth century, and these changes are documented in detail.

Francis Frith photographed Jerusalem, Damascus and Baalbec in the late 1850s. These are signed and numbered in the negatives. Also not to be overlooked are the excellent views by Frank Good—the "Eastern Series" on yellow mounts. Less common are the views by Felix Bonfils.

E. & H. T. Anthony, "Glories of the Yosemite, California," #42, "Cathedral Rocks, 2670 ft. high," issued on yellow mounts. This was a popular series in the 1870s. $4–8 each.

The British War Office conducted a topographical survey of the Sinai in 1868–1869. A series of views were issued but are rarely seen in the United States.

Edward L. Wilson's "Scenes in the Orient" (negatives by William H. Rau) and William E. James's series of the Holy Lands show the influence of missionaries in the area. Charles Bierstadt made a few views, especially in what is now Israel in the early 1870s. These were later published by Underwood and Underwood in the 1890s.

Most of the major publishers offered views of the area (*see* Boxed Sets in Chapter 6). The most popular subjects among collectors are those showing Judaica, occupationals (people working) and local native life (lepers, street vendors and so on).

Pre-1870 views by Frith, Good, Bonfils and others	6–12.00
1870–1890 views, Bierstadt, E. L. Wilson and others	5–10.00
Post-1890 views	
Underwood & Underwood, View of lepers, Jerusalem	1–3.00
H. C. White, Underwood & Underwood, Keystone, etc.	1–2.00

Niagara Falls

(See Daredevils and Wire Walkers, and Glass Stereo Views in Chapter 5)

This scenic wonder is possibly the most stereo-photographed subject encountered by collectors. Thousands of views were made of the falls, Whirlpool Rapids, Goat Island, Cave of the Winds and Prospect Point. The photographers were fascinated with the changes of the falls in different seasons. There are outstanding views of frozen foliage, ice arches, deep caves and snow piled on fences. Several times during the nineteenth century, the Niagara River froze over and formed an ice bridge. A number of fine views were made of this event with people frolicking on the high hills of ice.

All major publishers offered Niagara Falls stereos, from the Langenheims in 1854 through the Keystones in the 1930s. The first Langenheim issues are on ivory mounts with gold trim framing the prints. The views have manuscript titles and are dated. The earliest known example is dated on the reverse "Spring 1854" and shows the American Falls with snow on the ground, indicating the view was taken early that spring. These early views are calotypes, a process pioneered in the United States by the Langenheims. The prints are a grayish tan color. The 1855–1857 issues are on enameled ivory mounts and usually have the Langenheim blindstamp at one end. The 1858–1861 issues are on ivory enameled mounts with a paper label on reverse for "American Stereoscopic Co./copyright 1858 by Langenheim & Loyd."

E. Anthony (1859–1862)	
#156, Photographic stand by falls, 1859	12–20.00
No number, "Niagara in Winter," typical	6–8.00
E. & H. T. Anthony (1862–1870s), #7743, American falls, 1870s	2–4.00
George Barker	
Prospect Point, falls in winter, typical	2–4.00
#966, Photographer at work on Luna Island with camera on tripod, winter, 1875	10–12.00
Charles Bierstadt, #163, Bridge and Terrapin Tower, typical	4–6.00
George Curtis, #264, Whirlpool Rapids with suspension bridge, typical view	2–4.00
S. Davis, #426, New suspension bridge, typical	3–5.00
Keystone (1893–1930s), #161, Home of Jack Frost, Prospect Park, typical view	2–3.00
B. W. Kilburn, #7765, Table Rock, Canada side, typical view	2–3.00
Langenheim	
1854 issue, American Falls	150–200.00
1855–1857 issues, Often blindstamped	75–100.00
1858–1861 issues (American Stereoscopic Co.), Langenheim & Loyd, 1858	25–35.00
J. J. Reilly, #335, Side view of Second Sister Bridge, typical	10–12.00
John P. Soule, #783, Moonlight view of American Falls, typical view	4–6.00
Underwood & Underwood	
Large crowd at Prospect Point, 1893, typical	2–4.00
Sold/Published views by George Barker, Charles Bierstadt and J. F. Jarvis (1888–1900)	2–4.00
Universal Photo Art (C. H. Graves), #5611–5643, Falls, rapids, etc.	2–4.00
L. E. Walker, #833, Falls from suspension bridge, 1870s, typical	4–6.00
H. C. White, #306, Looking up gorge showing Upper Arch Bridge and distant falls, typical	2–4.00

Nudes

(See Risqué and Nudes in Chapter 5)

Occupationals

(See Cowboys, Farming and Oil Industry in Chapter 5)

A true occupational is one showing a worker in his work place, preferably at work. The slow speed of the photographic plates did not permit the making of many action scenes. The photographer often posed the workers as though they were operating machines, which one can clearly see are not in motion. Views with motion show blurs of whirling belt wheels or people moving on the mill or factory floor. The stereo photograph of the nineteenth and early twentieth century is one of our best visual tools for documenting the history of labor. Nearly all industries were stereo-photographed and many show working conditions. In the later Keystone views, machines are seen taking over jobs previously done by manual labor, for example, milking machines in a dairy.

Auto Industry
    Keystone, #33143, Workers leaving Ford Plant, Detroit, Mich., common ———————————— 1–2.00
    Keystone, Engine assembling ——————— 2–4.00
Baking
    Keystone, #V29230, Men in dough mixing room, large bakery ——————— 6–7.00
Barber
    J. S. Moulton, Mass., #361, Studio-posed boy seated, barber cutting hair, 1870s ———————————— 25–30.00
Blacksmith
    Keystone, #18206, Shows many tools ————————————————— 4–5.00
Clothing
    Keystone, #22260, Women folding, ironing collars, Troy, N.Y. —————— 2–4.00
Commercial Fishing
    Kilburn, #10540, Salmon fishermen with catch on Columbia River, Oreg. ————————————————— 10–15.00

Keystone, #13884, Fish drying, Perce, Quebec, Canada —————— 1–3.00
Dairy
    Keystone
        #6658, Creamery, East Aurora, N.Y. ———————————— 1–2.00
        #16750, Machines filling bottles ——— 1–2.00
        #16756, Machines washing churned butter, Cohocton, N.Y. ——— 1–2.00
Doll Making
    Underwood & Underwood, #10436, Women making dolls in German factory ——————————————— 12–15.00
Grocery Store
    Keystone, #18200, Interior of store with kids buying bread and milk from grocer ——————————— 25–30.00
Ice Cutting
    Whitney & Zimmerman, Men cutting ice blocks, Minn., 1870. ———— 10–12.00
Lace Making
    Underwood & Underwood, #9617, Women making lace in France ———— 4–6.00
Milkman
    Keystone, #P-26392, Horse-drawn wagon ——————————————— 8–12.00
Mill
    Underwood & Underwood, Linen factory, typical industrial view ———— 2–3.00
Paper making
    Underwood & Underwood, #7984, Men operating machines in Marinette, Wis. ———————————— 2–3.00
Porcelain Making
    Underwood & Underwood, Men turning cups on lathes, Worcester, England ———————————————— 4–6.00
Rubber Industry, Tire Making, etc.
    Keystone, #22329, Tread being put on tire at Akron, Ohio, factory ———— 2–3.00
Textile Industry
    Keystone, #20301, Sorting silk skeins, South Manchester, Conn., typical ——————————————— 2–4.00
    Keystone, #V23231, Men in weaving room, cotton mill, S.C. ————— 2–3.00
    Kilburn, #613, Weaving machines,

Kilburn Bros., #1821, ''The Reapers,'' one of their better occupational views made in New Hampshire ca. 1870. $8.

H. C. White Co., #282, "Sausage drying room, where millions of sausages hang. Swift's Packing House, Chicago," one of many fine views showing the meat-packing industry, note the curved mount, 1905 issue. $4–6. (Gordon D. Hoffman Collection)

cotton mill, Fall River, Mass., typical _____ 4–5.00

Watch Making

T. Lewis, #25, Ladies working on watches from a series of forty-three views of the Waltham Watch Factory, 1873 _____ 12–18.00

Oil Industry

The oil boom in Pennsylvania at Pithole in the 1860s was the beginning of the petroleum industry in the United States and the stereo photographers were there to record the boom and then the bust. There are views of the Drake well, where it all began plus views on Oil Creek where shanty towns grew up among the derricks. These early views made in the 1860s are fairly uncommon. The most common of the nineteenth-century views of the oil industry in Pennsylvania are those by Detlor and Waddell of Bradford. Another fine series was made by Frank Robbins. These views show the oil industry from drilling to transport. There are nice views of towns and vast fields of storage tanks. Underwood and Underwood, Keystone and others made views of oil drilling after 1895. Most common is the Keystone view of the shooting well. A few views were also made in Ohio, but these are uncommon.

The oil boom at Beaumont, Texas, was stereophotographed by Keystone with a small series showing derricks and storage tanks. A small series of oil strikes in California was made about 1910.

California, International, Keystone and others _____ 10–12.00

Ohio, Local makers, 1870s–1880s, scarce _____ 15–20.00

Pennsylvania

J. A. Mather, Titusville, views of derricks, tanks, etc., 1860s–1870s. _ 15–25.00

Detlor & Waddell, #76, Burning tanks _____ 12–20.00

Robbins, #32, Triumph Hill, typical _____ 12–20.00

Robbins, #88, Gas well _____ 10–15.00

B. W. Kilburn, #16696, "California Oil Wells in the Bakersfield District." $12.

Detlor & Waddell, Bradford, Pa., Close view of oil riggers in drilling operation, ca. 1880. $20.

Wilt Brothers, Allegheny area,
1880s _____ 8–10.00
Keystone, #20352, Shooting a
well _____ 3–4.00
Texas
   Keystone
     #20054, Oil derricks, early
     automobile _____ 3–6.00
     #20354, Crude oil stills and fac-
     tory, Port Arthur _____ 2–3.00
     #34864, Tanks near Kilgore,
     common _____ 3–6.00

Palestine
(See *Near East in Chapter 5*)

Panama Canal
(See also *Personalities, [Goethals, Colonel George W.]*)

The idea of building a connection between the Atlantic and Pacific oceans intrigued engineers from the mid-nineteenth century until it was finally accomplished in 1914. One of the main purposes of the Selfridge Darien Expedition in the early 1870s was to survey the terrain for the future construction of a waterway between the great oceans (*see* Expeditions and Surveys in Chapter 5). Selfridge discovered that Darien was a rugged part of the world with dense rain forests and small mountains.

With the success of the Suez Canal in the late 1860s, the French, under the direction of Ferdinand De Lesseps, made an effort to dig a canal starting in 1881. After seven years and the loss of nearly $300 million, not to mention the loss of 20,000 lives, the French gave up. As far as can be determined, there are no views of this failed effort.

After 1901, there was renewed interest, this time by the United States. Panama gained independence in 1903 from Colombia with the help of United States political interests. The new Republic of Panama, to the delight of President Theodore Roosevelt, agreed to allow its country to be split by a strip of land called the Canal Zone. Colonel George Washington Goethals of the Army Corps of Engineers was placed in charge of digging the Panama Canal. Stereo photographers were on hand from nearly the beginning and made a remarkable record of the construction as well as scenes of local natives, working conditions and even views of the old French dredging machinery that had been abandoned in 1888 (*see also* Boxed Sets in Chapter 6).

Canal Construction
   Keystone, #21745, Near Gatun, 1913,
   common _____ 6–8.00
   Stereo-Travel, #57, Steam shovel
   on canal bottom, Culebra Cut, gray
   mount _____ 8–10.00
   Underwood & Underwood, Culebra
   Cut, showing depth _____ 8–10.00
   H. C. White, #11526, Work train in
   Culebra Cut _____ 10–12.00
   Printed litho views, sepia color,
   white card _____ 1.00
Canal in operation
   Keystone and Underwood & Under-
   wood, Ship in lock, Gatun _____ 5–8.00
   Stereo-Travel _____ 6–8.00
Local native life
   Keystone, Stereo-Travel and Under-
   wood & Underwood _____ 2–4.00
   H. C. White, #11545, Busy life
   among market boats in harbor,
   typical _____ 3–5.00
   Printed litho views _____ 1.00

Personalities

(See also *Glass Stereo Views, Langenheim* in Chapter 5)

One of the most popular types of view collected is famous people. The photographers and publishers photographed nearly every major personage of the nineteenth and early twentieth centuries. Most common are views of President McKinley (1896–1901). The rarest stereo views of United States presidents are Chester A. Arthur and Benjamin Harrison. The most sought-after president is Abraham Lincoln. United States western personalities also are very popular. Many collectors seek the views of George A. Custer taken during the Civil War and until his death in 1876 at the Battle of Little Big Horn.

Publishers issued "skeleton leaves," starting in the 1860s, whenever a portrait from life was not available. They are arrangements of thin, almost transparent leaves with a photo of the person in the middle. These are not as popular with collectors and are collected more for their stereoscopic effect. In the late 1870s, another type was introduced with a portrait of the person framed in flowers or flags. These, too, are not taken from life and were sold by publishers when a stereo portrait from life was not available. Some publishers issued flat portraits of famous persons simply mounting two identical, nonstereo images together. Portraits of P. T. Barnum, President Arthur, Wild Bill Hickock and others were sold as flat images. Actual stereo portraits of these three men are rare.

There are many distant views for which a magnifying glass is needed to see the personality. Examples are President Harrison's in-auguration and Chester A. Arthur at Garfield's funeral.

Every United States president from Lincoln to Bush has been stereo-photographed. It is possible that a portrait of James Buchanan, the fifteenth president (just before Lincoln), may exist but none has been located. Buchanan died in 1868.

There is interest in related views that do not show the personality. Views of funeral processions, homes and places related to their careers are sought to round out a collection (*see* Photographic Related Views Photographers at Work in Chapter 5).

Amundsen, Roald, Keystone, #13327,
View of explorer inspecting ice fields
in Antarctic ⎯⎯⎯⎯⎯⎯⎯ 4–6.00
Arthur, President Chester A.
  Skeleton leaves, framed in flow-
  ers, etc. ⎯⎯⎯⎯⎯⎯⎯ 4–6.00
  Close portrait flat, nonstereo ⎯⎯ 6–10.00
  F. Jay Haynes, President Arthur
  in Yellowstone
    Views of members of party, not
    Arthur ⎯⎯⎯⎯⎯⎯⎯ 60–100.00
    Views of tent camp, pack
    mules, etc. ⎯⎯⎯⎯⎯⎯ 30–40.00
    President Arthur with Robert
    Lincoln, Philip H. Sheridan and
    others at Upper Geyser Basin ⎯ 600–800.00
  Close portrait, in stereo, not
  known to exist ⎯⎯⎯⎯⎯⎯ 1000.00+
  Garfield's funeral, Cleveland,
  1881, Ryder and Liebich photog-
  raphers, distant ⎯⎯⎯⎯⎯ 15–20.00
Barton, Clara, founder of American
Red Cross
  Littleton View Co. (sold by Un-
  derwood & Underwood), #1970,
  Nonstereo portrait framed in
  flowers ⎯⎯⎯⎯⎯⎯⎯ 4–6.00

Littleton View Co. (sold by Underwood & Underwood), #1816, "McKinley & Hobart," 1896, typical view of nonstereo portraits framed in flowers when a view from life was not available. $5.

B. W. Kilburn, #12000, "European Queens and Princess, Coronation, Moscow, Russia," 1897. $12.

Littleton View Co. (sold by Underwood & Underwood), #1970, "Miss Clara Barton, President of the Am. National Red Cross," 1898. $4–6.

Keystone, #V28008, Seated at
desk ————————— 40–60.00
Bryan, William Jennings,
Keystone, #15539, on way to
hotel in New York City ————— 25–30.00
Underwood & Underwood, at
home in Nebraska ————— 10–15.00
Various makers, framed in flow-
ers, nonstereo ————————— 1–3.00
Black-and-white printed litho-
graph, at Castle Garden, N.Y. ———— 1.00
Buntline, Ned J., J. Gurney, por-
trait ——————————— 150–200.00
Burbank, Luther, Keystone,
#16746, posed with cactus at Santa
Rosa, Calif., this may not be
Burbank ————————— 4–6.00
Burroughs, John, Keystone,
#V18500, Portrait outdoors in
woods ————————— 20–30.00
Cleveland, Grover
  Underwood & Underwood,
  #10027, Posed in his hunting
  gear, S.C., 1907, ex-president
  view ——————————— 40–60.00
  Various makers, Nonstereo por-
  trait with or without his wife,
  Frances, framed in flowers ——— 1–3.00
Cody, William F. (Buffalo Bill),

C. W. Woodward, #1392, Close-up
on horseback ————————— 20–30.00
Colfax, Schuyler, vice president,
A. J. Russell, #885, Posed with
party during the inspection tour of
western rail-mail routes ————— 45–60.00
Coolidge, Calvin
  Keystone
  #26303, With cabinet ————— 20–30.00
  #28004, In his White House
  office ——————————— 15–25.00
  #29472, And his cabinet,
  common ————————— 6–8.00
Custer, George Armstrong
  F. Jay Haynes, #1206, People
  posed in front of Monument to
  Custer, Little Big Horn ———— 35–40.00
  Lovejoy & Foster, With bear he
  killed ————————— 350–500.00
  Taylor & Huntington, #2438,
  With his dog in camp during
  Civil War, 1862, 1880s reprint —— 500–600.00
  E. & H. T. Anthony, "War
  Views," #2438, Above in vintage
  issue, yellow mount, 1860s ——— 600–700.00
Czar Nicholas of Russia, Under-
wood & Underwood, With presi-
dent of France ————————— 8–12.00
de Gerlache, Commander Adrien,

*Underwood & Underwood, #8007,
"Ex-President Cleveland, honored and
beloved—in his study, at home, Prin-
ceton, N.J.," 1906. $50. (Gordon D.
Hoffman Collection)*

Keystone, #13328, Posed on ice,
South Pole with killed seal _____ 4–5.00
Dewey, Admiral George, Under-
wood & Underwood, On flagship
Olympia, Manila Bay, 1899 _____ 8–10.00
Edison, Thomas A.
   Keystone, #V28007, In labora-
   tory _____ 85–100.00
   Underwood & Underwood, In
   laboratory _____ 100–125.00
Edison, Henry Ford and Harvey
Firestone, Keystone, #18551, At
Harding's funeral, Ohio _____ 70–75.00
Eisenhower, Dwight D., Keystone,
At table with microphones, ca.
1954 _____ 150–250.00
Farragutt, Admiral, Anthony,
#2280, "Prominent Portraits." _____ 40–50.00
Ford, Henry, Keystone, #28023,
Showing a telebinocular stereo
viewer to Anton Lang _____ 35–45.00
Gandhi, Mahatma, Keystone,
#33852, Seated on floor _____ 15–20.00
Garfield, James A.
   J. F. Jarvis, Delivering inaugural
   address, 1881 _____ 50–75.00
   James F. Ryder
      Garfield seated on porch of his
      Mentor, Ohio, home, preelec-
      tion, ca. 1880 _____ 75–100.00
      Stern & Gates, Garfield and
      Rudolph families posed outside
      at Hiram, Ohio, ca. 1881 _____ 200–300.00
      Liebich, Close view of casket,
      Cleveland _____ 10–15.00
      Liebich, Moore, Ryder, etc.,
      Guard at vault _____ 10–12.00
      Kilburn, #4608, Monument at
      Cleveland (Tomb) _____ 1–3.00
Gehrig, Lou (baseball player), Key-
stone, #32597 _____ 200–250.00
Gilbert, Mrs. John (actress), Anthony "Prominent Portraits,"
#2846–2848, Typical, posed in
costume _____ 15–25.00
Goethals, Colonel George Washington (engineer), Keystone, #28010,
Seated at desk _____ 15–25.00

Grant, Ulysses S.
   Anthony, #2965, 3877 and 3878,
   Lieutenant General Grant in uni-
   form, studio posed _____ 70–80.00
   Bierstadt Bros., Close-up of Grant
   and party on top of Mt. Washington, N.H. _____ 45–75.00
   J. Gurney & Son, Standing vig-
   netted portrait _____ 75–90.00
   G. W. Pach, Grant with wife and
   son posed before their cottage at
   Long Branch, N.J., 1872 _____ 45–65.00
   Joseph W. Warren, Posed with
   party at Martha's Vineyard (sev-
   eral versions), 1874 _____ 30–35.00
   Parade of troops on Pennsylvania
   Avenue, second inauguration,
   1873, very scarce _____ 70–80.00
   Various makers, Portrait in skele-
   ton leaves or framed in flowers,
   nonstereo _____ 2–4.00
Greeley, Horace
   Anthony, #2932, Studio portrait ____ 80–90.00
   Close view, standing on a porch,
   1870s _____ 70–80.00
   Portrait framed in flowers, skele-
   ton leaves _____ 2–4.00
Harding, Warren G. (*see* Alaska in
Chapter 5)
   Keystone
      #17392, With wife at Marion,
      Ohio, home _____ 20–25.00
      #18518, Addressing boy scouts
      in Butte, Mont., western/Alaska
      tour _____ 15–20.00
      #18521, Posed with members
      of Old Oregon Trail Associa-
      tion, Meachem, Oreg., tour _____ 15–20.00
      #18539, Seated aboard stage-
      coach, Meachem, Oreg., west-
      ern/Alaska tour _____ 15–20.00
      #18591, Driving last spike on
      Alaskan Railroad at Tanana
      River, photographer in view _____ 30–35.00
Harrison, Benjamin
   Close view or portrait _____ 300–350.00
   Inauguration, at distance _____ 30–35.00
   Centennial of Washington's inau-

Keystone View Co., #17423, "President and Mrs. Hoover, Mr. and Mrs. Edison and Mr. Ford [not in view] Boarding a Train of 1879 Model— Light's Golden Jubilee," 1929. $70. (Gordon D. Hoffman Collection)

guration in far distance, New
York City ⎯⎯⎯⎯⎯⎯⎯⎯ 10–15.00
Portrait in skeleton leaves, framed
by flowers ⎯⎯⎯⎯⎯⎯⎯⎯ 3–4.00
Funeral Parade, Indianapolis,
Whiting and others made views ⎯⎯ 10–15.00
Hayes, Rutherford B.
George O. Bartlett, close portrait ⎯⎯ 80–90.00
E. W. Beckwith, #3, "The Wyoming Massacre Centennial,"
Plymouth, Pa., seated with officials, 1878 ⎯⎯⎯⎯⎯⎯⎯⎯ 175–200.00
J. F. Jarvis, delivering inaugural
address, Washington, D.C. ⎯⎯⎯⎯ 65–75.00
North & Oswald, With wife posed
with the members of 23rd Ohio
Volunteer Infantry at Reunion,
near Toledo, 1877 ⎯⎯⎯⎯⎯⎯ 100–125.00
Posed with party at Hastings,
Minn., western tour ⎯⎯⎯⎯⎯⎯ 125–150.00
Holmes, Oliver Wendell
Keystone, #32726, Home in Boston, 1920s ⎯⎯⎯⎯⎯⎯⎯⎯ 5–7.00
No known stereo portraits, many
portraits known on cartes-de-visite and cabinet cards.
Hoover, Herbert, Keystone,
#28012, Very close portrait ⎯⎯⎯⎯ 30–35.00
Ingersoll, Robert G. (Republican
party leader)
Posed with family outdoors,
1880 ⎯⎯⎯⎯⎯⎯⎯⎯⎯⎯ 20–25.00
Various makers, nonstereo portrait framed in flowers or skeleton
leaves ⎯⎯⎯⎯⎯⎯⎯⎯⎯⎯ 1–2.00
Irving, Washington (*see* Glass
Views, Langenheim in Chapter 5),
Copy view of Grave, Sleepy Hollow,
N.Y. ⎯⎯⎯⎯⎯⎯⎯⎯⎯⎯ 1–2.00
Jefferson, Thomas, M. P. Simons,
Tomb at Monticello, Va., 1870s ⎯⎯ 5–7.00
Johnson, Andrew, Anthony,
"Prominent Portraits," Seated
portrait ⎯⎯⎯⎯⎯⎯⎯⎯⎯⎯ 100–125.00
King Haakon (Norway), Keystone,
#13489, With Grand Duke Michael
of Russia at boat landing, Norway ⎯⎯ 4–6.00
Lane, Miss Harriet, Anthony,

"Prominent Portraits." ⎯⎯⎯⎯⎯⎯ 40–60.00
Lee, Robert E.
Kilburn, #4604, Portrait in skeleton leaves ⎯⎯⎯⎯⎯⎯⎯⎯ 6–8.00
Portrait in stereo, vintage print ⎯⎯ 600–800.00
Lincoln, Abraham
Portraits, vintage
Anthony, (*see* illustration) ⎯⎯ 600–1200.00

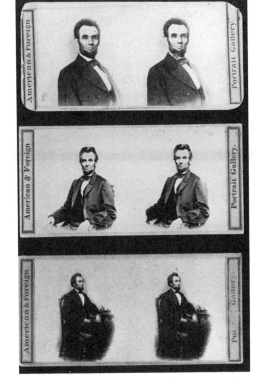

Three E. & H. T. Anthony "Portrait Gallery" views of President Abraham Lincoln. The bottom portrait, #2968, on the yellow mount recently sold for $1100. Depending on condition (note top view is trimmed at the corners), Lincoln vintage portraits like these normally sell in the $600–1200 range.

Brady Album Gallery, Alexander Gardner _____ 1000–2000.00
Taylor & Huntington, 1880s reprint from original negatives, orange cabinet mounts _____ 300–600.00

(*Note:* Taylor & Huntington issued a nonstereo flat portrait in their series, which has limited collector interest.)

Keystone, #28016, copied in 1930s from the Library of Congress original "fuzzy hair." _____ 60–70.00

(*Note:* Keystone offered a nonstereo flat portrait from a painting. It has limited collector interest.)

Lincoln's Funeral (1865)
Anthony, #2948–2955, 2957–2958, 2987, Scenes in New York City and Washington, D.C. _____ 40–65.00
Ridgeway Glover (Philadelphia), Views in Philadelphia, Chicago and Springfield, Ill. _____ 75–100.00
J. Gurney (New York), Views in New York City _____ 65–85.00
J. Q. A. Tresize (Springfield) _____ 75–100.00
Various local photographers,

Baltimore, Albany, Cleveland, Columbus, Indianapolis (staged), Michigan City (Ind.), Chicago (Carbutt) and Springfield _____ 100–125.00
Post-1865 views, not from life
Keystone, #12455, Presidents Lincoln, Garfield and McKinley, memorial tableau of little girls praying before photos of "Martyred Presidents" _____ 2–4.00
I. L. Rogers "Phantom Leaves," 1872 _____ 2–4.00
Lincoln, Mary Todd, Anthony, #2970, "Prominent Portraits." _____ 50–60.00
Lindbergh (*see* Aviation in Chapter 5)
Longfellow, Henry Wadsworth, Keystone, #32727, Seated in study _____ 50–60.00
Maharaja of Gwalior, Underwood & Underwood, #3485, At home in India, 1903 _____ 3–5.00
Marconi, M. G. (inventor of wireless telegraphy)
Keystone, #V11969 _____ 35–45.00
Underwood & Underwood, Close-up seated pose, 1903 _____ 40–50.00

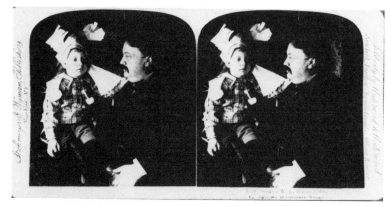

Underwood & Underwood portrait of United States Senator W. E. Mason and his son, Lowell, 1898. Part of a series by Henry Strohmeyer of leading political leaders. $35. (Gordon D. Hoffman Collection)

E. W. Kelley, "Inaugural Ball Room, March 4, 1897, Washington, D.C.," decorated for McKinley's inaugural event, offered both tinted and untinted. $5.

Mason, United States Senator
W. E., Underwood & Underwood
(Henry Strohmeyer), Seated with
son, Lowell, 1898 _____ 35.00
McKinley, William
  Keystone
  #2474, Portrait with wife,
  framed in flowers _____ 1–3.00
  #2477, Delivering his Inaugural Address, 1897 _____ 4–6.00
  #2479, Overall view of inauguration, 1897 _____ 4–6.00
  #2480, Ohio Regiment march-
  ing in inaugural parade, 1897 _____ 4–5.00
  #2481, Men carrying flags, inaugural parade _____ 4–5.00
  #2482, Pennsylvania in Honor
  of Her Neighbor, inaugural parade, 1897 _____ 4–5.00
  #2484, ''The Bravest of the
  Brave,'' inaugural parade _____ 4–5.00
  #2490, Before taking Oath of
  Office, 1897 _____ 4–5.00
  #2497, Inaugural Ballroom,
  Washington, 1897 _____ 4–5.00
  #(2), 4861 (Underwood & Underwood negative) Seated at
  head of council table _____ 2–3.00
  #6078, Brass band passing before McKinley at Grand Army
  of the Republic reunion, Buffalo, 1897 _____ 4–6.00
  #6079, Veterans passing before
  McKinley at Grand Army of
  the Republic reunion, Buffalo,
  1897 _____ 5–6.00
  #6083, In carriage heading
  procession, Grand Army of the
  Republic reunion, Buffalo,
  1897 _____ 5–6.00
  #9513, Framed in flowers and
  flags, 1899 _____ 1–2.00
  #9649, National Guard passing
  before McKinley, unveiling
  Grant's Monument, Philadelphia, 1899 _____ 3–4.00

Admiral Dewey Sword Presentation, Washington, October 3,
1899, #10519–10526 _____ each 3–4.00
#11604, Seated at desk, White
House, 1900 _____ 3–4.00
#11663, Overall view, second
inauguration, 1901 _____ 4–6.00
#11698, With General Shafter,
San Francisco, 1901 _____ 4–6.00
#12454, Cleveland, Ohio, Dec-
orated in mourning during funeral week, 1901 _____ 4–6.00
#V226135, Taking Oath of Of-
fice, 1901, Teddy Roosevelt in
view, later issue of Underwood
& Underwood, #5587 _____ 10–15.00
B. W. Kilburn
  #11429, Close portrait, flat,
  nonstereo, 1896 _____ 2–4.00
  #12717, Close view, reading
  dispatches, image is flat, nonstereo effect, 1898 _____ 5–6.00
  #14472, People waiting to see
  McKinley at Pan-American Exposition, 1901 _____ 4–5.00
  #14539–14541, 14546–14547
  Last address, Pan-American Exposition, 1901, several variants
  exist _____ 5–8.00
  #14543, 14549, 14550 Mc-
  Kinley at Pan-American Exposition Stadium, 1901, last
  stereo view of him _____ 3–4.00
Underwood & Underwood
  #5587, Chief Justice Fuller ad-
  ministering Oath of Office,
  1901, T. Roosevelt in view _____ 10–15.00
  #(1) Close-up at his desk in
  White House _____ 5–6.00
  #(2) At head of council table,
  White House _____ 4–5.00
  Speaking from rear of railroad
  car, Decatur, Ala., typical from
  tour series, 1901 _____ 8–10.00
Funeral views, Buffalo, Washington, D.C., and Canton, Ohio,

B. W. Kilburn (sold by James M. Davis), #14582, ''Carrying the Body of President McKinley into the Church, Canton, O.,'' one of a large series of the 1901 funeral. There are variants of most negatives. $3–6 each.

B. W. Kilburn, #14600, "The Automobile ambulance which conveyed our martyred President [McKinley] from the Temple of Music to the Hospital." $8.

1901, Kilburn, Keystone, etc.
Views of processions, crowds _____ 3–4.00
Views of casket _____ 5–6.00
Interior of Temple of Music
where he was shot, Kilburn,
#14562, Boys seated in chairs _____ 4–6.00
Doctors and nurses at operating
table where his wounds were
treated, Kilburn, #14598–
14599 _____ 8–10.00
Ambulance that carried him
from Temple of Music with
drivers _____ 12–15.00
Receiving vault in Canton with
guards, several makers _____ 2–4.00
McKinley's House, Canton,
Ohio _____ 2–4.00
Milburn House, Buffalo, where
he died _____ 4–6.00
Floral tributes, Canton (some
tinted) _____ 1–3.00
McKinley, Mrs. William, Underwood & Underwood, Seated in
White House conservatory _____ 1–3.00
Morse, Samuel F. B.
Anthony, #2873, "Prominent
Portraits." _____ 175–200.00
J. Gurney, Close portrait _____ 200–250.00

Parker, Alton B. (presidential candidate), Underwood & Underwood,
On piazza of his home, Rosemont,
N.Y. _____ 20.00
Pershing, General John J., Keystone, #19133, With Marshall Foch
and others at Paris, World War I _____ 2–4.00
Prince Henry (United States visit,
several publishers)
On launching platform of German Emperor's Yacht, christening, with Alice Roosevelt, 1903 _____ 12–15.00
Views of tour, Underwood & Underwood, H. C. White, etc. _____ 5–6.00
Queen Victoria
Kilburn, #12076, Canadian
mounted troops passing reviewing stand, Diamond Jubilee,
typical _____ 3–5.00
Underwood & Underwood,
Seated at breakfast, Nice, France _____ 30–40.00
Rogers, Will, Keystone, #32796, At
1932 Chicago Democratic
Convention _____ 65–75.00
Roosevelt, Franklin D., Keystone,
#33535, Typical, scarce _____ 65–75.00
Roosevelt, Theodore
Griffith, #3070, Seated at desk,

Underwood & Underwood, Portrait of Chief Justice Alton B. Parker on the piazza of his home at Rosemount, Esopus, N.Y., 1904. $20. (Gordon D. Hoffman Collection)

H. C. White, #8188, "Prince Henry, Members of his Suite and the Reception Committee [including President Teddy Roosevelt] on the Bridge of the Deutschland," 1902. $15.

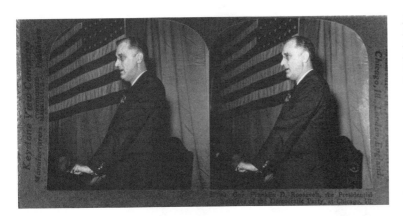

Keystone View Co., #32790, "Gov. Franklin D. Roosevelt, the Presidential Nominee of the Democratic Party, at Chicago, Ill.," scarce prepresidential view. $75. (Gordon D. Hoffman Collection)

Keystone View Co., #11914, "President [Teddy] Roosevelt signing an important Bill—President's Office, White House, Washington, D.C.," 1903. $12.

White House	8–10.00

Keystone
  #11911, Portrait framed with
  flowers ————————— 2–4.00
  #11915, At desk dictating to
  Secretary William Loeb, 1903 —— 10–12.00
Underwood & Underwood
  Standing portrait in White
  House office ————————— 8–10.00

With Speaker Cannon and Republican Committee in front of decorated Sagamore Hill, Oyster Bay ————————————— 15–20.00
Large crowd in Providence, R.I., listening to speech, not in view ————————————— 5–6.00
Close full-length pose at Old Mission in Santa Barbara,

Calif., 1903 _____ 15–20.00

Close view speaking in Concord, N.H., 1905 _____ 25–30.00

At Glacier Point, Yosemite, Calif. _____ 20–30.00

#7660, On horseback with hunting party, Yellowstone, typical western tour _____ 12–20.00

#10003, With family at Sagamore Hill, Oyster Bay, N.Y., 1907 _____ 12–18.00

H. C. White

#9911–9928 Inauguration, 1905 _____ each 8–12.00

#9929–9947, Hunting trip in Colorado _____ 15–25.00

Various makers, Color-printed lithographs, most of 1905 inauguration _____ 1–2.00

Ruth, Babe (baseball player), Keystone, #32590 _____ 200–250.00

Sandburg, Carl, Keystone, #34503, Posed in study, stereo viewer and views in front of him on table _____ 125–150.00

Shaw, George Bernard, Keystone, #34505, Posed on ship _____ 50–60.00

Smith, H. G. (senator and nominee

for vice-president), H. C. White, Close portrait _____ 40.00

Stanley, Henry M. (explorer), In a tent, Upper Congo _____ 30–35.00

Stanton, Edwin M. (Lincoln's secretary of war), Anthony, #3876, "Prominent Portraits," vignetted _____ 65–75.00

Stowe, Harriet Beecher

Identified local photographer, seated on her porch or under tree, Fla., 1870s _____ 25–30.00

Pirated copy, no photographer noted _____ 3–4.00

Taft, William Howard, Underwood & Underwood, #10062, Seated at desk, typical _____ 15–25.00

Thomas, Lowell (newsman and travel expert), Keystone, #32812 _____ 40–50.00

Tom Thumb

Anthony, "The Fairy Wedding Party." _____ 30–40.00

Underwood & Underwood, With Commodore Nut and wives _____ 10–15.00

Truman, Harry S.

Keystone, Seated in office _____ 150–200.00

Lynn Skeels, Baseball outing, in office _____ 200–250.00

H. C. White, portrait, "Ex-Senator H. G. Davis, nominee for Vice President of the United States on the Democratic Ticket," 1904. $40. (Gordon D. Hoffman Collection)

Lynn Skeels, Portrait of President Harry S. Truman, ca. 1948. Skeels made a number of views of Truman including the one published by Keystone. $250. (Gordon D. Hoffman Collection)

Underwood & Underwood, #8010, "The great humorist 'Mark Twain' (S. L. Clemens) and his peculiar method of work, New York," 1906. $200.

Twain, Mark (Samuel Clemens)
Evans & Soule, J. Gurney, etc.,
pre-1880 ————————— 300–350.00
Underwood & Underwood,
#8010; H. C. White, #13055;
and Keystone, #V34494, Seated
in bed writing ————————— 200–250.00
Washington, Booker T.
Keystone, #V11960, With An-
drew Carnegie ————————— 50–70.00
Underwood & Underwood, with
President McKinley and governor
of Alabama on podium, Tuske-
gee, 1899 ————————— 35–45.00
Washington, George (*see* Southern
United States in Chapter 5)
Rogers, skeleton leaves, 1874,
portraits of George and Martha ——— 2–4.00
Underwood & Underwood,
#11165, Headquarters at New-
burgh, N.Y. ————————— 1–3.00
Wright Brothers (*see* Aviation in
Chapter 5)
Young, Brigham
C. W. Carter, Vignetted bust por-
trait ————————— 10–15.00
Savage & Ottinger, Seated studio
pose, 1870s ————————— 35–45.00

Philippine Islands

(See also *Wars, Spanish-American War* in
Chapter 5)

Pre-1898 views of the islands are extremely
rare. The Spanish-American War (1898)
brought interest to the area. Soon after the
quick victory of the United States Navy at Manila, the war was over and the islands were
ceded to the United States. Stereo photographers arrived within the year and began documenting the war and the local native life. The
best series was made by James Ricalton for
Underwood and Underwood. The views were
sold in large quantities and there are very few

rarities. The most popular are views of native
lifestyles and industries. There also are a number of fine scenes of busy wharves and crowded
streets.

Underwood & Underwood
#4557, Filipino school for girls ——— 2–4.00
#4579, Natives before small hut ——— 1–3.00
Universal Photo Art (Graves) ————— 2–4.00
#8911, Rampart of Fort Guadeloupe,
Cavite, Luzon
#8920, Looking across Manila Bay
from walls of Fort Malate, Manila
#8950, Making Manila rope
H. C. White, #3526, A Filipino beauty,
Manila, typical ————————— 3–4.00

Photographic Related Views

Popular among collectors are those views
showing photographers at work or the photographic business. The early stereo photographers turned the cameras on themselves to
show their studios, wagons, camps and equipment. Some of the studio exteriors appear in-
cidentally in a street scene, only visible with
a magnifying glass.

Major photographic exhibits and conventions were documented. There are excellent
views of the various exhibits at expositions
plus much rarer views of the National Photographer's Association annual conventions
starting in 1868. The most photographed convention was at Cleveland, Ohio, in 1870.

Values are influenced by regional interests
and subject content and condition.

Camp Scenes with Equipment
W. M. Chase of Baltimore, #1272,
"Artists Camp," close-up of man
and boy, tent and equipment ——— 20–30.00

No maker, staged view of a photographer and his curious customer, ca. 1870. This is not a true photo studio—the camera may be fake—but it is of interest to collectors. $30.

Unpublished Underwood & Underwood view of the printing department in the Underwood factory, ca. 1902. This is probably a one-of-a-kind view. $200. (Gordon D. Hoffman Collection)

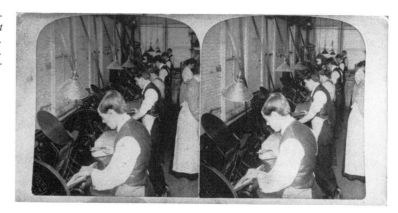

John P. Soule, #117, In White Mountains, camera and equipment _____ 60–70.00
Conventions
  Cleveland (1870)
    Anthony, #6792, Interior of exhibits hall _____ 125–150.00
    Johnson, Close view of Jeremiah Gurney exhibit _____ 150–175.00
    Thomas T. Sweeny, Group poses before Perry Monument, camera in foreground _____ 300–350.00
  Cincinnati, Delegates with banner in front of Music Hall, 1880s _____ 100–150.00
Dark tents
  G. F. Gates, In Freers Glen, N.Y., 1867 _____ 10–15.00
Exhibits, at Expositions, Fairs, etc.
  London Stereoscopic Co., #54, French photographic gallery, exhibition of 1862, tinted _____ 75–100.00
Interior of Studio
  Cameras on tripods, large skylight _____ 150–200.00
Photographers at work
  Harwood & Mooney, Charles City, Iowa, Posed in woods with equipment _____ 30–40.00

Keystone, #34419, Man with folding stereo camera talking to two French children, one with a viewer _____ 20–25.00
Kilburn, #5496, "Our Trip to the Mines," near Ouray, Colo., Kilburn on horse, equipment in view _____ 10–20.00
Underwood & Underwood, Man with box camera taking photo of kids on Brooklyn Bridge, New York City _____ 10–15.00
F. G. Weller, #333, "The Young Photographer," boy playing photographer _____ 20–30.00
Photographic Personalities
  Brigandi, Keystone, #26965, Keystone photographer holding a 32 pound, 9 foot Python snake, Fla. _____ 35–45.00
  Burton Holmes, Keystone, #18292, Author for Keystone View Co. standing in home holding a stereo viewer _____ 75–100.00
  James Ricalton, Underwood & Underwood photographer, Posed with 7½ foot Chinaman, 1900 _____ 30–35.00
Photo Wagons

Lockwood, Ripon, Wis., Interior of Lockwood's photo operating room showing posing chairs and large portrait camera, ca. 1878. $200. (Gordon D. Hoffman Collection)

Underwood & Underwood, #8288, Classic view of the stereo photographer perched out over Fifth Avenue, New York City. $45. (John Weiler Collection)

Centennial Photographic Co., #2854, at 1876 Exposition _____ 45–50.00

W. M. Green's "Reliable Photographing Travelling [sic] Gallery," trailor parked in Paris, Maine, 1870s _____ 85–100.00

Stereo Photography
(*See* Advertising in Chapter 5)

English Classic, Tinted view of couple in parlor, Brewster Stereoscope on table, 1860 _____ 10–15.00

Keystone, Tinted close portrait of two costumed Japanese girls looking at stereo views _____ 50–60.00

Pirated copy, #68, "Oh! Oh! Oh!" girl looking in large table model stereoscope, tinted _____ 25–30.00

Studio Exteriors

Gallery Row, Cleveland, Ohio, Signs for various photo studios, Superior Street, 1870s _____ 15–20.00

Thomas Houseworth, San Francisco, #150, View of building with sign, photos in windows ____ 100–150.00

J. Thurlow, #85, "Cameron's Cone," near Manitou, Colo.,

large sign on building reads "Photographs." _____ 50–60.00

Photo stand, Niagara Falls, sign reads "Stereoscopic Views of the Falls." _____ 10–15.00

Various Related Views

H. C. White, #5213, Little girl taking picture of her doll with folding camera _____ 12–15.00

Political
(See *Personalities* in Chapter 5)

Presidents
(See *Personalities* in Chapter 5)

Puerto Rico
(See *Caribbean and Cuba* in Chapter 5)

Railroads

All areas of railroading are portrayed in stereo views. There are excellent views of locomotives, passenger cars (including interiors), trains, repair shops, construction scenes and depots. The most sought after by collectors are close views of locomotives, especially in the American west.

The most stereo-photographed railroad is the Cog Railway on Mount Washington. An entire history of this railroad can be assembled from stereo views. There are excellent early construction views (1860s), including views of workers sliding down the cog tracks, the locomotives and the depots at the base and summit. The best series of the Mount Washington Cog Railway was taken by Kilburn Brothers (later B. W. Kilburn).

Views of eastern United States railroads are fairly easy to find, and as one moves further west, the supply of good railroad views tends to diminish. An exception is the building of the Transcontinental Railroad, which was completed at Promontory Point, Utah, in 1869. Alfred A. Hart of Sacramento made an excellent series of the Central Pacific Railroad. The negatives were obtained by C. E. Watkins in 1869 and published by him without credit to Hart. Watkins added to the negative file, but in 1871 his negatives were seized for nonpayment of debts by I. W. Taber of San Francisco. Taber issued the series without credit to Hart or Watkins. Watkins issued a "New Series" in the 1870s, which includes a few railroad views. A. J. Russell photographed the Union Pacific Railroad, which constructed the transcontinental route toward the west. Russell's series usually can be found with a listing on the reverse of the yellow mounts. S. J. Sedgwick obtained the negatives in 1873 and published

the series without credit to Russell. The negatives passed to O. C. Smith in about 1875, and he offered them with credit to himself into 1878. The Russell views were sold on plain yellow mounts with manuscript titles. The most sought after views from the transcontinental series show the "Joining of the Rails." C. R. Savage of Salt Lake City and A. J. Russell both recorded the historic event. "East and West shaking hands, May 10, 1869," showing the locomotives head to head and the large crowd, is the most famous view and equally the most sought after by collectors.

Other fine western railroad views were made by Thomas Houseworth, J. J. Reilly, F. Jay Haynes, Charles Weitfle, Elmer and Tenney and William H. Jackson. Many local makers photographed "the first train into town" or the newly finished depot.

One series of stereo views is difficult to categorize. This is John Carbutt's "Union Pacific Railroad Excursion to the 100th Meridian" in 1866. The series on yellow mounts includes excellent railroad views plus views of steamboats, Indians, Nebraska Territory and famous personalities. The Union Pacific reached 247 miles west of Omaha by October 1867. To promote their progress and to assure stockholders of their investment, the Union Pacific Railroad (U.P.R.R.) directors invited leading businessmen and political leaders on an excursion to the wilderness. John Carbutt, the noted Chicago photographer, was hired to make a visual record of the event. More than 200 men and their wives made the trip in the luxury Palace cars of the U.P.R.R. Thirty-six stereo

A. W. Manning of Edina, Mo., View of train at station, Hurdland, Mo., ca. 1880. $75. (Gordon D. Hoffman Collection)

views were issued on yellow mounts and are highly prized by collectors.

The major publishers, Keystone, Underwood and Underwood, Universal Photo Art, H. C. White and others made excellent railroad views after 1890. Keystone issued a boxed set of the B.&O. Railroad centenary (*see* Boxed Sets in Chapter 6) and an educational set called "Rail Transportation." (*See also* Transportation, Street Cars in Chapter 5.)

Anthony, #753, Locomotive near Port Jervis on Erie Railroad, 1860s, typical _____ 20–30.00

C. E. Brown of Boston, "View at Asbury Grove, Hamilton, Mass.," typical 1870s view by local maker in east _____ 45–60.00

John Carbutt, "Union Pacific Railroad Excursion to the 100th Meridian, Oct. 1866" (#198–233), yellow mounts

   #204, "Group of Pawnee Warriors and Palace Cars of U.P.R.R." _____ 100–150.00

   #219, "The Directors of the U.P.R.R. at the 100th Meridian," in front of train _____ 150–200.00

   #224, "T. C. Durant, Engs. & Heads of Depts., U.P.R.R.," posed by diamond stack locomotive _____ 200–225.00

Centennial Photographic Co., Locomotive on display, 1876 Centennial Exposition _____ 40–50.00

Elmer & Tenney, "Minnesota Snow View Series of 1881," blockade of Winona and St. Peter Divisions of the Central and Northwest Railroad, snow gang at work, locomotive in background _____ 45–60.00

W. A. Faze, "Local Freight between Akron and Cuyahoga Falls," Ohio,

1870s, typical Midwest local maker _____ 65–75.00

Alfred A. Hart, #47, Secrettown, Central Pacific Railroad construction site, typical _____ 200–300.00

W. H. Jackson, #98, "1,000 Mile Tree," railroad workers laying track _____ 35–40.00

Keystone

   #2367, Loop at Georgetown, Colo., common _____ 4–5.00

   #7090, Interior of Baldwin Locomotive Works _____ 7–9.00

   #37509, The chief, 1930s _____ 40–45.00

Kilburn

   #101, Close view of locomotive and crowd on trestle, Mt. Washington Railway, N.H. _____ 15–20.00

   #186, "The Engine," Mt. Washington _____ 25–30.00

   #432, Large side view of locomotive _____ 30–35.00

   #522, Mt. Washington Railway and Summit House _____ 4–7.00

   #779, Train with engineer posed, 1870 _____ 45–50.00

   #5612, Passenger train on steep ledge above Rio de Las Animas, Durango and Rio Grande Railroad, Colo. _____ 6–8.00

   Mt. Washington Cog Railway, on Jacob's ladder, workers sliding down, pushing up car, etc. _____ 4–6.00

F. A. Nims, #193, Railroad workers at handcar near Marshall Pass, Colo., 1880 _____ 20–25.00

Notman (Canada), Locomotive, tender and two cars loaded with men on frozen river, St. Lawrence _____ 15–20.00

Pirated copies, Mt. Washington Railway, no photographer noted _____ 2–3.00

Purviance, Rear of locomotive at middle distance on Pennsylvania Central Railroad, Osceola, Pa. _____ 6–8.00

W. A. Faze, Painesville, Ohio, "Local Freight between Akron and Cuyahoga Falls," Ohio, 1870s, typical Midwest local maker. $65–75.

Kilburn View Co., #186, "The Engine, Mt. Washington." $25–30.

A. J. Russell
  Great trestle near tunnel #2,
  Union Pacific Railroad _____ 12–15.00
  Train coming through cut #4,
  West of Wasatch _____ 35–45.00
  Train stopped at entrance to Echo
  Canyon tunnel #2, Union Pacific
  Railroad, west from Omaha _____ 30–40.00
  "Joining of the Rails." _____ 300–400.00
Underwood & Underwood
  Distant view of train on George-
  town Loop, Colo. _____ 4–6.00
  Passenger train on Bridge, Royal
  Gorge, Colo. _____ 4–6.00
  Train going through Pillars of
  Hercules, common _____ 6–7.00
Union View Co.
  #1411, Grand Central Depot,
  New York City _____ 7–9.00
  #1848, Railyards along Missis-
  sippi River, St. Paul _____ 1–3.00
Universal Photo Art (C. H. Graves)
  #2876, Columbian Express, Pacific Railroad, Seventy miles per
  hour _____ 15–20.00
  #4069, The great Pack Saddle on
  the Pennsylvania Railroad _____ 5–6.00
C. E. Watkins (negatives by A. A.
Hart; Central Pacific Railroad)
  #12, Bloomer Cut _____ 12–15.00
  #44, Very close view, locomotive
  Huntington _____ 70–75.00
  #153, Close view of train in Hogs
  Back Cut, Alta, Calif. _____ 60–65.00
  #339, Close view of train in Pali-
  sades, Ten Mile Canyon _____ 50–60.00
Charles Weitfle, Central City, Colo.,
1878–1881
  #251, General Grant's train in
  Royal Gorge, Colo. _____ 70–80.00
  #410, Two diamond stack locomotives on Dale Creek Bridge,
  near Sherman, Wyo. _____ 40–50.00
H. C. White, #13250, Fast express
rounding the bend, Horseshoe
Curve, Pa. _____ 8–10.00
Whitney & Paradise (negatives
probably by Hart), Bloomer Cut,
Central Pacific Railroad _____ 40–45.00

Trainwrecks

(See also Disasters)

Many wrecks were stereo-photographed, especially in the 1870s and 1880s. Few wrecks
were stereo-photographed after 1900. There
are some views of submerged or damaged locomotives and cars in Johnstown, Pennsylvania and in Kansas City.

Eastern United States, pre-1890, Wreck
near Hartford, Conn., typical, 1870s _____ 15–25.00
Midwestern United States, pre-1890,
Great Ashtabula, Ohio, bridge col-
lapse _____ 20–30.00
Western United States, pre-1890, William Caswell, Duluth, Minn., Wreck
of bridge across Mississippi, wrecked
locomotive and tender, 1875, typical _____ 25–35.00
Post-1890 views _____ 20–30.00

Risqué and Nudes

The photographing of nudes began soon after
photography and the daguerreotype were announced in 1839. Stereo daguerreotypes of
nudes were available in France and England
in the early 1850s. Paper prints of female nudes
are known from the 1850s and early 1860s
but are rarely seen in the United States. After
the Civil War, a few of the French views were
brought back to the United States by travelers.
No known United States photographers made
nudes until a series was offered by I.M.R.C.
Company in the mid-1920s. Little is known
about this company. They offered views on
gray mounts and many were in offered sets to
be used in arcade machines as "peep shows."
Most have mild nudity (bare breasts and but-
tocks); full-frontal nudity is rare. A French
photographer made a series of erotic scenes
with both male and female nudes in various

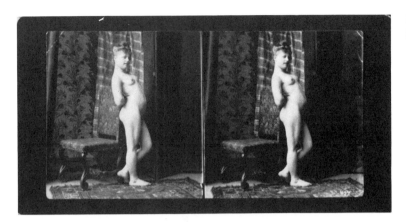

Fully nude female model in "artistic" pose, ca. 1890s. $90.

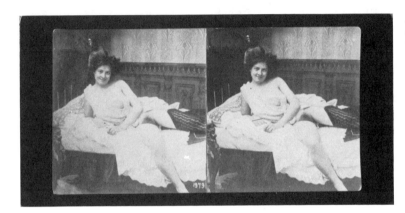

Model in erotic pose. Full-frontal nudity from unretouched negatives are rare, ca. 1890s. $175–200.

sexual acts. These are rare, especially in excellent condition. The quality of these views is generally low.

More commonly encountered are what are collectively called "risqué" views. These were made by several photographers in the United States as well as in Europe. Most are of young ladies in scanty clothes, showing stockinged legs, bare backs and the tops of their breasts. These were banned in some cities and on occasion one may find a censor's seal on the reverse of the mounts.

Nudes, Female
(*See* Stereo Ambrotypes, Daguerreotypes and Tintypes in Chapter 5)
  Pre-1875, French or English
    Breasts exposed, usually
    tinted _____ 200–250.00
    Full-frontal nudity _____ 300–400.00
  Post-1875, usually on thick buff
  or gray mounts
    Breasts exposed _____ 75–90.00
    Full nudity, not frontal, artistic

pose _____ 75–90.00
  Frontal nudity, erotic pose,
  open legs, etc. _____ 175–200.00
Risqué, various makers, U.S. and
European, no nudity
  Pre-1890, Various tease poses,
  showing stockings, etc. _____ 8–12.00
  Post-1890, Usually a comic theme
  or "naughty" ladies smoking and
  drinking _____ 6–10.00
"Lunch Time," women nursing,
usually blacks, many different
versions _____ 15–20.00

Russia
(See *Europe in Chapter 5*)

Ships and Maritime
(See *Transportation and Whaling in Chapter 5*)

Maritime history is one of the most popular categories for collectors of views. All kinds of ships, from 1850s sailing vessels through the development of steam vessels are documented in detail. The most sought are the views of the

Underwood & Underwood, #11118, Tall ships at the wharf in Montevideo, Uruguay, ca. 1910. $15. (Gordon D. Hoffman Collection)

steamship *Great Eastern*. There are views published by London Stereoscopic Company of its construction in the late 1850s plus an extensive series of the complete ship. The *Great Eastern* was the largest ship in the world and was a symbol of England's leadership in transatlantic mail and passenger service. Upon arrival in New York City in 1860, Stacy made views of the massive ship at the wharf plus a few distant views of the *Great Eastern* in New York Harbor.

There are excellent views of sailing ships including tall "Men o' War" in the 1860s, which would soon be replaced by iron steamships. The great ships of the China trade are seen in the harbors of New York, Boston, New Bedford and other seacoast cities.

The Civil War brought the need for stronger and faster ships. Steel hulls replaced wood, and steam began to replace sails. Ships of the 1870s period are seen with both sail and funnel stacks.

River steamers were documented by a number of local photographers. There are many views of the *Bristol*, a large sidewheeler. Ships of the Fall River and Hudson River Lines were photographed by Anthony and others.

Collectors seek out views of stern-wheelers on the Ohio and Mississippi rivers. Views of steamers on the far western rivers are rare but can be found with persistent hunting. There are many fine views of the busy docks in St. Louis and New Orleans and the most photographed ship of that region, the *Grand Republic*.

After 1890, there are excellent views of steamships and the few full-rigged sailing vessels then in service. Nearly every United States naval vessel in 1898 was stereo-photographed

including a large series by Underwood and Underwood. The most common is the *Oregon*, at the time the finest warship in the United States fleet.

Oceanliners were photographed leaving the ways at shipyards in England and at the docks in Hoboken, New Jersey. There are also some fine deck scenes and interiors.

Great Eastern, late 1850s–1860s
  London Stereoscopic Co. (negatives by Howlett)
    Close-up of "The Old Rigger" in rain gear posed on deck ———— 125–150.00
    General view of engine room, 1862 ———— 250–275.00
    I. M. Brunel, Builder of *Great Eastern*, seated posed with top hat in hand aboard ship, 1860 _ 550–575.00
    Maiden voyage, showing view of deck from the bow with many dignitaries ———— 100–150.00
    Viewing looking aft on deck ——— 100–150.00
    View of wrecked forward funnel after explosion ———— 50–75.00
  George Stacy, New York City
    Side view of *Great Eastern* at dock, New York ———— 100–150.00
    View of ship at distance in harbor ———— 35–50.00
  G. W. Wilson, #221, Distant view in Southampton waters, England ———— 25–30.00
Sailing Vessels
  Anthony, Vessels in New York Harbor, seen from the Battery, many versions, 1859–1873 ———— 15–20.00
  Alfred S. Campbell, #215, Racing yacht *Defender*, America's Cup race, 1895 ———— 8–12.00
  J. Carbutt, Chicago, #284, Ore dock at Escanaba, Mich., 1867, showing ship masts ———— 12–18.00
  Keystone, #V27198, Whaling

ships *Diana* and *Nova Zembla* _____ 10–15.00
Kilburn
   #772, Tudors Wharf, Charlestown, Mass., tall ships _____ 15–20.00
   #774, Tall ships at Charlestown, Mass. _____ 8–12.00
   #775, Close view of deck,
   sail/steamship, Boston _____ 15–25.00
   #776, View across decks of tall
   ships _____ 8–12.00
   #1886, View of Navy Yard,
   Ireland Island, Bermuda _____ 35–40.00
   #4138, View from Pier 11,
   many tall ships in old slip and
   South Street, New York City,
   considered one of Kilburn's
   best _____ 15–20.00
   #4970, Two-masted sailing
   vessel under Brooklyn Bridge,
   New York City, 1888 _____ 6–8.00
   #6508, View of bows of tall
   ships, New York City _____ 4–6.00
Langenheim, Packet ships tied up
at Pier 2, East River, New York
City, rare, 1856 _____ 100–125.00
H. A. Mills, Camden, Maine, two-
masted sailing vessel with town
behind, typical _____ 35–40.00
J. W. & J. S. Moulton, #44, Long
wharf and tall ships at Boston _____ 20–25.00
Franklin White of Lancaster,
N.H., 1858, South Street docks,
New York City, *Ocean Belle* dis-
plays banner for trip to Calif. _____ 75–100.00
G. W. Wilson, "HMS *Cambridge*—
gun practice," 1857, scarce view
of British Man 'O War _____ 50–75.00
Steam-Powered ships (*See* the *Great
Eastern*)
America Illustrated, yellow
mounts, negatives by Seaver,
published by Pollock in Boston
(not copies)
   End view of Brooklyn ferry
   boat under way, the *New York*,
   1870s _____ 15–20.00
   Steamer *Scythia*, Cunard Line,
   New York City docks _____ 20–25.00
   #35, Steamer *Planter* loaded
   with cotton next to tall ships,
   Charleston, S.C., 1870s _____ 20–25.00
Anthony
   #894, Ferry boat under way in
   New York harbor _____ 8–12.00
   #3942, East River, New York
   City, side-wheel steamer *City of
   Boston* _____ 15–25.00
S. T. Blessing, New Orleans,
#525, New Orleans and Mobile
Railroad station, tall stacked riv-
erboats behind station, unusual
combination _____ 35–45.00
B. F. Childs, Mich., close-up of a
Lake Superior Palace steamer,
1870s _____ 15–25.00
W. H. Cushing, Fla., Men and

women posed on deck of St.
Johns River steamer, Palatka,
1870s _____ 12–18.00
Griffith & Griffith
   #1572, (negatives by Rau)
   United States battleship *Iowa* _____ 1–2.00
   #9570, Steamer *Okahumpkee*
   on Ocklawaha River, Fla. _____ 4–6.00
   Zahner negatives Spanish-
   American War
      Reina Mercedes, Santiago Har-
      bor, 1899 _____ 2–4.00
      SS *Rio de Janeiro*, bound for
      Manila _____ 1–2.00
A. Hatch, Bath, Maine, *Eastern
City* side-wheeler of the Bath and
Boston Line _____ 60–65.00
W. H. Illingworth, St. Paul,
Minn., Steamboat landing, St.
Paul, several steamers at docks _____ 25–35.00
International View Co. (Wasson)
   #233, Sailors on United States
   cruiser *Brooklyn* _____ 1–3.00
   #528, Wreck of *Maine*, Havana, Cuba _____ 1–3.00
James F. Jarvis (Underwood &
Underwood), Sailors with dog
mascot, USS *Monitor Terror*. _____ 6–8.00
Keystone
   #9347, United States battleship
   Oregon, visitors on board at
   guns _____ 4–6.00
   #9391, Transport ship *Pennsylvania*, bound for Manila, Spanish-American War _____ 1–2.00
   #10534, Admiral Dewey's flagship *Olympia* in New York
   Harbor _____ 5–7.00
   #11269, German troops going
   to China on *Grefeld*, Bremerhaven, Germany _____ 7–9.00
   #P-26391, Mississippi steamboat at Memphis, Tenn. _____ 16–20.00
   #28890, Shipbuilding docks in
   Belfast, Ireland _____ 8–10.00
   #32042, Great Lakes steamer
   Tionesta at pier _____ 6–8.00
Kilburn
   #2058, Side-wheel steamer
   Mt. Washington, Centre Harbor,
   N.H. _____ 20–25.00
   #5160, Bow view of steamer
   Belle of Lake Minnetonka, Minn.,
   1889 _____ 6–8.00
   #10209, Tugboat under way,
   Hudson River and New York
   Harbor, 1895 _____ 6–8.00
M. Nowack, Docked steamship in
the St. Croix Dalles, crowd on
board _____ 20–25.00
Pirated Copies, without credit to the
photographers, 1870s–1880s
   Side-wheeler *Grand Republic*,
   1880s _____ 10–12.00
   Stern-wheeler *J. E. McDonald* at
   shore, 1880s _____ 5–7.00

Stereo-Travel Co., #45, of the steamer
"Roosevelt *leaving Chicago for hol-*
iday trip." 1909. $15. (Gordon D.
Hoffman Collection)

Underwood & Underwood, #13735,
SS Cleveland *during launching of her*
hull at San Francisco. Ship launch-
ings were photographed by numerous
stereo publishers. $12. (Gordon D.
Hoffman Collection)

Whaleback boat *Christopher Co-*
lumbus, 1890s _____ 2–4.00
F. A. Schelfield, Westerly, R.I., Two
side-wheel steamers, 1860s _____ 16–20.00
George Stacy, #368, South ferry
boat in the dock, New York City,
1860s _____ 16–20.00
Sterro-Photo Co. [sic], #889, Head-
on view of stern-wheel steamer,
Wisconsin Dells _____ 8–10.00
Underwood & Underwood
  Bow view of steamer *Rosa Rion,*
  Manila, 1899 _____ 1–3.00
  Stern-wheeler unloading sugar,
  New Orleans, 1890 _____ 12–15.00
  United States battleship *Oregon,*
  many different views _____ 3–5.00
  United States battleship *Indiana*
  returning from war _____ 1–2.00
Universal View Co. (William H.
Rau)
  Sailors by guns on United States
  battleship *Kentucky* _____ 4–6.00
  United States battleship *Massa-*
  chusetts _____ 1–3.00
  United States battleship *Texas* _____ 4–5.00
L. E. Walker, Two steamships
docked on Chautauqua Lake, New

York _____ 15–20.00
C. E. Watkins, San Francisco
  Yacht race, *Centennial Celebration,*
  San Francisco, 1876 _____ 40–50.00
  Ships, ferry boats in San Francisco _____ 40–60.00
H. C. White
  #7405, Bow of cruiser *Olympia,*
  1901, typical _____ 5–7.00
  General Slocum Disaster, New
  York, 1904 _____ each 15–20.00
  #8298, The *General Slocum* the
  morning after the disaster, bodies
  on the beach in background
  #8299, Divers going down for
  bodies in upper saloon, out of
  which more than 175 bodies
  were taken
  #8400, The mass of burned tim-
  bers and ruined metal, showing
  broken paddle wheel shaft
  #8401, Among the oil barrels,
  where the fire started
  #8402, All that was left of the
  boat that carried more than 1000
  souls to destruction
  #8403, On the deck of the *Slo-*
  cum, showing the effects of the

fire on metal work and steel
#8404, Stern view of the *Slocum*
#8405, Port view of the *General Slocum*

South Africa
(See *Africa and Wars in Chapter 5*)

Southern United States

Alabama
(*See also* Blacks in Chapter 5)
  Pre-1890 views
    Views of cities and towns, Montgomery, etc. _____ 15–20.00
    Scenic studies, landscapes _____ 6–8.00
  Post-1890 views
    Keystone, Birmingham, Muscle Shoals, etc. _____ 1–3.00
    Underwood & Underwood, Tuskegee _____ 8–12.00
Arkansas
  Pre-1890 views
    Eureka Springs, various makers, 1870s–1880s _____ 8–12.00
    Other towns, cities, Hot Springs, etc. _____ 15–20.00
  Post-1890 views, Keystone and others _____ 1–3.00
Florida
  Northern Part
    Fernandina, Engle & Furlong, Seaver and others _____ 6–8.00
    Gainesville, scarce _____ 15–20.00
    Jacksonville, common, many makers, 1860s–1910 _____ 2–4.00
    Lake City, scarce _____ 8–12.00
    Ocala, C. H. Colby, 1870s _____ 6–10.00
    Palatka
    (*See* Ships and Maritime views, Steam-Powered Ships in Chapter 5),
    J. G. Mangold, W. H. Cushing, J. P. Mears, Green Cove Springs

area _____ 6–8.00
    St. Augustine, Bloomfield Guide series, common, cabinet mounts _____ 1–3.00
    Florida Club (most negatives by George Pierron)
      Spanish Cathedral, Ft. Marion, etc. _____ 2–4.00
      Street scenes, people views _____ 4–6.00
    W. H. Cushing, Ober Bros. and others, 1870–1889
      Fort Marion (*see* Indians in Chapter 5), scenes of empty fort, parapets, etc. _____ 4–6.00
      Street scenes, people views _____ 5–8.00
    St. Johns River, Ocklawaha River, etc., views of moss-covered trees, palms, etc. _____ 1–3.00
    Tampa, J. C. Field and others, 1870s–1880s _____ 8–10.00
    Views of flowers, palms, palmettoes, etc. _____ 1–2.00
  Southern Part
    Pre-1890, Towns, people, etc. _____ 10–15.00
    Post-1890, Towns and people, etc. _____ 5–8.00
    Views of trees, plants, etc. _____ 1–3.00
Georgia
(*See* Expositions and Fairs, and Blacks in Chapter 5)
  Atlanta, M. M. Gardner, W. J. Land and others _____ 15–20.00
  Macon, Seaver, yellow mounts with list on reverse _____ 15–20.00
  Savannah, Havens, Ryan, Wilson and others _____ 8–15.00
  Scenes at Bonaventure, Wilson and others _____ 1–3.00
  Scenics in North Georgia, Schaub and others _____ 2–4.00
  Various other towns, local makers, 1860s–1889 _____ 15–20.00
Kentucky
  Pre-1890, Lexington, Louisville, etc., town views _____ 20–30.00
  Pre-1890, Scenics, Mullen and oth-

Bloomfield's Historical Guide series, these are fairly common on red, gray or yellow cabinet mounts with paper title labels on the reverse. $1–3 each.

Mugbier, New Orleans, La., "Clay Statue & Touro Building," ca. 1880. $20.

ers, often tinted ⸻ 8–12.00
Post-1890 Views ⸻ 3–4.00
Louisiana
(*See also* Ships and Maritime Views, Steam-Powered Ships in Chapter 5)
Pre-1890, Blessing, Lilienthal, Mugnier and others usually of New Orleans ⸻ 10–20.00
Post-1890
New Orleans, Keystone, Underwood & Underwood, etc. ⸻ 5–8.00
Views of sugarcane fields, deltas, etc. ⸻ 2–4.00
North Carolina
Asheville, Morgan, Robertson, Taylor and others, Town views, usually on cabinet mounts ⸻ 15–20.00
Pre-1890, Other town views ⸻ 20–25.00
Scenic studies, French Broad River, etc. ⸻ 2–4.00
Various post-1890 views, Keystone, etc. ⸻ 2–4.00
South Carolina
(*See* Blacks, Ships and Maritime Views and Wars, Civil War in Chapter 5)
Aiken and area, J. A. Palmer, usually on cabinet mounts, paper labels on reverse ⸻ 10–15.00
Charleston, Barnard, Newell, Quinby & Co., etc. Town views, 1860s–1880s ⸻ 15–25.00
Other town views, 1860s–1880s ⸻ 15–20.00
Various scenic studies ⸻ 4–8.00
Tennessee
(*See* Wars, Civil War in Chapter 5)
Lookout Mountain, Anthony, Linn and others ⸻ 2–4.00
Nashville and area
R. Poole and others, City view, 1860s–1880s ⸻ 15–25.00
The Hermitage, Andrew Jackson's home ⸻ 12–15.00
Webster & Albee, low-quality copies ⸻ 1–3.00
Other town views, Chattanooga,

Memphis, etc. ⸻ 15–20.00
Scenic studies ⸻ 1–3.00
Texas
(*See* Cowboys, Disasters, and Oil Industry in Chapter 5)
Austin, H. B. Hillyer and others ⸻ 25–35.00
Dallas, pre-1890 town views, rare ⸻ 35–45.00
Galveston, P. H. Rose and others, pre-1900 ⸻ 15–20.00
San Antonio, J. Hardesty, H. A. Doerr and others ⸻ 25–30.00
Various other pre-1890 town views ⸻ 35–45.00
Various scenic studies ⸻ 3–5.00
Post-1890 views
San Antonio Floral Carnival, Kilburn, People in flower-decorated wagons and carriages, 1905 ⸻ 2–6.00
San Antonio, Keystone, #32335, 34885, etc., Alamo Mission, typical ⸻ 5–6.00
Virginia
(*See also* Washington, D.C., in Chapter 5)
Arlington National Cemetery, 1866–1930s ⸻ 2–4.00
Mount Vernon, Washington's Home Langenheim, 1856–1858, ivory mount, blindstamped or with 1858 label ⸻ 40–50.00
Anthony, Bell & Bro., pre-1865
View of mansion ⸻ 10–15.00
View of tomb ⸻ 4–6.00
Alexander Gardner "The Home of Washington Illustrated" (1861–1865) ⸻ 15–30.00
N. G. Johnson (1878–1883)
East front portico of the mansion ⸻ 6–8.00
East parlor ⸻ 6–8.00
State dining room ⸻ 6–8.00
Washington's family dining room ⸻ 6–8.00
Washington's room at Mt. Vernon ⸻ 6–8.00

Various exterior views, the
tomb, etc. ———————— 4–6.00
Luke C. Dillon, James F. Jarvis,
1883–1893 ———————— 4–6.00
Various makers, Keystone, etc.,
1893–1930s ———————— 3–5.00
Pirated copies, litho printed
views, etc. ———————— 1.00
Natural Bridge
  Kilburn and others, yellow
  mounts, 1870s ———————— 2–4.00
  Various post-1890 makers, Un-
  derwood & Underwood, etc. ——— 1–3.00
Richmond
(*See* Wars, Civil War in Chapter 5)
  D. H. Anderson, Cook, Cook &
  Anderson, Selden & Co. and oth-
  ers, 1860s–1880s
    State House, Washington
    Statue, etc. ———————— 5–8.00
    Various buildings, Lee Man-
    sion, etc. ———————— 8–12.00
  Various other towns, 1870–1890 —— 12–20.00
  Various scenic studies, 1860s–
  1880s ———————— 2–4.00
West Virginia
(*See* Disasters, [Huntington, W.V.])
  Pre-1890 views ———————— 12–20.00
  Post-1890 views, Keystone, etc. ——— 6–8.00

Sports
(See also *Personalities in Chapter 5*)

Views of sporting events such as baseball games, horse races and the like are uncommon. Posed scenes and portraits of teams and individuals are more likely to be encountered. Most popular with collectors are baseball, golf and rowing. Pre-1890 views of these sports are uncommon but can be found.

The Olympics were not covered in detail until they were held in Los Angeles in 1932. Philip Brigandi made a scarce series, which he published on Keystone-type gray mounts. One of his views was offered by Keystone on their own mount (#32803). The 1936 Olympiad in Berlin, and 1952 in Helsinki were stereo-photographed by Raumbild of Germany. These are on unmounted smaller format prints in sets. The Raumbild sets were sold with a special book (the views were placed in slots in the back of the book) with a metal folding viewer (*see* Chapter 6).

Auto Racing
  Stereo-Travel, Atlanta and In-
  dianapolis races, 1909 ——— each 40–60.00
  Underwood & Underwood,
  New York to Paris "Great
  Race," 1908 ———————— each 40–60.00
Baseball
(*See* Personalities, Gehrig and
Ruth in Chapter 5)
  Lloyd's Art Gallery, Waterford,
  N.Y., local team, 1880, typical ——— 40–60.00
  Distant view of ball game and
  parks ———————— 6–10.00
Boxing
  Keystone, #V19239, Soldiers
  boxing on troop ship, World
  War I, common ———————— 4–6.00
  Views of noted boxers, fights ——— 20–25.00
Croquet players
  Kilburn, #4809, Close view of
  two couples, 1888 ———————— 8–10.00
  Mid-distance view of people
  playing ———————— 4–6.00
English Soccer
  Littleton (published by Under-
  wood & Underwood), #5297,
  Goalkeeper posed with team,
  Sheffield ———————— 5–7.00
Football
  Keystone, #26426, Yale Bowl
  during game, does not show
  game ———————— 3–5.00
  View of game in progress or
  players ———————— 10–15.00

Stereo-Travel Co., #25, "Waiting call to race," 1909 Indianapolis 500. $60. (Gordon D. Hoffman Collection)

Underwood & Underwood, #10063,
"The Thomas car (American) starting
from New York on the race to Paris,"
1908, rare view of the winning Thomas
Flyer of the "Great Race." $60. (Gor-
don D. Hoffman Collection)

Keystone View Co., #V19239 (from
Underwood & Underwood negative),
"A Friendly Bout among Our Boys,
on Transport returning from France,"
1918. #W290, in the World War I
book-boxed set. $6.

Golf
  Bay State Publishing Co., In-
  structional, close view of noted
  golfers ———————————— 20–35.00
  Keystone (from fifty-view
  boxed set)
    Bobby Jones swinging club ——— 25–40.00
    Other golfers, instructional ——— 10–15.00
Horse Racing
  Baker & Record, Saratoga,
  N.Y., View of crowded grand-
  stand, 1870s, typical ——————— 8–10.00
  Races in progress ————————— 12–15.00
Olympics, 1932, Keystone,
#32803, Opening ceremonies ——— 25–30.00
Rowing, Close view of team with
oars, 1870s ——————————————— 15–20.00

Statuary and Sculpture

Views of classic statuary and noted sculpture of the nineteenth century were very popular with customers from the 1850s through the 1890s. Fewer views were made after 1900. Today, these are not generally very popular with collectors but are excellent examples of stereo photography. Most popular with collectors are the plaster casts of John Rogers ("Rogers Groups"), which were sold in large quantities by several publishers from the 1860s into the 1890s. Rogers made statuary of familiar folksy subjects, which were sold in plaster form to decorate parlors throughout the United States.

Roger Fenton, William England and others made many views of statuary in the late 1850s into the 1870s. Views of sculptors at work are very uncommon although there are good views of marble quarries in Italy.

An excellent series was made by Powers of "Palmer's Marbles." These were done in Italy mainly for resale in the United States. Other classic Italian work is documented by dozens of makers and a large collection could be assembled at a low cost.

Most of the public statues were photographed by stereo photographers. Notable is Greenough's *George Washington*, which stood in front of the United States Capitol; St. Gauden's *Abraham Lincoln*, in Chicago; and the many works in Central Park. A collector also should look into the many series of views of World's Fairs and Expositions for additional fine examples on display, many for the first public exhibit.

Rogers Groups, many makers, including
J. B. Aiken, Charles Bierstadt (later sold
by Underwood & Underwood), J. Gurney & Son, B. W. Kilburn and John P.
Soule _____ 4–6.00
   Courtship in Sleepy Hollow
   School Examination
   Sharpshooters
   The Checker Players
   The Council of War (Lincoln and Grant)
   The Photographer
   The Slave Auction
   The Town Pump
   The Village Schoolmaster
   The Wounded Soldier
Rogers Groups, low-quality pirated
copies _____ 1–2.00
Various sculpture and statues _____ 1–3.00

Stereo Ambrotypes, Daguerreotypes and Tintypes

Collectors usually call these "hard images." None are common and the vast majority are portraits. The earliest are stereo daguerreotypes. Examples from the early 1850s exist, although earlier examples may possibly be found, primarily in European collections. Two major English makers are usually encountered in the pre-1855 examples—those by Claudet and Williams. The Claudet stereo daguerreotypes are usually beautifully composed, tinted portraits. Williams took some outdoor scenes and classic statuary; all are rare in the United States. Stereo daguerreotypes of nudes are highly prized by collectors and examples always command high prices when they reach the market. Most are not credited to the daguerreotypist, but are believed to be of French origin.

In the United States, several daguerreotypists offered stereo daguerreotypes, again mostly portraits. These were made to fit the Mascher case. Some of the Mascher stereo daguerreotypes are found without credit to the photographer or the subject. They are known in two sizes: sixth plate ($2\frac{3}{4}$" by $3\frac{1}{4}$") and quarter plate ($3\frac{1}{4}$" by $4\frac{1}{4}$"). J. F. Mascher patented this combination case and stereoscope March 8, 1853. This date often appears on the case, but most likely a particular image is from 1854 to 1858.

Stereo ambrotypes are actually much scarcer than stereo daguerreotypes; however, they usually do not command the same values. Portraits are the most common, but outdoor scenes also are known.

Stereoscopic tintypes are usually found in two forms, either as an uncut pair (pseudoscopic) or as a cut pair—mounted or unmounted. Most examples are portraits, but outdoor scenes are not uncommon. Examples identified as to photographer are rare.

Stereo Daguerreotypes
   Antonine Claudet, finely tinted _ 800–1200.00
   Williams, Mayall and others,
   English, 1851–1856 _____ 800–1200.00
   Nudes, identified outdoor scenes
   or occupationals _____ 1500–3000.00
   United States makers in Mascher
   cases _____ 500–900.00
Stereo ambrotypes
   Portraits in Mascher cases _____ 250–300.00
   Uncased (but sealed) _____ 100–200.00

No maker, probably English, ca. 1855, Stereo daguerreotype of classic nude statuary, a typical example. $800.

Stereo daguerreotype in Mascher case. The lens board at bottom flips up making the case a viewer, ca. 1855. $500–900.

Stereo tintypes
  Pairs separated and mounted
  (vintage mount) _____ 75–100.00
  Pairs separated, modern mount _____ 50–75.00
  Unmounted pair, not separated,
  pseudoscopic _____ 35–60.00

Surveys and Expeditions
(See Expeditions and Surveys in Chapter 5)

Syria
(See Near East in Chapter 5)

Tintype Stereo
(See Stereo Ambrotypes, Daguerreotypes and Tintypes in Chapter 5)

Tissues

The tissue stereo view (hold to light) is highly popular among collectors. Constructed of a four-part sandwich of die-cut cardboard with a paper positive on a thin tissue paper, the tissue stereo view is as fragile as the name implies. Many have not survived the handling of more than one hundred years of existence, and they are often found with their tissue torn beyond repair. Unfortunately, many have been repaired with cellophane tape, which has caused additional damage. Thus undamaged examples are eagerly sought by collectors. By reflected light, the tissue looks much like any other view but when backlighted, the tissue can come to life; often bright colors and pinpricks were used to simulate lights to add to the deep three-dimensional effect.

Little is known of the early makers, but by examining large collections, it has been possible to gain some insight into the manufacture of tissues. The majority made before 1895 were produced in France, thus the term "French tissues" is used. The leading makers identified themselves by blindstamping the embossed mounts with their initials such as B. K., J. A., L. L., E. L., J. Q. and G. A. F. Many are found without any imprint. Most of the French tissues are found beautifully hand tinted and pinpricked. The tinting may be a bit blotchy or sloppy on some of the lesser makers.

The most common are scenes of tourist attractions in and around Paris. There are many fine exteriors and interiors of Versailles, the Fontainebleu and various other royal residences.

Very popular with collectors are the theatrical and "Diableries" views. Several plays in Paris theaters were reproduced in sets in a diorama format. B. K. was the best maker of these. Complete sets in their original boxes are extremely rare. The "Diablo" or "Diableries" are possibly the most fascinating: They show scenes, which have been made with clay figures, that depict the Devil in hell. B. K. made a series of seventy-two views on yellow-embossed mounts. The Devil and his cohorts, their eyes ablaze in red and their jewels glittering, are seen tempting young women. These were primarily made in the 1870s but were for sale in Paris as late as 1900. In the early 1880s B. K. issued "Diableries, du Voyage Dans L'Autre Monde" on off-white mounts with red printing. These are found in boxes of six or twelve. Complete sets with undamaged boxes are very uncommon. Although B. K. issued

B. K. of Paris, #21, "La Loterie Infernale," pin-pricked and tinted, an example of a Diableries tissue, ca. 1870s, in near excellent condition (no tears). $20–30.

many tissues of plays, operas and ballets, the Diableries remain the favorite of collectors.

Hidden-subject or trick tissues are also encountered. The most common is the daylight scene that when held to the light reveals a night scene with a moon, stars and light coming from windows and streetlights. Rarer are scenes that when held to the light show fires, often with flames coming from the windows. Hidden balloons are also very popular and eagerly sought.

R. Y. Young of the American Stereoscopic Company issued tissues in the United States from about 1897 to 1905. These are on a creamy buff mount and are the same subjects as in his regular card-mounted views. They often are nicely hand tinted. He also issued a "Life of Christ," using detailed clay figures. These religious views are not popular with collectors, but have excellent stereo effect.

Condition is very important in evaluating tissues. Finely tinted, pinpricked, undamaged and near-new appearing tissues are always sought by collectors. Tissues that are damaged, stained, soiled or badly tinted have minimal value.

The American Stereoscopic Company was a major publisher from about 1897 to 1905, producing a wide variety of subjects. Of particular interest are the tinted and untinted tissues. Subjects include President McKinley, comics, children, the Los Angeles Floral Parade (1901), the Alaska Gold Rush and views of major United States cities. There is an extensive series of very realistically posed animal specimens plus "The Life of Christ."

Collectors value these tissues at about 25 to 50 percent more than the same subject on a regular mount. The American Stereoscopic Company has no relation to the Langenheim and Loyd or the New England companies of the same name.

American Stereoscopic Co. (R. Y. Young), Tissue stereo "A Marvel of Beauty—The Golden Temple, Kyoto, Japan." Offered tinted or untinted and also as a regular stereo print. $8–10 each for the tinted tissue version.

European Tissues, usually made in France
Balloon, close view _____ 60–70.00
Diableries, B. K., usually yellow embossed or white mounts, Devil, skeletons, etc., no tears or soil _____ 20–30.00
Interior or exterior scene, pinpricked with no tears, 1870s _____ 10–20.00
Interior of exterior, minor tears, but viewable with nice tinting, 1870s _____ 6–8.00
Hidden subject or "surprise" _____ 20–30.00
G. A. F.
 #25, "Tour Saint-Jacques," nicely tinted _____ 6–8.00
 #180, Palace of Senah, nicely tinted _____ 4–6.00
 #601, Tomb of Emperor Napoleon, nicely tinted _____ 8–12.00
Hanriot, #3362, Salon, Palace of St. Cloud _____ 12–15.00
Tinted view, large group of uniformed firemen with a fire wagon __ 25–30.00

Transportation

(See also Aviation, Bicycles, Railroads, and Ships and Maritime Views in Chapter 5)

This section deals with the wide range of transport seen in stereo views. Collectors are interested in all aspects of wheeled transportation but place the greatest value on views where the subject is the center of interest. There are many views where wagons, automobiles, boats and so on are incidental to the main subject. The following views are close to medium-close views, where the item of transportation is the main subject.

Automobiles
(See also Occupationals and Sports in Chapter 5)
 Close view of identified automobile _____ 15–30.00
 View of automobile as main subject, middle distance _____ 8–12.00

Not part of main subject, incidental ____ 4–6.00
Color lithograph _____ 1.00
Boats
 Ferry
  New York Harbor, identifiable ____ 10–15.00
  San Francisco, pre-1890 _____ 30–40.00
  Various locations, east of Mississippi River _____ 10–15.00
  Various locations, west of Mississippi River _____ 35–45.00
 Rowboats, Small Craft, Canoes, etc. _____ 6–8.00
Horse-drawn Vehicles, Main Subject
 Covered Wagon
  Eastern United States, pre-1890 __ 10–15.00
  Keystone, carrying supplies to Perry, Lake Erie _____ 4–6.00
  Western United States, pre-1890 _ 25–35.00
 Delivery wagons _____ 10–15.00
 Horsecars (Trolleys) _____ 15–20.00
 Omnibus (Station Wagon) _____ 8–12.00
 Stagecoach, Main Subject
  Eastern United States, pre-1890 __ 10–15.00
  Western United States _____ 65–95.00
 Surrey, Carriage, Main Subject
  Goat carriage, Central Park _____ 6–8.00
  Eastern United States, pre-1900 ___ 8–12.00
  Western United States _____ 10–15.00
  Royal coach, usually in museums and expositions _____ 5–8.00
 Two-Wheel Cart
  Canada, Ireland, 1870s–1880s _____ 6–8.00
  Red River carts, usually by Minnesota photographers _____ 15–20.00
  Various locations in the United States _____ 6–8.00
 Street Cars, Main Subject
  Cable cars, San Francisco, pre-1890
   Views by Houseworth, Watkins, etc. _____ 60–80.00
   Pirated copies _____ 5–10.00
 Electric Railways, Main Subject
  United States Cities
   New York City, Chicago, Washington, D.C. and other major cities _____ 5–8.00
   Hartford, Harrisburg, Cleveland

Keystone View Co., #17497, "733 Phaeton, 4-Passenger," scarce advertising view of the Reo automobiles known, beautifully hand colored. $30. (Gordon D. Hoffman Collection)

Leo Daft of Troy, N.Y., Buffalo East Side Railway car ready for shipment, ca. 1878, a scarce "builder's" view. $45. (Gordon D. Hoffman Collection)

"American Scenery," attributed to Seaver of Boston. This is not a pirated copy, which is indicated by separated print pairs, #31, "Mauch Chunk, Switch Back Railroad," Pa. $8.

and other medium-size cities _____ 8–12.00
Western cities, pre-1890
    Denver, San Francisco, etc. ____ 25–35.00
Post-1890 views, Underwood &
Underwood and Keystone, San
    Francisco is most common _____ 5–8.00
Foreign cities _____ 3–5.00
Various Inclined Planes
    Cincinnati, Ohio, Muhrman, Waldack and others _____ 20–25.00
    Lookout Mountain, Tenn., Linn, showing car _____ 20–25.00
    Mauch Chunk, Pa., Gates, Kleckner and others _____ 5–8.00
    Mount Holyoke, Mass., Knowlton and others _____ 8–12.00
    Pittsburgh, Pa., Albee, Purviance and others _____ 25–35.00
    Various foreign locations _____ 4–6.00
    Various other United States sites ___ 20–25.00

Tunis

(See *Africa in Chapter 5*)

Wars

Nearly every armed conflict from the 1850s to 1945 has been photographed in stereo. The slow plates and cumbersome equipment made it nearly impossible for the early photographers to capture any action scenes or actually document a battle.

The first war to be photographed during the age of the stereo view was the War with Russia—the Crimean War (1854–1856). Evidence that stereo views were made is difficult to verify. It is likely that the three major photographers who documented the conflict—Fenton, Robertson and Szathmari—made stereo views, but examples of their work are so rare that it is unlikely the general collector would ever encounter them. There are views of British troops taken in the 1855–1860 period, but these were probably made in England. There are examples in United States collections of the Austro-Italian war (1859). Views examined did not give credit to the photographer, but they are clearly marked as to subject showing troops at rest.

The American Civil War (1861–1865) is the earliest armed conflict most likely to be encountered by collectors. There are excellent views of the leading personalities, including portraits of most of the generals and politicians. There are no views of battles in progress, but many views were taken soon afterward and show the dead in the field, broken earthworks, bombed buildings and occupied forts. In addition, there are views of wagontrains moving supplies to the front and artillery brigades being brought into position. There also are excellent "camp scenes," that show cooks and their mess, field hospitals, infantry encampments and supply depots.

After Fort Sumter fell in the spring of 1861, regiments of local volunteers were established to answer the call to arms from both sides. The New York Seventh Regiment was sent to defend Washington, D.C., and set up at Camp Cameron. T. C. Roche was employed by Edward Anthony to make a record, which became a series called "Camp Life." Bierstadt Brothers of New Bedford, Massachusetts made a small series showing troops on picket duty; the views were offered both on glass and as paper prints. A number of local photographers made views of troops leaving for training camps or joining army units that were assembled in their areas. Such an example is the view by J. Q. A. Tresize of troops marching off to war in Zanesville, Ohio, in 1861. Ironically, Tresize would stereo-photograph Lincoln's funeral in his new home in Springfield, Illinois, in 1865.

The most famous series was that made by the company of stereo photographers assembled by Mathew Brady. Brady had galleries in both New York and Washington, D.C., and was already established as a supplier of photographs to the major weekly illustrated publications. At the time, it was not possible to reproduce photos directly into printed form. Instead, teams of engravers converted the images onto wood blocks for printing. Seeing the war as the news event of the century, Brady contracted to supply photos plus stereo views for commercial sale to the public. Edward Anthony was the major supplier of wet-plate photographic equipment and helped Brady by supplying materials in exchange for commercial sale of stereo views under the Anthony label for Brady and Company. The principal photographers for Brady were Alexander Gardner, Timothy H. O'Sullivan, James F. Gibson, George N. Barnard and William Bell. At first, Brady offered the stereo views as "Brady's Album Gallery" and E. and H. T. Anthony offered the series along with views by T. C. Roche as "War Views." Early in 1863, Alexander Gardner, disenchanted with Brady's handling of the business, left to go on his own, taking with him his brother, James; Timothy H. O'Sullivan; George N. Barnard; and, eventually, James F. Gibson. Gardner, O'Sullivan and Gibson were the first to document the aftermath of the Battle of Gettysburg, making approximately sixty stereo negatives. After he lost most of his best photographers, Brady was thrust into financial trouble. Beginning in July 1864, several suits were filed against Brady in Washington, D.C., for being unable to pay his rent, for nonpayment of wages to his employees as well as for money owed for work done on improving his gallery. E. and H. T. Anthony attached the stereo negatives to cover the large debt Brady owed to them for apparatus and supplies. These are the negatives now in the Library of Congress. E. and H. T. Anthony also

Alexander Gardner, #277, Dead Confederate soldier, Devil's Den, Gettysburg, July 6, 1863. $45.

E. & H. T. Anthony & Co., "War Views," #2515, "Gen. Grant's Rail Road, City Point, Va., looking South." One of the better railroad views from the Anthony Civil War series issued ca. 1864. $150. (Gordon D. Hoffman Collection)

acted as a wholesale agent for the views published by Gardner as "Photographic Incidents of the War." In 1864, Anthony issued the views as "Photographic History/The War for the Union" with paper labels on the reverse. The views were also issued on glass, but are extremely rare in this form.

Sam. A. Cooley and George S. Cook were the most famous of the stereo photographers in the South. Sam A. Cooley is best known for his views with the Tenth Army Corps in South Carolina. John P. Soule made a small series in Charleston, South Carolina, at the time of the flag raising at Fort Sumter in April 1865.

The Civil War views sold briskly during the conflict but after the surrender and the sad assassination of Lincoln, the country was thrust into a melancholy. Anthony issued Civil War views taken in the southern states as "Southern Scenes," without mention of the war. After the financial depression of 1873, Anthony curtailed much of its stereo views business and put the war negatives in storage. In 1880, two private collectors, General Albert Ordway of Washington, D.C., and Colonel A. Rand of Boston obtained the Anthony war negatives. They attempted to sell the negatives to the United States government, but without success. Sometime between 1881 and 1884, John C. Taylor of Hartford, Connecticut, purchased the negatives. With a partner, a man named Huntington, Taylor established the publishing firm Taylor and Huntington, which was located at 2 State Street in Hartford. Using the original negatives, the series can be found on orange or cream cabinet mounts as "1861 The War for the Union. 1865/1861 Photographic

War History. 1865." In approximately 1885, the business was moved to 21 Linden Street in Hartford and became "The War Photograph & Exhibition Company." There was much resistence to the price of $0.30 for each view at a time when most views were selling for $1.50 per dozen. Taylor wrote "A Word as to Prices" on the back of the mounts. Although of high quality, sometimes printed better than the vintage views, the Taylor and Huntington reprints were not very successful.

There is a misconception that the Taylor and Huntington views are very common. In the mid-1970s, a large hoard of the series was discovered in New England. These apparently were unsold stock and most of the views were in excellent condition. This large group was broken into smaller lots and sold by at least a dozen dealers. These views are now in collections throughout the United States. In the next ten to twenty years, these collections will come back into the market and the views will again be available in excellent condition. In the early 1980s, most Taylor and Huntington reprints sold for about one-fourth to one-half of their vintage versions. But in the last two years, the reprints are, in some cases, being offered at prices equal to the vintage Anthony and Gardner views. Collectors will always want the first issues, much as book collectors want first editions.

Gettysburg Battlefield has always been a popular tourist attraction and from 1865 into the early 1900s, many different views of the battlefield were sold. C. J. Tyson, Levi Mumper and W. H. Tipton all issued fine views of Gettysburg, including some made from negatives obtained in 1863. Many major publish-

Taylor & Huntington, Reprint Civil War issue, #740, 'Hospital at Fredericksburg, Va., May, 1864.'' $45.

Taylor & Huntington, reprint Civil War issue, #2531, ''Embalming Surgeon at Work,'' $65.

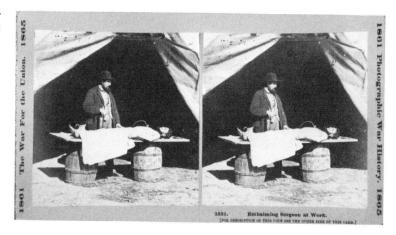

ers issued views copied from popular prints of battles by Prang and others. These are not in stereo.

Veterans of the Civil War began meeting for reunions in the 1870s, some of which are documented by local makers. Grand Army of the Republic (G.A.R.) reunions were covered in detail by the major publishers after 1890. These usually show parades and rarely include close views of veterans at encampments.

In the 1930s, Keystone sold a few views copied from vintage views in the Library of Congress, including the "fuzzy hair" portrait of Abraham Lincoln and Lincoln seated with McClellan in a tent at Antietam.

The Franco-Prussian War (1870–1871) was not covered in the detail of the American Civil War. Views of bombed cities and towns are fairly common. Rare are views of troops in camp or in close formations. Like the Civil

War, battle scenes were not possible. At least one posed scene has been examined. The Battle of Champigny, where the German infantry killed or captured 20,000 French troops, was the Gettysburg of this conflict. The Paris Commune shows the famous city under arms with ruins, street barricades and scenes of riots. Many of these views are posed but still are interesting. E. Linde made the largest series, which are usually on yellow mounts.

The Greco-Turkish War (1897) was best stereo-photographed by Bert Underwood. Less common are the views by Keystone and Kilburn, many of which are posed, showing, for example, a Greek soldier at the scene of a former battle.

The Boer War (British Colonial War in South Africa) took place from 1899 to 1902. This conflict had been brewing since 1834, when the British in Cape Colony freed the slaves of the Dutch settlers of South Africa (the Boers). Rather than conform, the Boers resettled in two republics, the Transvaal and Orange Free State. After gold was discovered in Transvaal in 1895, foreigners (Uitlanders), who were mostly British subjects, poured into the independent country. The Boers refused to grant these people—mostly prospectors—political rights but taxed them anyway. The British protested and the Boers sent an army into British territory in South Africa.

The Boers at first overwhelmed the British troops, but the tide turned when Lord Roberts was sent with crack troops to end the siege. Most of the stereo views show Lord Roberts's troops and include numerous views of camps and supply depots. Excellent views were offered by Keystone, Kilburn, Underwood and Underwood and H. C. White. Most of the battle scenes are staged but appear very realistic.

The Spanish-American War (1898–1899) and the insurrection in the Philippines (1899–1901) were covered in detail by most of the major publishers. There are excellent views of United States naval vessels, wrecks of Spanish ships in Manila and Puerto Rico plus the wreck of the *Maine* in Havana Harbor. Most of the ''battle'' scenes are actually practice exercises in Georgia or Florida. There are some gruesome postbattle scenes in the Philippines where the bloody insurrection continued after Spain sued for peace. Kilburn made the best views in the Philippines, although there are views by others.

The Russo-Japanese War (1904–1905) was the first conflict with stereo view coverage of actual battle scenes. Most of the views center around the Battle of Port Arthur, which lasted

eight months affording the photographers an opportunity to make many fine views. There also are excellent views of the fall of Mukden in Manchuria and the defeat of the Russian fleet in the Strait of Tsushima. In addition, several photographers made views in Japan showing troops at the emperor's birthday celebration as well as views in hospitals.

World War I (1914–1918) was covered in a documentary style by stereo photographers. The first American stereo photographer on the scene was Albert K. Hibbard, who was in Europe at the outbreak of the war making a series of industrial and occupational views for Underwood and Underwood. He rushed to the Serbian front and made views of the overwhelmed and outmoded Serbian army. He then worked his way back to France to cover the early days of the conflict. In December 1914, seeing that the conflict was going to last longer than a few months, Kaiser Wilhelm announced that journalists and photographers could not be guaranteed protection. Upon hearing of this, Bert Underwood ordered Hibbard home. He arrived in the United States about January 1, 1915, and Underwood and Underwood soon afterward issued their boxed set ''The European War,'' without credit to Hibbard.

Realistic Travels Company in England issued a fine set that showed the British side of the war. A few French photographers issued views, some as stereo postcards.

W. E. Troutman of Reading, Pennsylvania, issued a series of at least 300 views after the war. Many of these are copies of Realistic Travels views plus some staged scenes made in Pennsylvania. There are a few in this series

Keystone View Co., #18632, ''Zeppelin Wrecked and Burned—Ruins Being inspected by French Troops.'' $4.

that appear only under his name but may have been obtained from amateurs or local photographers in Europe.

The most common World War I views are those issued by Keystone View Company. The Keystone View Company views show the battlefields soon after the Armistice was signed. Andrew S. Iddings was hired to photograph the battlefields not covered by Hibbard in 1914. About 1919, Keystone had obtained the Underwood and Underwood negatives of the war. These were renumbered and given the prefix *V.* Early examples issued by Keystone give copyright credit to "Underwood & Underwood," again not mentioning Hibbard. In addition to the Hibbard negatives, Underwood and Underwood had obtained other war negatives, apparently from a British photographer. These show the battles for the Dardanelles. In addition to the Iddings negatives, Keystone added negatives purchased from an unknown French photographer (or photographers) as well as made views of training in the United States and of installations at places like Fortress Monroe, Virginia. Keystone sent a photographer to the Peace Conference in Paris. Later they made a series of the American Legion reunion in the 1920s. Unlike the Civil War views, the World War I views remained popular sellers in the years following the war (*see* Chapter 6).

World War II was covered by the Raumbild firm in Germany. The firm was founded by Otto Wilhelm Schonstein in the early 1930s as Raumbild-Verlag. The views were in a smaller than standard 6 cm by 13 cm size on unmounted print paper (similar to the Keystone Junior). They were sold as part of books with a folding metal viewer (*see* Sports in Chapter 5). Raumbild covered the rise of the Nazi Third Reich including the Reichsparteitag Convention and the invasion of Poland in 1939.

Keystone offered some rarely seen views of postwar ruins plus B-36 airplanes (*see* Aviation in Chapter 5). According to the files of the company, now in California, the wartime views were censored by the War Department and not issued until after the Armistice.

World War II was the last commercial venture for stereo photography. There may exist amateur views of Korea, Vietnam and the Arab-Israeli Six-Day wars. View-Master issued a three-reel packet of Vietnam, which shows the influence of the war and the United States presence.

Crimean War (1854–1856)
  Examples are rare to nonexistent. Anyone having such views should have them expertized by an authority on British military history.
Austro-Italian War (1859)
  View of troops in camp, ivory mounts, rare _____ 50–75.00
Civil War, American War between the States (1861–1865), Vintage views from original negatives
  Anthony (issued until 1873), Three-digit numbers are from negatives supplied by Alexander Gardner as "Photographic Incidents of the War" (*see* Gardner below)
    #2282, Block house near Aqueduct Bridge, Arlington Heights _____ 20–25.00
    #2311, Interior of Fort Richardson, Va., soldiers and cannons _____ 35–45.00
    #2339, Fort Sumner on the Chickahominy, Va. _____ 20–25.00
    #2392, Wheatfield where General Reynolds was killed (Gettysburg, mistitled, is actually McPherson's Woods. Man in midforeground is Mathew Brady) _____ 125–150.00
      Version without Brady _____ 15–20.00
    #2397, Rebel Prisoners, Gettysburg, (negative by Brady) _____ 25–30.00
    #2442, Colonel Chapman and staff at his headquarters in the field, Army of the Potomac, Va. _____ 30–40.00
    #2495, Thirteenth New York Artillery winter quarters before Petersburg, Va. _____ 30–40.00
    #2497, Negro children, Aikin's farm, James River, Va. _____ 40–50.00
    #2509, Bodies laid out for interment at the burial ground, Fredericksburg, Va., (dead rebels) _____ 15–20.00
    #2542 and 2543, Celebrated Aikins Landing, where all the Rebel prisoners are exchanged on James River near Dutch Gap, the double-turreted monitor *Onondaga* at anchor in the river _____ 30–40.00
    #2591, Jefferson Davis, one of General Grant's saddle horses at City Point, Va. _____ 20–30.00
    #2635, View from an elevation in front of the Capitol, Nashville, Tenn. _____ 20–30.00
    #2676, Group of scouts, City

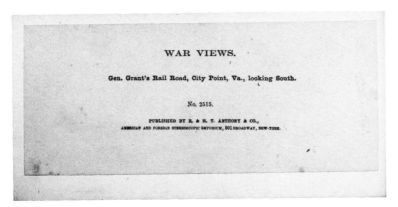

WAR VIEWS.

Gen. Grant's Rail Road, City Point, Va., looking South.

No. 2515.

PUBLISHED BY E. & H. T. ANTHONY & CO.,
AMERICAN AND FOREIGN STEREOSCOPIC EMPORIUM, 501 BROADWAY, NEW-YORK.

E. & H. T. Anthony, "War Views" label. Fronts of the yellow or orange mounts are usually imprinted "Photographic History, The War for the Union." These are vintage prints sold during or just after the Civil War. Some were still available as late as 1873.

Point, Va. _____ 30–40.00
#2692, Monitor *Casco*, James River, Va. _____ 25–30.00
#2728, Park of captured Rebel guns, Richmond, Va. _____ 20–30.00
#2908, Portrait of Commodore Theodore Bailey, United States Navy _____ 20–25.00
#3031, Front view of Dunlop house, Petersburg, Va., showing effect of shot and shell, typical view _____ 25–35.00
#3071, Graves of the Union soldiers who died at the race course, Charleston, S.C. _____ 15–20.00
#3103, Broad Street, Charleston, S.C., looking east _____ 25–35.00
#3139, Interior of Fort Sumpter [*sic*], Charleston Harbor, S.C., April 14, 1865, pending ceremony raising the old flag _____ 20–25.00
#3174, Ruins in the burned district, Richmond, Va. _____ 20–25.00
#3178, A dead Rebel soldier, as he lay on the foot passage in the trenches of Fort Mahone. Bloody soldier after Petersburg, Va., April 2, 1865 _____ 70–75.00
#3181, Rebel artillery soldiers, killed in the trenches of Fort Mahone, two dead Confederates, close-up after Petersburg, 1865 _____ 75–80.00
#3187, This view was taken in the trenches of Fort Mahone after the storming of Petersburg, Va., Rebel dead in trenches _____ 15–25.00
#3188, This view was taken in the Rebel trenches after the storming of Petersburg, shows dead Rebel soldier _____ 25–35.00
#3199, Bomb proofs in the Union Fort Sedgwick, called by the Rebel soldiers "Fort Hell," Petersburg, Va., April 2, 1865, morning after it was taken by

Union soldiers _____ 40–50.00
#3200–3202, Union picket line in front of the rebel Fort Mahone _____ 15–20.00
#3206–3208, "Chevaux de Frise," in front of the rebel works at Petersburg, Va., morning after storming, 1865 _____ 20–25.00
#3243, Ruins in the burned district, from the Petersburg railroad depot, portion of arsenal grounds, Richmond _____ 20–25.00
#3267, Double pontoon bridge on the James River, Richmond, Va. _____ 20–25.00
#3291 and 3292, The Custom House, Bank Street, Richmond, Va. _____ 20–25.00
#3334 and 3335, Interior view of Fort Sedgwick, Petersburg, Va. _____ 20–25.00
#3364 and 3365, Libby Prison, Richmond, Va. (negative by Brady), typical _____ 20–30.00
#3387, Colonel Ord at the mansion formerly occupied by Jefferson Davis, Richmond, Va., in the doorway is the table on which the surrender of General Lee was signed (the table is now at the Chicago Historical Society) _____ 30–40.00
#3405–3407, The chair that President Lincoln occupied at the time of his assassination at Ford's Theater _____ 50–70.00
#3436, Unitarian and German Lutheran churches, Archdale Street, Charleston, S.C. _____ 20–25.00
#3505, View on the blockade runner *Ruby*, on Morris Island, S.C. _____ 30–40.00
#3572, View near Savannah, Ga. _____ 15–20.00
#3602, The original Swamp Angel gun, Morris Island, S.C. _____ 20–25.00
#3622, Panoramic view of

Richmond, Va. _____ 20–25.00
#3880, Major General Philip
H. Sheridan, seated portrait _____ 65–75.00
#3882, Major General Oliver
O. Howard, 1865 _____ 70–80.00
#3900, Brigadier General C. R.
Wood, 1865 _____ 85–95.00
#4004, Fort McAlister, Ga.,
showing the place where General Sherman's men carried the
fort by storm _____ 20–25.00
#4013, Colonel Burk and staff,
taken at Fort Hamilton _____ 50–70.00
Bierstadt Bros., Pickets on the
alert, Lewisville, Va. _____ 25–35.00
Brady, "Brady's Album Gallery"
#197, Beauregard gun, Fort
Pulaski, Georgia _____ 40–50.00
#326, Lewis House, near Bull
Run _____ 35–45.00
#350, General McClellan's
tent, Camp Winfield Scott, near
Yorktown, May 1, 1862 _____ 45–60.00
#357, Group: Comte de Paris,
Duc de Chartres, Prince de
Joinville and friends at Camp
Winfield Scott, near Yorktown,
May 1, 1862 _____ 60–70.00
#359, Group: Servants of officers of staff, Camp Winfield
Scott, near Yorktown, 1862 _____ 60–70.00
#412, Front line of Confederate works, showing General
McClellan's Battery No. 1 _____ 50–60.00
#414, Water Battery, Yorktown, looking toward
Gloucester _____ 35–45.00
#436, General Stoneman and
staff, at his headquarters near
Fair Oaks _____ 70–80.00
#441, General Caldwell and
staff, at Fair Oaks, June 1862 ____ 70–80.00
#496, General Fitz John Porter
and Staff, at headquarters, Westover Landing, Va., 1862 _____ 80–90.00
#500, Panoramic view from
the center of battlefield of Cedar Mountain, Union Camp in
the foreground, mountain in
distance _____ 50–60.00
#554, Confederate soldier,
who, after being wounded
dragged himself to a little ravine where he died, Antietam ____ 60–70.00
Gardner "Incidents of the War,"
E. & H. T. Anthony, wholesale
agents (photographer's name in
parenthesis)
#158, Moss-covered tomb,
more than 150 years old, on
Port Royal Island, S.C.
(O'Sullivan) _____ 20–25.00
#204, Fort Beauregard, Bay
Point, S.C. (O'Sullivan) _____ 35–45.00
#228, "Farmers' Inn and Hotel, Emmitsburg, where our

special Artist was captured,"
July 5, 1863 (Gibson) _____ 50–60.00
#237, The Home of a Rebel
sharp-shooter, on the Battlefield of Gettysburg (Gibson) _____ 45–50.00
#246, Scene near the woods
on Confederate center, at the
Battle of Gettysburg (Gibson) ____ 25–30.00
#249, Scene in the woods at
the foot of Round Top, at the
Battle of Gettysburg (Gibson),
group of dead bodies _____ 45–50.00
#274, War, effect of a shell on
a Confederate soldier at the
Battle of Gettysburg (Alexander
Gardner), gruesome, soldier's
dismembered hand next to gutted body _____ 45–50.00
#294, Headquarters *New York
Herald,* Army of the Potomac
(O'Sullivan) _____ 50–60.00
#300, Forts on Heights of
Centreville (Barnard) _____ 45–50.00
#327, Beauregard's Headquarters, Manassas (Barnard) _____ 45–50.00
#334, Fort on Heights of
Centreville, mounting Quaker
Guns, March 1862 (Barnard) ____ 45–50.00
#351, Group: T. Anderson,
Esq., Lieutenant Colonels
Fletcher and Neville, Major
Pearson, Prince de Joinville,
Comte de Paris, General Van
Vliet, G. Sheffield, S. L. Arny
and Duc de Chartres, at Camp
Winfield Scott, near Yorktown
(Gibson) _____ 60–70.00
#361, View of Gloucester and
Yorktown (Gibson) _____ 35–45.00
#379, Battery No. 4, near
Yorktown, mounting ten 13"
mortars, each weighing 20,000
pounds, east north end
(Gibson) _____ 60–70.00
#389, Group of General Andrew Porter's staff, May 20,
1862 (Gibson) _____ 60–70.00
#428, Lieutenant Washington,
a Confederate prisoner, and
Captain Custer (Gibson) _____ 700–800.00
#439, Major Robertson's Battery of Horse Artillery, near
Richmond, June 1862 (Gibson) ____ 70–80.00
#460, Water Battery, Gloucester, mounting fifteen heavy
guns (Barnard) _____ 30–40.00
#465, Main entrance, Hampton Church, Va., July 2, 1862
(Barnard) _____ 25–35.00
#516, Ambulance train, Falmouth (O'Sullivan) _____ 60–70.00
#517, Rappahannock Bridge,
south view (O'Sullivan) _____ 30–40.00
#557, Gathered together for
burial, after the Battle of Antie-

tam (O'Sullivan) _____ 50–60.00

#566, Confederate soldiers as they fell at the Battle of Antietam (Gardner) _____ 40–60.00

#576, General Hooker's headquarters during the Battle of Antietam (Alexander Gardner) ____ 50–60.00

#605, Group: President Lincoln, Generals McClellan, McClernand and Marcy, and Garrett, Hatch, Lamon, Kennedy and others before reviewing the troops on the Battlefield of Antietam, Oct. 3, 1862 (Alexander Gardner) _____ 1500–2000.00

#611, Antietam Bridge, south view (Gibson) _____ 40–60.00

#635, General Averill and staff, Westover Landing, August 1862 (Gardner) _____ 60–70.00

#641, Benson's Battery of Horse Artillery near Fair Oaks, June, 1862 (Gibson) _____ 90–100.00

#645, Scene at Blackburn's Ford, July 4, 1862 (O'Sullivan) _____ 20–25.00

#683, View at Fredricksburg (Gardner) _____ 40–60.00

#777, Union soldier at Charles City Courthouse, Va., 1864 _____ 30–40.00

R. Newell, Philadelphia (typical local maker) Rosedale destroyed by Rebels, Chambersburg, Pa., July 30, 1864, often tinted _____ 20–30.00

John P. Soule, #370, Mills House amid ruins of Charleston, 1865, black and white men seated _____ 25–30.00

C. J. Tyson, Gettysburg, Pa., #573, General Lee's headquarters _____ 10–15.00

Taylor & Huntington, War Photograph & Exhibition Co., Hartford, Conn., reprints from original negatives

#217, Close-up of officer's mess, Co. D, Ninety-third New

York Infantry, tents behind ____ 130–150.00

#274, Effect of a shell on a Confederate soldier at the Battle of Gettysburg, gruesome, dismembered hand next to gutted body (negative by Alexander Gardner) _____ 25–30.00

#458, Magruder Battery at Yorktown (negative by G. N. Barnard) _____ 20–30.00

#2289, Chain Bridge near Washington, D.C., close view ____ 15–20.00

#2557, Pontoon Boats on the way to Dutch Gap _____ 20–30.00

#3679, Ft. McAllister, Ga. _____ 10–15.00

#6705, Powder Magazine with soldiers _____ 30–40.00

Postwar

Gettysburg Battlefield

Mumper, Tipton and other local makers, View of monument _____ 4–6.00

Keystone, Underwood & Underwood and others _____ 2–4.00

Related views, no stereo effect (post-1890)

Griffith/William H. Rau, drawing of Sheridan's Charge, often tinted _____ 2–4.00

Universal View Co./William H. Rau, drawing, Battle of Antietam, often tinted _____ 2–4.00

The Franco-Prussian War (1870–1871)

J. Andrieu (J. A.), E. Linde and others

Bombed buildings, typical _____ 6–8.00

Views showing troops close-up _____ 12–15.00

Greco-Turkish War (1897)

Underwood & Underwood, #(62), Large crowd at demonstration before Royal Palace after Grecian defeat, Athens, 1897, typical _____ 4–6.00

Taylor & Huntington, reprint Civil War issue, #163, "General I. I. Stevens and Staff, Beaufort, S.C., March, 1862." $45.

Taylor & Huntington, reprint Civil War issue, #6258, ''A Crippled Locomotive in Richmond.'' $75.

James F. Jarvis (sold by Underwood & Underwood), ''Gen. Grant's Brigade leaving Newport News for Porto [sic] Rico,'' 1899. $6.

Spanish-American War
(1898–1899), Insurrection in the
Philippines (1899–1901)
  Jarvis (Underwood & Underwood)
    Kentucky volunteers in camp _____ 4–6.00
    Large formation of Fourth
    Ohio, Newport News, Va. _____ 2–4.00
    Soldiers on review for President
    McKinley, Camp Alger, Va.,
    1898 _____ 3–5.00
  Keystone View Co. _____ 2–4.00
    #9120, Troop K, Tenth U.S.
    Cavalry
    #9246, ''Some of Our 'Heroes'
    of the War Bound for Cuba,''
    mules and horses on dock
    #9250, Boarding the transport
    boats for Santiago
    #9387, Soldiers and their
    sweethearts on the eve of departure for Manila
    #9520, Officers Third U.S. Engineers at mess, Chaplain Sam
    Small at Head of Table
  Underwood & Underwood
    A hot time on the firing line,

    Philippines _____ 3–5.00
    A problem the Filipinos
    couldn't solve _____ 3–5.00
    Co. H, Fighting Washington
    Volunteers at Taquig,
    Philippines _____ 3–5.00
    Co. G., Washington Volunteers,
    Pasig _____ 5–7.00
    Dead Filipino on battlefield _____ 2–4.00
    Gun crew with cannon,
    Philippines _____ 5–7.00
    Men posed before General
    McArthur's Headquarters _____ 4–6.00
    Ninth Infantry, formation, Las
    Pinas _____ 1–3.00
    Soldiers firing rifles, Philippines _____ 1–3.00
    Troops on street in Pasay,
    Philippines _____ 4–6.00
    Troops rest on firing line,
    Philippines _____ 1–3.00
  Whiting View Co., #571, Flag
  draped-caskets, burial of *Maine*
  victims, Arlington Cemetery _____ 1–3.00
Boer War (South African War, 1899–1902)
  Keystone
    #11814, British cavalry at

Pretoria _____ 1–3.00
#11836, British camp, 1900 _____ 1–3.00
#11840, Formation of cavalry,
1900 _____ 3–5.00
#11844, British cavalry seen
across Veldt, 1900 _____ 1–3.00
#11881, Imperial army wagons
pulled by oxen _____ 3–5.00
Underwood & Underwood
Artillery firing, typical _____ 5–7.00
Draught bullocks (oxen) captured by Gordon Hussars on
Modder River _____ 4–6.00
Fording Modder with army
supplies _____ 4–6.00
New Zealand Hill defenders firing rifles from behind sand-
bags _____ 3–5.00
H. C. White _____ 5–8.00
#8051, Medical Corps exercis-
ing on deck of troopship *Nor-
man*
#8055, "Cleaning the equip-
ments [sic]," Greenpoint Camp,
Cape Town
Boxer Rebellion (1900)
Kilburn
#13904, Close view of Boxers
posed with long flintlock rifles,
1900 _____ 8–12.00
#14356, Close view of man
holding severed head of a
Boxer, pile of heads at his feet,
gruesome _____ 25–35.00
#14890, Beheaded Boxers laid
out on the ground, severed
heads at sides _____ 35–45.00
Underwood & Underwood (negatives by Ricalton)
Beheading scenes, gruesome _____ 35–45.00
Most others, bombed towns,
etc. _____ 4–7.00
H. C. White _____ 5–8.00
#3817, Village of Fung Chow,
showing complete destruction
by "Allied" force
#3829, Queen's Indian Troops
(Sikhs) on guard in grounds of
summer palace near Peking
Russo-Japanese War (1904–1905)
Underwood & Underwood
#4380, General view of Port
Arthur, typical _____ 4–6.00
#7559, Shell being fired at Port
Arthur _____ 4–5.00
#7595, Japanese soldiers dig-
ging trench _____ 1–3.00
#14501, Russian soldiers on
Parade, Port Arthur _____ 1–3.00
H. C. White
#8311, Japanese soldiers with
rifles _____ 2–4.00
#8317, Field Marshal Marquis
Oyama and his wife in Tokyo
Garden _____ 3–5.00
Whiting View Co., #9041, Japa-

nese soldiers on review _____ 1–3.00
World War I
(*See* Boxed Sets in Chapter 6)
Keystone (*V* prefix are from Underwood & Underwood nega-
tives) The views were primarily
sold in sets; views without position numbers are scarce and may
not have appeared in a set.
#19133, Marshall Foch, Gen-
eral Pershing and others at
Paris, typical _____ 2–4.00
#V19234, United States Army
tractor negotiating steep declivi-
ties of Rhine, typical reissue
from Underwood negative, this
view was #43 in the 48-view
set, #91 in the 100-view, #182
in the 200-view and #276 in
the 300-view set _____ 2–4.00
Realistic Travels, Sold in sets, not
common in the United States,
most views show British troops _____ 3–5.00
Troutman, Sold in sets. Print
quality varies from excellent to
poor, scarce _____ 3–5.00
Underwood & Underwood,
Found with and without position
numbers on gray mounts, although most were sold in sets,
scarcer than Keystone regular or
the *V* prefix reissues
#12022, Driving out the in-
vader—fighting the Germans
house to house _____ 4–6.00
#12303, In a French trench—
sandbag protected, men pose
by early rockets _____ 4–6.00
#12339, At Mass in the allied
trenches on the Western front _____ 3–5.00
Various other makers _____ 6–8.00
Color lithographs from drawings
and black-and-white lithographs
from unknown source _____ 0.50–1.00
World War II
(*See* Aviation in Chapter 5 and
Boxed Sets in Chapter 6)
Keystone, usually with paper title
label on reverse, bombed London,
etc. _____ 10–15.00
Raumbild-Verlag, sold only in
sets.

Washington, D.C.
(See also *Southern United States in Chapter 5*)

Our nation's capital has been continuously
stereo-photographed from 1855 to date. The
Langenheims made a series in 1855, which
was updated in 1858. John McClees made a
rare series in 1857. By 1861, a number of stereo
photographers had made views of the city,
mostly of the famous public buildings such as
the Capitol and White House. Most notable

are the views by Anthony, New York Stereoscopic Company, Mathew Brady and George Stacy. Some of these early views show the Capitol building without a dome or in the construction stages of the new dome. During the Civil War, Alexander Gardner and George N. Barnard (for Brady) made views of the city plus scenes of fortifications at the bridges over the Potomac River.

After the Civil War, the leading makers of stereo views of Washington, D.C., were the Bell Brothers (F. A. and C. M.), who made a remarkable series of most of the major buildings, streets and the newly developing street railway system. About 1870, James F. Jarvis opened a photoprinting establishment and was responsible for printing many of the western survey views (*see* Expeditions and Surveys in Chapter 5). Jarvis issued an extensive series of the city, including one of the best series of the White House. In addition, Jarvis photographed many historical events (*see* personalities in Chapter 5). In the late 1880s, Jarvis signed an agreement with Underwood and Underwood for them to publish and sell his views.

There were many local makers who made significant views, including C. S. and L. Cudlip, M. P. Rice, T. W. Smillie (many fine views of the Smithsonian) and G. D. Wakely.

Other nice series were published by D. Barnum, the Kilburn Brothers (later B. W. Kilburn), W. M. Chase, J. W. and J. S. Moulton and John P. Soule. After 1890, every major publisher offered Washington, D.C., views. Keystone was still adding negatives as late as 1952!

Collectors seek out views of the Capitol under construction, historic events in the city, the Smithsonian, the Washington Monument (in unfinished form or being completed) and busy street scenes. The most common street scene was published by J. F. Jarvis from the early 1870s to about 1897. This is a scene of busy Pennsylvania Avenue looking toward the Capitol from the Treasury Building. There are dozens of versions showing various types of street cars as well as wagons and carriages.

Anthony
#283, Military asylum, close view	25–30.00
#914, Pennsylvania Avenue, from Willard's Hotel	12–15.00
#1309, South front of the White House	10–12.00
#1311, Encampment on White House grounds	30–40.00
#2987, Treasury Building draped for the funeral of President Lincoln, 1865	40–45.00
#3000, View of Georgetown, the Potomac and Chesapeake Canal, from rear of the Observatory	12–15.00

D. Barnum, View of White House, ca. 1860, uncommon _____ 10–15.00

Bell Brothers
Corcoran Art Gallery, 1860s	5–7.00
Interior of Senate Chamber, 1867	8–9.00
Library of Congress in Capitol, men at reading tables	8–12.00
Old Capitol Building, 1866	6–8.00
United States Patent Office, interior with models in cases between columns	10–12.00
Various exterior views of Capitol and White House	4–6.00

"Brady's Album Gallery," rare
Capitol from near Trinity Church	40–60.00
Willard's Hotel, and Treasury	20–30.00

W. M. Chase
#1012–1015, Statuary, United

E. & H. T. Anthony, #11034, "Interior of Smithsonian Institute," showing mounted dinosaur skeleton, ca. 1873, a scarce subject. $40.

Keystone View Co., #11938, "President-elect Wilson and President Taft Coming to the Front of the Inaugural Stand—Inauguration Ceremonies, March 4, 1913, Washington, D.C." $12.

States Capitol _____ 2–3.00
#1066, United States Treasury _____ 4–6.00
#1119, Corcoran Art Gallery _____ 5–7.00
C. S. & L. Cudlip (1870s) Exterior
of White House, typical _____ 4–6.00
Alexander Gardner, rare
  #1, Capitol Building (negative by
  Barnard) _____ 40–60.00
  Views of the city _____ 25–35.00
James F. Jarvis (*See also* Underwood
and Underwood in Chapter 4)
  Pennsylvania Avenue looking to-
  ward the Capitol, common, often
  tinted _____ 5–8.00
  The White House, interiors,
  tinted _____ 3–5.00
  Various public buildings _____ 6–8.00
Langenheim (also available on
glass)
  Capitol Building showing Bul-
  finch Dome intact, 1855, rare _____ 200–300.00
  Views of the city _____ 40–60.00
Keystone View Co.
  #186, Garfield Monument and
  Capitol _____ 2–4.00
  #220, Pension Building _____ 3–5.00
  #224, The Capitol _____ 2–4.00
  #8057, United States Treasury
  Building _____ 2–4.00
  #8086, The Reading Room,
  Congressional Library _____ 3–5.00
  #8097, United States Treasury,
  $1,600,000 _____ 6–8.00
Kilburn
  #7257, View from Agricultural
  Department _____ 2–4.00
  #7630, Bird's-eye view _____ 3–5.00
  #7631, War Department and
  White House _____ 3–5.00
John McClees, Views of the city,
1850s, rare _____ 60–80.00
J. W. & J. S. Moulton of Salem,
Mass.
  #1, The Capitol (front view) _____ 2–4.00
  #20, Long Bridge _____ 4–6.00
  #76, Fresco painting, dome of
  Capitol _____ 1–2.00

#109, Pennsylvania Avenue _____ 6–8.00
New York Stereoscopic Co., Views
of the city, often tinted, 1850s,
rare _____ 25–35.00
M. P. Rice (1870s) Views of public
buildings _____ 5–7.00
T. W. Smillie
  Smithsonian, exterior views _____ 5–7.00
  Smithsonian, interior views _____ 10–12.00
  Various public buildings _____ 4–6.00
George Stacy, often on yellow
marks without credit imprint
"American Scenery" with neg.
number & manuscript title on re-
verse. Views of city, ca. 1860 _____ 12–15.00
Underwood & Underwood
(1888–1897; from Jarvis nega-
tives) _____ 2–5.00
Universal Photo Art (C. H. Graves)
  #3760, East Room, White
  House _____ 3–4.00
  #3784, Fourteenth Street, or
  Thomas Circle _____ 4–6.00
G. D. Wakely (1865), View of the
city _____ 8–10.00
Richard Walzl of Baltimore, published views from Chase negatives
(*See* W. M. Chase in Chapter 4).
H. C. White
  #101, The Treasury Building _____ 3–4.00
  #131, The Green Room, White
  House _____ 2–4.00
  #157, Statue of Garfield _____ 1–3.00
  #8174, East Room decorated for
  Prince Henry's visit, common _____ 1–3.00

Western United States

Arizona Territory Views (1863–1890)
  Flagstaff
    Wittick & Russell of Albuquer-
    que, Views of town, early
    1880s _____ 45–50.00
  Florence
    D. F. Mitchell, View of town,
    late 1870s. _____ 45–50.00
  Fort Yuma
    G. H. Rothrock, Views of Fort,

1870s _____ 75–85.00
Grand Canyon (*See also* Arizona
Territory Views [post-1890] be-
low)
  J. C. Burge, Scenic studies,
  1880s _____ 10–15.00
  Mohave County
    G. H. Rothrock, Scenics, late
    1880s _____ 10–15.00
  Phoenix
    J. C. Burge, D. F. Mitchell,
    Rothrock & Barnett, Views of
    town _____ 45–50.00
    Scenic studies in vicinity _____ 10–15.00
  Prescott
    D. P. Flanders, D. F. Mitchell
    and G. H. Rothrock, Views of
    town _____ 50–60.00
  San Xavier (views of Mission)
    Charles O. Farciot, D. P. Flan-
    ders and G. H. Rothrock, Exte-
    rior view _____ 12–15.00
    Views of shrubbery, cactus, etc. _____ 6–8.00
Arizona Territory Views (post-1890)
  Grand Canyon and area
    Keystone, #29093, El Tovar
    Hotel as seen from Hopi House,
    Indians in lower foreground,
    late 1920s _____ 3–5.00
    Kolb Brothers (1910–1930s),
    Views of canyon _____ 6–8.00
    Underwood & Underwood,
    Rapids of Colorado River as
    seen from Pine Creek, 1903 _____ 2–4.00
    Universal Photo Art (C. H.
    Graves), #5675 and 5676, Ti-
    tan of Chasms _____ 2–4.00
    H. C. White
      #12206, Scenic, looking
      down Granite Gorge from
      below Bright Angel _____ 1–3.00
      #12215, Low storm clouds
      hanging across Grand
      Canyon _____ 1–3.00
      #12217, Study of the canyon
      from Grand View Point,
      1906 _____ 4–5.00
      #12219, Pack horses de-
      scending Copper Mine Trail,
      1905 _____ 3–5.00
  Non–Grand Canyon Views (*See*
  Mining in Chapter 5)
    Keystone
      #13718, Man with horse-
      drawn disk cultivator in Salt
      River Valley _____ 3–5.00
      #32705, Coolidge Dam, near
      San Carlos, 1930s _____ 4–6.00
California
(*See also* Logging and Lumbering,
Mining, and Railroads in
Chapter 5)
  Alta
    A. A. Hart, #70, Blasting Chalk
    Cliffs, many workmen _____ 50–70.00
  Berkeley

Keystone, #13299, Earthquake
fissure, 1906 _____ 3–5.00
Big Trees (Mariposa Grove)
  Keystone _____ 5–7.00
    #5006, The Wawona Tree
    #5007, The Fallen Monarch
  C. E. Watkins, #1163, Looking
  up big tree _____ 20–25.00
  H. C. White _____ 6–8.00
    #694, Cabin in the Upper
    Grove
    #701, Looking through Wa-
    wona Tunnel
    #704, Looking down trunk
    of fallen monarch with cav-
    alry on horseback
Calaveras Grove
  Keystone, #9471, Group at
  "Pioneers Cabin." _____ 3–5.00
  C. L. Pond, Pioneers Cabin
  with people _____ 15–25.00
Cascades on Chilnoalna River
  C. Bierstadt, #1210, Scene on
  river _____ 10–12.00
Farallone Islands
  Watkins _____ 10–12.00
    #2012, Natural Arch
    #2015, Sugar Loaf
Geysers (Sonoma County)
  J. C. Brayton, Witches' Caul-
  dron _____ 7–9.00
  Thomas Houseworth _____ 10–15.00
    #1158, Witches' Cauldron
    and Group of People
    #1159–1162, The Witches'
    Cauldron
    #1163 and 1164, The
    Witches' Cauldron and
    Devil's Pulpit
  Andrew Price, #13, Devil's
  Laboratory _____ 15–20.00
  C. E. Watkins
    #1284, Geyser Hotel, with
    carriage _____ 25–35.00
    #1572, Devil's Canyon _____ 8–10.00
    #1574, Steamboat Geysers _____ 10–12.00
    #1583, Geyser Hotel _____ 35–40.00
    #1592, Calistoga Hotel _____ 10–15.00
    #1593, Calistoga Hotel _____ 25–30.00
Hollywood
  Keystone, #V26385, Overview
  of Universal City movie studios,
  1920s _____ 8–12.00
La Jolla
  H. C. White _____ 3–5.00
    #649, Sculptured by the
    sea—natural arch in the cliffs
    #650, A curiously carved
    cliff
Los Angeles
  Anthony, #10805, Grading
  Fort Hill _____ 35–45.00
  Keystone, #32331, City Hall
  Building _____ 2–4.00
  Kilburn #9968 and 9969,
  Overview of city from hills,

1895 _____ 12–18.00
Mount Shasta
  Underwood and Underwood,
  #6014, Snowcapped mountain
  seen from valley _____ 3–5.00
Oakland
  Houseworth, #1426, Brayton
  Hall, Oakland College, 1870 _____ 20–30.00
Pasadena
  Keystone
    #9034, Man posed in floral
    park, often tinted, 1898 _____ 3–5.00
    #13528, Boy and girl watch
    as baby ostriches hatch _____ 3–5.00
Redlands
  Underwood & Underwood
    #5956, Overview of orange
    grove _____ 2–4.00
    #32319, Overview from
    Twin Peaks _____ 3–5.00
  Kilburn
    #984, Russian Hill, pano-
    rama _____ 8–12.00
    #4411, Cliff House and Sea
    Lion Rocks _____ 3–5.00
  Lawrence & Houseworth,
  #480, View on Harrison Street,
  Rincon Hill _____ 20–30.00
  A. J. McDonald, Fisherman's
  Wharf, many small boats,
  1885 _____ 50–60.00
  Muybridge
    #162, Alcatraz from Black
    Point _____ 45–60.00
    #389, California Street, busy
    scene _____ 100–125.00
    #626, Telegraph Hill from
    wharf, 1870s _____ 20–30.00
  J. J. Reilly, #121, Market
  Street _____ 25–30.00
  Universal Photo Art (C. H.
  Graves)
    #5513, Chinese on China-
    town street _____ 15–20.00
    #5515, Moonlight on San
    Francisco Bay _____ 1–2.00
    #5558, Seal Rocks, moon-
    light _____ 1–3.00

C. E. Watkins
  #701, Overview from Rincon Hill _____ 20–25.00
  #768, Panorama from Russian Hill _____ 15–20.00
  #973, Panorama from Pine
  and Stockton Streets _____ 20–25.00
  #1744, Lick House dining
  room _____ 35–40.00
  #3679, California Street
  from Montgomery Street,
  with horse car (New Series) ____ 20–25.00
  #3684, United States Branch
  Mint _____ 20–25.00
  #3685, Mercantile Library
  Building _____ 30–35.00
Pirated copies
  Cable Car, Clay Street Hill
  from 1868 view _____ 20–25.00
  Chinese store, Chinatown _____ 4–6.00
  Pacific Insurance Co. Building _____ 2–4.00
  Pacific mail steamer in
  drydock _____ 4–6.00
  Top floor, Palace Hotel _____ 1–3.00
  Seal Rocks _____ 1.00
Riverside
  Underwood & Underwood
  Man working sluice, orange
  grove _____ 3–5.00
  #5959, Man in carriage,
  Magnolia Avenue _____ 6–7.00
Sacramento
  E. Anthony (negative by Weed)
  #67, Overview of city,
  1860s _____ 40–45.00
  #77, State House _____ 45–50.00
San Bernardino Springs
  New York View Co., Overview
  of buildings _____ 3–5.00
San Diego
  Parker & Parker, #6, City seen
  from hill, several Victorian
  houses, 1870s _____ 40–50.00
San Francisco
  (*See also* Disasters in Chapter 5)
  Continent Stereo Co., #76,
  Ferns, Woodward's Garden _____ 5–7.00

*Lawrence & Houseworth, #203,
"Portsmouth Square or Plaza, San
Francisco," 1866. $50.*

Thomas Houseworth
(*See also* Lawrence & House-
worth in Chapter 4)
#210, Bank of California,
northwest corner of Califor-
nia and Sansome streets _____ 20–25.00
#355, From corner of Cali-
fornia and Powell Streets
looking northeast _____ 25–30.00
#462, Interior of the old
Mission Church, Mission Do-
lores _____ 40–50.00
J. F. Jarvis (Underwood & Underwood)
Chinatown scene, 1892 _____ 12–18.00
View of Seal Rocks, Cliff
House _____ 1–3.00
Keystone View Co.
#5045, Cliff House and Seal
Rocks, moonlight _____ 2–4.00
#5060, Market Street, cable
cars in front of "welcome"
arch, 1899 _____ 10–15.00
#16507, Overview of city
showing rebuilding after
earthquake and fire, 1908 _____ 15–20.00
#16743, Overview of city
showing Market Street _____ 6–8.00
San Gabriel
Keystone, #13555, Ladies in
front of San Gabriel Mission _____ 2–4.00
San Jose
Watkins, #192, Academy of
Notre Dame _____ 15–20.00
Santa Barbara
Hayward & Muzzall, Falls in
Mission Canyon _____ 6–8.00
Tuttle & Lee, #17, Fountain
Head, Hot Springs, men and
boy in view _____ 8–12.00
Sonoma
(*See* Geysers, page 166)
Yosemite
(*See* National Parks in Chapter 5)
Colorado
Arapahoe Peak
Keystone, #11646, Man and

pack horses on a slope _____ 2–4.00
Box Canyon
Underwood & Underwood,
#10644, Boy stands at
walkway _____ 1–3.00
Cathedral Spires
Keystone, #2410, People in
surrey _____ 1–2.00
Clear Creek
Continent Stereo Co., Big Hole
in the Rock _____ 1–3.00
Kilburn, #2939, Railroad
tracks _____ 2–4.00
Weitfle, #53, Railroad tracks,
scene below falls _____ 5–7.00
Colorado Springs
Gurnsey, #112, Cupola from
school building _____ 15–20.00
Denver
Kilburn, #5650, Interior of
Trinity M. E. Church _____ 3–5.00
Alexander Martin, #154, Six-
teenth Street, close street view
with horse-drawn trolley _____ 75–85.00
C. Weitfle, #245, Overview,
east from Tower _____ 40–50.00
Garden of the Gods
Keystone, #W23252, Gateway,
Garden of the Gods _____ 1–3.00
Kilburn, #5559, "The Ship,"
rock formation _____ 1–2.00
Savage of Salt Lake, Scenic
study of rocks _____ 2–4.00
Underwood & Underwood,
People at Balancing Rock _____ 1–2.00
Georgetown
Kilburn, #5542, Overview of
city, 1890 _____ 7–9.00
Georgetown Loop
W. H. Jackson, #1735, Train
stopped on track _____ 30–35.00
Keystone, Kilburn and others,
showing train on the loop _____ 5–7.00
Color litho of train on loop _____ 1.00
Guadelupe
William H. Jackson, #5197,
Interior of Chapel of the

Strohmeyer & Wyman (published by Underwood & Underwood), view of Pike's Peak, from Peep-Hole, Colo., 1894. This view has many variants and is very common. $2.

Spring ——————————— 15–20.00
Leadville
William H. Jackson, #1108,
Harrison Avenue, street scene,
very dramatic ——————— 75–85.00
C. Weitfle, #42, Chestnut
Street, men in street ———— 45–50.00
Manitou Springs, J. Thurlow
(1870s)
#86, Interior Manitou House
with Christmas tree decorated
with United States flags, 1875 —— 15–20.00
Mesa Verde
Underwood & Underwood,
#10652, canyon scene ————— 1–3.00
Palmer Lake
Keystone, #2403, Phoebe's
Arch, 1898 ———————— 1–3.00
Pike's Peak
J. Collier, #117, Overall view
from valley ——————— 3–5.00
Keystone, #26908, As seen
from plains ——————— 1–2.00
Underwood & Underwood, As
seen through "Peephole," kids
in foreground, several variants
exist ————————— 1–3.00
Quaker Rocks
Charles Bierstadt, #10, Scenic
study ————————— 1–2.00
Royal Gorge (Grand Canyon of
Arkansas)
Underwood & Underwood,
Railroad tracks and bridge ——— 1–3.00
Ute Pass
J. Thurlow, supply train in
Pass, covered wagons on grade
(1870s) ————————— 20–30.00
Vulcan's Anvil
Keystone, #2434, Boy in front
of rock formation ————— 2–4.00
Dakotas
Dakota Territory
(*See* Expeditions and Surveys in
Chapter 5)
Deadwood
Melander (negatives by Ro-
dacker & Blanchard), Albert
Pollock and others, Boom
town, town views in Gulch ——— 40–50.00
Fargo
F. Jay Haynes
#17, Railroad tracks
showing locmotive ———— 65–75.00
#310, Grandin Elevator,
by river ——————— 20–25.00
Groton
F. Q. Miller and C. H. Carli,
View of town, 1880s ———— 30–40.00
Mitchell
C. W. Johnson, the "Corn
Palace," ca. 1900 ————— 30–40.00
Yankton
Delong, S. J. Morrow, Views
of town ——————— 40–50.00

Post-1890 views
W. R. Cross views of Dead-
wood, Lead City Town views —— 20–30.00
Scenic studies, Hot Springs,
etc. ————————— 8–10.00
Keystone, Black Hills, etc. ——— 1–2.00
Idaho
Pre-1890 views are uncommon
Town views, Muskogee, Silver
City, etc. ——————— 20–30.00
Scenic studies, Snake River,
etc. ————————— 6–8.00
Post-1890
Keystone, #37581, People in
heated outdoor pool, Sun Val-
ley, 1930s ——————— 3–5.00
Others ————————— 5–8.00
Kansas
Pre-1890 views are uncommon
"Life and Scenes in Kansas,"
Conklin & Kleckner of
Atchison ——————— 30–40.00
J. R. Riddle, Scenes of Topeka
and area ——————— 25–30.00
Military installations, E. E.
Henry at Fort Leavenworth,
etc. ————————— 35–45.00
Scenic studies ————— 6–8.00
Post-1890
Local makers —————— 6–8.00
Major publishers, Keystone,
etc. ————————— 2–4.00
Montana (Territory)
Butte (City) (*See* Mining in Chap-
ter 5)
N. A. Forsyth, views of town —— 15–20.00
Bozeman
Calfee & Catlin, Street views
with mule teams, etc. ———— 125–150.00
Columbia Gardens
N. A. Forsyth, #21, Men in
rowboat, typical ————— 3–5.00
Scenic studies —————— 3–5.00
Nebraska
Lincoln
Clements, State buildings,
1870–1880s —————— 20–25.00
Omaha
J. Carbutt, Hamilton, Jackson
Bros., town views, 1865–
1870s. ———————— 40–50.00
Other town views ————— 20–30.00
Post-1900 views, scenic studies,
etc. ————————— 5–8.00
Nevada (*See also* Mining in Chap-
ter 5)
Carson City
Thomas Houseworth, #695,
City and valley from the west —— 20–30.00
C. E. Watkins, #4071, Capitol
Building, 1876 ————— 45–60.00
Las Vegas and Area
Town views, very uncommon —— 45–50.00
Scenic studies, cactus, etc. ——— 6–8.00
Lake Tahoe and area

Thomas Houseworth, #677,
Summit of Cave Rock _____ 8–10.00
Virginia City
Continent Stereo Co., C Street
with wagons and horses _____ 30–35.00
Lawrence & Houseworth
#709, Wells Fargo & Co.'s
express office, C Street, busy
scene, stagecoach _____ 300–400.00
#715, View from Interna-
tional Hotel _____ 45–50.00
Watkins, #217, "All Aboard
for Virginia City," three stage-
coaches loaded and ready to
roll, in front of Wells Fargo _____ 125–175.00
Post-1890 views, Keystones, Sce-
nic studies _____ 4–6.00
New Mexico
(*See* Expeditions and Surveys in
Chapter 5)
Albuquerque
Continent Stereo Co., Street
scenes _____ 10–15.00
Santa Fe
Bennett & Brown, W. Henry
Brown, Town views, usually
yellow cabinet mounts _____ 35–45.00
Gurnsey, #220, San Francisco
Street with group of donkeys _____ 12–18.00
H. T. Hiester, Town views,
1870s _____ 45–50.00
Taos
W. H. Jackson, #2701, Pueblo
de Taos, 1880s _____ 60–70.00
Scenic studies, shrubbery, cactus _____ 6–8.00
Post-1890 views, Keystone, etc. _____ 3–5.00
North Dakota (*See* Dakotas above)
Oklahoma
Pre-1900 views (rare)
Fort Sill (*See also* Indians in
Chapter 5) Will Soule, Views of
fort _____ 75–100.00
Town views _____ 50–75.00
Post-1900 Views
Keystone view of Oklahoma
City, common _____ 3–5.00
Views by local makers _____ 10–15.00

Oregon
Columbia River
C. E. Watkins
#1244, Castle Rock _____ 5–7.00
#1297, The Tooth Bridge _____ 8–10.00
Portland
Crawford & Paxton, #117,
Overview of city showing
buildings, late 1880s, scarce _____ 50–70.00
C. E. Watkins, #1206, Pano-
rama of city _____ 25–30.00
Willimette Falls
C. E. Watkins, #1221, Mill and
town, 1869 _____ 20–30.00
Scenics of the falls _____ 4–8.00
Post-1890 Views
Mount Hood, Waterfalls, etc. _____ 2–5.00
Town views _____ 8–10.00
South Dakota (*See* Dakotas, page 169)
Texas (*See* Southern United States
in Chapter 5)
Utah
Pre-1900 Views
Ogden Canyon, Johnson,
#3723, scenic study _____ 2–4.00
Ogden City, C. E. Watkins,
Overview of town _____ 35–45.00
Salt Lake City
C. W. Carter, Interior of
Tabernacle _____ 7–12.00
C. L. Clement, New city and
county building, 1905 _____ 4–6.00
C. R. Savage, Two boys by
shore of lake _____ 2–4.00
Woodward, #1901, Taber-
nacle _____ 7–9.00
Pre-1880s, Street scenes,
construction scenes, etc. _____ 35–45.00
Post-1900 Views
Keystone, Underwood & Un-
derwood, etc. _____ 3–5.00
Washington (*See* Farming in Chap-
ter 5)
Baker Lake, Mt. Baker
Darius Kinsey, Scenic studies _____ 8–10.00
Seattle
Ball & Sons, Peterson Bros. and

*J. J. Reilly & J. P. Spooner, #396,
"Salt Lake City, Utah," ca. 1870s,
scarce view by California maker. $35.*

Darius Kinsey, #458, "Mt. Baker, 11,500 feet high, from Baker Lake, Wash.," 1903. $10. (John Weiler Collection)

others, Views of city	20–25.00
F. Jay Haynes, Front Street "after the fire," 1890	35–45.00
Keystone and others, post-1890	6–10.00

Spokane
Kilburn, #10510, High Bridge at Spokane Falls, 1896	15–20.00

Tacoma
Haynes, Looking north on Pacific Avenue	45–50.00
Others, post-1890s	8–10.00

Walla Walla (*See* Farming in Chapter 5)
S. W. Beers, views of town	20–25.00
Scenic studies, waterfalls, etc.	4–6.00

Wyoming (*See* National Parks, Yellowstone in Chapter 5)
(Town views are rare)
Cheyenne
Colorado View Co., #220, Carnegie Library, ca. 1905, light gray mount	8–12.00
C. D. Kirkland, D. S. Mitchell, Town views	45–50.00
Other town views	50–60.00
Scenic studies	5–6.00

Whaling

The whaling industry was documented in detail by several stereo photographers. Most notable is the series by J. Freeman of Nantucket. Now a major tourist attraction, Nantucket was a busy whaling center and drew summer residents who visited the island village. The Freeman views are uniform in tone and quality and rarely one finds an uninteresting subject. There are outstanding views of beached whales, skinning blubber (some tinted), lifesaving crews and equipment plus views of the town and local resident "types."

Bierstadt Brothers and later S. F. Adams made fine views of whaling ships at New Bedford.

These are not nearly as common as the J. Freeman series, but they are worth looking for and will add to a collection.

Shute and Son of Edgartown, Massachusetts made a twelve-view set "A Whaling Voyage," which used models on a tabletop and realistic scenes made with clay and oil cloth. Variations exist within the set, so more than twelve views can be obtained.

G. H. Nickerson made a few whaling views as part of his extensive maritime series at Provincetown, Massachusetts.

All of the above-mentioned series were made before 1880. By the 1880s, the whaling industry had declined and there were fewer views to be made. Keystone issued a view of a modern steel-hauled whaler towing a catch near Spitzbergen, Norway, and Underwood and Underwood made a view of a large beached whale being skinned on Long Island.

Bierstadt Bros. (later S. F. Adams), whaling ships at New Bedford, very uncommon	65–75.00

J. Freeman, Nantucket (*See* Eastern United States in Chapter 5)
Beached whales	35–50.00
"Cutting in" a finback whale, by ship	50–60.00

Keystone
#14768, Floating whale station, common	6–8.00
#V27198, (reissue of Underwood & Underwood view), whalers cruising, common	4–6.00

Nickerson, Provincetown, Mass., Cutting off blubber at side of ship, 1870	40–50.00

Underwood & Underwood
Whalers cruising in Dexterity Harbor	4–6.00
#4700, Gunner on Arctic whaler	10–15.00

#11232, Skinning whale, Long
Island _____ 8–12.00

Wire Walkers
(See *Daredevils and Wire Walkers in Chapter 5*)

Zoos
(See *Animals in Chapter 5*)

F. Jay Haynes scenic study of falls in Oregon from scarce northwest series of Yellowstone cabinet mount, circa 1880. $10.

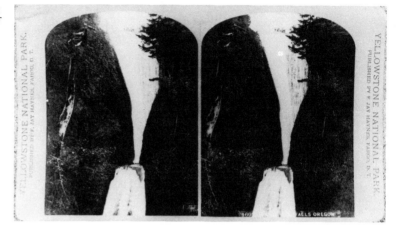

6

BOXED SETS

This chapter deals with sets sold in special containers as a unit. There are many sets or "series" made from the 1850s on that were sold as groups. The earliest known boxed set was issued by Edward Anthony. This was the twelve-view "The Place of Prayer or Stereoscopic Illustrations of the Fulton St. Prayer Meeting" (1857). The set was made just a few blocks from Anthony's New York City Gallery at the North Dutch Church, of which Edward Anthony was a member. It is believed this may have been a fund-raising campaign. The set of twelve in a special box with a paper label sold for $3 or individual views could be had for $0.30 each. Apparently other small sets were offered in boxes by E. Anthony but examples have not been examined.

Delos Barnum issued a set of historic scenes in Boston (1859), and a thin cardboard folder was issued to hold one dozen selected views from the series. A. J. Fisher of New York City issued green-and-buff boxes, but these were not made for special sets. C. E. Watkins sold views in a special box that held up to twenty-four views. Again, the box was not specifically made for a particular set.

The first company to systematically sell boxed sets was Underwood and Underwood. In 1897, the Underwoods issued their first set in a slip-

case box. This was a set of seventy-two views that comprised a "Tour of the World." Up until 1900, stereo views were sold in dozens or half dozens. Thus the seventy-two views were equivalent to six dozen, or half a gross. The set sold briskly from the start, and they soon added other sets of individual countries plus a tour of the United States. About the turn of the century, the Underwoods began offering the sets in "volume boxes" or "book boxes." They also added descriptive books, written by noted authorities, to the most popular sets.

Unfortunately, most of the early Underwood and Underwood stereographs are unnumbered. Numbers within a set appear either imprinted at the top or reverse center or in parentheses just before the title at the bottom front. The Underwood salesmen were able to offer special sets that could be ordered for a customer. These can be found with numbers marked with either a rubber stamp or hand-script ink.

The Underwoods' chief competitors saw the success of this selling strategy and began issuing sets. The only major company that failed to follow the Underwoods' lead was B. W. Kilburn View Company of Littleton, New Hampshire. James M. Davis was in charge of distribution, and apparently he thought the boxes

Lynn Skeels of Washington, D.C., photographed his personal collection of book-boxed sets, ca. 1945. This would be regarded by collectors as a photographica view. Skeels was a professional stereo photographer plus an avid collector. He made most of the sets for Stereo-Travel Co. as well as his own published views of the airship USS Macon *and views of President Truman.*

were nothing more than a sales gimmick. Although Kilburn made a number of unified series, they never issued a boxed set. Keystone, H. C. White, Universal Photo Art, Griffith and Griffith, Stereo-Travel and Whiting View Company all issued boxed sets. The Griffith and Griffith and Whiting View Company sets are rare. Lynn Skeels broke from the Stereo-Travel Company about 1912 and issued his own sets as the Globe Stereoscopic View Company. These sets are also rarely offered.

It is reported that Underwood and Underwood's production was 25,000 stereographs per day in 1901. A large portion of these were sold in boxed sets. Hundreds, maybe thousands, of boxed sets have been broken up over the years, and the views have been sold individually. Thus some sets are scarce.

Keystone View Company took the boxed set idea one step further by developing an educational system. Much of their success after 1902 was the sale of this system. Thousands of sets were sold to schools, public libraries and larger churches for Sunday School lessons. The Keystone system got away from the twelve/twenty-four/thirty-six/seventy-two concept of selling in dozens to selling sets of fifty or one hundred views, along with the special guidebooks and maps. They hired the noted world traveler Burton Holmes to edit the system. Later in the 1930s, Lowell Thomas was hired to follow Holmes.

Collecting boxed sets can be a good way to obtain a fine collection at a low price. Few sets sell for as much as their combined parts, which is another reason so many sets have been broken up. Furthermore, there is confusion regarding the numbering of these sets. For the

Keystone sets, there can be a number of editions of the same set. There were at least a dozen editions of the "Tour of the World" set, which makes it very difficult to know what views are missing when a set is incomplete. A view may have been in position #9 in the earliest edition but could have become position #23 in the next edition—the position number usually appears at the top center on the front. In about 1920, Keystone printed a "position number box" on the reverse of the mounts for sets sold in more than one size. Different negatives also would replace a position, making another change.

Between 1912 and 1921, Keystone obtained the Underwood and Underwood negatives and reassigned their negative numbers with a V prefix. For example, #V23927 T, "Life in the Land of Confucius—Street scene in Canton, China" can be found as position #141 or #282 in the "Tour of the World." As the V prefix indicates, this view is from an Underwood and Underwood negative and appeared earlier in the "China" set issued by that company. A collector missing position #282 from his 400-view set might not realize that #141 in the 200-view "Tour of the World" is the same view. Therefore, even though a common view may be found to be missing, it could be difficult to find one with the correct position number. As a result, collectors prefer complete sets, as issued, with all the correct numbers. About 1921, Keystone expanded the "Tour of the World" from 100/200/400 views to 600 views. The set was completely overhauled; outdated views were replaced with "modern" scenes. They had obtained excellent negatives of the H. C. White Company of North Bennington,

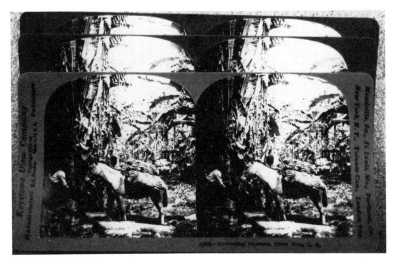

Keystone View Co., #12804, "Harvesting Bananas, Costa Rica, C.A.," is a very common view and was used in a number of boxed sets. Here the view is seen without a set position number, #35 is as it appeared in the 400-view "World Tour" and #294 is the position in the 600-view "World Tour."

SERIES	400	200	100
POSITION	35	20	13

would ripen too fast. In the United States there are large warming-houses in the large railroad centers where the fruit has the chill taken off if it has traveled in our winter cold.

The tree-like banana plant is a great sucker or shoot from an underground rootstock. It bears from 50 to 150 flowers in a cluster— blossoms each with a long, tube-like ovary crowned by colored petals. After the petals have fallen the energy of the plant goes to

A detail of the reverse of Keystone, #12804, showing the box at upper-right corner that indicates set positions. This appears on Keystone sets in the late 1920s. As can be seen, the view was also #20 in the 200-view "World Tour" and #13 in the 100-view "World Tour." Thus to complete a set, one must have the correct numbered views. This is a frustration for collectors who find their missing view but without the correct number corresponding to their incomplete set.

Vermont. These were renumbered and given a *W* prefix.

In about 1929, Keystone began issuing a 1200-view "Tour of the World." They also added an oak cabinet for storage, mainly aimed at schools and libraries. The 1200-view tour was still being updated and offered in the early 1950s! Like the 600-view tour, the 1200-view tour was made in a number of editions. In the early 1930s, the economic depression made the $600 1200-view "Tour of the World" a luxury item. The sets were renumbered; a single asterisk prefix indicated the view was in the 600 set and two asterisks indicated that the view was from the 1200 set. These were

replaced with diamonds in about 1932. As a result, a 600-view "Tour of the World" can be found "complete" today with numbers ranging from 1 to 1200. This was a sales ploy that permitted the salesman to offer one-half of the 1200-view set, and once sold he could return a few months later to sell the missing 600 views to complete the set. Unfortunately many customers could not afford the second 600 views.

Also during the Depression, Keystone came up with the idea of selling personal sets. A salesman would call on the customer to sell them a 600- or 1200-view "Tour of the World" and offer to have a stereo photographer visit their home to make views of the family. Furthermore, a preference for a particular subject was answered by removing less interesting subjects from the set and replacing them with views of greater interest. Therefore, an Italian-American could remove views of China or England and replace them with Italian views from the large Keystone inventory. A 600-view set was recently examined from a Pittsburgh estate that had a large run of coal mining views which replaced the South American views. Also in the box were six views of the family in their living room.

In 1933, Keystone began offering the "Keystone Junior" sets. These are sets of twenty-five views on thick, unmounted print paper in a smaller format than the standard-mount views. They were sold with a metal viewer. The Junior views are not as popular as the full-size views, but often contain subject matter difficult to find in the standard size.

Other sets of interest were made from 1914 to 1952. A German company offered a smaller format set of thirty-six views of the "Berkshire Knitting Mills of Reading, Pa.," which came in a green book box with a folding metal viewer. The same company made sets, but not in boxes, of cities in California as well as a rare set showing the filming of the classic silent film "The Hunchback of Notre Dame" in the 1920s.

Possibly the most unique sets sold in the period just prior to World War I and into the 1920s are those by the Corte-Scope Company of Toledo and later Cleveland, Ohio. The Corte-Scope photographer traveled throughout the Midwest selling large manufacturing concerns on the idea of a commercial package that included the folding Corte-Scope viewer and a series of views illustrating their factories and products. This package was then distributed to salesmen who used the viewer and views as a selling tool. The Corte-Scope Company be-

The Corte-Scope folding viewer and a box set of views. The viewer was made in several versions in several different size boxes and set sizes. Most complete sets, $250–300.

gan in Toledo, Ohio, in 1911 as the American Corte-Scope Company. The early sets are of low quality and are uncommon. In 1915, the company was reorganized in Cleveland, Ohio, and hired Albert K. Hibbard as the chief photographer (*see* Wars in Chapter 5, pages 157–158). The Corte-Scope views are standard size on unmounted thick print paper and were sold in sets of various sizes with a folding Corte-Scope metal viewer. They were packaged in black leather-covered boxes. Most of the sets were made from 1915 to 1921, but one set is dated as late as 1928.

Another interesting series of stereo view sets were made by Raumbild-Verlag of Germany (*see* also Sports, 1936, 1952 Olympics in Chapter 5). Using the 6 cm by 13 cm smaller format, the Raumbild views are on thick unmounted print paper. These are not found in boxes but are included here because they were sold as a complete package, which included the views (usually one hundred) housed in deep slots in the back of a descriptive book along with a folding metal viewer.

These are often called the "Nazi views" because they document the Third Reich in Germany in the 1930s. In addition there were sets of the Zeppelin factory with outstanding views of the LZ 127, the 1936 and 1952 Olympics and scenes at the Paris World Exposition (1937). Collectors seek out the various Nazi sets, which include views of Hitler, Mussolini and others.

A number of lithographic sets were issued in boxes. The most common is the tour that Sears, Roebuck and Company, issued in 1906 to promote the popular mail-order firm from Chicago. The set of fifty black-and-white lithographs show all aspects of the business including the printing of the famous catalog. View #1, a portrait of Richard Sears, was distributed in huge quantities to promote the set. The set came in a black cardboard box with a flip top. Other travel sets were sold by Sears and some were sold in cardboard folder boxes. Because there is very little interest in these sets with collectors, they are not listed here.

Berry, Kelley and Chadwick made many fine stereo views, but as far as can be determined, they never made any boxed sets. They did issue a set of the Ohio flood of 1913 but no box has ever been located.

Dr. Rainforth's Skin Clinic is a color lithograph set sold in a special box with a Holmes-type viewer. The 160-card set shows vividly various acute skin conditions. It has limited appeal among collectors. The Edinburgh Stereoscopic Atlas of Anatomy is a boxed set with views on 7″ by 9″ heavy cards. These sets came in various sizes up to ten volumes and sold in large quantities to medical schools and doctors. They, too, have limited collector appeal.

Boxed Sets, Book-Boxed Sets and Sets in Special Packaging

Note: Values are for complete box sets in excellent condition in boxes with little or no wear. For worn views or damaged boxes, deduct 50 percent. Sets missing views or with the wrong views, deduct 25 percent. Numbers in parentheses are the total number of views in the set.

Africa, Underwood & Underwood, (100), 1909	100–150.00
Air Transportation	
Keystone (50), Historic and classic planes	300–350.00
Keystone (50), Different views, commercial planes	200–250.00
Keystone (25), Junior format	100–125.00
Alaska, Underwood & Underwood (12)	50–75.00
"American Volunteer," Underwood & Underwood (6), Sentimental set	25–30.00
Animals, Underwood & Underwood (184)	200–225.00
Art, Underwood & Underwood (60)	100–125.00
"Artisque Coleur," H. C. White (100), Hand-colored miscellaneous subjects on black mounts with gold lettering	400–500.00
Austria, Underwood & Underwood (84)	200–225.00
Baltimore & Ohio Railroad Centenary	
Keystone (50)	300–350.00
Keystone (100)	700–800.00
Belgium, Underwood & Underwood (24)	50–75.00
Berkshire Mills (36), With metal viewer	125–175.00
Bernese Alps (*see* Switzerland below)	
Birds (usually hand colored)	
Keystone (25) *B* prefix on position numbers	100–125.00
Keystone (100) *B* prefix	400–450.00
Underwood & Underwood (92)	125–175.00
Boats	
Keystone (25), In regular box (not book box)	125–175.00
Keystone (25), Junior format, with viewer	25–30.00

Boer War (British South African)
Underwood & Underwood
(36) —————————— 150–200.00
Underwood & Underwood
(60) —————————— 275–300.00
Boxer Rebellion (*see* China below)
Bridges
Keystone (25), In regular box,
not book box —————— 75–100.00
Keystone (25), Junior format,
with viewer —————— 40–50.00
British Isles, H. C. White (100) ——— 275–300.00
Burma, Underwood & Underwood (50) —————————— 150–200.00
Burma and Ceylon, H. C. White
(100) —————————— 275–300.00
Butterflies and Moths, Keystone
(25), hand colored in regular
box, not book box ————— 100–125.00
California
H. C. White (100) ————— 275–300.00
Keystone (50) —————— 150–200.00
Canada
H. C. White (100) ————— 300–400.00
Keystone (100) —————— 250–300.00
Underwood & Underwood
(72) —————————— 150–200.00
Central America, Keystone (50) ——— 150–200.00
Ceramics, Underwood & Underwood (44) —————————— 100–125.00
Ceylon
Keystone (30) —————— 100–125.00
Underwood & Underwood
(30) —————————— 75–100.00
Chicago and Central States, H. C.
White (100) —————— 300–400.00
Childhood, Universal Photo Art
(100) —————————— 400–500.00
Children's tour ("Real Children
in Many Lands")
Underwood & Underwood
(18) —————————— 35–40.00
Guidebook —————— 17–20.00
China
H. C. White (100) ————— 400–500.00
Keystone (100) —————— 300–400.00
Stereo-Travel (100) ———— 350–450.00
Underwood & Underwood
(100) —————————— 275–300.00
Guidebook —————— 25–30.00
Subsets
Boxer Uprising (26),
#43–68 of China set ——— 150–200.00
Guidebook ————— 35–40.00
Hong Kong to Canton
(15), #1–15 of China set ——— 45–50.00
Guidebook ————— 35–40.00
Peking (32), #69–100 of
China set ————— 100–125.00
Guidebook ————— 35–40.00
Universal Photo Art
Vol. I (100) —————— 300–400.00
Vol. II (100) —————— 400–500.00
Colorado, Keystone (36) ———— 100–125.00

Colorado and southwestern
states, H. C. White (100) ———— 300–400.00
Costumes, Keystone (100), hand
colored —————————— 400–500.00
Cowboys, Keystone (50) ———— 275–300.00
Cuba, Stereo-Travel (100) ———— 300–400.00
Cuba and Porto Rico [*sic*], Underwood & Underwood (100) ———— 300–400.00
Czechoslovakia
Keystone (50) —————— 150–200.00
Keystone (100) —————— 350–450.00
Denmark
Underwood & Underwood
(36) —————————— 100–125.00
Universal Photo Art (30) ———— 200–300.00
Ecuador, Underwood & Underwood (42) —————————— 150–200.00
Edinburgh Stereoscopic Atlas of
Anatomy, sold in several
volumes —————— per volume 50.00
Egypt
H. C. White (100) ————— 200–225.00
Keystone (100) —————— 175–200.00
Universal Photo Art (100) ——— 225–250.00
Guidebook —————— 15–20.00
Subsets
Ancient Egypt (21) ———— 50–60.00
Cairo and the Pyramids
(27) —————————— 60–70.00
Universal Photo Art (100) ——— 250–300.00
Elephants, Underwood & Underwood (12) —————————— 20–30.00
England
H. C. White (100) ————— 200–300.00
Keystone (100) —————— 175–200.00
Stereo-Travel (100) ———— 250–300.00
Underwood & Underwood
(100) —————————— 175–200.00
(*See also* British Isles above and
Great Britain below)
Eskimos, Keystone (50) ———— 275–300.00
Eye-Training, Keystone (12),
With viewer, in shoe-box shaped
box, 1937 —————————— 50–60.00
Flax and Linen Industries, Underwood & Underwood (30) ———— 60–70.00
Flora (Wildflowers) Underwood
& Underwood, (66), Hand
colored —————————— 100–125.00
Florida, Keystone (50) ———— 250–300.00
Flowers, Keystone (100), Hand
colored —————————— 275–300.00
France
H. C. White (100) ————— 300–400.00
Keystone (100) —————— 250–300.00
Stereo-Travel
(30) —————————— 70–80.00
(100) —————————— 300–400.00
Underwood & Underwood
(100) —————————— 250–275.00
Guidebook —————— 25–30.00
The French Cook
(*See* Comics and Sentimentals in
Chapter 4 for unboxed set)
Underwood & Underwood (10),

Regular box, not book box _____ 50–60.00
Fuel Industries, Underwood &
Underwood (19) _____ 50–60.00
Germany
  H. C. White (100) _____ 300–400.00
  Keystone
    (50) _____ 100–125.00
    (100) _____ 200–250.00
  Underwood & Underwood
    (100) _____ 250–275.00
Gettysburg Battlefield
  Underwood & Underwood
    (12) _____ 75–100.00
  Underwood & Underwood
    (18) _____ 100–125.00
Glacier National Park
  N. A. Forsyth (30) _____ 125–150.00
  Keystone (36) _____ 90–100.00
  Underwood & Underwood
    (30) _____ 90–100.00
Golf, Keystone (50) _____ 300–400.00
Gold Rush, Alaska, Keystone
(100) _____ 500–600.00
Grand Canyon
  Keystone (36) _____ 60–70.00
  Underwood & Underwood
    (18), 1903 _____ 40–50.00
    Guidebook _____ 15–20.00
Great Britain, Universal Photo
Art (48) _____ 175–200.00
Greece
  H. C. White (100) _____ 350–400.00
  Keystone
    (50) _____ 100–125.00
    (100) _____ 200–250.00
  Underwood & Underwood
    (100) _____ 250–275.00
    Guidebook _____ 25–30.00
    Subset
      Athens (27), Positions
      #1–27 in set _____ 75–90.00
Hand colored (*See also* "Artisque
Coleur" above)
  Underwood & Underwood
  Series #1 (100) _____ 400–450.00
  Underwood & Underwood

Series #2 (74) _____ 300–350.00
  Underwood & Underwood
  Series #3 (36) _____ 175–200.00
  Underwood & Underwood
  Series #4 (24) _____ 100–125.00
Hawaii
  Universal Photo Art (50) _____ 250–300.00
Hawaiian Islands-Philippines
  Underwood & Underwood
    (100) _____ 300–400.00
History
  Keystone, *H* prefix on position
  numbers
    (100) _____ 500–600.00
    (300) _____ 800–900.00
    (400) _____ 1200–1500.00
Holland
  Keystone (50) _____ 150–200.00
  Underwood & Underwood
    (24) _____ 75–85.00
Hunting
  Keystone
    (50) _____ 85–100.00
    (100) _____ 260–285.00
  Underwood & Underwood
    (30) _____ 50–75.00
  Universal Photo Art (24) _____ 100–125.00
India
  H. C. White (100) _____ 250–275.00
  Keystone (100) _____ 150–175.00
  Underwood & Underwood
    (100), 1903 _____ 180–250.00
    Guidebook _____ 35–40.00
    Subset
      Bombay to Cashmere (27),
      #1–27 in set _____ 50–75.00
Indians
  N. A. Forsyth (30) _____ 250–275.00
  Keystone (100) _____ 600–700.00
Ireland
  Underwood & Underwood
    (100) _____ 275–300.00
    Guidebook _____ 20–25.00
    Subset
      Queensland, Cork and
      Dublin (36), #1–36 in

Keystone View Co., #W26097, "Old South Meeting House, Boston, Mass.," #H 50 in the Keystone "History" boxed set, ca. 1920. The print is from the earlier H. C. White negative obtained about 1908.

set _____ 90–125.00
Universal Photo Art (48) _____ 150–200.00
Iron and Steel Manufacture
  Underwood & Underwood
    (60) _____ 150–200.00
    (67) _____ 175–225.00
Iron Horse (*See also* Baltimore &
Ohio Railroad Centenary above)
  Keystone
    (25), Regular box, not book
    box _____ 100–120.00
    (25), Junior format, ca.
    1935 _____ 50–60.00
"Is Marriage a Failure?" comic
set
  Underwood & Underwood (18)
  In regular box, not book box _____ 50–60.00
Italy
  H. C. White (100) _____ 175–200.00
  Keystone
    (50) _____ 75–100.00
    (100) _____ 150–175.00
  Stereo-Travel (100) _____ 200–300.00
  Underwood & Underwood
    (100) _____ 150–175.00
    Guidebook, 1908 _____ 40–45.00
    Subset
      A Visit to Pope Pius X
      (12) _____ 40–45.00
  Universal Photo Art (48) _____ 150–200.00
Jamaica
  H. C. White (100) _____ 300–375.00
  Keystone (36) _____ 75–100.00
  Stereo-Travel (100) _____ 300–375.00
  Underwood & Underwood
    (24) _____ 50–75.00
  Universal Photo Art (100) _____ 400–500.00
Japan (*See also* Russo-Japanese
War below)
  H. C. White
    (100) _____ 300–400.00
    (200) _____ 600–800.00
  Keystone
    (50) _____ 75–100.00
    (100) _____ 150–200.00
  Stereo-Travel (100) _____ 300–400.00
  Underwood & Underwood
    (100) _____ 300–350.00
  Universal Photo Art
    Vol. I (100) _____ 350–450.00
    Vol. II (100) _____ 450–550.00
Java
  Keystone (100) _____ 200–300.00
  Underwood & Underwood
    (36) _____ 75–100.00
  Universal Photo Art (100) _____ 300–400.00
Jerusalem (*See* Palestine below)
Keystone Junior (usually half
value of full-size views except the
following)
  Century of Progress Exposition,
  Chicago, 1933
    General views (60) with
    viewer _____ 175–200.00
    "Wings of a Century" (25) ____ 100–125.00
    "Midget Village" (25) _____ 200–250.00

Figure three times value of
full-size views on gray
mounts (50-view boxed set
known)
Korea (Chosen)
  Underwood & Underwood
    (48) _____ 175–200.00
  Universal Photo Art (25) _____ 150–175.00
Last of the Buffalo, N. A. Forsyth
  (50) _____ 500–600.00
Life of Jesus (*See* Palestine below)
London, England, Underwood &
Underwood (30) _____ 100–125.00
Louisiana Purchase Exposition
(St. Louis World's Fair), 1904
  H. C. White (100) _____ 500–600.00
  Keystone
    (36) _____ 100–125.00
    (200) _____ 600–700.00
  Underwood & Underwood
    (48) _____ 175–200.00
    (55) _____ 200–250.00
    Guidebook _____ 45–50.00
  Universal Photo Art (100) _____ 500–600.00
Lyndhurst (Tarrytown, N.Y.,
1905), Underwood & Underwood
(42) _____ 175–200.00
Manchuria
  Keystone (18) _____ 75–100.00
  Underwood & Underwood
    (18) _____ 75–100.00
Manchuria and Korea
  Keystone
    (50) _____ 175–200.00
    (100) _____ 275–300.00
Martinique, Underwood & Un-
derwood (18) _____ 75–100.00
Martinique-St. Vincent, Keystone
(100) _____ 275–300.00
Mass and Benediction, Keystone
(100) _____ 100–150.00
Mathematical Series (Diagrams),
Underwood & Underwood (25) _____ 50–75.00
Mesopotamia
  Keystone
    (50) _____ 150–200.00
    (84) _____ 200–225.00
  Underwood & Underwood (84) __ 200–225.00
Mexico
  Keystone (100), *MX* prefix _____ 200–250.00
  Stereo-Travel (100) _____ 250–300.00
  Underwood & Underwood
    (100) _____ 200–250.00
Mont Blanc (*See* Switzerland be-
low)
Moscow (*See* Russia below)
Morrison Cave (Montana)
  N. A. Forsyth
    (25) _____ 100–150.00
    (30) _____ 175–200.00
Motor, Stereo-Travel (60), Forty
views of 1909 Indianapolis "500"
and twenty views of balloon race __ 600–700.00
Mt. Rainier National Park, Key-
stone (30) _____ 100–125.00
Mr. & Mrs. Newlywed, Under-

wood & Underwood (10) _____ 40–60.00
National Costumes (*See* Costumes above)
National Parks
  Keystone
    (100) _____ 200–300.00
    (110), Includes Canadian
    views _____ 250–275.00
New York City
  Stereo-Travel (100), Includes
  mostly Hudson-Fulton Celebra-
  tion, 1909 _____ 500–600.00
  Stereo-Travel (100), Includes
  only a few Hudson-Fulton and
  many views of street life,
  1913–1915 views, published
  1916 _____ 750–850.00
  Underwood & Underwood
    (30) _____ 100–125.00
    (36) _____ 125–150.00
New York State, H. C. White
(100) _____ 300–400.00
Niagara Falls
  Keystone (18) _____ 25–30.00
  Underwood & Underwood (18) _____ 30–35.00
  Universal Photo Art (36) _____ 75–100.00
Niagara in Winter, Underwood &
Underwood (12) _____ 20–25.00
Norway
  Keystone (100) _____ 200–250.00
  Underwood & Underwood
    (100) _____ 180–200.00
    Guidebook _____ 20–25.00
    Subset
      Hardanger and Bergen (27),
      #26–52 of set _____ 60–75.00
  Universal Photo Art (100) _____ 300–400.00
Our Cruise series, Underwood &
Underwood, no two sets alike,
trips around the world, to the
Mediterranean or the Orient, ships
include SS *Arabic, Kurfurst, Presi-
dent Cleveland,* etc., usually in half
dozens, 18, 24, 36 and up to more
than 200 views in each set, typical
100-view set _____ 250–300.00
Our Pilgrimage to California, Cus-
tom set, 1904, typical example,
Underwood & Underwood (36) _____ 100–125.00
Our Pacific Possessions
  H. C. White (100) _____ 300–400.00
Palestine (Holy land)
  Keystone
    (100) _____ 125–150.00
    (200) _____ 250–300.00
  H. C. White (100) _____ 200–300.00
  Underwood & Underwood
    (100) _____ 125–150.00
    Guidebook _____ 15–20.00
    (139), Comprises the above
    plus ''Life of Jesus'' and ''Old
    Testaments,'' all duplicates
    omitted _____ 150–175.00
    Guidebook _____ 15–20.00
    Subsets

Jerusalem
  Keystone (30) _____ 30–40.00
  Underwood & Under-
  wood (27), #9–35 of
  set _____ 30–40.00
Life of Jesus
  Keystone (24) _____ 25–30.00
  Underwood & Under-
  wood (24) _____ 30–40.00
Universal Photo Art (100) _____ 225–250.00
Panama (Canal)
  Keystone
    (24) _____ 75–100.00
    (35) _____ 150–175.00
    (100) _____ 300–400.00
  Stereo-Travel (100) _____ 400–500.00
  Underwood & Underwood
    (36) _____ 100–125.00
    (45) _____ 125–150.00
Panama-California Exposition,
Keystone (72) _____ 300–400.00
Panama-Pacific Exposition, Key-
stone (100) _____ 500–600.00
Paris, Underwood & Underwood
(36) _____ 50–75.00
Paris Exposition, 1900
  Underwood & Underwood
    (36) _____ 100–150.00
    (60) _____ 175–200.00
Peking (*See* China above)
Peru
  Keystone (60) _____ 175–200.00
  Underwood & Underwood (60) _____ 175–200.00
Pets
  Keystone
    (25), Regular box, not book
    box _____ 30–35.00
    (25), Junior format _____ 15–20.00
Philippines
  H. C. White (100) _____ 300–400.00
  Keystone
    (50) _____ 125–150.00
    (100) _____ 250–300.00
  Underwood & Underwood
    (100) _____ 250–300.00
  Universal Photo Art (100) _____ 400–500.00
Philippine Islands, Hawaii, Samoa
  Keystone (100) _____ 200–250.00
  Underwood & Underwood
    (100) _____ 250–275.00
Pilgrimage to see the Holy Father
  Underwood & Underwood (36) _____ 50–75.00
    Guidebook _____ 15–20.00
  (*See also* Italy above)
Pope Pius X (*See* Italy above)
Portugal
  Keystone
    (36) _____ 50–75.00
    (60) _____ 100–125.00
  Underwood & Underwood
    (60) _____ 100–125.00
Precious Metal Industry, Under-
wood & Underwood (34) _____ 100–125.00
President Harding's Alaskan Trip
  Keystone

Boxed set by Underwood & Underwood, "Stereograph Record, William McKinley, Beloved by all the People." Twenty-four-view set with book (views numbered 1 to 60). $155. The complete sixty-view set with book, $300–330.

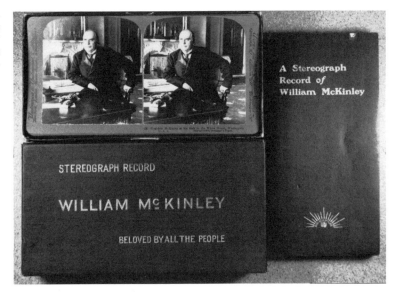

(50), Includes funeral	400–500.00
(100), Includes funeral	900–1000.00

President McKinley
Underwood & Underwood

(12)	50–60.00
(24)	100–125.00
(48)	200–250.00
(54)	225–275.00
(60)	275–300.00
Guidebook	25–30.00

President Roosevelt (Theodore),
Underwood & Underwood (36) —— 300–400.00

Primary Sets, *P* prefix
Keystone

(100)	200–300.00
(200)	400–500.00
(300)	650–750.00

Public Helpers, Keystone (25),
Regular box —— 75–100.00

Puerto Rico, Keystone (36) —— 75–100.00

Queenstown, Cork and Dublin
(*See* Ireland above)

Real Children in Many Lands (*See*
Children's Tour above)

Rhine, Underwood & Underwood
(24) —— 50–75.00

Dr. Rainforth's Skin Clinic (160),
Color lithos with Holmes viewer
in box —— 75–100.00

Raumbild-Verlag (*See* separate listing below)

Railroads, Keystone (25), Regular
box —— 100–125.00

Rice Industry, Underwood & Underwood (24) —— 50–75.00

Rome (Italy)

Keystone (46)	50–75.00
Underwood & Underwood (46)	50–75.00
Guidebook	20–25.00

Rubber manufacturing, Underwood & Underwood (49) —— 100–125.00

Russia

H. C. White (100)	400–500.00

Keystone

(50)	150–175.00
(100)	300–400.00

Underwood & Underwood

(100)	300–400.00
Guidebook	30–40.00

Subsets
Moscow

Keystone (27)	75–100.00

Underwood & Underwood
(27), #47–73 from set —— 75–100.00

Guidebook	30–40.00

St. Petersburg, Underwood & Underwood (39), #8–46 in
set —— 100–125.00

Guidebook	30–50.00

Russo-Japanese War, 1905

H. C. White (100)	400–500.00

Underwood & Underwood
(100) —— 400–500.00

Saint Louis Fair (*See* Louisiana
Purchase Exposition above)

Saint Petersburg (*See* Russia
above)

St. Pierre and Mt. Pelée

Underwood & Underwood (18)	50–75.00
Guidebook	20–25.00

Salt Manufacture, Underwood & Underwood (30) —— 50–75.00

San Francisco Earthquake
Underwood & Underwood

(36)	225–250.00
(51)	300–400.00

Scandinavia

H. C. White (100)	300–400.00
Keystone (100)	250–300.00

Underwood & Underwood
(100) —— 250–300.00

Scenic America

Keystone
(100) _____ 200–300.00
(300) _____ 500–600.00
Scotland
Keystone (100) _____ 150–200.00
Underwood & Underwood (84) __ 100–125.00
Scotland and Ireland, H. C. White
(100) _____ 250–300.00
Sears, Roebuck & Co., Black-and-
white lithos, flip-top black box,
common (50) _____ 25.00
Selected Subjects, Keystone (100),
Custom made, 1930s, typical
version _____ 100–150.00
Ship and Boat Construction, Un-
derwood & Underwood (20) _____ 75–100.00
Ship Life, Keystone (25), Regular
box _____ 125–150.00
Sicily
Stereo-Travel (100), Includes
immigrant views _____ 300–400.00
Underwood & Underwood (54) ___ 75–100.00
Silk Industry
Keystone (25) _____ 45–60.00
Underwood & Underwood (15) _____ 30–35.00
Solid Geometry, Keystone (50) _____ 50–75.00
South America
Keystone
(50) _____ 50–75.00
(100), several versions or
editions _____ 150–200.00
Underwood & Underwood (54) __ 100–125.00
South Sea Islands
Keystone
(50) _____ 200–225.00
(100) _____ 400–450.00
Spain
Keystone (100) _____ 200–300.00
Underwood & Underwood
(100) _____ 200–300.00
Spanish-American War
Keystone (100) _____ 400–500.00
Underwood & Underwood
(72) _____ 350–400.00
(100), More than one
version _____ 450–500.00
Spanish Bull Fight
Keystone (12) _____ 75–125.00

Underwood & Underwood (12) ___ 75–125.00
"Stereographs," custom made,
Underwood & Underwood, thirty-
six and one hundred, typical ex-
ample in book box _____ 75–125.00
Sweden
Keystone (50) _____ 75–100.00
Stereo-Travel (100) _____ 200–300.00
Underwood & Underwood
(100) _____ 150–200.00
Universal Photo Art (72) _____ 200–300.00
Switzerland
Keystone
(50) _____ 50–75.00
(100) _____ 100–150.00
Underwood & Underwood
(100) _____ 150–175.00
Guidebook _____ 20–25.00
Textile Industries, Underwood &
Underwood (116) _____ 250–300.00
Tombstones, Keystone (48) _____ 50–75.00
Tour of the World
Keystone (many versions,
1902–1952)
(72) _____ 50–75.00
(100) _____ 100–125.00
(200) _____ 200–225.00
(400) _____ 450–500.00
(600), Common _____ 600–650.00
Oak storage cabinet, three
sections _____ 200–300.00
(1200), With metal telebin-
ocular viewer _____ 1200–1300.00
Guidebooks, numerous
editions _____ 20–25.00
H. C. White
(100) "Trip Around the
World." _____ 150–175.00
(100) "Trip to Europe." _____ 150–175.00
Underwood & Underwood (72)
"Trip Around the World." _____ 75–100.00
Guidebook _____ 15–20.00
Universal Photo Art (60)
"Around the World." _____ 150–175.00
Traveling in the Holy Land (*See*
Palestine above)
Travel Lessons in the Life of Christ
(*See* Palestine above)

Lynn Skeels's view of his Keystone viewers and a volume from the 1200-view "Tour of the World." This view was made about 1945.

Underwood & Underwood, #11252, "Woodrow Wilson, 28th President of the United States," appeared as #11 in the 100-view "United States" set. Complete set $200. (Gordon D. Hoffman Collection)

Travel Lessons, Old Testament
    Keystone (51) _____ 50–75.00
    Underwood & Underwood
        (27) _____ 25–30.00
        (51) _____ 50–75.00
Tree Products, Underwood & Underwood (24) _____ 35–50.00
Trees (native)
    Keystone
        (24) _____ 35–50.00
        (25), 1930s edition _____ 70–80.00
        (100) _____ 100–125.00
Trip around the World (*See* Tour of the World above)
Turkey
    Keystone
        (50) _____ 70–80.00
        (72) _____ 125–150.00
    Underwood & Underwood (72) __ 150–175.00
United States
    H. C. White (100) _____ 200–250.00
    Keystone (100) _____ 150–175.00
    Underwood & Underwood
        (100) _____ 175–200.00
        (200) _____ 350–450.00
U.S. History, American History (*See* History above)
Utah Parks
    Keystone
        (36), Usually tinted _____ 75–100.00
        (50), Usually tinted _____ 125–150.00
Vienna to the Orient, H. C. White (100) _____ 350–400.00
Volcanoes and Volcanic Action, Underwood & Underwood (60) ____ 100–125.00
Washington, D.C.
    Keystone
        (24) _____ 25–30.00
        (42) _____ 50–75.00
        (50) _____ 50–75.00
    Underwood & Underwood
        (36) _____ 50–65.00
        (42) _____ 65–75.00
        Guidebook _____ 20–25.00
Washington and South, H. C. White (100) _____ 250–300.00
Watkins and Havana Glen, Under-

wood & Underwood (18) _____ 20–25.00
West Coast of South America, Keystone (43) _____ 50–75.00
West Indies
    Keystone
        (72) _____ 100–125.00
        (100) _____ 150–175.00
West Indies Cruise, H. C. White (100) _____ 250–300.00
Whiting's Universal Library, 318 color lithos trimmed and notched for use in the Whiting Sculptoscope viewing machine in black box _____ 50–75.00
Wild Animals (*See also* Animals above)
    Keystone (100) _____ 100–125.00
    Underwood & Underwood
        (100) _____ 100–125.00
Wild Birds (*See* Birds above)
World's Fair (*See* Louisiana Purchase Exposition above)
World Tour (*See* Tour of the World above)
World War I, the European War
    Keystone
        (36) _____ 35–45.00
        (50) _____ 50–75.00
        (100) _____ 225–250.00
        (200) _____ 300–350.00
        (300) _____ 400–450.00
    Underwood & Underwood
        (100) _____ 250–300.00
        (200) _____ 400–450.00
        (250) _____ 500–550.00
    Realistic Travels (100) _____ 225–250.00
    W. E. Troutman
        (100) _____ 300–400.00
        (300) _____ 800–900.00
    45 cm by 107 cm Glass transparencies (100) _____ 400–450.00
    Color or black-and-white lithos, usually in sets of 25 _____ 10–15.00
    Color lithos made from drawing, no 3-D (25) _____ 5.00
World Visualized for the Classroom

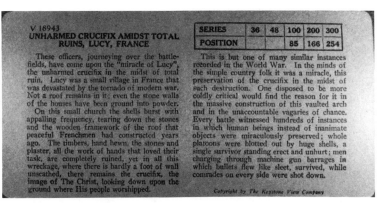

Keystone View Co., #V18943, "'Miracle of Lucy,' France—Unharmed Crucifix Amidst Total Ruin," from the "World War" book-boxed set. Reverse shows this view appeared as #85 in the 100-view set, #166 in the 200-view set and #254 in the 300-view set. It does not appear in the 36- or 48-view sets. Also the V prefix indicates the view is from an Underwood & Underwood negative. Most Keystone World War I views are $1–4 each, if sold individually.

Underwood & Underwood
(600) _____ 600–700.00
(1000) _____ 1100–1200.00
Yellowstone National Park (*See also* National Parks above)
H. C. White (100) _____ 275–300.00
Keystone
(18) _____ 20–25.00
(30) _____ 35–45.00
(36) _____ 50–60.00
(50) _____ 65–75.00
Stereo-Travel (100) _____ 350–400.00
Underwood & Underwood
(30) _____ 90–100.00
(50) _____ 125–150.00
Guidebook _____ 25–30.00
Yellowstone-Grand Canyon, Keystone (36) _____ 50–60.00
Yosemite
Keystone
(24) _____ 50–60.00
(36) _____ 100–125.00
Underwood & Underwood
(24) _____ 50–60.00
(30) _____ 90–100.00
Guidebook _____ 20–25.00
Zermatt and the Matterhorn (Switzerland)

Keystone (15) _____ 20–25.00
Underwood & Underwood (15) ____ 20–25.00

Corte-Scope Sets

Note: Values are difficult to determine because so few have been offered for sale at auction. I have most of the sets represented in this listing and have paid or traded at a variety of values. Furthermore, there are very few known sets duplicated in collections and there are variants in both size and subject. On average, the views have sold at about $3 each in sets. One set of fifty sold for $150. This price included the viewer; viewers have sold for $35 to $50 each when sold as a separate piece. Therefore, a reasonable value for a fifty-view set with the viewer in the box would be $200 to $250. Sets that do not have the box; that are missing the viewer; or consist of soiled, damaged or missing views would be valued at 25 to 50 percent less.

Views are standard size on thick unmounted print paper with the number and title printed in the lower margin of the view. They have the Corte-Scope logo imprinted on the reverse. Boxes are black, pebble-grained leather, covered with a flap top with metal snap closures.

Corte-Scope Co., #3, "Felling Timber" (black lumberjacks at work), from a set on various lumbering processes made for the Chicago Mill & Lumber Co.

The viewer is steel or aluminum and folds to fit into the box along with the views.

Adams X-Ray Co., Detroit (29), Dental X ray

A. I. Root Co., Medina, Ohio (25), Beekeeping

Allen Herschell Co., North Tonawanda, N.Y., carousels, number in set unknown, extremely rare

American Seeding-Machine Co., Springfield, Ohio (61), Horse-drawn farm implements

Baker Valve Gears, Railroad locomotive gears (8)

Bauer Bros. Co., Springfield, Ohio (19), Grain milling

Beardslee Chandelier Mfg. Co., Chicago, Ill. (22), Lighting fixtures

Bostwick-Braun Co., Toledo, (35 in continuous roll in wood holder), ca. 1911, Hardware

Cadillac Motor Car Co., Detroit (65), Auto plant

Chalmers Motor Co., Detroit (45), Auto plant

Chambers Valve Co., N.Y. (16), Railroad locomotive valves

Chandler Motor Car Co. (39), Auto plant

Chicago Mill & Lumber Co.
  Lumbering (23)
  Lumber mill (12)
  Making saws (15)
  Making veneer (30)
  Paper making (50)

Cincinnati Wire Box Co. (17), making boxes

Davis Manufacturing Co., Dayton, Ohio, Bicycles and sewing machines, number in set unknown, rare

Diamond Match Co., New York City, other United States locations (87), Making matches

Equipment Improvement Co., New York (15), Railroad locomotive valve gears

Heath and Milligan Manuf. Co., Chicago, Ill. (40), Paint

Hudson Motor Car Co., Detroit, Mich. (54), Auto plant

Installation of First Bishop of Toledo, Ohio, 1911 (53), Event, views bound as book, thin cardboard box

Libbey Glass Co., Toledo, ca. 1911 (11), Glass products, views on continuous roll in wood holder

Marion-Handley (Mutual Motors Co.), Jackson, Mich., (29), Auto plant

Corte-Scope Co., #53, from a set of the Diamond Match Co. These men are operating machines that make book matches, ca. 1916.

Morgan & Wright, Detroit (32), Rubber tires and tubes

Morgan Door and Milling Co. (63), Doors, sashes

1918 United States Lawn Tennis Championships, Forest Hills, N.Y. (50), Event

Paige-Detroit Motor Co., Detroit, Mich. (90), Auto plant

Patterson-Sargent Co., Cleveland, Ohio (50), Paint making

Standard Tool Co., Cleveland, Ohio (30), Machine drills

Studebaker (78), Auto plant

Thomas E. Wilson & Co. "Corte-Scope Golf" (59), Golf instruction with "Jock" Hutchinson

Timken Roller Bearing Co., Canton, Ohio and Detroit, Mich., (25), Roller bearings

United States Rubber Co., Ball Band Rubber Boot [*sic*] Plant, Mishawaka, Ind. (49), making rubber boots and shoes

Waite (Wire) Grass Carpet Co., Oshkosh, Wisc. (28), Grass carpets

Warner and Swasey Co., Cleveland, Ohio (30), Tools

Willard Storage Battery Co., Cleveland, Ohio (16), Batteries

Willys-Overland Co., Toledo, Ohio, (47), Auto plant

Raumbild-Verlag

Like the Corte-Scope sets, very few of the Raumbild sets have been sold at auction in the United States. A large hoard of these sets was found in the mid-1980s in Germany. The owner traded these sets to collectors in the United States. The most common sets are "Der Kampf Im Westen" (one hundred views in a book with a viewer) and "U.S. Occupied Zone of Germany" (thirty-six in a booklike box with viewer). The latter was purchased in quantity by G.I.s after World War II. The sets usually change hands at $2.50–3.00 per view. Thus a set in excellent condition, complete with one hundred views and the viewer usually retails at $250–$300.00.

Note: Views are 6 cm by 13 cm photos on thick print paper (unmounted).

"A Tour through the Franke & Heidecke Precision Camera Works, Braunschweig" (30), Special edition, ca. 1937

"Aus der Lebensgemeinschaft des Waldes" (Forest Ecology) (100), 1939, Rare

"Der Kampf Im Westen" (The Western Front) (100), 1940

"Die Olympischen Spiele 1936" (The 1936 Olympic Games) In book (100)

"Dictatorship, War, Disaster" (300), 1954, in English

"Die Soldaten des Fuhrers Im Felde" (The Fuhrer's Soldiers in the Field) (100)

"Deutsche Gaue" (German Districts) (200)

"Grossdeutschlands Wiedergeburt" (The Rebirth of Greater Germany), in at least three different editions (100 or 120)

"Flight and Might, A Raumbild Portrait of our Luftwaffe," (100) and eight color plates

"Historische Bauten Deutschland vor und nach der Zerstorung," (Historical Buildings of Germany before and after Their Destruction) (100).

Raumbild-Verlag "Die Olympischen Spiele 1936" (The 1936 Olympic Games). The book set has one hundred views plus a folding medal viewer. $250–300. (Courtesy Stereo World *magazine)*

"Histoire de Paris des origines a nous jours" (Paris in relief, the history of Paris from the beginning to today), limited, signed edition of 500 (100).

"Hitler—Mussolini, The State Visit of the Fuhrer to Italy" (100), 1937

"Learn First Aid" (60), 1952

"Munich, Capital of the Movement" (100), 1937

"Skulls and Skeletons: A Pleasant Chat about a Bony Subject" (18), 1951

"So They Battled, The XV Olympic Games at Helsinki" (100), 1952

"The Paris World Exhibition, 1937," (100)

"Traditionsgau Munchen-Oberbayern" (The Traditional District, Munich and Upper Bavaria) (100), No book issued

"Treasures of the Baroque" three volumes, each (24), 1948–1950

"U.S. Occupied Zone of Germany," (36), 1946, in English, common, in red-white-and-blue folder box.

"Venedig-Em Raumer lebnis" (Venice, A Spatial Experience) (60), 1935.

"Vienna, The Pearl of the Reich" (100), 1941

The Raumbild magazine *Das Raumbild*, published high-quality reproductions of Raumbild views. The first issue was January 1935. The magazine was issued until December 1937 and then it was not issued for three months. It was restarted with the April 1938 issue and was published to 1939. The magazine was made in small print runs of no more than 1500 of each, thus the magazines are very uncommon, especially in the United States.

7

THE MODERN ERA OF 3-D VISUAL COLLECTIBLES

After World War I, the standard format card-mount stereo view began a quick decline. Most of the major publishers were bought out by the Keystone View Company of Meadville, Pennsylvania. Stereo photography was used by a few specialty companies, such as the Corte-Scope Company of Cleveland, Ohio, and Raumbild-Verlag in Germany. These companies made print views but their distribution was generally limited. Keystone stressed the educational aspects of their views, keying their sets to schools and libraries. The 1929 financial depression caused Keystone to reevaluate their business. The "Tour of the World" set was revised and a custom division was established to sell special "personal" views to wealthy families. They also expanded the eye-testing area of the business, which eventually became their main source of sales, especially after 1939.

The 1920s and 1930s saw the development of smaller roll film in 35-, 16- and 8-mm sizes. Kodachrome color film was a major breakthrough in the late 1930s and made possible high-quality transparencies, especially in the 35-mm size.

Although the major publishing of card-mount stereo views had declined, amateur stereo photography remained vital and active with the introduction of new cameras and films.

Several commercial ventures emerged and these will be discussed at length in this section.

TRU-VUE "PICTURES WITH DEPTH"

This company had an unlikely chance of survival when it was founded as a branch of the Rock Island Bridge and Iron Works in Rock Island, Illinois, at the height of the Great Depression in 1931. But the company did survive and brought stereo photography into the new era of commercial sales. The use of 35-mm film had been developed in the 1920s and made a workable format. The Tru-Vue filmstrips are printed on Kodak positive/gold-base print safety film. The copper/gold chemistry gives the views a rich brownish tone. The original views were made with a 5" by 7" Stereo Graflex camera and mounted as black-and-white prints. The prints were then copied onto the 35-mm film. The filmstrip usually contains fourteen stereo pairs.

The summer of 1933 saw a major breakthrough for the company. In Chicago, the Century of Progress Exposition was drawing huge crowds and Tru-Vue produced a series showing the attraction; they also issued a spe-

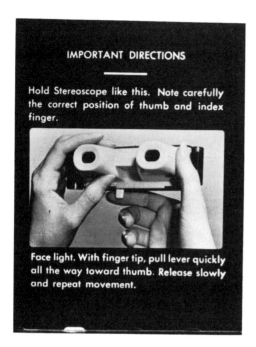

Instruction frame from the Tru-Vue "Depth Photography" film showing proper use of the Tru-Vuer.

cial version of their viewer. In addition, a "gift pak" was developed using the Century of Progress logo; inside the pack was the listing of available films. From the start, the Century of Progress films had brisk sales, and orders soon arrived in Rock Island for other subjects. New films were added and major department stores offered selections. By 1949, sales were more than a million filmstrips a year.

Freelance photographers made most of the views and receive credit at the beginning of the filmstrip. Many were made by Stereoscopic Society members (*see* Amateur Views in Chapter 5). Notable were George Brookwell, Elliot Fisher, T. J. Hileman, A. W. Luce, Alexis McKinney, Gabriel Moulin and James Sawders. Also each filmstrip is dated at the end. The subject matter and quality of the stereo photography are not always up to the standards set by Keystone and others, but for the social historian they provide a remarkable record of the 1930s and 1940s. There are many street scenes and people views.

In August 1933, Tru-Vue issued a test reel called "Tru-Vues of Current Events." The plan was to issue the films as a monthly news "magazine" showing famous people, events, beauty queens and so forth. Unfortunately, the project was not met with any enthusiasm and was dropped. There apparently are "test" reels in the market; however, they are very rare. The boxes are simply marked "TV-1, TV-2, TV-3" and so on.

The original Tru-Vue boxes are a simple red-and-white or blue-and-white (often the white over the years has turned to a light buff color). The logo "Pictures with Depth" appears on these early boxes. About 1940, Tru-Vue issued the more common red-and-silver or red-and-white boxes with stripes and no logo. The boxes contain the roll of film wrapped in a small ad flyer tied together with a tiny rubberband or an inner cardboard holder. The boxes and films are fragile and should be handled with care.

The variety of subject matter is remarkable. They claimed more than 400 titles. Some of the best are "A Night at the Carnival" (#201 and 202), "Navaho [*sic*] Lands" (#803), "*Normandie*" (the fabulous ocean liner, #1803) and the "1939 New York World's Fair" (#1205–1212, eight films).

Collectors seek out the many advertising films that were not sold to the general public. These were used to promote products or companies. They were used by salesmen or given to potential customers. These are often longer than the standard fourteen views and are scarce.

A number of films were geared to children. My personal favorite is "Santa Claus' Workshop (for boys)" (#223), featuring Santa working with his elves in the American Flyer factory. He is seen with rows and rows of now highly collectible toy trains.

The viewer (Tru-Vuer) was made in two basic models, which have color variants. The earliest is in a dark brown plastic with a metal front that is screwed on. The standard model has "Tru-Vue" on a diagonal in a box with triangles at the top left and bottom right. These were made in huge quantities and are common. The rare version has the "Century of Progress" logo on the front. In the mid-1940s (about 1946) Tru-Vue issued the all plastic model viewer. Most common is the dark brown front with a cream back. They also made an

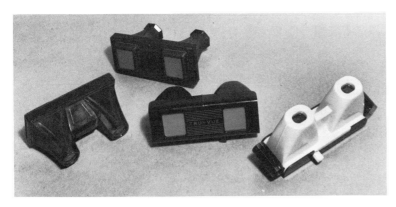

Original Tru-Vuer at rear, left to right, viewers from the 1930s, mid-1940s and late 1940s to 1951. (Photo courtesy of John Dennis, Stereo World *magazine.)*

all brown and an all black viewer with thin red embossed lines on the front.

To compete with View-Master, Tru-Vue issued "Stereochromes" in color in 1950. These films had nine views and round perforations along the bottom and came in bright yellow, red, and blue boxes. Ansco film was used.

It is interesting to note that Ansco was a direct descendent of the firm of E. and H. T. Anthony Company, which produced many nineteenth-century stereos. Unfortunately, the Ansco transparency color positives are not very permanent. Most Stereochromes have lost much of their color and have become magenta (pink). The color films came too late to keep View-Master from dominating the market.

Earlier, Tru-Vue had signed a long-term contract with Walt Disney Productions, which gave them rights to the many popular Disney cartoon characters in a 3-D format. Sawyer's (parent company of View-Master) saw the marketing potential of the Disney products and made a bid for the Tru-Vue Company. In 1951, Tru-Vue sold all of their assets to Sawyer's, who moved them to Beaverton, Oregon.

TRU-VUE FILMSTRIP PRICE GUIDE

Condition

Values are given for filmstrips that are complete and excellent: There are no knicks in the perforations or tears and the boxes are clean and complete with all of the flaps. Tru-Vue films and boxes are fragile and should be handled with care. Do not touch the film surface with your fingers. Remember: *handle with care.*

Note: The early Tru-Vue filmstrips were not numbered. There is little if any premium paid for the earlier version or those in the earlier-type boxes, except the following:

Bobby Jones Golf, six different films	each 25–30.00
Bonneville Dam, #1, scarce	10–15.00
Day at the Circus	12–15.00
Depth Photography, many different versions	each 2–4.00
Dam, #15, on Mississippi (River)	12–15.00
California Exposition (California-Pacific International Exposition,	

Original Tru-Vue box and sleeve at left—(blue-and-white) and later 1930s version in red-and-white. The red with silver stripes is from the 1940s, and the color filmstrip box with sleeve at the right is from 1950. (Photo courtesy of John Dennis, Stereo World *magazine.)*

San Diego, 1935), 1 and 2 (two films) _____ each 35–40.00
CP-1 to CP-4 (Century of Progress, Chicago, 1933) _____ each 20–25.00
CP-5 to CP-8 (Century of Progress, Chicago, 1933, scarce second group of four films) _____ each 30–35.00
    Special viewer in box _____ 50–60.00
Grand Coulee, #1, scarce _____ 15–20.00
New York City, #1–6, Different from later films _____ each 10–15.00
"Tru-Vues of Current Events," extremely rare, 1933 _____ 60–70.00
TV (#1–6, extremely scarce, early test films) _____ 50–60.00

See listings at end of numbered films for *C* and *X* prefix color films and advertising films.

Animal, Bird and Marine Life

101, Animals of the World _____ 2–4.00
102, Aquarium (New York) _____ 6.00
103, Birds from Everywhere _____ 4.00
104, Bronx Zoo (New York) _____ 4.00
105, Brookfield Zoo (Chicago) _____ 4–5.00
106, London Zoo, no. 1 _____ 5–6.00
107, London Zoo, no. 2 _____ 5–6.00

Children

201, A Night at the Carnival, no. 1 _____ 5.00
202, A Night at the Carnival, no. 2 _____ 10.00
203, Blondie (cartoon) _____ 20.00
204, Cinderella, part 1 _____ 10.00
205, Cinderella, part 2 _____ 10.00
206, Days of '49 _____ 5.00
207, Fairyland, no. 1 _____ 2.00
208, Fairyland, no. 2 _____ 2.00
209, Fairyland, no. 3 _____ 10.00
210, Goldilocks, part 1 _____ 4.00
211, Goldilocks, part 2 _____ 4.00
212, Jack and the Beanstalk (cartoon) ___ 6–8.00
213, Land of the Little Wooden People (Olvera St. Puppet Theatre, Los Angeles, Calif.) _____ 6–8.00
214, Little Orphan Annie (cartoon) _____ 10.00
215, Night Before Christmas (live action) _____ 4–5.00
216, Popeye (cartoon) _____ 5–7.00

Ringling Brothers and Barnum and Bailey Circus

217, no. 1, Early Morning Arrival _____ 6–8.00
218, no. 2, The Menagerie _____ 6–8.00
219, no. 3, Under the Big Top _____ 6–8.00
220, no. 4, Clowns and Side Show _____ 6–8.00

Miscellaneous

221, Pendleton Round-up, no. 1 _____ 5.00
222, Pendleton Round-up, no. 2 _____ 5.00
223, Santa Claus' Workshop (for boys), Santa in the American Flyer toy train factory _____ 12–15.00
224, Santa's Workshop (for girls), Santa making dolls _____ 6.00
225, Smilin' Jack _____ 7–8.00
226, Smokey Stover _____ 5–7.00
227, Three Little Pigs _____ 4.00
228, Toyland _____ 10–12.00
229, The World A Million Years Ago ____ 7–8.00
230, Susann's Doll House [*sic*] _____ 10–12.00
231, Keep 'em Flying _____ 10–12.00
232, Dick Tracy _____ 10–12.00
233, Sandy's Railroad _____ 20–25.00

National Parks

301, Black Hills, no. 1 _____ 4.00
302, Black Hills, no. 2 _____ 4.00
303, Black Hills, no. 3 _____ 4.00
304, Bryce Canyon _____ 4.00
305, Carlsbad Cavern, no. 1 _____ 6.00
306, Carlsbad Cavern, no. 2 _____ 9.00
307, Crater Lake _____ 9.00
308, Glacier, no. 1 _____ 3.00
309, Glacier, no. 2 _____ 3.00
310, Glacier, no. 3 _____ 3.00
311, Grand Canyon of Ariz., no. 1 _____ 2.00
312, Grand Canyon of Ariz., no. 2 _____ 3.00
313, Grand Canyon of Ariz., no. 3 _____ 5.00
314, Grand Canyon of Ariz., no. 4 _____ 5.00
315, Grand Canyon (North Rim) _____ 5.00
316, Grand Tetons _____ 5.00
317, Great Smoky Mountains, no. 1 _____ 2.00
318, Great Smoky Mountains, no. 2 _____ 2.00
319, Kings Canyon _____ 5.00
320, Mesa Verde, no. 1 _____ 4.00
321, Mesa Verde, no. 2 _____ 4.00
322, Mesa Verde, no. 3 _____ 6.00
323, Mount Rainier _____ 4.00
324, Rocky Mountains, no. 1 _____ 3.00
325, Rocky Mountains, no. 2 _____ 4.00
326, Sequoia, no. 1 _____ 5–6.00
327, Sequoia, no. 2 _____ 5–6.00
328, Shenandoah (Skyline Drive) _____ 5–6.00
329, Western Vacation by Air _____ 10–12.00
330, Yellowstone, no. 1 _____ 2.00
331, Yellowstone, no. 2 _____ 2.00
332, Yellowstone, no. 3 _____ 2.00
333, Yellowstone, no. 4 _____ 3.00
334, Yosemite, no. 1 _____ 2.00
335, Yosemite, no. 2 _____ 4.00
336, Yosemite, no. 3 _____ 4.00
337, Zion _____ 5.00

Pacific Northwest Region

401, Columbia River Highway _____ 5.00
402, Oregon Caves, no. 1 _____ 6.00
403, Oregon Caves, no. 2 _____ 6.00
404, Oregon Coast Highway _____ 5.00

California

501, Along the Pacific _____ 4–5.00
502, California Missions _____ 6.00

503, Chinatown (San Francisco) _____ 12.00
504, Death Valley, no. 1 _____ 4.00
505, Death Valley, no. 2 _____ 4.00
506, Death Valley, no. 3 _____ 4.00
507, Hancock Park _____ 8.00
508, High Sierra Region _____ 4.00
509, Hollywood, no. 1 _____ 4.00
510, Hollywood, no. 2 _____ 5.00
511, Lake Arrowhead _____ 10–12.00
512, Long Beach _____ 8–10.00
513, Los Angeles, no. 1 _____ 10–12.00
514, Los Angeles, no. 2 _____ 10–12.00
515, Monterey Peninsula _____ 6.00
516, Mount Wilson Observatory _____ 12.00
517, Palm Springs _____ 8–10.00
518, Ramona's Marriage Place _____ 6–8.00
519, Redwood Highway, no. 1 _____ 4.00
520, Redwood Highway, no. 2 _____ 5.00
521, San Diego, no. 1 _____ 6.00
522, San Diego, no. 2 _____ 6.00
523, San Francisco, no. 1 _____ 5.00
524, San Francisco, no. 2 _____ 5.00
525, San Francisco, no. 3 _____ 15.00
526, San Juan Capistrano _____ 5.00
527, Santa Barbara, no. 1 _____ 6.00
528, Santa Barbara, no. 2 _____ 6.00
529, Santa Catalina Island, no. 1 _____ 8.00
530, Santa Catalina Island, no. 2 _____ 8.00
531, Santa Catalina Island, no. 3 _____ 10.00
532, Santa Cruz _____ 5.00
533, Santa Monica, Westwood, Beverly Hills _____ 5.00
534, Tournament of Roses (Shirley Temple, image is "flat") _____ 10.00
535, U.S. Naval Training Station (San Diego) _____ 10.00

Great Basin Region

601, Boulder Dam, no. 1 _____ 2.00
602, Boulder Dam, no. 2 _____ 2.00
603, Boulder Dam, no. 3 _____ 2.00
604, Boulder Dam, no. 4 _____ 2.00
605, Cedar Breaks National Monument _____ 4.00
606, Salt Lake City _____ 3–4.00

Colorado

701, American Alps, no. 1 _____ 6.00
702, American Alps, no. 2 _____ 6.00
703, Arches National Monument _____ 5.00
704, Beyond the Rockies _____ 5.00
705, Black Canyon, no. 1 _____ 5.00
706, Black Canyon, no. 2 _____ 5.00
707, Central City _____ 8.00
708, Colorado National Monument, no. 1 _____ 5.00
709, Colorado National Monument, no. 2 _____ 5.00
710, Crest of the Continent _____ 5.00
711, Denver _____ 7–8.00
712, Denver Mountain Parks _____ 6.00
713, Estes Park Region _____ 6.00
714, Grand Mesa, no. 1 _____ 7–8.00

715, Grand Mesa, no. 2 _____ 7–8.00
716, Great Sand Dunes Nat'l Monument _____ 6.00
717, Gunnison—Lake City—Crede _____ 10.00
718, Pikes Peak by Auto _____ 2.00
719, Pikes Peak Region, no. 1 _____ 3.00
720, Pikes Peak Region, no. 2 _____ 3.00
721, Royal Gorge _____ 5.00
722, Salida _____ 6.00

Scenic Highways of Colorado

723, no. 1, Crossing Continental Divide _____ 10.00
724, no. 2, Gunnison River Route _____ 10.00
725, no. 3, Colorado River Canyon _____ 10.00
726, no. 4, Shadow of the Rockies _____ 10.00
727, no. 5, River of Lost Souls _____ 10.00

Colorado

728, Seven Falls, Cheyenne Canon [sic] _____ 4.00
729, Switzerland of America, no. 1 _____ 4.00
730, Switzerland of America, no. 2 _____ 5.00
731, Switzerland of America, no. 3 _____ 5.00
732, Through the Rockies _____ 5.00
733, White River National Forest _____ 6.00
734, Will Rogers' Shrine and Broadmoor _____ 8.00

Southwest Region

801, Aztec Ruins _____ 5–6.00
802, Great Southwest, no. 1 _____ 4.00
803, Great Southwest, no. 2 (Navaho lands) _____ 4.00
804, Great Southwest, no. 3 _____ 4.00
805, Kaibab National Forest _____ 4.00
806, Navaho and his Country (train scene) _____ 8–10.00
807, Old Santa Fe and Vicinity _____ 4.00
808, Palo Duro Canyon (Texas) _____ 6.00
809, Petrified Forest and Painted Desert of Ariz. _____ 2.00
810, San Antonio, Texas _____ 4.00
811, Tucson, Ariz. _____ 6.00

Central States

901, Chicago, no. 1 _____ 2.00
902, Chicago, no. 2 _____ 3.00
903, Dells of Wisconsin _____ 3.00
904, Detroit, no. 1 _____ 6.00
905, Detroit, no. 2 _____ 5.00
906, Greenfield Village (Detroit) _____ 5–6.00
907, Louisville, Kentucky _____ 7–8.00
908, Michigan's Mackinac Island _____ 6.00
909, Starved Rock Park, no. 1 _____ 2.00
910, Starved Rock Park, no. 2 _____ 3.00
911, Great Lakes, United States Naval Training Station, no. 1 _____ 15.00
912, Great Lakes, United States Naval Training Station, no. 2 _____ 15.00

Eastern Region

1001, Atlantic City _____ 6.00
1002, Boston, no. 1 _____ 4.00
1003, Boston, no. 2 _____ 4.00
1004, Cape Cod Country _____ 5.00
1005, Howe Caverns _____ 6.00
1006, Jones Beach State Park _____ 6.00
1007, Lake Placid, no. 1 _____ 6.00
1008, Lake Placid, no. 2 _____ 6.00
1009, New York City, no. 1 _____ 3.00
1010, New York City, no. 2 _____ 3.00
1011, New York City, no. 3 _____ 3.00
1012, New York City, no. 4 _____ 3.00
1013, Niagara Falls _____ 3–4.00
1014, Old Salem, Mass. _____ 5.00
1015, Philadelphia, no. 1 _____ 6.00
1016, Philadelphia, no. 2 _____ 6.00
1017, Rockefeller Center _____ 8.00
1018, Statue of Liberty _____ 6–8.00
1019, Washington, D.C., no. 1 _____ 2.00
1020, Washington, D.C., no. 2 _____ 2.00
1021, Washington, D.C., no. 3 _____ 3.00
1022, Washington, D.C., no. 4 _____ 3.00
1023, West Point _____ 10.00
1024, White Mountains _____ 3.00

South Eastern Region

1101, Asheville, N.C. _____ 5.00
1102, Beauty Spots of Central Florida _____ 2.00
1103, Charleston, no. 1 _____ 5.00
1104, Charleston, no. 2 _____ 5.00
1105, Charleston, no. 3 _____ 6.00
1106, Endless Caverns of Virginia _____ 3.00
1107, Jacksonville, Fla. _____ 4.00
1108, Key West, Fla., no. 1 _____ 6.00
1109, Key West, Fla., no. 2 _____ 6.00
1110, Land of the Sky _____ 4.00
1111, Lost Colony of Fort Raleigh _____ 6.00

1112, Miami _____ 3.00
1113, Miami Beach _____ 6.00
1114, Miami, Round About _____ 8.00
1115, New Orleans, La. _____ 6.00
1116, Norris Dam _____ 5.00
1117, St. Augustine _____ 2.00
1118, Savannah, Ga. _____ 5.00
1119, Shenandoah Valley _____ 4.00
1120, Silver Springs, Fla. _____ 3.00

World's Fairs

Golden Gate International Exposition, San
Francisco (1940)
   1201, no. 1, General Views _____ 25.00
   1202, no. 2, Flowers, Aviation _____ 30.00
   1203, no. 3, Gayway _____ 25.00
   1204, no. 4, Street of Nations _____ 25.00
New York World's Fair
   1205, no. 1, General Views _____ 25.00
   1206, no. 2, Foreign Exhibits _____ 25.00
   1207, no. 3, Foreign Exhibits _____ 25.00
   1208, no. 4, Court of States _____ 25.00
   1209, no. 5, Social Exhibits _____ 25.00
   1210, no. 6, Industries _____ 25.00
   1211, no. 7, Transportation _____ 25.00
   1212, no. 8, Amusements _____ 25.00

Stage and Screen

1301, A Circus at Michael Todd's _____ 35.00
1302, A Night at the College Inn,
scarce _____ 40.00
1303, Back Stage at Earl Carroll's _____ 35.00
1304, Back Stage at the Florentine
Gardens, Hollywood _____ 35.00
1305, Chez Paree After Dark _____ 22–25.00
1306, Gypsy Rose Lee (two versions)
   Personal Appearance _____ 45.00
   Strip and Not a Tease _____ 35.00

Rephotographed and mounted pair from the Tru-Vue filmstrip of Sally Rand's Bubble Dance, #1312. Film- strip in like-new condition and in a clean, undamaged box, $50.

1307, Hollywood Personalities (includes Cary Grant, Jack Oakie, Spencer Tracy, etc.) _____ 50.00
1308, Ice Follies _____ 12–15.00
1309, Mississippi River Show Boat _____ 25–30.00
1310, Movies in the Making _____ 25.00
1311, Movie Stars' Homes _____ 40.00
1312, Sally Rand (Bubble Dance) _____ 40–50.00
1313, Sally Rand Dude (Nude) Ranch [at 1940 Golden Gate Exposition] _____ 35.00
1314, Sally Rand (Fan Dance) _____ 75–80.00

Historical

1401, Battlefield, Gettysburg _____ 6.00
1402, Plymouth and the Pilgrims _____ 5–6.00
1403, Valley Forge _____ 5.00

Abraham Lincoln

1404, Life of Lincoln, part 1 _____ 3.00
1405, Life of Lincoln, part 2 _____ 3.00
1406, Life of Lincoln, part 3 _____ 4.00
1407, Lincoln in Illinois _____ 4.00
1408, Lincoln's New Salem, part 1 _____ 4–5.00
1409, Lincoln's New Salem, part 2 _____ 4–5.00

Historic Virginia

1410, no. 1, Jamestown & Yorktown _____ 2.00
1411, no. 2, Williamsburg _____ 3.00
1412, no. 3, Williamsburg _____ 3.00
1413, no. 4, Along the Potomac and Rapahannock Rivers _____ 10.00
1414, no. 5, Monticello _____ 6.00
1415, no. 6, Richmond _____ 6.00

Foreign and United States Possessions

1501, Agua Caliente _____ 5.00
1502, Air Voyage to Jamaica _____ 10.00
1503, Along the Nile _____ 5.00
1504, Around the World, no. 1 _____ 4.00
1505, Around the World, no. 2 _____ 4.00
1506, Around the World, no. 3 _____ 4.00
1507, Budapest _____ 10.00
1508, Colombia _____ 10.00
1509, Egypt _____ 8–10.00
1510, Finland _____ 8.00
1511, Ganges Country _____ 8.00
1512, Haiti _____ 8.00
1513, Havana _____ 12.00

Hawaiian Islands

1514, Beauty of Hawaii _____ 2–3.00
1515, Honolulu _____ 4.00
1516, National Park _____ 6.00
1517, People of Hawaii _____ 5–6.00

Miscellaneous Foreign

1518, India, no. 1 _____ 6.00
1519, India, no. 2 _____ 8.00

1520, Islands of South Seas _____ 15.00
1521, Jamaica _____ 10.00
1522, Japan _____ 15.00
1523, Land of the Buccaneers _____ 7–8.00
1524, Mexico City, no. 1 _____ 3–4.00
1525, Mexico City, no. 2 _____ 3–4.00
1526, Nassau _____ 6.00
1527, Native Haiti _____ 8.00
1528, Norway _____ 6.00
1529, Orient _____ 12–15.00
1530, Panama _____ 7–8.00
1531, Rome, Italy _____ 10.00
1532, San Juan, Puerto Rico _____ 8.00
1533, Santo Domingo _____ 6.00
1534, Siam, no. 1 _____ 6.00
1535, Siam, no. 2 _____ 6.00
1536, South America, West Coast _____ 4–5.00
1537, Sweden _____ 16–20.00
1538, Venice, Italy _____ 6.00
1539, Around the World, no. 4 _____ 6.00
1540, Around the World, no. 5 _____ 6.00
1541, Around the World, no. 6 _____ 6.00
1542, China _____ 10–12.00

Canada

1601, Alberta _____ 5.00
1602, Banff National Park, no. 1 _____ 2.00
1603, Banff National Park, no. 2 _____ 2.00
1604, Banff National Park, no. 3 _____ 2.00
1605, Banff National Park, no. 4 _____ 3.00
1606, Banks of the Saskatchewan _____ 5.00
1607, Gaspe Peninsula _____ 5.00
1608, Jasper National Park, no. 1 _____ 5.00
1609, Jasper National Park, no. 2 _____ 5.00
1610, Jasper National Park, no. 3 _____ 5.00
1611, Jasper National Park, no. 4 _____ 5.00
1612, Kootenay National Park _____ 8.00
1613, Montreal _____ 12.00
1614, Old Caribou Road, no. 1 _____ 6.00
1615, Old Caribou Road, no. 2 _____ 6.00
1616, Quebec _____ 4.00
1617, Vancouver, no. 1 _____ 6.00
1618, Vancouver, no. 2 _____ 6.00
1619, Victoria _____ 6.00
1620, Waterton—Glacier Peace Park _____ 6.00
1621, Winnipeg _____ 8–10.00
1622, Yoho National Park _____ 8.00

England

1701, Coronation _____ 25.00
1702, Coronation (Aldershot Tattoo) _____ 25.00
1703, Hampton Court Palace _____ 5.00
1704, Kew Gardens and Richmond _____ 5.00
1705, London Parks _____ 10.00
1706, London "The City" _____ 8–10.00
1707, London "West End" _____ 8–10.00
1708, Windsor Castle, no. 1 _____ 2.00
1709, Windsor Castle, no. 2 _____ 3.00

France

1801, Fontainebleau, no. 1 _____ 6.00
1802, Fontainebleau, no. 2 _____ 6.00

1803, *Normandie* (ocean liner) _____ 35.00
1804, Paris Exposition, no. 1 _____ 30.00
1805, Paris Exposition, no. 2 _____ 30.00
1806, Paris (Left Bank) _____ 15.00
1807, Paris (Right Bank), no. 1 _____ 6.00
1808, Paris (Right Bank), no. 2 _____ 8.00
1809, Paris (along the Seine) _____ 8.00
1810, Paris Park _____ 6.00
1811, Versailles _____ 6.00

Religious Films

1901, Passion Play, part 1 _____ 4–5.00
1902, Passion Play, part 2 _____ 4–5.00
1903, Passion Play, part 3 _____ 4–5.00
1904, Society of the Atonement (Gray-
mour Ave Maria Hour) _____ 15.00

Army and Navy

2001, Our New Army _____ 15.00
2002, Army Life Today _____ 15.00

Advertising Films

These come in a variety of lengths and subjects. So few have been sold with recorded
sales that I have decided not to place individual values. Generally, complete films in excellent condition (no tears, knicks or scratches)
in a clean and complete box sell for $25 to
$35 each. Listed here are those known to me
but there are many more.

Arthur Walter Seed Co., Grand Ridge, Ill. (two films
   in color)
   "Scientific Processing—Arthur Walter Seed Co."
   "Seed Corn in the Making"
Beech-Nut
Elgin Watches
ESSO Oil
Ford Motor Co. (1949, in color)
General Motors Corp.
Hughes' Tool Co., Houston, Tex.
Pop-Sycles [*sic*] (color)
The Agfa Co.
The Borden Co. (Elsie, the cow)
White Trucks

Color "Stereochromes"

C 1250, *Ile de France* (ocean liner) _____ 45–50.00
C 1251, *Queen Mary* (ocean liner) _____ 35–45.00
C 6033, Railway Fair, Chicago, ex-
tremely rare
   A, Rail Fair Exhibits _____ 50–60.00
   B, Rail Fair Trains _____ 60–70.00
   C, Rail Fair "Wheels a' Rollin'" _____ 60–70.00
X 54, Disney's Mickey Mouse _____ 30–35.00
Other Disney characters _____ 20–30.00

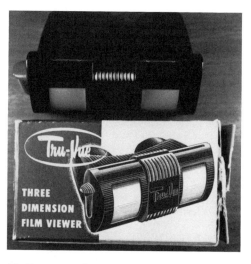

The Tru-Vue Card viewer with the original box. $12.

TRU-VUE CARDS

After Sawyer's purchased the Tru-Vue Company, they moved the manufacturing operations to their Beaverton, Oregon, plant near
Portland. They developed a new format that
fit the merchandising methods of the View-
Master system. The Tru-Vue cards eventually
replaced the filmstrips. Unfortunately, Sawyer's did not use Kodachrome color in the Tru-
Vue cards and as a result they are found today
missing most of the yellow and blue colors
leaving the images a light magenta (pink).

Values

There are three basic types of viewers and several different colors. The card is inserted in the
top and is advanced down through the viewer.
Most viewers, in the original box and in excellent condition, sell for $10–12 each.

The cards came in envelopes and were available in card sets (or albums), which had an
outer envelope. Complete cards in the envelopes sell from $2 to $5 each. Premiums are
paid for television shows. The Disney cards are
all fairly common.

Children's Albums
(contain three cards in an envelope)

DA-1, Disney Album (D-1, 2 & 3)
FA-1, Fairy Tale Album (F-1, 2 & 3)

Tru-Vue Gift set, which includes the Tru-Vue card viewer and a sampler of three cards in the original box. $20.

MA-1, Robin Hood (M-1, 2 & 3)
MA-2, Robinson Crusoe Album (M-4, 5 & 6)
MA-3, Tom Sawyer Album (M-8, 9 & 10)
TA-1, Television Album (T-1, 2 & 3)
WA-5, Western Roundup (C-3, 11 & 12)

Children's Subjects

C-1, Day at the Zoo
C-2, American Indians
C-3, Wild West Rodeo
C-4, Children's Fairyland
C-6, Circus Parade, 1954
C-21, 22 & 23, Space Travel
C-51, 52 & 53, Air Travel
C-54, 55 & 56, Modern Machine Marvels
D-1, Mickey Mouse in "Mickey's Birthday Party"
D-2, Donald Duck in "Deep Sea Diver"
D-3, Pluto in "Baseball Catcher"
D-4, Pinocchio Comes to Life
D-6, Peter Pan

D-7, Lady and the Tramp
D-8, Disneyland Park, Main Street U.S.A.
D-9, Disneyland Park, Frontierland
D-10, Disneyland Park, Adventureland
D-22, Mickey Mouse Club Circus Mouseketeers
D-23, Bambi
D-24, Zorro
F-1, Cinderella
F-2, Little Red Riding Hood
F-3, Jack and the Beanstalk
F-4, The Three Little Pigs
F-5, Goldilocks and the Three Bears
F-6, The Sleeping Beauty
F-7, Hansel and Gretel
F-8, Little Black Sambo
M-1, Robin Hood, Fights Little John
M-3, Robin Hood meets Friar Tuck
M-5, Robinson Crusoe Battles a Shark
M-9, Tom Sawyer, Pirate Adventure
M-10, Tom Sawyer, Treasure Cave
M-12, Jim Bowie, The Runaway Slave

Tru-Vue "Scenic Adventure" card and
envelope, #106, "Carlsbad Caverns
(1), New Mexico." $2.

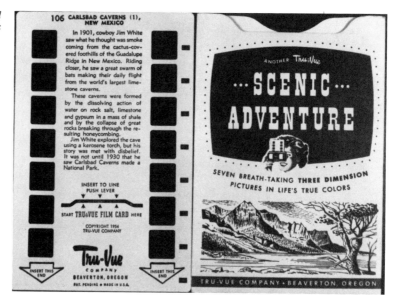

M-13, Sir Lancelot, Knights in Chains
S-1, Frosty, the Snow Man
S-5, The Littlest Snowman by Charles Tazewell
T-1, Kukla, Fran and Ollie
T-2, Wild Bill Hickok and Jingles
T-3, Buck Rogers
T-4, Howdy Doody and Clarabell the Clown
T-12, The Mask of the Lone Ranger
T-14, The Lone Ranger and the Phantom Raiders
T-16, Roy Rogers in Three-to-One Odds
T-19, Wild Bill Hickok and the Swindlers
T-21, Circus Boy and Bimbo, the Elephant

Scenic Subjects

106, Carlsbad Caverns (1), New Mexico
107, Carlsbad Caverns (2), New Mexico
108, Carlsbad Caverns (3), New Mexico
117, Grand Canyon National Park—South Rim (1)
118, Grand Canyon National Park—South Rim (2)
119, Grand Canyon National Park—Bright Angel
   Trail, Ariz.
125, Great Smoky Mountains (1), Tenn. and N.C.
154, Yellowstone National Park—Grand Canyon
   Area, Wyo.
155, Yellowstone National Park—Old Faithful Area,
   Wyo.
156, Yellowstone National Park—Lower Basin Area,
   Wyo.
159, Yosemite National Park (1), Calif.
160, Yosemite National Park (2), Calif.
161, Yosemite National Park (3), Calif.
205, Chicago, Ill.
217, Hollywood, Calif.
218, Homes of Movie Stars, Hollywood, Calif.
221, Los Angeles, Calif.
225, Miami and Miami Beach, Fla.

232, New York City (1)
233, New York City (2)
241, St. Augustine, Fla.
246, San Francisco, Calif.
250, Washington, D.C. (1)
251, Washington, D.C. (2)
301, Black Hills of South Dakota
312, Garden of the Gods, Colo.
319, Lookout Mountain—Chattanooga, Tenn.
324, Mount Vernon, Va., Home of George Washington
325, Niagara Falls, N.Y.
328, Petrified Forest and Painted Desert, Ariz.
330, Pike's Peak, Colo.
334, Royal Gorge, Colo.
604, Lake Louise, Canadian Rockies

Unnumbered Scenic Foreign Country Cards

Austria
Bermuda
Canada
Ecuador
Greece
India
Indonesia
Ireland
Peru
Portugal
Puerto Rico
Scotland
South Sea Islands
Spain
Switzerland
Thailand
Turkey

Tru-Vue "Magic Eyes" Gift Sets (contain three cards)

Bonanza (TV show)
Lassie (TV show)
The Monkees (TV show)
The Munsters (TV show)
Wizard of Oz

NOVELVIEWS

A product of Novelart Company of Long Island, New York, the Novelview filmstrips were a direct, but far less successful, competitor to Tru-Vue. The format of the Novelview was nearly identical with at least two different styles of viewer (with and without an advance knob). The films came in boxes of the same size as Tru-Vue. The quality does not seem to be up to Tru-Vue standards but they did make some subjects not available in any other 3-D format. The most sought after are the baseball films, which include 1936 Yankees and World Series plus an instructional film featuring pitcher Dizzy Dean. They also made cartoon films of Popeye, Joe Palooka and Katzenjammer Kids. The information about the company is sketchy but we do know they were active only a short time from the mid- to late-1930s. They had a promotion on the Jack Armstrong radio program, which featured a giveaway through the sponsor, Wheaties cereal. With a boxtop from Wheaties and two three-cent stamps, Novelview sent a film featuring Jack Armstrong on the Congo River. The Novelviewer was also called a "Moviescope" in this promotion. All Novelview items are rare and seldom come into the market. Therefore, I will not set values. In small groups I have seen the films in excellent condition in the boxes sell for as much as $20 each and even more for the baseball films. The Novelviewers usually sell in the $15 to $20 range, depending on condition. Listed here are the known Novelview filmstrips. I have been told there are commercial filmstrips that advertise products, but I have not examined any.

American Museum of Natural History

100A, Behind the Scenes—Gorillas
101, American Birds in their natural settings
104, The Planetarium—General Views
112A, Reptiles and How They Live

Fairy Tales and Famous Stories

300, Sleeping Beauty and the Handsome Prince
301, Three Little Pigs and the Big Bad Wolf
303, Goldilocks and Three Bears
304, Cinderella and the Glass Slipper
305, Puss in Boots and the Ogre
306, Hansel and Gretel and the Wicked Witch
307, Red Riding Hood and the Big Bad Wolf
308, Ali Baba and the Forty Thieves, part I, "Open Sesame"
308A, Ali Baba and the Forty Thieves, part II, The Robbers Destroyed

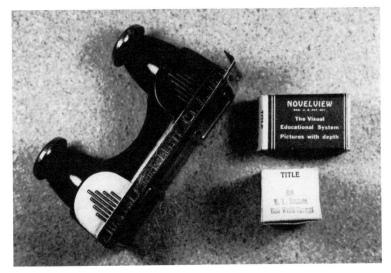

The Novelviewer and boxes of films. The Novelview was a direct competitor to Tru-Vue in the late 1930s but is much scarcer. Shown is the most desirable film, #835, "N.Y. Yankees, 1936 World Champs." The viewer in excellent condition is valued at about $20. The Yankees filmstrip is rare, complete (no tears or scratches) in the box, it is valued at $100. (Gordon D. Hoffman Collection)

310, Robin Hood, part I, His Adventurous Band
310A, Robin Hood, part II, His Prowess Rewarded
311, Treasure Island, part I, Jim Inherits the Secret Map
311A, Treasure Island, part II, The Pirates Attack
311B, Treasure Island, part III, The Pirates Outwitted and the Treasure Saved

Scenics and Points of Interest

400, Niagara Falls—American and Canadian
423, Battle of Gettysburg, part I, Civil War's decisive battle

American Cities

501, New York City—Skyline and famous buildings
501F, Radio City—Scenes from observation roof
501G, Empire State Building—World's highest structure

Foreign Countries

600, Rio de Janeiro—World's Most Beautiful Harbor
602, Paris—Heart of French National Life
605, London—City of Eight Million
609, Havana, Cuba—Metropolis of the West Indies

Ringling Bros., Barnum & Bailey Circus

702, The Clowns Who Make Us Laugh
707A, Under the Big Top—Thrilling Acts
708, Circus—Backstage
709, Circus Animals—The "Hippo" and Giraffe

Baseball

803, "Dizzy" Dean—How He Pitches
833, 1936 World Series, part I
835, 1936 Yankees—World's Series Champions

North American Indians

9001, Pueblos of San Ildefonso and Isleta, N.Mex.
903, Mexican Indians—Their arts and crafts
906, Seminole Indians—Their homes in the Everglades

Cartoons

1400, Scrappy's Ducky Prank
1401, Scrappy's Surprise
1402, Scrappy's Fish Story
1403, Popeye in "I'm Insulked"
1404, Popeye in "Within the Law"
1405, Joe Palooka "The Young Defender"
1406, Flash Gordon "Into the Water World"
1407, Flash Gordon "The Monster of the Deep"
1408, Katzenjammer Kids in "Love"
1413, Katzenjammer Kids on Strike

Special Film

Jack Armstrong Jungle Adventure

VIEW-MASTER

More than one billion View-Master reels have been sold since the first reels were placed on public sale more than fifty years ago in 1939. The idea for the View-Master came from William Gruber, a Portland, Oregon, piano tuner. He constructed a stereo rig that consisted of a pair of Kodak Bantam Specials he carried on his shoulder. He had been experimenting with the new Kodachrome color film and had in mind a device for viewing seven pairs on a card disk. By chance Gruber met Harold Graves, president of Sawyer's, a Portland photo-finishing and postcard company. Graves was impressed by Gruber's idea, and together they worked out the details of the now familiar View-Master format using 16 mm transparencies. Approximately $50,000 were borrowed for machinery, which was designed by Gruber.

Patents for the special stereoscope were filed on January 20, 1939, after several months of testing. The original viewer is called the *A* model and is recognized by the flip-front opening and straight "barrels" for viewing. In 1943, the improved Model *B* was introduced, which has a streamlined design, but still has the flip-front. The Model *A*, in nearly all cases, is found today with a warped front and often the mechanism is jammed. The Model *B*, a bit heavier and made in a better grade of plastic with a stronger hinge on the bottom, is not as likely to warp.

The first View-Master packages consisted of fifteen scenic reels and the stereoscope in a special woodlike paper-covered gift box. These were offered for sale at first in Portland in mid- to late-1939 and along with a special reel at the 1939 and 1940 World's Fairs in New York City and San Francisco. By 1941, a thousand dealers around the United States were actively selling the new viewers and reels to an eager public.

During World War II, View-Master produced special training reels for the United States Navy and the Army Air Corp. The various known sets are described at the end of the "Three-Reel Packets" section.

Model A View-Master "stereoscope" with earliest (gold) reel envelope. The viewer is a speckled color variant, $50 in a box. (Courtesy of John Dennis, Stereo World magazine.)

After the war, View-Master introduced the familiar square Model *C* viewer (1946–1956). By far, this is the most common viewer; it came in several slight variations of color and design. It was also in this period that Sawyer (abbreviated SAW in checklists) expanded View-Master by adding more subjects (worldwide coverage of scenics) and developing new products—a stereo camera called "The Personal," a film cutter and a projector called the Stereomatic 500. An extensive series of single-lens projectors was produced, mainly geared to the children's market.

Public demand for View-Master products soared after 1946. Production barely satisfied the needs of the original 1000-dealer network.

Repackaging of the single reels into the three-reel packets made the product more appealing to department stores and many added large View-Master sections next to their camera departments.

In October 1966, General Aniline and Film Corporation (GAF) bought Sawyer's and revamped the View-Master line. GAF introduced new 2-D projectors and the 3-D Talking View-Master.

In late 1980, GAF sold the View-Master portion of their company to a limited partnership headed by businessman Arnold Thaler. Further acquisitions resulted in the purchase of Ideal Toys. Recently, View-Master Ideal, Inc. was purchased by TYCO. This guide deals with View-Master products made before 1981. There are collectors for current products but most collectors prefer the earlier material.

The following pages will describe most of the View-Master material made before 1981. There are hundreds of special reels plus foreign-language reels that are rarely encountered by collectors.

View-Master Viewers (Stereoscopes)

Model A, plastic, black, round front flips open, "to change view pull to stop then

Black Model A viewers with large-lens version at the left ($25), regular version at the right ($15). (Courtesy of John Dennis, Stereo World magazine.)

Left, black Model B (British eyecup design), right, blue-and-black Model B with United States eyecup design, $20–35. (Courtesy Stereo World magazine, Wolfgang Sell photo.)

release'' imprinted above title window. Excellent condition, very clean lenses and mechanism works, 1938–1944 ___ 15–25.00

Model B, black Bakelite with more streamlined design, flip-front, 1944–1948 _____ 20–35.00

Model C, black Bakelite, insert in top, 1946–1956

Regular model with box, common ___ 2–4.00

With light attachment including batteries, no corrosion inside ___ 20–25.00

With transformer for light attachment _____ 30–35.00

Model D (Focusing) in the box _____ 85.00

Model E, top in wide, dipped *V* design. Made in brown and black, ivory or red knob _____ 8–10.00

Model F, lighted viewer in dark brown plastic with pressure bar on top _____ 15–20.00

Model G, common, ''Standard,'' at least thirteen color variations, 1959–1977

Off-white, dark brown lever ''albino'' _ 10–15.00

Beige, Sawyer's or GAF logos _____ 2–3.00

Red/white/blue (Bicentennial, 1976) _____ 3–4.00

Red with blue knob, scarce _____ 15–20.00

Model H, lighted, round bottom, Sawyer's or GAF logo on front, 1967–1981 _____ 10–15.00

Most modern viewers _____ 1–2.00

Projectors

S-1, metal, brown, single lens, carrying case _____ 45–50.00

Stereomatic ''500'', 3-D, two lens, carrying case _____ 200–300.00

Sawyer's or GAF plastic single lens ___ 8–12.00

Cameras

Personal 3-D with custom film cutter _____ 150–200.00

Mark II with film cutter, made in Europe _____ 175–225.00

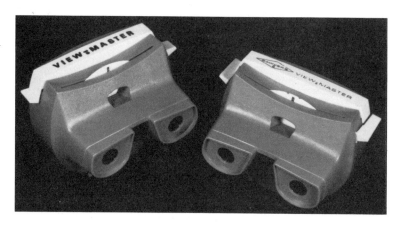

Left, GAF Model H viewer, right, Sawyer's version, Model H. $10–15. (Courtesy John Dennis, Stereo World magazine.)

Advertisement for the View-Master Personal Stereo Camera. The camera with the film cutter, $150–200.

COLLECTOR'S GUIDE TO VIEW-MASTER SINGLE REELS

The earliest View-Master reels are a dark blue with gold foil centers (1939–1941), which are often found warped. The envelopes are gold foil with blue lettering. The blue-and-gold reels were replaced by a dark blue-and-buff reel. During the early 1940s Sawyer's went to an off-white or buff reel and by 1946 had switched all production to the standard white reel design we know today. Up to about 1945, the reels were "hand-lettered" and did not have position numbers. After 1946, all reels had typeset lettering and position numbers were printed above the titles for each pair. There are many different reel lettering designs. In evaluating single reels, prices given are for both hand-lettered (HL, left price column) and standard white reels (SWR, right price column). All will be found in blue-and-white envelopes (BWE). Add 25 percent for buff-and-blue reels and 50 percent for blue-and-gold foil center reels. Values are given for reels in like-new condition. Deduct 50 percent for worn or soiled reels. Reels that are badly worn, stained, bent or have scratched or missing images are of little value.

Reel Numbering

The lowest known reel number is 4, "Boulder Dam, Scenic Auto Tour." Reels numbered 1,

Various View-Master reel lists issued by Sawyer's, Inc. $1–3 each.

2 or 3 are advertising reels first made in the 1950s (*see* Advertising Reels in Chapter 7). There are many variations of the single-reel titles. Only the reels with major changes are listed.

4, Boulder Dam, Scenic Auto Tour _____ 5.00 —
4, Boulder Dam, Nevada, USA, Scenic Auto Tour _____ — 1.00
5, Boulder Dam, Canyon Cruise No. 1 _____ 10.00 —
5, Boulder Dam, Nevada, Canyon Cruise _____ — 4.00
6, Boulder Dam, Canyon Cruise, No. 2 _____ 10.00 —
7, Boulder Dam, Lake Mead Drive _____ 10.00 —
8, Boulder Dam, Powerhouse Tour _____ 5.00 —
8, Boulder Dam, Nevada, Powerhouse Tour _____ — 1.50
8, Hoover [Boulder] Dam, Nev., Powerhouse Tour _____ — 1.00
9, Boulder Dam, Boat Trip to Dam _____ 10.00 —
10, Boulder City, The Desert Oasis _____ 10.00 —
10, Boulder City, Nev. _____ — 4.00
11, Boulder Dam, Nev. _____ 2.50 1.50
11, Hoover [Boulder Dam] Nev. ___ — 1.00
13, Virginia City _____ 8.00 1.00
14, Reno, "Biggest Little City in the World" _____ — 8.00
15, Las Vegas _____ — 8.00
16, Bryce Canyon National Park, Utah _____ 10.00 1.00
17, Bryce Canyon National Park ___ 2.00 1.00
21, Crater Lake, Oreg. _____ 2.00 1.50
22, Crater Lake, Oreg. _____ 3.00 1.50
23, Crater Lake National Park, Boat Trip _____ — 8.00
23, Crater Lake National Park III, Oreg. _____ — 5.00

26, Grand Canyon, Ariz. _____ 2.00 1.00
27, Grand Canyon, El Tovar to Yavapai Point _____ 3.00 —
27, Grand Canyon National Park, South Rim II _____ — 1.00
28, Grand Canyon, West Rim Drive _____ 3.00 1.00
29, Grand Canyon, East Rim Drive _____ 3.00 1.50
30, Grand Canyon , Ariz., Bright Angel Trail _____ 2.00 —
30, Grand Canyon National Park, Ariz. _____ — 1.00
31, Grand Canyon, Kaibab Trail ___ 3.00 1.00
32, Grand Canyon, River Trail ___ 2.00 1.00
36, Grand Canyon, North Rim ___ 2.00 1.00
37, Grand Canyon National Park, Meteor Crater _____ — 50.00
41, Grand Teton National Park ___ 2.00 1.00
42, Grand Teton National Park, Wyo. _____ 2.00 1.00
43, Grand Teton National Park III, Wyo. _____ — 5.00
46, Glacier National Park, Mont. ___ 4.00 1.00
47, Glacier National Park _____ 3.00 1.00
48, Glacier National Park, Going-to-the-Sun Highway _____ 2.00 1.00
49, Mountain Trip, Glacier National Park _____ 2.00 2.00
51, The Garden of the Gods, Colo. _____ 3.00 1.00
52, Frontier Town, in the Adiron-dacks _____ — 10.00
53, Park of the Red Rocks _____ 3.00 1.00
56, Golden Gate Exposition, For-eign Exhibits _____ 30.00 15.00
57, Golden Gate Exposition, Buildings _____ 20.00 15.00
58, Golden Gate Exposition, Flow-ers and Landscaping _____ 14.00 10.00
59, Golden Gate International Expo, at Night _____ 10.00 8.00
61, Hawaiian Hula Dancers, Hawaii _____ 4.00 2.00

View-Master, #16, "Bryce Canyon Nat'l Park, Utah," in early hand-lettered version with envelope. The reel is dark buff on the front and has a deep blue back. $10.

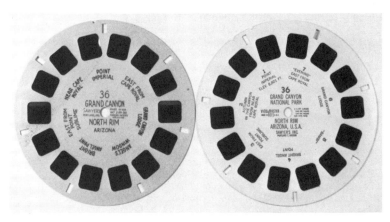

View-Master, #36, "Grand Canyon, North Rim, Arizona," at left in early hand-lettered version. Value $2. To the right is the later version, which is more common. Value $1.

62, Hawaiian Hula Dancers	3.00	1.00
63, Honolulu	4.00	1.00
64, Island of Oahu, Hawaii	3.00	1.00
65, Island of Hawaii, Kona Side	6.00	3.00
66, Island of Hawaii	5.00	1.00
67, Island of Maui, Hawaii	1.00	3.00
68, Hawaiian Flowers, Hawaii	4.00	1.00
69, Hawaiian Flowers	3.00	1.00
70, Hawaiian Flowers, Hawaii	10.00	3.00
71, Hawaii National Park, Island of Hawaii	8.00	1.00
72, Island of Kuai, Hawaii	3.00	6.00
73, Waikiki, Island of Oahu, Hawaii	2.00	1.00
74, Lee Mansion, Arlington National Cemetery, Va.	—	10.00
75, (Title unknown—from Packet A814)	Extremely rare	
76, Mount Vernon	10.00	1.00
77, Interior, Washington's Home, Mount Vernon, Va.	—	3.00
79, Natural Bridge	10.00	1.00
81, Niagara Falls	4.00	1.00
82, Niagara Falls in Winter, N.Y.	3.00	1.00
83, Old Fort Niagara, Youngstown, N.Y.	—	10.00
84, Edison Institute Museum	9.00	10.00
85, Edison Institute, Greenfield Village	15.00	10.00
86, Franklin D. Roosevelt's Home, Hyde Park, N.Y.	—	2.00
86, World's Fair, New York, Sculpture, 1939	15.00	—
87, World's Fair, Foreign Exhibits, 1939	15.00	—
87, Statue of Liberty National Monument	—	10.00
88, New York World's Fair, 1939	30.00	25.00
89, New York World's Fair, 1939–1940 II	20.00	10.00
91, Oregon Caves	2.00	1.00
92, Oregon Caves National Monument	2.00	2.00
93, Oregon Caves National Monument III	—	4.00
94, Storytown, USA, Lake George, N.Y.	—	10.00
96, Oregon's Coast	2.00	1.00
97, Oregon's Coast, Southern Section	16.00	—
101, Rocky Mountain National Park, Colo.	2.00	1.00

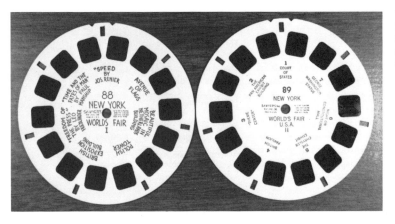

View-Master, reels #88 and 89, "New York World's Fair," comparing the earlier hand-lettered version at left with the later typeset version. $30 and $10 respectively.

102, Rocky Mountain National Park	3.00	1.00
104, Seattle, Wash.	—	10.00
105, Mt. Rainier National Park, Glaciers	4.00	1.00
106, Mt. Rainier National Park, Wash., Sunrise Side	2.00	1.00
107, Mt. Rainier National Park, Paradise Side	2.00	1.00
108, Mt. Rainier National Park, Paradise Side	2.00	4.00
109, Mt. Rainier National Park, Paradise Side	10.00	—
110, Mt. Rainier National Park, Wild Flowers	10.00	4.00
111, Redwood Highway	3.00	1.00
112, Redwood Highway, Calif.	2.00	1.00
113, Redwood Highway III, Calif.	—	5.00
115, Sequoia National Park	2.00	2.00
116, Sequoia National Park, Calif.	2.00	1.00
117, Sequoia National Park, Calif.	4.00	1.00
118, King's Canyon National Park, Grant Grove	10.00	2.00
121, Salt Lake City	11.00	1.00
122, Morman Temple, Tabernacle and Grounds, Salt Lake City	11.00	1.00
124, The Dells of the Wisconsin River	2.00	1.00
126, Yellowstone National Park	3.00	1.00
127, Yellowstone National Park	2.00	1.00
128, Yellowstone National Park	2.00	1.00
129, Yellowstone National Park	2.00	1.00
129, Yellowstone National Park, Geysers and Pools	4.00	1.00
131, Yosemite National Park	10.00	1.00
132, Yosemite National Park, Calif.	10.00	1.00
133, Yosemite National Park III, Calif.	—	1.00
136, Washington, D.C.	3.00	1.00
137, Washington, D.C.	3.00	1.00
139, United States Naval Academy, Annapolis, Md.	—	3.00
141, Zion National Park, Utah	3.00	1.00
142, Zion National Park	2.00	1.00
144, Palm Beach and West Palm Beach, Fla.	—	10.00
145, Sanctuary of Our Sorrowful Mother, Portland, Oreg.	10.00	2.00
145, Hollywood, Fla.	—	10.00
146, Sanctuary of Our Sorrowful Mother	3.00	2.00
146, Fort Lauderdale	—	15.00
147, The Seven Dolors Sanctuary of Our Sorrowful Mother	3.00	1.00
147, Fort Myers, Fla.	—	10.00
148, Sanctuary of Our Sorrowful Mother, The Grotto and Grounds	10.00	5.00
148, Clearwater, Fla.	—	10.00
149, Sanctuary of Our Sorrowful Mother, Monastery and Grounds	10.00	5.00
149, Rare Bird Farm, Fla.	—	9.00
151, Columbia River Highway, Oreg.	4.00	1.00
152, Water Falls along Columbia Highway	5.00	—
152, Bonneville Dam and Columbia River Highway, Oregon.	5.00	2.50
152, Columbia River Highway, Falls	10.00	5.00
153, Bonneville Dam, Columbia River Highway	10.00	—
154, Atlantic City	—	1.00
155, Miss America Beauty Pageant, Atlantic City, N.J., 1954	—	15.00
156, New York City, N.Y.	3.00	1.00
157, New York City II, 1946	—	1.25
157, New York City II, 1948	—	2.00
157, New York City II, 1950	—	1.00
158, Florida Flowers	5.00	—
158, Rockefeller Center, Empire State Building, New York City, 1946	—	5.00
158, Rockefeller Center, Empire State Building, New York City, 1948	—	1.00
158, New York City III, 1952	—	2.00
158, New York City III, 1958	—	5.00
159, Fruits and Flowers, Fla.	4.00	—
159, Florida Flowers, 1955	—	5.00
160, St. Augustine, Ostrich, Alligator Farm	2.00	1.00
160, St. Augustine, Fla.	—	1.00
161, Silver Springs, Fla.	3.00	1.00
162, St. Augustine	4.00	—
162, Overseas Highway and Key West	1.25	2.00
162, Highway US 1, Daytona Beach to Key West, Fla.	—	2.00
163, Scenes of Florida	4.00	2.00
163, Miami Beach, Fla.	—	3.00
164, Cypress Gardens and Bok Tower	2.00	1.00
165, Miami and Miami Beach	3.00	1.00
166, Marine Studios, St. Augustine	—	1.00
167, Marine Studios, St. Augustine	5.00	—
167, Bok Tower and Florida Flowers, Fla.	—	3.00
168, Miami Beach	5.00	—
168, Water Skiing, Cypress Gardens, Fla.	—	2.00
169, Palm Beach	4.00	—
169, Everglades National Park, Fla.	—	5.00
170, Key West and Overseas Highway	6.00	—
170, Sarasota, Fla.	—	5.00
171, McKee Jungle Gardens, Vero Beach	5.00	—
171, Spanish Monastery, North Miami Beach, Fla.	—	5.00
172, Parrot Jungle, Miami, Fla.	—	5.00
173, Bok Tower	4.00	2.00
174, Seminole Indians and the		

Everglades _____ 8.00 —
174, Monument Valley, Ariz. and
Utah _____ — 1.50
175, Navajo Indians, N. Mex. and
Ariz. _____ — 2.00
176, Petrified Forest _____ 5.00 1.00
177, The Painted Desert _____ 4.00 1.00
178, Desert Scenes _____ 10.00 1.00
179, Tucson _____ 4.00 1.25
180, Phoenix _____ 2.00 2.00
181, Colonial Williamsburg, Va. __ 10.00 1.00
182, (Title unknown—
from packet A814) _____ Extremely rare
183, Lake Tahoe, Calif. _____ 3.00 1.00
184, The Monterey Peninsula,
Calif. _____ 2.00 1.25
186, Palm Springs _____ 3.00 1.00
187, The Mariner's Museum,
Newport News _____ 10.00 5.00
188, Santa Barbara, Calif. _____ 4.00 1.50
189, Mission San Juan Capistrano __ 2.00 2.00
191, Lambert Gardens, Portland ___ 5.00 —
192, Cave of the Mounds, Blue
Mounds _____ — 10.00
193, Lambert Gardens _____ 5.00 —
194, The Beautiful Caverns of
Luray, Va. _____ 5.00 1.50
195, Beautiful Caverns of Luray ___ 5.00 2.00
196, Grand Coulee Dam _____ 3.00 1.50
198, San Francisco _____ 6.00 1.00
201, Santa Catalina _____ 3.00 1.00
202, The Corn Palace, Mitchell _____ — 10.00
203, The Black Hills, S. Dak. _____ 2.00 1.00
204, Badlands National Monument,
S. Dak. _____ — 2.00
205, Duluth and North Shore Drive,
Minn. _____ — 1.00
206, Sun Valley, Idaho _____ 3.00 1.00
207, Sun Valley, Idaho _____ 5.00 1.00
208, Sun Valley, Idaho _____ 10.00 5.00
211, Timberline Lodge and Mt.
Hood, Oreg. _____ 4.00 2.00
212, Mt. Hood, Oreg. Loop Trail ___ 3.00 —
212, Mount Hood, Oreg. _____ — 1.00
215, Farmer's Market, Los Angeles __ — 5.00

216, Knott's Berry Farm I, Ghost
Town, Calif., near Los Angeles _____ — 4.00
217, Knott's Berry Farm II, Ghost
Town, Calif., near Los Angeles _____ — 5.00
218, Knott's Berry Farm III, Ghost
Town, Calif., near Los Angeles _____ — 5.00
219, Hollywood, Calif. _____ 10.00 1.50
220, Homes of Hollywood Movie
Stars _____ 5.00 4.00
221, Los Angeles, Calif. _____ 4.00 2.00
222, Tournament of Roses, Pasadena, Calif. _____ — 10.00
223, Los Angeles Area, Coastal
Towns, Calif. _____ — 15.00
226, Dioramas, Mesa Verde
National Park, Colo. _____ 5.00 1.00
227, Mesa Verde National Park _____ 2.00 1.00
231, Cedar Breaks National
Monument, Utah _____ — 2.00
234, Cave of the Winds, Colo. _____ 5.00 1.00
236, The Million Dollar Highway ___ 4.00 1.50
237, Berthoud Pass Highway 40,
Rocky Mountains _____ 4.00 2.00
238, Royal Gorge, Colo. _____ 10.00 1.00
239, Monarch Pass, U.S. Highway
50, Colo. _____ — 5.00
240, Central City, Colo. _____ — 10.00
241, North and South Cheyenne
Mountain, Colo. _____ 10.00 2.00
243, Broadmoor—Cheyenne
Mountain, Colo. _____ 3.00 1.00
245, Pike's Peak _____ 4.00 1.00
246, Denver and Denver
Mountain Parks _____ — 1.00
248, Upper Michigan _____ — 1.00
248, Mackinac Island and Vicinity,
Mich. _____ — 4.00
249, Iowa, The Hawkeye State _____ — 1.00
251, Carlsbad Caverns National
Park _____ 5.00 1.00
252, Carlsbad Caverns National
Park _____ 2.00 1.00
253, Carlsbad Caverns National
Park _____ 4.00 1.00
255, Skiing in New England, 1957 __ — 5.00

View-Master, #194, "The Beautiful Caverns of Luray, Va.," 1939 issue in deep blue with gold foil center and gold foil and blue envelope. $7.50. (Gordon D. Hoffman Collection)

256, Mt. Lassen Volcanic National Park, Calif.	—	1.00
257, Acadia National Park, Maine	10.00	1.00
258, Cannon Mountain Aerial Tramway, Franconia Notch	5.00	1.00
259, Crawford Notch, Eastern Slope	5.00	4.00
260, Franconia Notch, Lost River, White Mountains	10.00	1.50
261, Shenandoah National Park, Skyline Drive, Va. (summer)	4.00	1.00
262, Shenandoah National Park, Skyline Drive, Va. (autumn)	10.00	2.00
262, Jamestown, 1955	—	10.00
263, Adirondack Mountains, N.Y.	4.00	5.00
263, Endless Caverns, Va., 1955	—	10.00
264, Ausable Chasm, N.Y.	2.00	4.00
265, White Mountains	4.00	1.00
266, Mount Washington	10.00	4.00
267, Cranmore Mt. Skimobile Tramway, White Mountains	8.00	4.00
268, The Mohawk Trail, Mass.	2.00	2.00
268, Santa's Village	—	10.00
269, Old Covered Bridges, New England	5.00	8.50
270, Lake George, N.Y.	10.00	5.00
270, Mount Sunapee State Park, N.H.	—	5.00
271, Mt. Mansfield and Smugglers Notch	10.00	5.00
271, Rural Connecticut, 1950	—	2.00
272, Vermont State, North Section	5.00	1.00
273, Maine Seacoast, York to Cape Porpoise	2.00	1.00
274, Autumn Foliage, Mt. Monadnock	4.00	4.00
275, The Mohawk Trail, Autumn Foliage, Mass.	3.00	1.00
276, Wild Flowers, Rocky Mountain Region	10.00	5.00
276, Cape Cod, Mass.	—	1.00
277, Autumn Foliage of New England	3.00	1.00
278, Boston, Mass.	4.00	1.00

280, Historic Plymouth, Mass.	10.00	1.00
281, Santa Fe, N.Mex.	2.00	4.00
281, Old Sturbridge Village, Sturbridge	10.00	5.00
282, Fiesta, Santa Fe, N.Mex.	5.00	—
282, Santa Fe, N.Mex., 1948	—	1.25
283, Taos, N.Mex.	3.00	5.00
284, Death Valley National Monument	5.00	1.00
285, Death Valley National Monument	3.00	1.00
286, Death Valley National Monument III	10.00	5.00
286, Indian Tribal Ceremonial, Gallup, N.Mex.	—	2.00
287, White Sands National Monument	5.00	2.00
288, Aztec Ruins National Monument, N.Mex.	2.00	2.00
289, Desert Cactus in Bloom	2.00	1.00
290, Desert Wildflowers in Bloom	2.00	1.00
291, California Wild Flowers	5.00	3.00
292, Oak Creek Canyon and Vicinity	8.00	4.00
293, Central and Southern Arizona	3.00	5.00
294, Zuni and Navajo Indian Crafts and Arts	5.00	2.50
294, Indian Arts and Crafts, N.Mex.	—	2.50
295, St. Louis Zoological Park	3.00	1.00
296, St. Louis Zoological Park	5.00	8.00
297, St. Louis Zoological Park III	10.00	5.00
298, Abe Lincoln's New Salem and Springfield, Ill., 1950	—	1.00
299, Hot Springs National Park, Ark.	5.00	1.00
301, Alaska Bound	4.00	1.00
302, Alaska, Ketchikan, Juneau	3.00	2.00
303, Alaska, Skagway, White Pass, West Taku Arm	4.00	2.00
304, Juneau and the Mendenhall Glacier, Alaska	—	1.00
305, Sitka, Alaska, 1950	—	2.00
306, Mount McKinley National Park, Alaska	—	1.00

View-Master, reel #284, "Death Valley Nat'l Mon., Calif. I," hand-lettered white reel. $5.

View-Master, reel #296, ''St. Louis Zoological Park No. II,'' hand-lettered white reel. $5.

307, Ketchikan and Vicinity, Alaska _____ —	2.00	
308, Anchorage, Alaska, 1950 _____ —	1.00	
309, The Eskimos, Alaska, 1950 _____ —	2.00	
311, Vancouver, B.C., Stanley Park _____ 10.00	5.00	
311, Vancouver, British Columbia, Canada _____ —	1.00	
313, Victoria, B.C. and Butchart's Gardens _____ 2.00	6.00	
313, Victoria and Vicinity, B.C. _____ 1.50	1.00	
314, Victoria, B.C., Butchart's Gardens _____ 9.00	5.00	
316, Jasper National Park, Canada _____ 2.00	1.00	
317, Jasper Nat'l Park, Canada _____ 10.00	1.50	
317, The Jasper Icefields, Canadian Rockies, Alberta, 1948 _____ —	1.00	
318, Banff National Park, Alta., Canada _____ 3.00	1.00	
319, Banff National Park, Canada, Lake Louise _____ 10.00	1.00	
319, Lake Louise, Canadian Rockies, Alta., Canada, 1948 _____ —	1.00	
320, Indian Days, Banff, Alta., Canada _____ —	6.00	
321, Waterton Lakes National Park, Canada _____ 3.00	1.50	
322, Calgary Stampede, Alta. _____ 10.00	5.00	
326, Rock City Gardens, Lookout Mountain, Tenn. _____ 3.00	3.00	
327, Scenes of Lookout Mountain, Chattanooga _____ —	4.00	
328, San Antonio, Tex. _____ 2.00	1.00	
330, The French Quarter, New Orleans, La. _____ —	5.00	
331, New Orleans, La. _____ 4.00	1.00	
332, The Mardi Gras, New Orleans, La. _____ —	3.00	
333, Chicago, Ill. _____ —	1.50	
334, Natchez, ''The Old South,'' Miss. _____ —	1.00	
335, Bellingrath Gardens, Mobile _____ —	10.00	

336, Great Smoky Mountains National Park, Tenn. _____ 10.00	1.00	
337, Great Smoky Mountains National Park, Tenn. _____ 3.00	1.00	
338, Lookout Mountain, Chattanooga, Tenn. _____ 2.00	1.00	
339, Mammoth Cave National Park _____ 6.00	1.00	
340, Mammoth Cave National Park _____ 10.00	1.00	
342, Race Horses of the Bluegrass Country, Ky. _____ —	3.00	
343, Roosevelt's Little White House, Warms Springs, Ga. _____ —	1.00	
344, Howe Caverns, N.Y. _____ 2.00	5.00	
345, Howe Caverns II _____ 3.00	1.00	
345, Home of Theodore Roosevelt, Sagamore Hill, Oyster Bay, N.Y. _____ —	10.00	
347, Gettysburg National Military Monument _____ 5.00	5.00	
348, Gettysburg National Military Monument, Pa., II _____ 10.00	5.00	
349, Amish Country, Pa. _____ —	1.00	
350, Philadelphia, Pa. _____ —	1.00	
351, Historic Philadelphia and Valley Forge, Pa. _____ —	1.00	
352, Independence National Historical Park, Philadelphia, Pa. _____ —	5.00	
358, Mobile, Ala., 1955 _____ —	10.00	
360, Historic Charleston, S.C. _____ —	1.00	
361, Castillo de San Marcos National Monument, St. Augustine, Fla. _____ —	10.00	
362, Carriage Cavalcade _____ —	15.00	
363, Ross Allen's Reptile Institute, Seminole Indian Village, Silver Springs _____ —	20.00	
365, Kansas, The Wheat State _____ —	1.00	
365, Historic Charleston _____ —	10.00	
366, The Great Masterpiece, Lake Wales, Fla. _____ —	10.00	
367, The Sunken Gardens, St. Petersburg _____ —	8.00	
368, The Florida Keys _____ —	8.00	

369, Will Rogers Memorial,
Claremore, Okla. _____ — 10.00
370, Oklahoma, The Sooner State ___ — 2.00
371, Tropical Hobbyland, Miami ____ — 15.00
372, The Colorful Ozarks _____ — 5.00
373, Mark Twain's Home Town,
Hannibal, Mo. _____ — 15.00
374, Onondaga Caves, Leasburg,
Mo. _____ — 30.00
375, Niagara Falls to Toronto,
Canada _____ — 1.50
375, Niagara Falls, Ont., Canada ____ — 1.00
376, Toronto, Ont., Canada _____ — 1.50
376, Toronto and Vicinity, Ont.,
Canada _____ — 1.00
377, Hamilton and Vicinity, Ont.,
Canada _____ — 10.00
378, Ottawa, Ont., Canada _____ — 1.00
380, Montreal, Que., Canada _____ — 1.00
381, Montreal and Vicinity, Que.,
Canada _____ — 5.00
382, Laurentian Mountain Area,
Que., Canada _____ — 1.00
383, Quebec City, Canada I _____ — 1.00
384, Quebec City, Canada II _____ — 2.00
385, Quebec City and Vicinity,
Canada _____ — 2.00
386, Ste. Anne De Beaupre, Que.,
Canada _____ — 1.00
387, Rural Quebec, Canada _____ — 2.00
388, Baspe Peninsula, Que.,
Canada _____ — 1.00
389, St. Joseph's Oratory, Mt.
Royal, Montreal, Que., Canada ____ — 10.00
391, Skiing in the Laurentians,
Que. _____ — 10.00
395, Greater Miami Area, Fla. _____ — 5.00
400, The Inauguration of President
Dwight D. Eisenhower, 1953 _____ — 10.00
401, Girl Scouts Serve Their
Country _____ — 35.00
405, The Coronation of Queen
Elizabeth II, London, England,
June 2, 1953 _____ — 2.50
406, The Coronation of Queen
Elizabeth II, London, England,
June 2, 1953 _____ — 2.50
407, The Coronation of Queen
Elizabeth II, London, England,
June 2, 1953 _____ — 2.50
501, Mexico City and Vicinity _____ 3.00 —
501, Mexico City I _____ — 1.00
502, Mexico City and Vicinity _____ 5.00 —
502, Mexico City, Mexico II _____ — 2.00
503, Mexico City and Vicinity _____ 6.00 —
503, Mexico City III _____ — 5.00
504, Taxco, Mexico _____ 4.00 2.00
505, Taxco, Cuernavaca _____ 10.00 —
505, Cuernavaca, Mexico _____ — 5.00
506, San Juan Teotihuacan Pyramids _____ 10.00 —
506, Pyramids of Teotihuacan and
Tenayuca _____ 3.00 3.50
507, Monte Alban Ruins,
Oaxaca _____ 10.00 —

507, Monte Alban and Mitla Ruins,
Oaxaca _____ 5.00 9.00
508, The Indians of Oaxaca _____ 6.00 4.00
509, Mitla Ruins, Oaxaca _____ 10.00 —
509, Monterrey and Pan-American
Highway, Mexico _____ — 2.00
510, Lake Patzcuaro and Paricutin
Volcano _____ 6.50 —
510, Paricutin Volcano, Mexico _____ — 3.00
511, Acapulco, Mexico _____ 3.00 1.50
512, Acapulco, Mexico _____ 10.00 —
513, Cholula and Tlaxlala,
Mexico _____ 5.00 —
514, Tule Tree Fair, Oaxaca _____ 10.00 —
515, Typical Scenes in Mexico _____ 4.00 3.00
516, Lake Patzcuaro, Mexico _____ — 5.00
517, Vicinity of Mexico City,
Mexico _____ — 10.00
517, Mexico City and Vicinity,
Mexico _____ — 6.00
518, Cuernavaca and Vicinity,
Mexico _____ — 8.00
519, Carnival at Amercameca,
Mexico _____ — 5.00
520, Chichen-Itza, Mayan Ruins,
Yucatan, Mexico _____ — 3.00
520, Mayan Ruins, Yucatan
Peninsula, Mexico _____ — 10.00
521, Yucatan Scenes and Uxmal
Ruins, Mexico _____ — 10.00
523, Mexican Bullfight _____ — 3.00
524, Charros Costumes and Dances
of Mexico, 1946 _____ — 4.00
524, Charros Costumes and Dances
of Mexico, 1948 _____ — 1.50
525, Puebla-Vera Cruz, Mexico _____ — 15.00
530, Panama City, Panama, 1946 ___ — 3.00
530, Panama City, Panama, 1948 ___ — 1.50
531, Panama City II, Panama,
1946 _____ — 6.00
532, Old Panama, Ft. San Lorenzo,
Panama _____ — 2.00
533, Balboa to Colon, Panama _____ — 2.00
533, Panama City to Colon,
Panama _____ — 5.00
534, Native Indians of Panama _____ — 10.00
541, San Jose, Costa
Rica _____ — 3.00
541, San Jose and Vicinity, Costa
Rica _____ — 8.00
542, Cartago and the Irazu Volcano,
Costa Rica _____ — 5.00
543, Scenes of Costa Rica _____ — 3.00
544, Costa Rica, Central America ___ — 7.00
548, San Salvador and Vicinity,
El Salvador (No position numbers) __ — 4.00
548, San Salvador and Vicinity,
El Salvador (with position numbers) _____ — 2.00
549, El Salvador _____ 10.00 5.00
551, Guatemala City, Guatemala ___ 5.00 2.00
552, Chichicastenango, Guate-
mala _____ 4.00 2.00
553, Antiqua and Lake Atitlan,
Guatemala _____ 7.00 10.00

View-Master, reel #521, "Yucatan Scenes and Uxmal Ruins, Mexico," 1946. $10.

553, Antiqua, Guatemala _____ —	4.00	
554, Lake Atitlan, Guatemala _____ —	7.50	
555, Highland Indians of Guatemala _____ —	3.00	
558, Tegucigalpa, Honduras _____ —	4.00	
559, Tegucigalpa, Silver Hill, Honduras _____ —	7.00	
561, Managua and Vicinity, Nicaragua _____ —	3.00	
562, Magnificent Managua, Nicaragua _____ —	4.00	
564, San Juan, Puerto Rico _____ —	1.00	
565, San Juan to Ponce, Puerto Rico (no position numbers) _____ —	5.00	
565, San Juan to Ponce, Puerto Rico (with position numbers) _____ —	4.00	
571, Morro Castle, Havana, Cuba ___ —	5.00	
571, Havana and Morro Castle, Cuba _____ —	4.00	
572, Havana, Cuba I _____ —	2.00	
573, Havana II, Cuba _____ —	4.00	
574, Havana, Cuba III _____ —	4.00	
577, Scenes of Cuba _____ —	3.00	
577, Scenes of Havana, Cuba _____ —	5.00	
581, Kingston, Jamaica _____ —	3.00	
582, Jamaica, North Coast _____ —	1.50	
585, Port of Spain and Saddle Road, Trinidad _____ —	2.50	
586, Port of Spain, Asphalt Lake, Trinidad _____ —	3.00	
587, Trinidad, Land of Calypso _____ —	5.00	
589, Port-au-Prince, Haiti (no position numbers) _____ —	3.00	
589, Port-au-Prince, Haiti (with position numbers) _____ —	1.50	
590, The People of Haiti (no position numbers) _____ —	5.00	
590, The People of Haiti (with position numbers) _____ —	4.00	
591, Haiti, Magic Island _____ —	8.00	
592, Ciudad Truijillo, Dominican Republic (no position numbers) ___ —	4.00	
592, Ciudad Truijillo, Dominican Republic (with position numbers) ___ —	2.00	

593, Santo Domingo, New World's Oldest City _____ —		5.00
595, Island of Bermuda _____ —		1.50
597, Nassau, Bahamas _____ —		1.00
598, Nassau, New World Riviera, Bahamas _____ —		4.00
601, Scenes of Colombia, Colombia _ —		3.00
602, Bogota, Colombia I _____ —		3.00
603, Bogota, Colombia II _____ —		10.00
604, Medellin, Colombia (no position numbers) _____ —		7.50
604, Medellin, Colombia (with position numbers) _____ —		10.00
606, Cartagena, Colombia _____ —		12.00
607, Barranquilla, Colombia _____ —		12.00
611, Quito, Ecuador _____	10.00	2.00
612, Rural Life in Ecuador (no position numbers) _____ —		4.00
612, Rural Life in Ecuador (with position numbers) _____ —		2.00
613, Scenes of Ecuador _____ —		3.00
615, Quito and the Equator, Ecuador _____ —		7.00
621, Lima, Peru _____	10.00	—
621, Lima, Peru I, 1946 _____ —		4.00
621, Lima, Peru I, 1948 _____ —		2.00
622, Arequipa to Cuzco, Peru _____	5.00	2.00
623, Ruins of Pachacamac, near Lima, Peru _____	21.00	4.00
623, Ruins of Pachacamac & Cajamarquilla, Lima, Peru _____ —		3.00
624, Ruins of Cajamarquilla, Lima, Peru _____	10.00	8.00
625, Ruins of Sacsahuaman Fortress, Cuzco, Peru _____	10.00	—
625, Ruins of Cajamarquilla, Lima, Peru _____		10.00
628, Lima II, Peru (no position numbers) _____ —		5.00
628, Lima II, Peru (with position numbers) _____ —		4.00
641, Santiago, Chile _____	4.00	1.50
642, Valparaiso and Vina Del Mar, Chile _____	4.00	3.00

643, Lakes Region, Chile (no position numbers) ———————— — 5.00
643, Lakes Region, Chile (with position numbers) ———————— — 6.00
651, La Paz, Bolivia ———————— 4.00 5.00
656, Buenos Aires, Argentina ——— 4.00 1.00
657, Buenos Aires, Argentina ——— 2.00 2.00
661, Caracas, Venezuela ———————— — 1.00
664, Willemstad, Curacao, Netherlands West Indies ———————— — 10.00
666, Santos and Sao Paulo, Brazil _ 10.00 —
667, La Plata, Argentina ————— 4.00 5.00

Reel #667, "La Plata, Argentina," is the highest numbered hand-lettered issue. All higher numbers are found on the standard white reels with typeset lettering.

669, Petropolis and Vicinity, Brazil ——— 2.50
670, Rio de Janeiro, Brazil ———————— 1.00
671, Rio de Janeiro and Copacabana Beach, Brazil ———————— 6.00
671, Rio de Janeiro II, Brazil ————— 3.00
672, Rio de Janeiro and Sugar Loaf Mountain, Brazil ———————— 7.00
673, Rio de Janeiro and the Corcovado, Brazil ———————— 4.00
675, Carnival, Rio de Janiero, Brazil ——— 4.00

691, Paramaribo and Natives of Suriname (Dutch Guiana) ———————— 10.00
697, Montevideo I, Uruguay ————— 4.00
698, Montevideo, Uruguay II ————— 6.00
701, A Day at the Circus I, Ringling Bros. and Barnum & Bailey ———————— 2.00
702, A Day at the Circus II, Ringling Bros. and Barnum & Bailey ———————— 2.00
703, A Day at the Circus III, Ringling Bros. and Barnum & Bailey ———————— 2.00
710, Fire Fighters in Action (with booklet) ———————— 10.00
715, Down on the Farm (with booklet) ——— 5.00
720, Bullfight in Spain (with booklet) ——— 4.00
725, Baseball Stars of the Major Leagues I (with booklet) ———————— 15.00
726, Baseball Stars of the Major Leagues II (with booklet) ———————— 15.00
727, Baseball Stars of the Major Leagues III (with booklet) ———————— 15.00
740, Movie Stars, Hollywood I ————— 15.00
741, Movie Stars, Hollywood II ————— 15.00
742, Movie Stars, Hollywood III ————— 15.00
742, Movie Stars, Hollywood III (Alan Ladd instead of Rod Cameron) ——— 20.00
745, Television Stars I ———————— 20.00
746, Television Stars II ———————— 20.00
747, Television Stars III ———————— 20.00
750, Pinky Lee's Seven Days (with booklet and special envelope) ———————— 25.00

View-Master, reel #710, "Fire Fighters in Action," with booklet. $10.

View-Master, reel #750, "Pinky Lee's Seven Days" with booklet and special envelope. $25. (Gordon D. Hoffman Collection)

800, Bugs Bunny and Elmer Fudd, The Hunter ____ 1.50

810, Tom and Jerry in "The Cat Trapper" ____ 1.50

820, Woody Woodpecker in "The Pony Express Ride" ____ 1.50

821, Woody Woodpecker in "The Bill Collector" ____ 2.00

822, Andy Panda in "Mystery Tracks" ____ 1.50

823, Chilly Willy the Penquin in "No Fishing" ____ 2.00

901, Wild Animals in Natural Habitats, Africa ____ 1.00

910, Zoo Animals I ____ 1.00

910, Wild Animals of Africa I, in Captivity ____ 1.00

911, Zoo Animals II ____ 1.00

911, Wild Animals of Africa II, in Captivity ____ 1.00

912, Zoo Animals III ____ 1.00

912, Wild Animals of India in Captivity ____ 1.00

913, Zoo Animals IV ____ 1.00

913, Wild Animals of North America in Captivity ____ 1.00

914, Zoo Animals V ____ 1.00

914, Wild Animals of South America in Captivity ____ 1.00

925, Performing Elephants, St. Louis Zoo, Mo. ____ 1.00

926, Performing Chimpanzees, St. Louis Zoo, Mo. ____ 1.00

927, Performing Lions, St. Louis Zoo, Mo. ____ 1.00

940, Life with the Cowboys, The Rodeo ____ 2.00

942, Life with the Cowboys, Cattle Roundup and Branding ____ 2.00

945, Roy Rogers, King of the Cowboys and Trigger ____ 5.00

946, Roy Rogers in "The Holdup" ____ 10.00

950, Gene Autry and his wonder horse Champion ____ 5.00

951, Gene Autry in "The Kidnapping" ____ 5.00

955, Hopalong Cassidy (William Boyd) and Topper ____ 5.00

956, Hopalong Cassidy (William Boyd) in "The Cattle Rustler" ____ 5.00

960, Cisco Kid (Duncan Renaldo) and Pancho (Leo Carrillo) ____ 5.00

967, Silver Springs Attractions ____ 10.00

975, Adventures of Tarzan (Rex Barker) "Tarzan Rescues Cheta" (with booklet) ____ 5.00

980, Garden Flowers of Spring ____ 1.00

981, Garden Flowers of Summer ____ 1.00

982, Garden Flowers of Autumn ____ 1.00

1001, London I, England, 1947 ____ 1.50

1001, London I, England, 1948 ____ 1.25

1002, London II, England, 1947 ____ 1.50

1002, London II, England, 1948 ____ 2.00

1003, London III, England ____ 9.00

1006, St. Paul's Cathedral, England ____ 13.00

1007, Changing of the Guard, Buckingham Palace, London, England ____ 15.00

1008, Trooping the Colour Ceremony, London, England ____ 15.00

1009, Kew Gardens, London, England ____ 13.00

1010, Hampton Court, Middlesex, England ____ 4.00

1011, London Planetarium, England ____ 7.00

1012, The Tower of London, England ____ 3.00

1013, Windsor Castle, Royal Residence, England ____ 1.50

1015, Dover, Kent, England ____ 1.00

View-Master, reel #821, "Woody Woodpecker in 'The Bill Collector,'" reel on left is like new while the reel on right shows wear and use. The like-new reel $2 and the other, $0.50.

1016, Ramsgate to Herne Bay, Kent,
England ⎯⎯⎯⎯⎯⎯⎯⎯ 5.00
1017, Folkstone and Dover, Kent,
England ⎯⎯⎯⎯⎯⎯⎯⎯ 5.00
1020, Cambridge University, Cambridge,
England ⎯⎯⎯⎯⎯⎯⎯⎯ 1.00
1022, Oxford, Oxfordshire, England ⎯⎯ 2.00
1025, Stratford-on-Avon, Warwickshire,
England ⎯⎯⎯⎯⎯⎯⎯⎯ 3.00
1025, Shakespeare's Stratford-on-Avon,
Warwickshire, England, 1948 ⎯⎯⎯⎯ 1.00
1027, Historic Canterbury, Kent, England ⎯ 5.00
1030, York, Yorkshire, England ⎯⎯⎯⎯ 9.00
1035, Somerset Scenes, England ⎯⎯⎯⎯ 4.00
1036, Wookey Hole Cave, Somerset,
England ⎯⎯⎯⎯⎯⎯⎯⎯ 6.00
1037, Cheddar Gorge and Caves, Somerset,
England ⎯⎯⎯⎯⎯⎯⎯⎯ 6.00
1038, Bath, Somerset, England ⎯⎯⎯⎯ 1.50
1040, Devon Scenes, England ⎯⎯⎯⎯⎯ 2.00
1041, Torquay, Devon, England ⎯⎯⎯⎯ 10.00
1042, Kent's Cavern, Torquay, Devon,
England ⎯⎯⎯⎯⎯⎯⎯⎯ 10.00
1045, Clovelly, Devon, England ⎯⎯⎯⎯ 7.50
1047, Sussex Scenes, England ⎯⎯⎯⎯⎯ 1.50
1048, Brighton, Sussex, England ⎯⎯⎯⎯ 12.00
1049, Eastbourne, Sussex, England ⎯⎯⎯ 12.00
1050, Cornwall Beauty Spots, England ⎯⎯ 12.00
1051, Cornwall II, England ⎯⎯⎯⎯⎯⎯ 15.00
1052, St. Ives to Newquay, Cornwall,
England ⎯⎯⎯⎯⎯⎯⎯⎯ 15.00
1053, Newquay, Cornwall, England ⎯⎯⎯ 15.00
1054, Lifracombe to Minehead,
England ⎯⎯⎯⎯⎯⎯⎯⎯ 15.00
1055, Weston-Super-Mare, England ⎯⎯⎯ 15.00
1056, Bristol, England ⎯⎯⎯⎯⎯⎯⎯⎯ 15.00
1057, Bournemouth, Dorset, England ⎯⎯ 15.00
1060, Blackpool and the Illuminations,
England ⎯⎯⎯⎯⎯⎯⎯⎯ 15.00
1065, The Peak District, Derbyshire,
England ⎯⎯⎯⎯⎯⎯⎯⎯ 15.00
1070, The Lake District I, England ⎯⎯⎯ 15.00
1071, The Lake District II, England ⎯⎯⎯ 15.00
1075, Medieval City of York, England ⎯⎯ 15.00
1075, Scarborough, Yorkshire, England ⎯⎯ 15.00
1076, Scarborough, Yorkshire, England ⎯⎯ 15.00

1079, The Duke of Bedford's Woburn Abbey, England ⎯⎯⎯⎯⎯⎯⎯⎯ 15.00
1080, Coventry Cathedral, England ⎯⎯⎯ 15.00
1081, Norwich and the Cathedral,
England ⎯⎯⎯⎯⎯⎯⎯⎯ 15.00
1082, Winchester and the Cathedral,
England ⎯⎯⎯⎯⎯⎯⎯⎯ 15.00
1083, Salisbury and the Cathedral,
England ⎯⎯⎯⎯⎯⎯⎯⎯ 15.00
1084, Clacton to Felixstowe, East Coast,
England ⎯⎯⎯⎯⎯⎯⎯⎯ 15.00
1090, The Isle of Wight I, England ⎯⎯⎯ 15.00
1091, The Isle of Wight II, England ⎯⎯⎯ 15.00
1092, Cowes Week, Isle of Wight,
England ⎯⎯⎯⎯⎯⎯⎯⎯ 20.00
1100, The Clipper *Cutty Sark*, Greenwich,
England ⎯⎯⎯⎯⎯⎯⎯⎯ 20.00
1101, H.M.S. *Victory*, Portsmouth,
England ⎯⎯⎯⎯⎯⎯⎯⎯ 20.00
1102, R.M.S. *Queen Mary*, England ⎯⎯ 20.00
1103, R.M.S. *Queen Elizabeth*, England ⎯ 20.00
1120, The Wedding of Princess Alexandra,
England, (1963) ⎯⎯⎯⎯⎯⎯⎯ 50.00
1150, Wales I ⎯⎯⎯⎯⎯⎯⎯⎯⎯ 10.00
1151, Wales II ⎯⎯⎯⎯⎯⎯⎯⎯⎯ 10.00
1153, Caldy Island, Wales ⎯⎯⎯⎯⎯⎯ 15.00
1170, Jersey, Channel Islands ⎯⎯⎯⎯⎯ 15.00
1200, Robert Burns's Country, Scotland ⎯ 2.00
1201, Loch Lomond, Scotland ⎯⎯⎯⎯⎯ 1.50
1208, Royal Deeside and Balmoral Castle,
Scotland ⎯⎯⎯⎯⎯⎯⎯⎯ 10.00
1210, Highland Scenes, Scotland ⎯⎯⎯⎯ 10.00
1211, Highland Games, Scotland ⎯⎯⎯⎯ 20.00
1213, Glen Coe, Western Highlands,
Scotland ⎯⎯⎯⎯⎯⎯⎯⎯ 10.00
1214, The Great Glen, Inverness to Fort
William, Scotland ⎯⎯⎯⎯⎯⎯ 10.00
1216, Northern Highlands, Scotland ⎯⎯⎯ 15.00
1220, Edinburgh, Scotland ⎯⎯⎯⎯⎯⎯ 10.00
1250, The Isle of Skye, Scotland ⎯⎯⎯⎯ 10.00
1301, Killarney, Ireland ⎯⎯⎯⎯⎯⎯⎯ 1.00
1302, Tipperary, Ireland ⎯⎯⎯⎯⎯⎯⎯ 1.00
1305, President Kennedy's Visit to Ireland,
June 1963 ⎯⎯⎯⎯⎯⎯⎯⎯ 75.00
1310, Cork, Cobh and Blarney Castle,
Ireland ⎯⎯⎯⎯⎯⎯⎯⎯ 10.00

1320, Dublin and the Wicklow Hills,
Ireland _____ 10.00
1330, Connemara, County Galway,
Ireland _____ 10.00
1335, Limerick and Shannon Airport,
Ireland _____ 25.00
1340, Donegal Scenes, Ireland _____ 10.00
1401, Paris I, France _____ 1.00
1402, Paris II, France _____ 1.00
1405, Montmartre, Paris, France _____ 10.00
1406, Notre Dame Cathedral, Paris,
France _____ 10.00
1407, Souvenir Tour Eiffel, Paris, France
(only sold at the Eiffel Tower, very
scarce) _____ 30.00
1407K, Monuments de Paris, Souvenir
Tour Eiffel (only sold at the Eiffel Tower) _ 40.00
1407L, Vedettes Paris, Tour Eiffel, Exclusi-
vite Souvenir (only sold at the Eiffel
Tower) _____ 40.00
1409, The Cathedral of Reims, France ____ 10.00
1410, Palace of Versailles, France _____ 1.00
1411, The Shrine of Our Lady of Lourdes,
France _____ 1.00
1412, Palace of Fontainebleau, France ____ 5.00
1413, The Cathedral of Chartres, France __ 5.00
1417, Environs of Lourdes, France _____ 5.00
1420, Battlefields of World War II, Normandy, France _____ 2.50
1422, Deauville, Trouville, France _____ 10.00
1423, Dunkerque-Calais-Boulogne,
France _____ 10.00
1425, The French Riviera (Cote De'Azur),
France _____ 2.00
1426, Cannes to Antibes, the Riviera,
France _____ 7.50
1427, Villefranche to Cap D'Ail, The
Riviera, France _____ 8.00
1429, Menton and Cap Martin, The
Riviera, France _____ 12.00
1430, Picturesque People of Brittany,
France _____ 6.00
1431, Mont St. Michel, Brittany, France ____ 6.00
1433, Mont St. Michel II, Brittany,
France _____ 8.00
1434, Royan, France _____ 5.00
1438, From Pornic to Les Sables, D'Olonne,
France _____ 5.00
1440, Nimes-Aries, Pont du Gard, Provence,
France _____ 6.00
1442, Carcassonne, Largest Fortress in
Europe, Fr. _____ 8.00
1444, The "Gorges of the Tarn,"
France _____ 8.00
1445, Avignon, Orange-Les Baux, The
Provence, France _____ 8.00
1448, Lyons, France _____ 8.00
1449, Evian and Lake Leman, France ____ 8.00
1450, Annecy and the Lake, France _____ 7.00
1451, The Lake of Annecy, France _____ 7.00
1452, In and Around Grenoble, France ____ 7.00
1453, L'Aple d'Huez, France _____ 8.00
1454, Summer Trips from Chamonix,
France _____ 8.00

1455, Chamonix, Mont Blanc in Winter,
France _____ 8.00
1456, Towards the "Roof" of Europe
from Chamonix, France _____ 8.00
1457, Hte. Savoie Les Contamines in Winter, France _____ 8.00
1458, Megeve in Winter, France _____ 8.00
1459, Megeve in Summer, France _____ 8.00
1460, Val d'Isere in Winter, France _____ 8.00
1461, Savoie, Courchevel in Winter,
France _____ 8.00
1462, The Grand Chartrouse, France _____ 8.00
1463, Land of the Mont Blanc, France ____ 8.00
1466, Strasbourg, France _____ 8.00
1467, Nancy, France _____ 8.00
1468, St. Odile and Surroundings, Alsace,
France _____ 10.00
1471, Eze, the Riviera, France _____ 10.00
1472, Cannes, the Riviera, France _____ 10.00
1473, "Route Napoleon," France _____ 10.00
1474, From Le Lavando to St. Tropez,
France _____ 10.00
1475, Esterel Coast, the Riviera, France ___ 10.00
1476, From Cassis to Hyeres, France _____ 10.00
1477, St. Paul-de-Vence, the Riviera,
France _____ 10.00
1478, Gorges of the River Loup, France ___ 10.00
1480, Corsica I, France _____ 12.00
1481, Corsica II, France _____ 12.00
1482, Corsica III, France _____ 15.00
1484, Valberg-Dalvis Gorges-Entrevaux,
France _____ 12.00
1487, Toulouse, France _____ 12.00
1490, The "Cote Vermeille," France _____ 10.00
1491, Perpignan, France _____ 12.00
1496, The Castle of Henry IV, Pau,
France _____ 12.00
1497, From Pau to Bagneres-de-Bigorre,
France _____ 12.00
1498, Luchon and the Pyrenees, France ___ 12.00
1500, West Berlin I, Germany _____ 8.00
1502, Allgau, Germany _____ 10.00
1503, Oberammergau _____ 10.00
1503, Oberstdorf, Kleinwalsertal Deutschland, Osterreich _____ 12.00
1504, Garmisch-Partenkirchen, in winter,
Germany _____ 12.00
1505, Garmisch-Partenkirchen and Mittenwald, Germany _____ 12.00
1505, Garmisch-Partenkirchen, Germany _ 12.00
1506, Zugspitze, Germany _____ 12.00
1507, Mittenwald, Germany _____ 12.00
1508, Bad, Reichenhall, Bavaria,
Germany _____ 10.00
1509, Herrenchiemsee, Royal Castle of
Bavaria, Germany _____ 10.00
1509, Royal Castles of Bavaria, Germany ___ 9.00
1511, Upper Bavaria I, Germany _____ 5.00
1512, Upper Bavaria II, Germany _____ 8.00
1513, Berchtesgaden Country I, Germany __ 7.50
1514, Berchtesgaden Country II,
Germany _____ 5.00
1515, The Rhineland I, Germany (with
booklet) _____ 10.00

1516, Heidelberg, Germany _____ 5.00
1517, Aachen, Germany _____ 10.00
1518, Nuremburg, Germany _____ 10.00
1519, Bayreuth, Germany _____ 10.00
1520, Bodensee, Germany _____ 4.00
1521, The Black Forest I, Germany _____ 4.00
1522, Baden-Baden, Black Forest,
Germany _____ 8.00
1525, Munich I, Germany _____ 8.00
1526, Munich II, Germany _____ 8.00
1527, Chiemsee, Bavaria, Germany _____ 10.00
1528, Oktoberfest, Munich, Germany _____ 15.00
1529, Tegernsee, Bavaria, Germany _____ 10.00
1530, Nordlingen, Germany _____ 6.00
1531, Dinkelsbuhl, Germany _____ 5.00
1532, Rothenburg on the Tauber,
Germany _____ 5.00
1534, Bundesgarlenschau Shellgart,
Germany _____ 10.00
1535, Stuttgart, Germany _____ 10.00
1536, Dieschwabische Alb, Germany _____ 10.00
1537, Hohenzollern Castle, Germany _____ 10.00
1538, Munster, Germany _____ 10.00
1539, Ulm and Its Cathedral, Germany _____ 10.00
1541, The Luneburg Heath, Germany _____ 10.00
1542, Bremen and Bremerhaven,
Germany _____ 10.00
1543, Teutoburg Forest and Spas of
Weserbergland _____ 10.00
1544, Hanover, Germany _____ 10.00
1545, Cuxhaven and Helgoland,
Germany _____ 10.00
1546, East Frisian Islands, Germany _____ 12.00
1547, North Frisian Islands, Germany _____ 12.00
1548, Lubeck, Germany _____ 12.00
1549, Travemunde, Germany _____ 12.00
1550, Passion Play, Oberammergau, Germany, 1950, Tableau (with booklet) _____ 1.00
1551, Passion Play, Oberammergau, Germany, Part I (with booklet) _____ 1.00
1552, Passion Play, Oberammergau, Germany, Part II (with booklet) _____ 1.00
1553, Oberammergau, Germany _____ 5.00
1554, Die Wieskirche, Oberbayern,
Deutschland _____ 15.00
1560, Liepzig, East Germany _____ 15.00
1562, Dresden, East Germany _____ 15.00
1563, Frankfurt on the Main _____ 10.00
1564, Wiesbaden and Mainz, Germany _____ 10.00
1566, Bonn and Rhine Panoramas,
Germany _____ 10.00
1567, Cathedral of Cologne, Germany _____ 8.00
1568, Dusseldorf and Cologne, Germany _____ 10.00
1569, The Lahn Valley, Germany _____ 10.00
1570, East Berlin, East Germany _____ 15.00
1573, San Souci Palace, Potsdam, East
Germany _____ 17.00
1576, Der Taunus, Germany _____ 15.00
1577, Das Ahrtal, Germany _____ 15.00
1578, Munster, Germany _____ 15.00
1579, Treves (Trier), Germany _____ 15.00
1580, Der Dom Von Trier Mit, Heiligem
Rock, Germany _____ 15.00
1581, Dusseldorf, Germany _____ 15.00
1584, The Harz Mountains, Germany _____ 15.00

1585, Harz Mountains in Winter,
Germany _____ 15.00
1586, Winterberg und Rahler Aster, Sav-
erland, Germany _____ 15.00
1589, Heiligenhafen und Fehmann,
Germany _____ 15.00
1601, Rome I, Italy _____ 2.00
1602, Rome II, Italy _____ 1.50
1603, Rome III, Italy _____ 4.00
1604, The Roman Forum, Rome, Italy _____ 1.50
1605, Holy Year, 1950, Rome, Italy _____ 3.00
1606, Venice, Italy _____ 2.00
1606, Tivoli and Villa D'Este, Italy _____ 7.00
1607, Milan, Italy _____ 5.00
1608, Florence, Italy (with translation
sheet in five languages; made in
Belgium) _____ 1.50
1609, Florence II, Italy _____ 3.75
1610, Pisa, Italy _____ 2.00
1611, Volterra and San Gimignamo, Italy _____ 3.00
1612, Naples, Italy _____ 1.00
1613, Musea of Naples, Italy _____ 5.00
1614, The Ruins of Pompeii, Destroyed 79
A.D., Italy _____ 5.00
1616, Mount Vesuvius near Pompeii,
Italy _____ 1.50
1617, Island of Ischia, Italy _____ 3.00
1618, The Riviera, Rapallo to Portofino,
Italy _____ 1.50
1619, Genoa, Italy _____ 5.50
1620, Bolzano, South Tyrol, Italy _____ 1.50
1620, Bolzano and Lake Carezza, South
Tyrol, Italy _____ 4.00
1621, Merano, South Tyrol, Italy _____ 4.00
1622, Dolomite Mountains, Northern
Italy _____ 2.00
1623, Cortina D'Ampezzo in Winter,
Italy _____ 8.50
1625, Stresa and the Borromee Islands,
Italy _____ 6.50
1626, Varees and Lake Orta, Italy _____ 10.00
1627, Cervinia and Aosta Valley, Italy _____ 10.00
1628, Valtellina and Splugen Pass Road,
Italy _____ 10.00
1629, Gardena Valley and Siusi Mountains, Italy _____ 10.00
1630, Venice, Italy _____ 1.00
1631, Venice II, Italy _____ 9.00
1632, Venice III, Italy _____ 10.00
1633, Venice, The Lagoon, Italy _____ 10.00
1634, Gondola Festival in Venice, Italy _____ 10.00
1635, Island of Capri, Italy _____ 6.00
1638, Ravenna, Italy _____ 10.00
1639, Trieste, Italy _____ 10.00
1640, Bologna, Italy _____ 8.00
1642, Rimini and Adriatic Riviera, Italy _____ 10.00
1643, Assisi, Italy _____ 10.00
1644, Perugia, Italy _____ 12.00
1645, Verona, Vicenza-Padua, Italy _____ 7.00
1646, Ferrara, Italy _____ 10.00
1650, Lake Garda, Italy _____ 6.00
1655, Lake Como, Italy _____ 6.00
1660, Sestriere in Winter, Italy _____ 10.00
1661, Island of Elba, Italy _____ 10.00
1662, Lucca and Montecatini, Italy _____ 10.00

1663, Siena, Italy ———————————— 10.00
1665, San Remo, The Riviera, Italy ——— 10.00
1666, Allasio to Ventimiglia, The Riviera,
Italy ———————————————————— 7.00
1667, From Viareggio to Carrara, Italy ——— 12.00
1670, Fiesole, Italy ——————————— 12.00
1675, Turin, Italy ————————————— 12.00
1680, Malta, The Island of Sunshine and
History ————————————————— 15.00
1685, Calabria and Puglie, Italy ————— 12.00
1691, Taormina, Sicily, Italy ——————— 12.00
1700, Romantic Seville, Spain ————— 1.50
1701, Old Castile, Spain ———————— 1.50
1702, Madrid, Spain ————————— 5.00
1703, Valencia, Spain ————————— 5.00
1704, Toledo, Spain ————————— 5.00
1705, The Alhambra Palace, Granada,
Spain ——————————————————— 1.50
1710, Montserrat, "The Mountain
Shrine," Spain ——————————— 10.00
1711, Monastery L'Escurial, Spain ——— 10.00
1712, Vallede Los Caidos, Spain ———— 10.00
1713, Segovia, Avila, Spain ——————— 10.00
1714, Salamanca, Spain ——————— 10.00
1715, Malaga to Gibraltar, Andalusia,
Spain ——————————————————— 10.00
1720, Holy Week, Seville, Spain ———— 10.00
1726, Barcelona, Spain ———————— 10.00
1730, Mayorca I, The Balearic Islands,
Spain ——————————————————— 10.00
1731, Mayorca II, The Balearic Islands,
Spain ——————————————————— 12.00
1732, Mayorca III, The Balearic Islands,
Spain ——————————————————— 12.00
1733, Palma de Mallorca, Spain I ——— 12.00
1734, Palma de Mallorca, Spain II ——— 12.00
1735, Paguera-Banalbufar, Majorca,
Spain ——————————————————— 12.00
1736, Valldemosa-Puerto de Soiler,
Majorca, Spain ———————————— 15.00
1737, La Calobra-Formentor, Majorca,
Spain ——————————————————— 12.00
1738, East Coast and Caves of Majorca,
Spain ——————————————————— 12.00
1739, Traditional Majorca, Spain ———— 12.00
1790, Tenerife, Canary Islands, Spain ——— 10.00
1799, Gibraltar ——————————————— 10.00
1801, Lisbon I, Portugal ——————— 7.00
1802, Lisbon II, Portugal ——————— 9.00
1805, "Costa Do Sol," from Eestoril to
Sintra, Portugal ——————————— 7.00
1806, From Peniche to Nazare, Portugal —— 10.00
1810, Oporto, Portugal ———————— 10.00
1820, Fatima and Batalha, Portugal ——— 6.00
1822, Pilgrimages and Sanctuary of Fatima, Portugal ———————————— 12.00
1850, Copenhagen, Denmark —————— 10.00
1850, Copenhagen II, Denmark ———— 10.00
1851, Copenhagen II, Denmark (with
booklet) ———————————————— 15.00
1852, Copenhagen's Tivoli, Denmark —— 12.00
1860, Hans Christian Andersen's Town,
Zealand Castles, Denmark ————— 12.00
1870, The Island of Bornholm, Denmark
(with booklet) ———————————— 15.00

1900, By the Zuider Zee, Holland ———— 1.50
1901, Windmill Land, South Holland ——— 2.00
1902, Volendam on the Zuyderzee,
Holland ——————————————————— 20.00
1903, Marken Island, Zuyderzee, Holland _ 20.00
1905, Amsterdam "Venice of the North,"
Holland ——————————————————— 20.00
1906, The Hague, Holland ——————— 15.00
1907, Madurodam, Miniature Town, The
Hague, Holland ———————————— 15.00
1908, Scheveningen Beach, Holland ——— 15.00
1909, Scheveningen Promenade Pier,
Holland ——————————————————— 15.00
1910, Alkmaar and the Cheese Market,
Holland ——————————————————— 15.00
1912, Zandwort Sea Resort, Holland ——— 12.00
1913, Aalsmeer Flower Auction,
Holland ——————————————————— 15.00
1915, Rotterdam, Holland ——————— 10.00
1916, Floriade and Euromast, Rotterdam,
Holland (Exposition, 1960) ————— 20.00
1920, Tulip Time, Holland ——————— 18.00
1922, Keukenhof Flower Exhibition,
Holland ——————————————————— 20.00
1928, East-Zuiderzee I, Holland ———— 8.00
1929, East-Zuiderzee II, Holland ———— 8.00
1931, Vacationland, Arnhem, Holland ——— 8.00
1935, Southern Limburg, Holland ———— 8.00
1938, Zeeland Scenes, Holland ————— 8.00
1941, Hertogenbosch and Oisteruyk,
Holland ——————————————————— 10.00
1942, Natuurpark "De Efteling,"
Kaalsheuvel I ————————————— 10.00
1943, Natuurpark "De Efteling,"
Kaalsheuvel II ———————————— 10.00
1944, Fresisland Beauty Spots, Holland —— 8.00
1947, Windmills of Holland ——————— 8.00
1950, Brussels, Belgium ——————— 5.00
1951, Brussels II, Belgium ——————— 8.00
1952, Medieval Bruges, Belgium ———— 5.00
1953, Historic Ghent, Belgium ————— 6.00
1957, Antwerp, Belgium ——————— 8.00
1960, The Meuse Valley and the Ardennes, Belgium (with booklet) ——— 12.00
1961, The Meuse from Namur to Hastiere,
Belgium ——————————————————— 8.00
1965, The Picturesque Bocq, Molignee
and Lesse Rivers, Belgium —————— 8.00
1966, Bouillon on the Semois, Belgium —— 8.00
1970, Province of Liege, Belgium ———— 8.00
1973, Ypres and the Hills of West-Flan-
ders, Belgium ————————————— 8.00
1977, King Baudouin of Belgium and his
Fiancee Dona Fabiola ———————— 35.00
1980, Ostend to Le Zoute, North Sea
Beaches, Belgium ———————————— 8.00
1981, Ostend, Belgium ———————— 6.00
1985, Napoleon's Waterloo, Belgium ——— 8.00
1987, Manneken Pis, Belgium ————— 8.00
1988, Grand Palace, Brussels, Belgium —— 8.00
1989, World's Fair Brussels-1958, The
Finnish Pavilion, Belgium —————— 16.00
1994, The Atomium World's Fair
Brussels-1958, Belg. ———————— 16.00
1995, Grand-Duchy of Luxemburg ——— 7.00

1996, King Baudouin's State Visit to
Grand-Duchy of Luxembourg _____ 35.00
1997, The City of Luxemburg, Grand-
Duchy of Luxembourg _____ 8.00
1998, Echternach and Surroundings,
Luxembourg _____ 8.00
2001, Zermatt I, Switzerland _____ 3.00
2001, The Matterhorn and Zermatt,
Switzerland, 1948 _____ 1.50
2001, The Matterhorn and Zermatt,
Switzerland, 1952 _____ 4.00
2002, Zermatt II, Switzerland _____ 3.00
2003, Bern, Switzerland _____ 2.00
2005, Zurich I, Switzerland, 1947 _____ 3.00
2005, Zurich, Switzerland, 1948 _____ 2.00
2006, Zurich II, Switzerland _____ 3.00
2006, Horticultural Exhibition, Zurich,
1959, Switz. _____ 20.00
2007, The Susten Pass, Switzerland _____ 8.00
2008, Grimsel, Furka and Oberalp Passes,
from Rhine to Rhone, Switzerland _____ 8.00
2009, Interlaken, Region I, Switzerland,
1947 _____ 2.00
2009, Interlaken, Region, Switzerland,
1948 _____ 1.50
2010, Interlaken Region II, Switzerland _____ 3.00
2011, Bernese Oberland in Winter,
Switzerland _____ 7.00
2012, The Bernese Oberland, Switzerland _____ 4.00
2013, William Tell's Country, Lake Lucerne, Switz. _____ 5.00
2014, Lucerne, Switzerland, 1947 _____ 3.00
2014, Lucerne, Switzerland, 1948 _____ 1.50
2015, Making Swiss Cheese, Switzerland _____ 2.00
2016, Davos in Winter, Switzerland _____ 4.00
2017, St. Moritz, Switzerland, 1947 _____ 2.00
2017, St. Moritz, Switzerland, 1948 _____ 1.00
2018, Winter Sports in St. Moritz,
Switzerland _____ 8.00
2019, Lugano and Locarno, Switzerland _____ 2.00
2020, Geneva, Switzerland, 1947 _____ 1.00
2020, Geneva, Switzerland, 1952 _____ 2.00
2021, Neuchatel Lake Area, Switzerland _____ 7.00
2022, Pontresina, Switzerland _____ 5.00
2025, Basle, Switzerland _____ 5.00
2026, Montreux to Lausanne "The Swiss
Riviera." _____ 7.00
2028, Montreux and Surroundings,
Switzerland _____ 10.00
2030, Winter in Arosa, Switzerland _____ 10.00
2031, Arosa, Switzerland _____ 10.00
2033, Flims, Switzerland _____ 10.00
2035, The Rhinefall, Schatthausen to Stein
A.R., Switzerland _____ 9.00
2037, Mosters, Switzerland _____ 10.00
2038, Schels, Tarasp, Vulpera,
Switzerland _____ 10.00
2039, Lugano, Switzerland _____ 12.00
2040, Lugano and Vicinity,
Switzerland _____ 12.00
2041, Locarno-Ascona-Brissago,
Switzerland _____ 12.00
2042, Locarno and Vicinity _____ 15.00
2044, Mount Pilatus, Switzerland _____ 15.00
2045, Santis and St. Gall, Switzerland _____ 13.00

2046, Santis and the Toggenburg,
Switzerland _____ 15.00
2047, Kussnacht and Weggis,
Switzerland _____ 15.00
2048, To the Top of Mount Rigi,
Switzerland _____ 15.00
2050, Upper Rhone Valley, Switzerland _____ 14.00
2052, St. Gothard Pass, Switzerland _____ 15.00
2054, Engelberg, Trubsee-Titlis,
Switzerland _____ 15.00
2056, The Jungfrau Railway, Switzerland _____ 20.00
2058, Famous Burgenstock Panoramas,
Switzerland _____ 15.00
2060, Oslo, Norway _____ 10.00
2065, Betgen, Norway _____ 10.00
2067, Stavanger and Haugesund, Norway
(with booklet) _____ 12.00
2070, From Molde to Kristiansund, More-
Romsdal, Norway (with booklet) _____ 10.00
2075, The Fjords, Norway _____ 5.00
2076, The Fjords Country, Norway _____ 5.00
2077, The Fjords II, Norway _____ 8.00
2080, Trondheim, Norway (with
booklet) _____ 10.00
2100, Stockholm I, Sweden _____ 5.00
2101, Stockholm II, Sweden _____ 4.00
2103, Millesgarden and Skansen,
Stockholm, Sweden _____ 9.00
2105, Gothenburg, Gateway to Sweden _____ 5.00
2106, By Gota Canal from Gothenburg to
Stockholm, Sweden (with booklet) _____ 8.00
2110, Skansen Open Air Museum, Zoological Gardens, Sweden _____ 10.00
2115, Midsummer in Datecarlia (Dalarna),
Sweden _____ 7.00
2116, Midsummer in Datecarlia (Dalarna)
II, Sweden _____ 10.00
2120, Visby Isle of Gotland, Sweden _____ 10.00
2125, Sweden I _____ 10.00
2126, Malmo, Sweden _____ 10.00
2128, Castles of Skane, Sweden (with
booklet) _____ 12.00
2130, Halsingborg and Molle, Sweden _____ 10.00
2151, Athens, Greece I _____ 10.00
2152, Athens, Greece II _____ 10.00
2154, Athens and Surroundings, Greece _____ 10.00
2157, Corinth and Epidaurus, Greece _____ 10.00
2159, Olympia and Mistra, Greece _____ 10.00
2160, Delphi and Mount Parnassus,
Greece _____ 10.00
2165, Cofu (Kerkyra), Greece _____ 10.00
2168, Thessalonika Surroundings, Mace-
donia, Greece _____ 10.00
2170, International Trade Fair, Thessalonika, Greece _____ 15.00
2171, Mount Athos I, Greece _____ 10.00
2172, Mount Athos II, Greece _____ 10.00
2180, Meteora, Greece _____ 10.00
2185, Costumes of Greece _____ 12.00
2195, Historical Island I, Rhodes, Greece _____ 10.00
2196, Historical Islands II, Delos-
Mykonos, Greece _____ 10.00
2197, Historical Islands III, Crete, Greece _____ 10.00
2300, The Tyrol, Austria _____ 2.00

2301, Bregenz on Lake Constance,
Austria _____ 6.00
2305, Festival in Austria _____ 4.00
2308, Kufstein and the Kaiser Mountains,
Austria _____ 4.00
2309, Salzkammergut, Austria _____ 8.00
2310, Romantic Salzburg, Austria _____ 5.00
2311, Kitzbuhel and St. Johann in Winter,
Austria _____ 8.00
2312, Grossglockner, Zell Am See to
Lienz, Austria _____ 6.00
2313, Badgastein and Hofgastein, Austria ___ 8.00
2314, Carinthian Lakes, Austria _____ 10.00
2315, Corpus Christi Day, Austria _____ 10.00
2318, Silvretta and Montafon, Austria ____ 10.00
2319, The Arlberg Area in Winter,
Austria _____ 10.00
2320, Innsbruck, Austria _____ 5.00
2322, The Arlsberg Area, Austria _____ 8.00
2325, Vienna I, Austria _____ 5.00
2326, Vienna II, Austria _____ 6.00
2327, Vienna II, Austria _____ 8.00
2335, Worthersee, Austria _____ 10.00
2337, Tauern Power Station, Kaprun,
Austria _____ 10.00
2338, Mount Dachstein and Aussee
Country, Austria _____ 10.00
2601, Helsinki, Finland I _____ 8.00
2602, Helsinki, Finland II _____ 8.00
2603, Turku Castle, Finland _____ 10.00
2604, Turku, Finland _____ 10.00
2605, Turku, Finland II _____ 10.00
2600, Tampere, Finland _____ 10.00
2608, Lahti, Finland _____ 10.00
2609, Savonlinna, Finland _____ 10.00
2610, To Aulanko and Tampers by Silver
Line, Finland _____ 8.00
2611, Kuopio and Surroundings,
Finland _____ 10.00
2612, Oulu and Surroundings, Finland
2613, Oulu and Surroundings II,
Finland _____ 12.00
2615, Vaasa, Finland _____ 12.00
2616, Jyvaskyla, Finland _____ 12.00
2617, Lappeenranta, Finland _____ 12.00
2618, Kotka, Finland _____ 12.00
2619, Hameenlinna, Finland _____ 12.00
2620, Aulanko Park, Finland _____ 12.00
2670, Principality of Andorra _____ 12.00
2680, Monaco and Monte Carlo,
Monaco _____ 2.00
2681, The Exotic Gardens of Monaco _____ 8.00
2690, Republic of San Marino _____ 8.00
2700, Principality of Liechtenstein _____ 4.00
2721, St. Peter's Basilica, Vatican State ____ 1.00
2722, Buildings and Swiss Guards, Vatican State _____ 2.00
2723, Museums and Galleries, Vatican
State _____ 2.00
2724, Art Treasures I, Vatican State _____ 5.00
2725, Art Treasures II, Vatican State _____ 5.00
2726, Holy Year, 1950, Vatican State _____ 2.50
3001, Capetown and Cape Peninsula,
Union of South Africa _____ 1.00
3002, Capetown II, Union of South Africa __ 5.00

3005, Table Mountain and Cableway,
Union of South Africa _____ 8.00
3011, The Cape of Good Hope and Groote
Schuur, Union of South Africa _____ 8.00
3015, The Kimberly Diamond Mine,
Union of South Africa _____ 25.00
3019, The Garden Route, Union of South
Africa _____ 5.00
3021, Durban, Natal, Union of South
Africa _____ 10.00
3024, Scenic Natal National Park, Union
of South Africa _____ 10.00
3025, Natal National Park, Union of
South Africa _____ 12.00
3027, Valley of a Thousand Hills, Natal,
Union of South Africa _____ 12.00
3029, Natives of Zululand, Union of South
Africa _____ 7.50
3029, Natives of Zululand, Union of South
Africa (Scene 7 "Cozy Back Seat") _____ 10.00
3031, Zululand, Union of South Africa ____ 12.00
3036, Pretoria, Union of South Africa ____ 12.00
3040, Johannesburg, Union of South
Africa _____ 12.00
3042, Gold Mining, Union of South
Africa _____ 50.00
3047, Natives of Transvaal, Union of
South Africa _____ 15.00
3100, Victoria Falls, Southern Rhodesia ____ 1.50
3110, Zimbabwe Ruins, Southern
Rhodesia _____ 8.00
3110, Victoria Falls, Southern Rhodesia ____ 5.00
3112, The Matopos, Southern Rhodesia ____ 5.00
3113, The Matopos Mountains, Southern
Rhodesia _____ 5.00
3115, Salisbury and Environs, Southern
Rhodesia _____ 5.00
3120, Copperbelt, Northern Rhodesia _____ 10.00
3200, Dar es Salaam, Tanganyika _____ 10.00
3203, Climbing Mt. Kilimanjaro,
Tanganyika _____ 5.00
3208, Zanzibar, Africa _____ 5.00
3210, Mombasa, Kenya _____ 10.00
3211, Nairobi, Kenya _____ 10.00
3212, Highlands of Kenya _____ 10.00
3213, Sisal Industry, Kenya _____ 12.00
3214, East African Safari _____ 12.00
3215, Coffee Industry in East Africa,
Kenya _____ 15.00
3216, Lake Victoria, Source of the Nile,
Kenya _____ 10.00
3216, Lake Victoria, East Africa (with
booklet) _____ 12.00
3217, Mount Kenya, Kenya _____ 10.00
3220, Mountains of the Moon,
Uganda _____ 10.00
3221, Kampala, Uganda _____ 10.00
3260, Addis Ababa, Ethiopia (includes
view of Emperor Haile Selassie) _____ 20.00
3265, Scenes of Ethiopia _____ 15.00
3301, Cairo, Egypt (with booklet) _____ 3.00
3302, The Famous Mosques of Cairo,
Egypt (with booklet) _____ 4.00
3303, The Great Pyramids and Sphinx,
Giza, Egypt (with booklet) _____ 3.00

3304, The Tombs of the Kings, Thebes, Egypt (with booklet) _____ 4.00
3305, Treasures of King Tut-Ankh-Amen, Cairo, Egypt (with booklet) _____ 7.00
3306, The River Nile, Assuan [sic] to Cairo, Egypt (with booklet) _____ 3.00
3307, The Valley of the Nile, Egypt (with booklet) _____ 4.00
3308, People of the Nile Valley, Egypt (with booklet) _____ 3.00
3309, Sakkara and Memphis, Egypt (with booklet) _____ 2.00
3310, Luxor and El Karnak, Egypt (with booklet) _____ 6.00
3311, Ancient Thebes, Egypt (with booklet) _____ 3.00
3312, Assuan [sic] on the Nile, Egypt (with booklet) _____ 4.00
3775, Brazzaville, French Equatorial, Africa _____ 10.00
3793, The Lake Area, Belgian Congo _____ 10.00
3810, Luanda, Portuguese West Africa _____ 12.00
4000, Jerusalem, The Old City, Palestine, 1948 _____ 3.00
4000, Jerusalem "The Holy City," Palestine, 1949 (with booklet) _____ 1.50
4001, Gethsemane to Calvary, Jerusalem, Palestine (with booklet) _____ 4.00
4002, Street Scenes in Old Jerusalem, Palestine (with booklet) _____ 2.00

4004, Moslem Temple Area, Jerusalem, Palestine (with booklet) _____ 4.00
4006, Bethlehem, Judea, Palestine (with booklet) _____ 2.00
4007, Nazareth, Galilee, Israel (with booklet) _____ 2.00
4008, Tel Aviv, Israel (with booklet) _____ 2.50
4009, The Sea of Galilee, Israel (with booklet) _____ 3.00
4010, Jaffa, Israel (with booklet) _____ 1.50
4012, Region of Haifa, Israel (with booklet) _____ 1.00
4013, Acre, Palestine (with booklet) _____ 3.00
4014, The Hula Valley, Galilee, Israel (with booklet) _____ 3.00
4015, The River Jordan, Palestine (with booklet) _____ 3.00
4016, The Samaritans, Samaria, Palestine (with booklet) _____ 4.00
4017, Wilderness of Judea, Palestine (with booklet) _____ 2.00
4050, The Arab Legion I, Transjordan _____ 2.00
4050, The Arab Legion, Jordan _____ 1.00
4051, The Arab Legion II, Transjordan _____ 6.00
4055, Scenes of Transjordan _____ 2.00
4141, Damascus, Syria _____ 3.00
4143, The Great Mosque Ommeyade, Damascus, Syria _____ 5.00
4151, Scenes of Lebanon _____ 2.00
4152, Baalbek, The Roman Ruins, Lebanon _ 5.00

View-Master, reel #4006, "Bethlehem, Judea, Palestine," with booklet, 1949. $2.

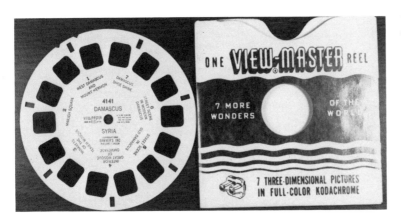

View-Master, reel #4141, "Damascus, Syria," 1950. $3.

4153, The Cedars of Lebanon	5.00
4285, Afghanistan, South Central Asia	5.00
4300, The Taj Mahal, Agra, India	3.00
4301, Agra, India	8.00
4302, Maharaja's Festival, Mysore, India	4.00
4303, At home with Jawaharlal Nehru, India's Great Leader	50.00
4304, People of China	6.00
4305, Calcutta, India, 1949	2.00
4305, Calcutta, India, 1952	3.00
4306, Old Delhi, India	5.00
4307, New Delhi, India	2.00
4308, Arts and Crafts of India	9.00
4309, Dances of India	10.00
4310, Madras, India	10.00
4311, Temples of South India	10.00
4312, Benares, India	10.00
4313, Darjeeling and the Himalayas, India	10.00
4314, Tea Industry, Darjeeling, India	15.00
4315, Jaipur, India	10.00
4316, Bombay, India	10.00
4317, Rural Scenes, India	10.00
4323, The People of Kashmir, India	12.00
4324, Srinagar, Kashmir, India	12.00
4351, Movie Stars of India I	35.00
4352, Movie Stars of India II	35.00
4353, Movie Stars of India III	35.00
4360, Prime Minister Nehru's United States Visit, India	50.00
4451, Lahore, Mosques and Antiquities, Pakistan	12.00
4452, Lahore, "The City," Pakistan	12.00
4453, Karachi, Pakistan	12.00
4552, Kelantan, Malaya	15.00
4553, Malacca, Malaya	15.00
4554, Malacca, Malaya	15.00
4560, Aborigines of Malaya	20.00
4810, Hong Kong Colony (China)	1.00
4811, Hong Kong	5.00
4814, Hong Kong	5.00
4820, Buddhist Temples of Bangkok, Siam	2.00
4824, Scenes and People of Siam	5.00
4825, Siamese Dance Drama, Siam	3.00
4871, Tokyo, Japan	1.50

4872, Mount Fuji and Rural Scenes, Japan	2.00
4873, Festivals of Japan	2.50
5001, Sydney, New South Wales, Australia	1.50
5001, Sydney I, New South Wales, Australia	7.00
5002, Sydney II, New South Wales, Australia	10.00
5003, Scenic Sydney, New South Wales, Australia	10.00
5005, The Beaches, Sydney, New South Wales, Australia	10.00
5006, Sydney Beaches and Surf Life Savers, Australia	10.00
5008, The Blue Mountain, New South Wales, Australia	5.00
5009, The Blue Mountain II, New South Wales, Australia	5.00
5010, The Great Barrier Reef, Queensland, Australia	2.00
5015, Ski Fields of Mt. Kosciusko and Thredbo Valley, Australia	8.00
5016, Summit of Australia, Mt. Kosciusko in winter	8.00
5020, Kangaroo Hunt with Aborigines of Australia (distant shots)	3.00
5020, Kangaroo Hunt with Aborigines of Australia (close-ups)	5.00
5025, Canberra, Capital of Australia	10.00
5026, City of Canberra, Australia	10.00
5026, Canberra, Australia	10.00
5041, Melbourne I, Australia	10.00
5042, Melbourne II, Australia	10.00
5043, City of Melbourne I, Australia	12.00
5043, Melbourne, Australia	12.00
5044, City of Melbourne II, Australia	12.00
5080, Brisbane, Queensland, Australia	12.00
5081, Brisbane, Queensland, Australia	12.00
5085, "Surfer's Paradise," Southern Queensland, Australia	15.00
5086, Gold Coast, Queensland, Australia	12.00
5121, Adelaide and Vicinity, Australia	12.00
5161, Alice Springs, Northern Territory, Australia	12.00
5201, Perth, Western Australia	12.00

5241, Tasmania, Australia I _____ 10.00
5242, Tasmania, Australia II _____ 10.00
5261, The Maoris, Natives of New
Zealand _____ 2.00
5270, Rotorua, North Island, New
Zealand _____ 4.00
5301, The Southern Alps, South Island,
New Zealand _____ 2.00
5311, Christchurch, South Island, New
Zealand _____ 8.00
5375, Tropical Tahiti, Society Islands,
South Pacific _____ 5.00
5425, Beautiful Bali, Indonesia _____ 6.00
5600, Manila, Philippine Islands _____ 1.00
5605, Moros of Zamboanga, Philippine
Islands _____ 10.00
5606, Igorot Natives, Philippine Islands ___ 10.00
5607, General Scenes, Philippine Islands ___ 8.00
5610, Baguio, Philippine Islands _____ 15.00

"9000" Series Reels

These single reels were sold only at or near
the site of the subject depicted. They are ex-
actly the same as the SP prefix reels, but are
much scarcer in some cases (see SP Prefix Reels
in Chapter 7).

9001, Skyline Caverns, Front Royal, Va. ___ 2.00
9004, Maligne Lake, Canadian Rockies,
Alta. Canada _____ 4.00
9008, Hoover [Boulder] Dam, Nev., Scenic
Auto Tour _____ 2.00
9028, Adirondack Mountains, N.Y. _____ 4.00
9034, Sea Lion Caves, Florence, Oreg. _____ 2.00
9037, St. Petersburg, Fla. _____ 2.00
9042, Estes Park and Big Thompson Canyon, Colo. _____ 3.00
9043, National Monuments of Western
Colo. _____ 4.00
9047, Gettysburg National Military Park,
Pa. _____ 3.00
9055, Prehistoric Cliff Dwellers of Mesa
Verde, Colo. _____ 5.00
9058, Home of Santa's Workshop, North
Pole, N.Y. _____ 4.00

9066, Cape Breton Highlands, N.S.,
Canada _____ 6.00
9067, Bird Sanctuary, Bonaventure Island,
Que., Canada _____ 6.00
9069, Kenora and Lake of the Woods,
Ont., Canada _____ 5.00
9071, Tulip Time in Holland, Mich. _____ 3.00

Single Reels with Prefix Letters Not Included in Sets

A1815, Queen Mary Souvenir (Ship at
Long Beach, Calif.) _____ 15.00
A4901, Wall Drug _____ 10.00
A5331, Chicago's Adler Planetarium and
Astronomical Museum _____ 10.00
A5821, Mackinac Island, Mich. _____ 10.00
A6631, Cathedral of St. John the
Devine _____ 10.00
A6702, New York World's Fair,
1964–1965 (in special folder envelope) ___ 15.00
A7024, Franconia Notch _____ 8.00
A8931, Tweetsie Railroad, Blowing Rock,
N.C. _____ 25.00
B0661, Brasilia, Brazil _____ 15.00
B3731, Robin Hood Meets Friar Tuck,
1956 _____ 10.00
B4721, Lassie and Timmy in "The
Runaway Mule." _____ 15.00
B5924, Partridge Family _____ 15.00
B6551, Vanguard Launching at Cape
Canaveral (in special folder envelope) ___ 27.00
B7284, Winnie Otou und Das Halbblut
Apanatschi _____ 15.00
B7604, World's Fair Brussels—1959 (in
special folder envelope) _____ 15.00
BC1, View-Master Special Reel, Not for
Resale, 3-D Pictures for Profit _____ 50.00
CD1, Your Product Come to Life in
Sawyer's Inc. View-Master (com-
mercial advertising demo) _____ 50.00
CDR78, Previews, Avant Premiere _____ 25.00
CH (*See* Bible Story Reels in Chapter 7)
DD (*See* American Geographical Society
Reels in Chapter 7)
DR (*See* Demonstration Reels in Chapter 7)

View-Master, special single reel #B6551, "Vanguard Launching at Cape Canaveral," in descriptive folder, 1958. $27. (Gordon D. Hoffman Collection)

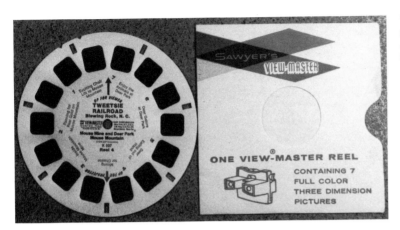

View-Master, single reel #K507, of the "Tweetsie Railroad, Blowing Rock, N.C.," 1979. $20. (Gordon D. Hoffman Collection)

DRE (*See* Demonstration Reels in Chapter 7)
E101, Mushrooms of the United States ____ 15.00
EA (*See* Easter Story Reels in Chapter 7)
FT (*See* Fairy Tale Reels in Chapter 7)
H107, Songs of Zion (nonstereo) _____ 5.00
H500, Roy Rogers "King of the Cowboys"
and Trigger _____ 4.00
J501, Dale Evans "Queen of the West." __ 10.00
J512, Mission San Juan, Capistrano _____ 4.00
J517, Ponderosa Ranch, Home of
"Bonanza" TV _____ 12.00
J518, Waltzing Waters, Fort Myers, Fla. __ 3.00
J529, Ripley's Museum, St. Augustine,
Fla. _____ 5.00
K507, Tweetsie Railroad, Blowing Rock,
N.C. _____ 20.00
K523, Potter's Wax Museum, St. Augustine, Fla. _____ 15.00
K525, Arizona, Sonora Desert Museum,
Tucson, Ariz. _____ 10.00
L501, Doll and Toy Museum at Hobby
City _____ 15.00
L506, Moaning Cavern, Vallecito, Calif. __ 8.00
L507, Farmer's Market, Los Angeles,
Calif. _____ 5.00
M500, Meteor Crater, Northern Ariz. ____ 10.00
M501, The Corn Palace, Mitchell, S.Dak. __ 5.00
MG (*See* Mother Goose Rhymes in
Chapter 7)
PR1, View-Master Preview Reel, Spring
Summer Release 1953 (Special envelope
"Demonstrate Stereo—and You Will Sell
Stereo!") _____ 50.00
S (lower case s—*See* World War II Military Training Reels in Chapter 7)
SP (*See* SP Prefix Reels in Chapter 7)
T (lower case *t*—*See* World War II Military
Training Reels in Chapter 7)

Bible Story Reels (CH prefix)

This series was produced by Churchcraft Pictures, St. Louis, Missouri, and features stories from the Bible performed by actors in authentic costumes. The reels come in special red-

GAF View-Master, #L-507 "Farmers Market, Los Angeles, California," in "Scenic America" single-reel packaging. $5.

and-white envelopes with a story booklet. Reel numbers: CH-1, CH-6A, CH-6B, CH-8, CH-15, CH-37, CH-40, CH-47, CH-49, CH-55A, CH-55B and CH-57.

Complete twelve-reel set _____ 40.00
Single reels with booklets, in special
envelopes _____ each 4.00

American Geographical Society Reels (DD prefix)

These are fourteen-scene nonstereo reels intended for projection in a single-lens View-Master projector. They were sold by subscription with sticker booklets. The reels generally sell from $4 to $9 each. Add 50 percent for the reels with an unused booklet and in ex-

Unauthorized View-Master reel of erotic female nude poses. Mounted in "Personal" reels in crude black-and-white envelope. These were not widely distributed and may be unique. Possibly as many as ten different reels were made. $100. (Gordon D. Hoffman Collection)

cellent condition. Booklets, without reels, are fairly common and have very little collector value.

Demonstration Reels (DR prefix)

The DR reels came free with viewers and were also given away by dealers as promotional items. They did not come in envelopes unless noted otherwise. An abbreviation code FV/NFS indicates "Free with Viewer—Not for Sale" imprinted on the outer edge of the reel. DRE prefix reels were made in Belgium and are listed after this section. Values are for reels in excellent condition. Lack of a protective envelope often allowed the DR reels to become scratched or soiled; deduct 50 percent for reels

showing minor use. Badly soiled or scratched reels have very little or no collector value.

DR-1, View-Master Demonstrator Reel, Self-Service Reel Sales Case (black ink) ———— 50.00
DR-1, The View-Master Personal Stereo Camera (red ink) ———— 35.00
DR-2, "Stereo-Matic 500" projector, Demonstration Reel, Special Reel, Not for Sale, Scenes from Stock View-Master Reels (black ink) ———— 50.00
DR-2, Stereo Showcase of View-Master Pictures (Belgian issue) ———— 25.00
DR-3, The View-Master Stereo Family (black ink) ———— 25.00
DR-4, Title Unknown ———— Extremely Rare
DR-5, Starred in View-Master 3-Dimensions (Scene 7 has a blank pocket to insert your own View-Master Personal

View-Master special single reel "Christmas Tour from Sawyer's." These apparently were distributed to employees and the dealer network. It shows a tour of the View-Master factory. $50. (Gordon D. Hoffman Collection)

stereo picture) —————————— 50.00
DR-6, View-Master, Stereo-Engineered,
Positive Alignment (black ink) ————— 35.00
DR-7, Boys and Girls, View-Master Three
Dimension Sample Reel, Not for Sale
(brown ink) —————————— 25.00
DR-8, Boys and Girls View-Master Three
Dimension Sample Reel, Not for Sale
(green ink with special Pinky Lee booklet
and envelope) ———————— 15.00
DR-9, Your Free View-Master "Fun Pa-
rade Reel," Sample Reel, Not for Sale
(green ink) ————————— 10.00
DR-10, View-Master Demonstrator Reel,
Sample Reel, Not for Sale (green ink) —— 15.00
DR-11, Atlas of Human Anatomy, Stereo
Demonstrator Reel (green ink with special
envelope folder) ———————— 15.00
DR-12, Stereos from the Atlas of Human
Anatomy (green ink) ——————— 15.00
DR-13, View-Master Scenic Wonders of
North America ————————— 5.00
DR-14, View-Master People of Other
Lands ——————————— 5.00
DR-15, Wonders of Nature ———— 5.00
   (DR-13–15 included in special gift
   three-reel packet, reels in green ink, the
   packet envelope is gold and red) ——— 30.00
DR-16, Beautiful North America (green
ink) ———————————— 4.00
DR-17, People Around the World (green
ink) ———————————— 5.00
DR-18, Animal and Flower Wonders
(green ink) ————————— 4.00
DR-19, North American Travel Scenes
(green ink) ————————— 3.00
DR-20, World Travel Wonders
(green ink) ————————— 3.00
DR-21, Highlights from Classic Stories
(green ink) ————————— 5.00
DR-22, Travelogues of North America
(green ink) ————————— 5.00
DR-23, Scenic Wonders of the World
(green ink) ————————— 5.00
DR-24, The World of Adventure (green
ink) ———————————— 5.00
DR-25, North American Wonderlands
(green ink) ————————— 5.00
DR-26, Scenes of Other Lands
(green ink) ————————— 5.00
DR-27, Highlights from Fairy Tales (green
ink) ———————————— 5.00
DR-28, What's New in View-Master Reels,
Spring 1959, Sample Reel, Not for Sale
(green ink) ————————— 15.00
DR-29, Stereo Seeing Is at Its Best in
View-Master Reels (green ink) ———— 10.00
DR-29, Stereo Seeing Is at Its Best in
View-Master Reels (black ink) ——— 12.00
DR-30, Examples of Scientific Uses of
Stereo Illustrations (green ink in special
envelope folder) ———————— 20.00
DR-35, Stereo Gives Your Product a Dra-
matic Presentation, View-Master Stereo is
Low Cost—High Value (black ink) ——— 35.00

DR-37, Stereo Showcase of View-Master
Pictures (black ink) ——————— 7.50
DR-38, View-Master International Series
"The World At Your Fingertips" (black
ink) ———————————— 5.00
DR-40, 1961 Annual Report to Stockhold-
ers of Sawyer's Inc., Portland, Oreg.
(black ink) ————————— 50.00
DR-43, Preview Reel, New Fall 1962
View-Master Packets, Seven Scenes, the
10 New Fall '62 Releases (black ink) —— 15.00
DR-44, Stereo Showcase of View-Master
Pictures (black ink) ——————— 6.00
DR-45, View-Master Preview Reel, Picture
Tour of United States Cities (red ink
FV/NFS) ———————————— 6.00
DR-46, View-Master Preview Reel, Picture
Tour of National Parks (red ink
FV/NFS) ———————————— 3.00
DR-47, View-Master Preview Reel, Picture
Tour of Vacationlands, Western United
States (red ink FV/NFS) —————— 8.00
DR-48, View-Master Preview Reel, Picture
Tour of Vacationlands, Eastern United
States (red ink FV/NFS) —————— 4.00
DR-49, View-Master Preview Reel, Picture
Tour of Scenic Wonders, United States
(red ink FV/NFS) ———————— 1.00
   Without FV/NFS ———————— 2.00
DR-50, View-Master Preview Reel, Picture
Tour of United States Tourist Attractions
(red ink FV/NFS) ———————— 10.00
   Without FV/NFS ——————— 10.00
DR-51, View-Master Preview Reel, Picture
Tour of Historical Landmarks (red ink
FV/NFS) ——————————— 10.00
   Without FV/NFS ———————— 4.00
DR-52, View-Master Preview Reel, Picture
Tour of Famous World Cities (red ink
FV/NFS) ———————————— 4.00
DR-53, View-Master Preview Reel, Picture
Tour of Nations of the World (red ink
FV/NFS) ———————————— 9.00
DR-54, View-Master Preview Reel, Picture
Tour of the World at Your Fingertips (red
ink FV/NFS) ————————— 5.00
   Without FV/NFS ———————— 4.00
DR-55, View-Master Preview Reel, Picture
Tour of Famous World Scenes (red ink
FV/NFS) ———————————— 8.00
DR-56, View-Master Preview Reel, Picture
Tour of People of Many Lands (red ink
FV/NFS) ———————————— 2.00
   Without FV/NFS ———————— 4.00
DR-57, View-Master Preview Reel, Picture
Tour of The Ancient World (red ink
FV/NFS) ———————————— 4.00
   Without FV/NFS ———————— 4.00
DR-58, View-Master Preview Reel, Picture
Tour of Classic Children's Stories (red ink
FV/NFS, SAW issue) ——————— 1.50
   Without FV/NFS, GAF issue ———— 4.00
DR-59, View-Master Preview Reel, Picture
Tour of Television & Cartoon Favorites
(red ink FV/NFS, SAW issue) ———— 4.00

Two versions of View-Master demonstration reel #DR-62, "What in the World Do You Want to See?" These came with the viewers and did not have envelopes. $2.00 each.

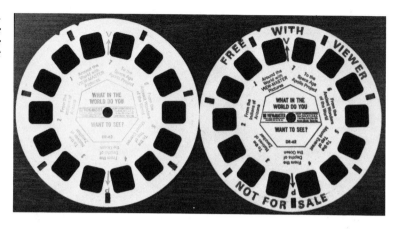

With FV/NFS, GAF issue _____ 2.00
Without FV/NFS, GAF issue _____ 2.00
DR-62, What in the World Do You Want to
See? (brown ink FV/NFS, SAW issue) _____ 3.00
GAF issue _____ 2.00
Without FV/NFS, red ink, GAF issue _____ 2.00
DR-63, What in the World Do You Want
to See? (red ink) _____ 10.00
Black ink _____ 7.00
S Suffix, Spanish Language version _____ 20.00
DR-64, View-Master Preview Reel, Picture
Tour of Famous World Cities (red ink
FV/NFS) _____ 8.00
Black ink _____ 10.00
DR-65, View-Master Preview Reel, Picture
Tour of Famous World Scenes (black ink
FV/NFS) _____ 8.00
S Suffix, Spanish language version _____ 15.00
DR-66, View-Master Preview Reel, Picture
Tour of People of Many Lands (Black ink
FV/NFS) _____ 8.00
DR-67S, View-Master, Estereorotos de
Cuentos Clasicos, Para Ninos (black ink
FV/NFS) _____ 15.00
DR-68, Highlights from the White House
twenty-one-scene Packet (blue ink
FV/NFS) _____ 8.00
DR-69, View-Master Preview Reel, Fairy
Tales (green ink FV/NFS) _____ 8.00
DR-70, View-Master Preview Reel, Scenic
Wonders, United States (green ink
FV/NFS) _____ 8.00
DR-71, View-Master Preview Reel, United
States Cities (green ink FV/NFS) _____ 8.00
DR-72, View-Master Preview Reel, TV
and Cartoon Favorites (green ink
FV/NFS) _____ 8.00
DR-73, View-Master Preview Reel, Cities
of the World (green ink FV/NFS) _____ 8.00
DR-76, View-Master Preview Reel, Space
Travel and Rockets (black ink FV/NFS) ___ 10.00
DR-77, Previews of View-Master Entertainment! (black ink) _____ 1.50

DR-78, Previews of View-Master Entertainment! (black ink) _____ 2.00
DR-82, View-Master Preview, Picture Reel
of Family Entertainment (red ink) _____ 1.50
S Suffix Spanish Language version _____ 5.00

Demonstration Reels (Belgian-Issue DRE prefix)

Similar to the United States issues, but these are very uncommon in this country. They were made in several different languages, which is indicated with the suffix code letter. Reels DRE-63 to DRE-66 appear to be the most common but there are only a few recorded sales.

DRE-1 to DRE-17 _____ each 10.00
DRE-22 to DRE-55 _____ each 4–8.00
DRE-63 to DRE-66 _____ each 2–5.00

Easter Story Reels (EA prefix)
(See *Three-Reel Packets, B-880 in Chapter 7*)

Fairy Tale Reels (FT prefix)

These were first offered in 1946 as single reels. The scenes were modeled in clay by Florence Thomas, a local artist and sculptor in the Portland, Oregon, area. Thomas's work is some of the best of the early clay animation artists. She developed special methods of close-up stereo photography and modeling, which is now in common use by major motion picture studios. Thomas trained Joe Liptak in her methods. Liptak became chief modeler at View-Master after Thomas retired and is responsible for the clay models in many of the later FT reels and

B packets. See appropriate B packets for FT reels and FT reels with letter suffix.

FT1, Little Red Riding Hood (with booklet) _____ 1.50
FT2, Hansel and Gretel (with booklet) _____ 1.50
FT3, Jack and the Beanstalk (with booklet) _____ 1.50
FT4, Snow White and the Seven Dwarfs (with booklet) _____ 1.50
FT5, Cinderella and the Glass Slipper (with booklet) _____ 1.50
FT6, Goldilocks and the Three Bears (with booklet) _____ 1.50
FT7, The Three Little Pigs (with booklet) _____ 1.50
FT8, Little Black Sambo (with booklet) _____ 10.00
FT9, The Ugly Duckling (with booklet) _____ 1.50
FT10, Sleeping Beauty (with booklet) _____ 5.00
FT11, The Pied Piper of Hamelin (with booklet) _____ 5.00
FT12, Thumbelina (with booklet) _____ 5.00
FT13, Rumpelstiltskin (with booklet, 1953) _____ 5.00
FT13, Rumpelstiltskin (without booklet, 1955) _____ 8.00
FT14, Goldilocks and the Three Bears (with booklet) _____ 5.00
FT25, Rudolph, the Red-Nosed Reindeer
   1939 copyright (with booklet) _____ 3.00
   1950 copyright (with booklet) _____ 4.00
   1952 copyright _____ 6.00
FT26, Rudolph, the Red-Nosed Reindeer and J. Baddy, the Brilliant Bear _____ 8.00
FT27, Rudolph, the Red-Nosed Reindeer and Uncle Bigby, the Blue-Nosed Reindeer _____ 8.00
FT28, Rudolph, the Red Nosed Reindeer, Shines Again _____ 8.00
FT30, The Night Before Christmas or a Visit from St. Nicholas (with booklet) _____ 2.00
FT51, The Magic Carpet (with booklet) _____ 1.50

Mother Goose Rhymes (all with booklets)

MG-1, Miss Muffet to Jack and Jill _____ 1.50
MG-2, Little Boy Blue to King Cole, 1950 _____ 1.50
MG-3, Bo-Peep to Cat and the Fiddle _____ 1.50

Sam Sawyer, Adventures of
(all with booklets)

SAM-1, Sam Flies to the Moon _____ 4.00
SAM-2, Sam Finds a Treasure _____ 4.00
SAM-3, In the Land of Giants _____ 4.00
SAM-4, Sam in Darkest Africa _____ 4.00
SAM-5, Sam in the Land of Ice _____ 4.00
SAM-6, Flying Saucer Pirates _____ 4.00

SP *Prefix Reels*

This series of reels was issued to be sold by the local distributors or at the attraction pic-tured. Most could also be ordered directly from the factory.

SP-1, Skyline Caverns, Front Royal, Va. ___ 20.00
SP-49, Glacier National Park, Mountain Trip IV _____ 5.00
SP-58, Golden Gate International Exposition, 1940 _____ 20.00
SP-59, Golden Gate International Exposition, Night Scenes, 1940 _____ 15.00
SP-67, Maui, The Valley Island, Hawaii, 1951 _____ 5.00
SP-72, Kauai, The Garden Isle, Hawaii, 1951 _____ 5.00
SP-72, Island of Kauai, Hawaii _____ 10.00
SP-88, New York World's Fair I _____ 20.00
SP-89, New York World's Fair II _____ 15.00
SP-92, Oregon Caves National Monument II _____ 8.00
SP-117, Sequoia National Park III _____ 8.00
SP-152, Bonneville Dam and Columbia River _____ 8.00
SP-152, Bonneville Dam, Oreg., 1952 _____ 4.00
SP-179, Tucson, Ariz. _____ 6.00
SP-180, Phoenix, Ariz. _____ 3.00
SP-184, Monterey Peninsula, Calif., 1949 ___ 6.00
SP-188, Santa Barbara, Calif., 1951 _____ 5.00
SP-189, San Juan Capistrano Mission, Calif. _____ 6.00
SP-207, Sun Valley, Idaho, Summer _____ 4.00
   Variant, scene 7: Opera House & Lodge _____ 8.00
SP-231, Cedar Breaks National Monument, Utah _____ 6.00
SP-236, Million Dollar Highway, Colo. ___ 2.00
SP-237, Berthoud Pass, Highway 40, Rocky Mountains _____ 4.00
SP-241, Cheyenne Canyons and Seven Falls, Colo. _____ 6.00
SP-243, Broadmoor, Cheyenne Mountains _____ 8.00
SP-282, Santa Fe, N.Mex., 1948 _____ 3.00
SP-285, Death Valley National Monument II _____ 10.00
Sp-287, White Sands National Monument, N.Mex. _____ 5.00
SP-288, Aztec Ruins National Monument, 1947 _____ 9.00
SP-305, Sitka, Alaska, 1950 _____ 8.00
SP-307, Ketchikan and Vicinity, 1950 _____ 8.00
SP-321, Waterton Lakes National Park, Alta. _____ 8.00
SP-9001, Skyline Caverns, Front Royal, Va. _____ 1.00
SP-9002, Trees of Mystery, Requa, Calif., 1948 _____ 1.50
   Variant, scene 1: "Babe" _____ 3.00
SP-9003, Butchart Gardens, Victoria, B.C., Canada, 1948 _____ 2.00
SP-9003, Butchart Gardens, Victoria, B.C., Canada, 1950 _____ 4.00
SP-9004, Maligne Lake, Jasper National Park, Alberta, Canada _____ 6.00

SP-9006, Fraser Canyon, B.C., Canada _____ 2.00
SP-9007, Indian Days, Banff, Alberta, Canada _____ 2.00
SP-9008, Hoover [Boulder] Dam, Nevada, Scenic Auto Tour, 1946 _____ 2.00
SP-9009, Hoover [Boulder] Dam, Nevada, Canyon Cruise, 1946 _____ 5.00
SP-9010, Virginia City, Nev. _____ 5.00
SP-9011, Taos, N.Mex. _____ 5.00
SP-9012, Natural Bridge of Virginia _____ 1.00
SP-9013, Sanctuary of Our Sorrowful Mother, Portland, Oreg. _____ 1.00
SP-9014, Sanctuary of Our Sorrowful Mother, Portland, Oreg. II _____ 1.00
SP-9015, Seven Dolors, Sanctuary of Our Sorrowful Mother, Portland, Oreg. _____ 1.00
SP-9016, Cranmore Mountain Skimobile Tramway, White Mountains, N.H. _____ 5.00
SP-9017, Cannon Mountain, Aerial Tramway, Franconia Notch, N.H. _____ 2.00
SP-9018, Ausable Chasm, N.Y. _____ 1.00
SP-9019, Mount Washington and Cog Road, N.H. _____ 3.00
SP-9020, Old Covered Bridges, New England _____ 5.00
SP-9021, Howe Caverns I, N.Y. _____ 4.00
SP-9022, Howe Caverns II, N.Y. _____ 1.50
SP-9023, Timberline Lodge and Mount Hood _____ 2.00
SP-9024, Rock City Gardens, Lookout Mountain, Tenn. _____ 3.00
SP-9025, Franconia Notch, Lost River, White Mountains, N.H. _____ 2.00
SP-9026, Beautiful Caverns of Luray I, Va. _____ 3.00
SP-9027, Beautiful Caverns of Luray II, Va. _____ 3.00
SP-9028, Adirondack Mountains, N.Y., 1950 _____ 3.00
SP-9029, Fort Ticonderoga and Crown Point, N.Y. _____ 3.00
SP-9030, Gloucester and North Shore, Mass. _____ 1.50
SP-9031, Petersen's Rock Gardens, Redmond, Oreg. _____ 2.00
SP-9032, Monticello, Charlottesville, Va. _____ 1.00
SP-9033, Water Skiing, Fla., 1949 _____ 1.00
SP-9034, Sea Lion Caves, Florence, Oreg. _____ 1.00
SP-9035, Crawford Notch, Eastern Slope, White Mountains _____ 1.00
SP-9036, Albuquerque, N.Mex., 1948 _____ 3.00
SP-9037, St. Petersburg, Fla., 1949 _____ 1.00
SP-9037, St. Petersburg, Fla., 1953 _____ 3.00
SP-9038, Ghost Town, Knott's Berry Farm, Buena Park, Calif. _____ 3.00
SP-9039, San Diego, Calif., 1949 _____ 2.00
SP-9039, San Diego, Calif., 1953 _____ 4.00
SP-9040, Badlands National Monument, S.Dak., 1949 _____ 1.00
SP-9042, Estes Park, Big Thompson Canyon, Colo. _____ 2.00
SP-9043, National Monuments of Western Colorado, 1949 _____ 3.00
SP-9044, Las Vegas, Nev. _____ 6.00

SP-9045, Oak Creek Canyon, Ariz., 1949 _____ 4.00
SP-9045, Oak Creek Canyon, Ariz., 1951 _____ 8.00
SP-9046, Weekiwachee Springs, Fla., 1949 _____ 3.00
SP-9047, Gettysburg National Military Park, Pa., 1950 _____ 2.00
SP-9048, Arches National Monument, Utah, 1950 _____ 3.00
SP-9049, Blue Ridge Parkway, N.C. and Va., 1950 _____ 1.00
SP-9050, Northern Maine, 1950 _____ 2.00
SP-9051, Martha's Vineyard Island, Mass. _____ 4.00
SP-9052, Florida Flowers and Bok Tower, 1950 _____ 2.00
SP-9052, The Bok Tower and Florida Flowers, 1951 _____ 1.00
SP-9053, The Everglades National Park, Fla. _____ 1.00
SP-9054, Big Bend National Park, Tex. _____ 4.00
SP-9055, Prehistoric Cliff Dwellers of Mesa Verde, Colo., 1950 _____ 4.00
SP-9056, Joshua Tree National Monument, Calif. _____ 5.00
SP-9057, Interior of George Washington's Mount Vernon home, Va., 1950 _____ 2.00
SP-9058, Home of Santa's Workshop, North Pole, N.Y., 1951 _____ 3.00
SP-9059, St. Louis, Missouri, 1951 _____ 3.00
SP-9060, The Cody Highway, Wyo. _____ 4.00
SP-9061, Big Horn Mountains, Wyo., 1951 _____ 2.00
SP-9062, Boys Town, Nebr., 1951 _____ 1.00
SP-9063, Baltimore, Md., 1951 _____ 1.00
SP-9064, Bellingrath Gardens, Mobile, 1952 _____ 3.00
SP-9065, Prince Edward Island, Canada, 1951 _____ 5.00
SP-9066, Cape Breton Highlands, N.S., Canada _____ 6.00
SP-9067, Bird Sanctuary, Bonaventure Island, Que., Canada, 1951 _____ 8.00
SP-9068, Canadian National Exhibitions, Toronto, Canada _____ 10.00
SP-9069, Kenora and Lake of the Woods, Ont., Canada, 1951 _____ 4.00
SP-9070, The Lakehead Region, Ont., Canada _____ 5.00
SP-9071, Tulip Time in Holland, Mich., 1952 _____ 2.00
SP-9072, Twin Cities and Southern Minnesota, 1952 _____ 4.00

VIEW-MASTER COMMERCIAL ADVERTISING AND SPECIAL-ISSUE REELS

Popular among View-Master collectors are the commercial advertising reels produced from 1946 to the present. These were not intended for general sale to the public or were given

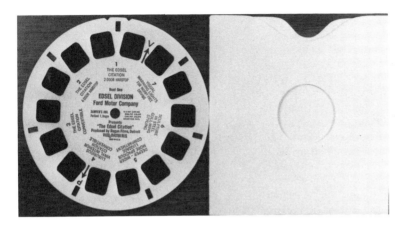

View-Master Advertising Reel, reel #1 of a set of five made for the Edsel division of the Ford Motor Company; they came in plain white envelopes. Complete set of five, $300.

away or sold as a promotional tool. Salesmen and factory representatives used the compact viewer and reels as an easy sale opener with their customers. As mentioned, View-Master reels were used during World War II for ship and aircraft identification and as a means for gunnery officers to teach correct sighting procedures. After the war, View-Master contracted with Three Dimension Company to make many of the commercial reels. The stereoscopic photography is outstanding and these reels are a visual record of the lifestyles of the years following World War II on into the 1950s when many new household products were introduced to an eager buying public.

The first commercial reels were made for the Steiner Cabinet Company in 1946. These were followed by reels for Brunswick, Bastian Blessing, Cosco, Mengel Cartons, Brown Shoe and Hanes Hosiery. Of particular note is the twenty different reels produced for Seven-Up, the popular soft drink. These were carried by delivery men who had the store owner view the reels while the shelves were being restocked. Standard Oil had a similar series made, which featured tires, batteries and accessories.

Some of the most sought after reels are those produced for the major automobile companies. Nash Motors used a set in the early 1950s, which was followed by a rare set for the Edsel. Buicks for 1960 and the new Lincoln-Mercury cars for 1962 were also shown in View-Master reels.

An extremely rare packet is the twelve-reel set made for Aero Mayflower moving vans in 1960. Only 1000 sets were made, and they feature a full-color packet envelope. The set shows a typical household move from estimate through packing to final delivery.

Other sets of reels were made for Anheuser-Busch, Fairbanks Morse (water softeners), Curtiss Candy Company (marshmallows), Sears (Twin-door Coldspot Refrigerators), U.S. Gypsum (acoustical tile), Golden Acres (sorgham), Clay Seed of Kentucky (tobacco), Restonic Mattress, Stitzel Weller Distillery and others.

In the early 1950s, Hollywood was swept up in the 3-D movie craze. The making of 3-D movies had been promoted from the late 1890s on into the 1940s but only a few shorts and special features were produced. The release of *Bwana Devil* in late 1952 in 3-D caught on immediately with the public and the major studios began production of more than sixty feature films to meet the public demand. View-Master created a special advertising package for theaters. National Screen Service, the distributor of lobby advertising posters, photos and so forth, made available a special viewing cabinet. The theater owner could show a set of View-Master reels of the coming attractions. The reels in this series are outstanding, showing leading movie stars such as Edward G. Robinson and Rita Hayworth in scenes from the 3-D films. These are called "movie preview reels" and are not to be confused with the View-Master *DR* prefix reels that are also called preview reels. Movie preview reels were clearly marked "Not for Resale" and gave credit to the studio or producer and the film process, such as Technicolor. Most of the 3-D movies were rushed into production and lacked technical quality. The public quickly grew tired of the gimmicks being used, and Hollywood shortened the release of many of the films, rereleasing them as flat movies. The reels are extremely rare and on most collector's want lists. There are thirty-one known titles.

An outstanding single reel is "Super Steelers," produced to benefit the Press Old Newsboys Children's Hospital Fund of Pittsburgh. This reel features the Pittsburgh Steeler football team photographed by Mike Chikiris, a professional photographer. Included are terrific views of Terry Bradshaw, Franco Harris, Jack Lambert, L. C. Greenwood, Mean Joe Greene and others. The production was limited to only 1000 reels, and it came in a plain white envelope.

Other special reels include "personal" sets of female nudes, which were not produced by View-Master. One set examined features six reels of "Betty Howard 'The Girl Who Has Everything.'" The set comes in a silver green personal folder box with a rubber-stamped imprint. Another set of more erotic View-Master reels were made in Europe in the 1960s, also as unauthorized "personal" reels. These are rare.

Evaluating These Reels

So few sales have been recorded for advertising reels that a price guide would be my best guess. Most commercial advertising reels have sold in the $15 to $25 range. Premium prices are paid for the automobile sets, especially the Edsel reels (five in the set). The movie preview reels have sold as high as $85 at auction. A complete set of thirty-one should easily bring more than $1000. The "Super Steelers" reel has sold as high as $17.50 at auction.

The Movie Preview Reels
(1953–1954, thirty-one known)

Issued as Movie Review Reels, these were not filmed in 3-D (although the reels *are* in 3-D).

Arena, MGM
Dangerous Mission, R.K.O. Radio Pictures
Devil's Canyon, R.K.O. Radio Pictures
Drums of Tahiti, Columbia Pictures
Flight to Tangier, Paramount Pictures
Fort Ti, Columbia Pictures
Gun Fury, Columbia Pictures
Hannah Lee, Jack Broder
House of Wax, Warner Brothers
Inferno, 20th Century Fox
It Came from Outer Space, Universal-International
Jesse James Vs. the Daltons, Columbia Pictures

Kiss Me Kate, MGM
Lost Treasures of the Amazon, Paramount
Miss Sadie Thompson, Columbia Pictures
Money from Home, Paramount Pictures
Sangaree, Paramount Pictures
Second Chance, R.K.O. Pictures
Son of Sinbad, R.K.O. Radio Pictures
Taza, Son of Cochise, Universal-International
The Charge at Feather River, Warner Brothers
The French Line, R.K.O. Radio Pictures
The Glass Webb, Universal-International
The Maze, Allied Artists
The Nebraskan, Columbia Pictures
The Stranger Wore a Gun, Columbia Pictures
They Called Him Hondo, Warner Brothers
Those Redheads from Seattle, Paramount Pictures
Wings of the Hawk, Universal-International
Beneath the 12-Mile Reef
The Robe

VIEW-MASTER THREE-REEL PACKETS

Beginning in 1950, Sawyer's started packaging the View-Master reels into special sets or packets of three. By 1956, the sale of single reels had nearly disappeared with production almost entirely in the three-reel packets. In 1958, a prefix began to appear, first with the letters *A* and *B* and over the years moving through the alphabet to *M*. Up to 1958, the numbering was confined to the reels. The earliest packets simply used reels already numbered such as "Los Angeles," which contained reels 219, 221 and 223 (1955–1956 issue). In 1957, Sawyer's began using a single number with an A, B and C suffix such as "Long Island, N.Y.," which contained reels 57A, 57B and 57C. About that time, the state packets were issued with abbreviations of the state as a prefix such as "Louisiana" LA1, LA2 and LA3.

Bill Wolf in his View-Master Reels series has given designation codes for the various packet types, which have become the standard for collectors. Some slight variations do exist, but they are not noted here. See the illustrated types and read the descriptions of each before using the price guide. Prices are for complete packets with a story booklet (BK) as noted in near-new condition with no tears to the packet envelope. Reels must be clean and show little or no use. Deduct 50 percent for torn packets or reels that show use. Add 25 percent for mint, never opened (MNO) packets with original cellophane wrap. Incomplete or badly damaged packets or reels have little or no collector value.

View-Master test packaging of three-reel packets. These packets were on store shelves and special hanging racks for a short time in the late 1950s. An early forerunner of the hanging card "blister" packs of the 1980s, this package was not tamperproof and was soon discontinued. Examples are usually valued 25 to 50 percent higher than their standard counterpart. (Gordon D. Hoffman Collection)

View-Master Packet Identification

Bill Wolf, a collector from Allentown, Pennsylvania, has devised a standard method of identifying View-Master packets. Walter Sigg, a major dealer has made some revisions to the Wolf method, which has been adopted by most dealers who sell the packets. The packets were first introduced in 1953 and proved to be an important marketing step for Sawyer's. Up until then, the reels had been sold as individual units. The packets featured three reels as a set. At first, Sawyer's simply used three reels already in their sales lists. For example the "Sequoia and Kings Canyon National Parks" packet included reel #115, 116 and 118. In late 1957, Sawyer's assigned a new numbering system to the packets and began to discontinue the sale of single reels. These transition packets are found with the letter prefix packet number rubber stamped on the packet's reverse side. As old stock was used up, the new packet number was printed on the newly designed packet envelopes.

Advanced View-Master collectors like to try to collect all of the packet designs. This is a challenge, because the company never kept accurate records of the different types of packet envelopes. Therefore, the collectors and dealers have attempted to identify the many variants.

About 1962, View-Master began inserting a picture, or story, booklet in each packet along with a packet order list. Thus for a packet to be complete it must include the three reels and the booklet and be in the original envelope. Packet lists are often missing and rarely add or subtract from the collector value.

An annoying design concept with the packet envelopes were the perforations in the envelopes developed in the early 1970s. These fine perforations (perfs) are so fragile that care must be taken in handling the later packet envelopes. Packets were originally sold shrink wrapped in cellophane. Collectors refer to these

(Continued on page 235)

View-Master, three-reel packet, "Tom Corbett, Space Cadet," type S1 packet. Line drawings with three reels and viewer at lower-left corner (1953–1954). $25. (Gordon D. Hoffman Collection)

View-Master, three-reel packet, A322 "Rocky Mountain National Park," type S3 at left, circle in upper-right corner with no numbers (1955–1957) and S4 at right, packet numbers in circle in upper-right corner (1958–1960). (Gordon D. Hoffman Collection)

View-Master, three-reel packet, A655, type S5 at left, pictures from photo, logo at lower right corner (1960–1963) and type G3, at right, GAF logo on front upper left for first time in lower case letters (1970–1975).

View-Master, three-reel packet, A813 "Colonial Williamsburg" from the "Historic America" series of packets. Type S6 Sawyer's issue, edition A. To be complete it must have a full outer envelope, a booklet, an inside envelope (sleeve) and the three reels. This was a popular packet and was issued in several different packet designs up to 1982. S6 characteristics—Lowell Thomas edition (1963–1966).

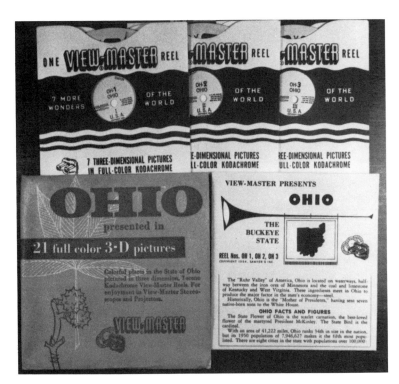

View-Master, three-reel packet, "Ohio," type S2 packet with booklet. Line drawings with reel numbers below logo on front (1954–1955). $6.

View-Master, three-reel packet, A179 "Disneyland, Tomorrowland," type G1, edition D, GAF in lower-case letters on back in black (1967–1969). This edition did not have a booklet. The Disneyland packets were issued in several different packet designs and editions and are still sold in the blister packaging.

View-Master, three-reel packet, A636 "Gettysburg National Military Park, Pennsylvania," type G2, edition A (note A in lower right corner), GAF logo in lowercase letters on back panel in red (1969–1970). G3, GAF in lower-case letter logo on front upper-left for first time (1970–1975), and G4, GAF in capital letters upper-left. (Gordon D. Hoffman Collection)

View-Master, three-reel packet, M36 "Era of the Space Shuttle," type V2, View-Master logo moved to far upper-left corner (1981–1982). Type V1 (View-Master International) is characterized by the blotted-out GAF logo (1981). (Gordon D. Hoffman Collection)

View-Master, three-reel packet, A669 "Operation Sail . . . The Tall Ships," type G5, redesigned back panel usually with dates (1977–1978). (Gordon D. Hoffman Collection)

A typical View-Master blister packet. The "E.T." packet was one of the first issued in this new packaging in 1982. Note that this guide does not go beyond 1982 in dealing with 3-D collectibles. The golden era of View-Master three-reel packets ended in 1982. The remaining packets were stapled to these hanging cards beginning in 1982. Some of the 1981 and 1982 packets are difficult to find without the staple holes.

View-Master, three-reel packet, J19 "Welcome Back Kotter," 1977, type G6, "3-D pictures" replaces "Stereo Pictures" below logo on back panel (1978–1981). This packet is Mint, never opened (MNO).

as mint, never opened (MNO). Once the cellophane wrap is removed, the packet envelope has a tendency to disintegrate along the perfs. Purchasers in the 1970s often used cellophane tape to repair the envelopes. As a result, many envelopes are found with brown tape stains. These stains detract from the appearance and the collector value.

View-Master Packet Collecting Hint

When purchasing already opened View-Master packets, be sure to check the reels and booklet. See if the packet is complete by reading the back panel. This panel will indicate the correct contents. Check to make sure the booklet is the correct one and has all the pages. The

reels should be clean with all film "chips" intact. It is recommended that the reels be viewed if possible, especially if they show use. The Kodak film base is surprisingly durable but can be scratched or nicked.

Unnumbered Three-Reel Packets, 1950–1957

Packets in this section were all published by Sawyer's and are designated S1 (1950–1954), S2 (1953–1955) and S3 (1955–1958).

Aircraft Carrier in Action at Sea, 760A, B & C	45.00
Alabama, ALA1, 2 & 3	8.00
Alaska, 304, 306 & 308	4.00
Alice in Wonderland, FT20A, B & C	8.00
Arabian Nights, FT50A, B & C	11.00

View-Master, six-reel packet, "Wild Animals," featuring reels #901 and 910–914. Although all fairly common individually, they are rarely seen as this packet. $25. (Gordon D. Hoffman Collection)

Rarely seen packets of out of print reels were offered through the View-Master dealer network, ca. 1960. Although the reels are fairly common, those in this type of envelope are very rare, $30–50 per packet. (Gordon D. Hoffman Collection)

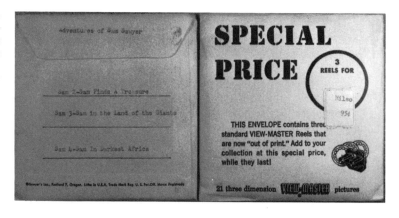

Arizona, ARIZ1, 2 & 3	3.00
Arkansas, AK1, 2 & 3	6.00
Atlantic City, N.J., 154A, B & C	40.00
Australia, 5001, 5020, 5041	9.00
Bambi (Disney), FT42A, B & C	11.00
Banff, Canadian Rockies, 318, 320, 9004	8.00
Baseball Stars, 725, 726, 727	60.00
Battle of the Monsters from the Animal World, 920A, B & C	35.00
Bellingrath Gardens, 355, 355B & C	10.00
Birth of Jesus, R1, 2 & 3	3.00
Black Hills and Badlands, S.Dak., 203A, B & 204	3.00
Blue Ridge Parkway, 78A, B & C	10.00
Bobby the Bunny, 830A, B & C	9.00
Boy Scout Jamboree, 8th World, 435A, B & C	40.00
Brave Eagle, 933A, B & C	25.00
Brazil, 670, 671 & 675	11.00

Brooklyn, 55A, B & C	30.00
Bryce Canyon National Park, 16, 17 & 231	9.00
Buffalo Bill, Jr., 965A, B & C	25.00
Butterflies, 890A, B & C	11.00
California, CALIF1, 2 & 3	3.00
California Missions, 190A, B & C	6.00
Canonization of Blessed Pius X, 410A, B & C	10.00
Carlsbad Caverns, 251, 252 & 253	6.00
Carnival of Nice, 1428A, B & C	25.00
Caverns of Luray, The Beautiful, 194A, B & C	9.00
Central Ontario, 376A, B & C	10.00
Cherokee Indians, 80A, B & C	15.00
Chicago, Illinois, 333A, B & C	4.00
Christmas Carol, A, FT31A, B & C	3.00
Christmas Story, XM1, 2 & 3	4.00
Church of Latter-Day Saints, 119A, B & C	14.00

View-Master, three-reel packet, ''Battle of the Monsters'' from ''The Animal World.'' Dramatic scenes from one of Irwin Allen's earliest films. Type S3 variant with line drawing. $35. (Gordon D. Hoffman Collection)

View-Master, three-reel packet, ''Carnival of Nice,'' type S3 variant with line drawings. $25. (Gordon D. Hoffman Collection)

View-Master, three-reel packet, ''Disneyland, 1. Main Street,'' contains reels 851A, B & C, type S3 pastel packet. Note the flap is torn, the only damage to this packet, although minor, it still lessens the value to collectors. This packet had no story booklet. $11.

Circus, 701, 702, 703		13.00
Colorado, COLO1, 2 & 3		6.00
Coney Island, N.Y., 56A, B & C		21.00
Connecticut, CONN1, 2 & 3		14.00
Coronation of Queen Elizabeth II, 405, 406 & 407		15.00
Cowboy Stars, 950, 955, 960		10.00
Crater Lake National Park, 21, 22 & 23		16.00
Cypress Gardens, Fla., Beautiful, 164A, B & C		3.00
Dale Evans "Queen of the West," 944A, B & C		25.00
Delaware, DEL1, 2 & 3		16.00
Denver and Mountain Parks, 237 and 246; the third reel is unknown (*See* packet A324, which is fairly common)		20.00
Denver Museum, 244A, B & C		13.00
Desert Wildflowers, 985A, B & C		7.00
Disneyland #1, Main Street USA, 851A, B & C		11.00
Disneyland #2, Frontierland, 852A, B & C		9.00
Disneyland #3, Adventureland, 853A, B & C		8.00
Disneyland #4, Fantasyland, 854A, B & C		9.00
Disneyland #5, Tomorrowland, 855A, B & C		22.00
Dolomite Mountains, 1622A, B & C		19.00
Donald Duck (Disney), 842A, B & C		3.00
Easter Story, EA1, 2 & 3		4.00
Eastern Ontario, 378, 379A & B		4.00
Egypt, 3300A, B & C		11.00
Fairy Tales I, FT1, 2 & 3		5.00
Fairy Tales II, FT4, 5 & 6		5.00
Fairy Tales II, FT5, 6 & 13		6.00
Fairy Tales III, FT7, 8 & 9		10.00
Fairy Tales IV, FT10, 11 & 12		11.00
Florida, FLA1, 2 & 3		3.00

Flowers of Hawaii, 68, 69 & 71		18.00
France, 1400A, B & C		4.00
Garden Flowers, 980, 981 & 982		10.00
Georgia, GA1, 2 & 3		6.00
Germany, 1575A, B & C		5.00
Glacier National Park, 46, 47 & 48		4.00
Goofy, Traveling Cameraman, 844A, B & C		7.00

View-Master, three-reel packet, ''Frontierland,'' Disneyland. This is the first issue of the Disneyland packets that was in this type S3 variant envelope. The reels have a D prefix. The packets usually have a value 50 percent higher than the later Disneyland editions (without the D prefix in the regular type S3 packet envelopes). (Gordon D. Hoffman Collection)

Grand Canyon I, 26, 27 & 30 _____ 8.00
Grand Canyon II, 31, 32 & 36 _____ 5.00
Grand Teton National Park, 41, 42 & 43 __ 11.00
Great Smokies National Park, 355A,
B & C _____ 5.00
Greater Miami Area, 163, 165 & 395 _____ 4.00
Greater Miami Seaquarium, 394A,
B & C _____ 11.00
Guatemala, 550A, B & C _____ 17.00
Hawaiian Medley, Life in Aloha Land, 62,
63 & 65 _____ 10.00
Historic Cities of Virginia, 75,
182 & 262 _____ extremely rare
Holy Land, The, 4000, 4006 & 4007 _____ 11.00
Hong Kong, 4810, 4811 & 4814 _____ 11.00
Hoover Dam and Lake Mead, 8, 11 &
SP9008 _____ 9.00
Hot Springs National Park, 299A, B & C __ 13.00
Hula Dancers, Oahu and Waikiki, 61, 64
& 73 _____ 8.00
Hunters of the Plains, 770A, B & C _____ 25.00
Ida Cason Callaway Gardens, 359A,
B & C _____ 16.00
Idaho, IDAHO1, 2 & 3 _____ 4.00
Illinois, ILL1, 2 & 3 _____ 5.00
In Darkest Africa, 3900A, B & C _____ 25.00
India, 4400A, B & C _____ 3.00
Indiana, IND1, 2 & 3 _____ 18.00
Inside Moscow, 2820A, B & C _____ 25.00
Iowa, IW1, 2 & 3 _____ 6.00
Island of Bermuda, 595A, B & C _____ 6.00
Islands of Romance, Hawaii, Maui, Kauai,
66, 67 & 72 _____ 11.00
Italy, 1600A, B & C _____ 11.00
Jamestown Festival, 77A, B & C _____ 18.00
Japan, 4900A, B & C _____ 10.00
Jesus Teaches Forgiveness, R7, 8 & 9 _____ 4.00

Johnny Moccasin, Jody McCrea in, 937A,
B & C _____ 20.00
Kansas, KN1, 2 & 3 _____ 6.00
Kentucky, KY1, 2 & 3 _____ 11.00
Kentucky Lake, 341A, B & C _____ 13.00
Knotts Berry Farm and Ghost Town, 216,
217 & 218 _____ 5.00
Lake Arrowhead and Santa's Village,
213A, B & C _____ 30.00
Lake Louise and Jasper, Canadian Rock-
ies, 316, 317 & 319 _____ 14.00
Las Vegas, Nev., 15A, B & C _____ 11.00
L'lle de Beaute Corsica, 1480, 1481 &
1482 _____ 20.00
Little Red Riding Hood (*See* Fairy Tales I
above)
Littlest Angel, The, FT32A, B & C _____ 6.00
Lone Ranger, 962A, B & C _____ 25.00
Long Island, NY, 57A, B & C _____ 35.00
Lookout Mountain, 327A, B & C _____ 5.00
Los Angeles, 219, 221 & 215 _____ 26.00
Los Angeles, 219, 221 & 223 _____ 11.00
Louisiana, LA1, 2 & 3 _____ 5.00
Lourdes Sanctuary and Pilgrimages,
France, 1415A, B & C _____ 5.00
Maine, MAINE1, 2 & 3 _____ 10.00
Mammoth Cave National Park, 339A,
B & C _____ 6.00
Marine Studios, Marineland of Florida,
166A, B & C _____ 10.00
Marineland of the Pacific, 244A, B & C _____ 6.00
Maritime Provinces, 396A, B & C _____ 12.00
Maryland, MD1, 2 & 3 _____ 10.00
Massachusetts, MASS1, 2 & 3 _____ 20.00
Mesa Verde, 226, 227 & SP9055 _____ 9.00
Mexico, 500A, B & C _____ 10.00
Michigan, MICH1, 2 & 3 _____ 6.00

View-Master, three-reel packet, "Long Island," type S3, $35.

Mickey Mouse Club Circus Visits Disney-
land, 856A, B & C _____ 25.00
Mickey Mouse Club Mouseketeers, 865A,
B & C _____ 25.00
Minnesota, MIN1, 2 & 3 _____ 8.00
Minnesota State Parks, 209A, B & C ____ 20.00
Miracles of Jesus, R10, 11 & 12 _____ 4.00
Mississippi, MISS1, 2 & 3 _____ 6.00
Missouri, MO1, 2 & 3 _____ 4.00
Montana, MONT1, 2 & 3 _____ 5.00
Monticello, 185A, B & C _____ 11.00
Montreal, 380A, B & C _____ 4.00
Mountain Rides of New Hampshire, 258,
266 & 267 _____ 7.00
Mother Goose Rhymes, MG1, 2 & 3 ____ 9.00
Mount Rainier National Park, 105, 106 &
107 _____ 13.00
Mount Vernon, 76A, B & C _____ 4.00
Movie Stars, 740, 741 & 742 _____ 50.00
Natural Bridge of Virginia, 79A, B & C ____ 15.00
Nebraska, NEBR1, 2 & 3 _____ 4.00
Netherlands, 1900, 1901 & 1920 _____ 13.00
Nevada, NEV1, 2 & 3 _____ 5.00
New England, 255, 273 & 277 _____ 6.00
New Fairy Tales (See Fairy Tales III)
New Hampshire, NH1, 2 & 3 _____ 4.00
New Jersey, NJ1, 2 & 3 _____ 8.00
New Mexico, NMEX1, 2 & 3 _____ 6.00
New Orleans, 330, 331 & 332 _____ 9.00
New York [State], NY1, 2 & 3 _____ 5.00
New York City, 156, 157 & 158 _____ 4.00
Niagara Falls, 81, 82 & 375 _____ 3.00
Niagara Peninsula and Southwestern
Ontario, 377, 377B & C _____ 12.00
Nice, The Riviera, France, 1424A & B
(Believed sold as a 2-reel
packet) _____ scarce 20.00
1955 Ghent Flowershow, Belgium, 1955A
& B (believed sold as a two-reel
packet) _____ scarce 20.00
North Carolina, NCAR1, 2 & 3 _____ 4.00
North Dakota, NDAK1, 2 & 3 _____ 20.00
Oberammergau Passion Play, 1550, 1551
& 1552 _____ 8.00
Ohio, OH1, 2 & 3 _____ 6.00
Oklahoma, OK1, 2 & 3 _____ 3.00
Ontario Vacationlands, 397A, B & C ____ 12.00
Oregon, OREG1, 2 & 3 _____ 4.00
Ozark Mountains, 372A, B & C _____ 3.00
Pacific Coast—Oregon Beaches, 96A,
B & C _____ 6.00
Painted Desert and Petrified Forest, 176,
177 & 178 _____ 8.00
Parables of Jesus, R4, 5 & 6 _____ 4.00
Park of the Red Rocks, 53, 237, 246 ____ 3.00
Parrot Jungle, 172A, B & C _____ 4.00
Passion Play (See Oberammergau Passion
Play above)
Pennsylvania, PA1, 2 & 3 _____ 5.00
People of Russia, 2810A, B & C _____ 25.00
Performing Animals, 925, 926 & 927 ____ 4.00
Peter Pan, FT40A, B & C _____ 6.00
Petersen's Rock Gardens, 99A, B & C ____ 13.00
Philadelphia and Valley Forge, 350, 351 &
352 _____ 5.00

Phipps Conservatory, 353A, B & C _____ 25.00
Pike's Peak, 51, 234 & 245 _____ 5.00
Prairie Provinces, 323A, B & C _____ 13.00
Quebec City, 383, 384 & 387 _____ 5.00
Rainier National Park (See Mount Rainier
National Park above)
Redwood Highway, 111, 112 & 113 ____ 11.00
Reno, 13, 14 & 183 _____ 11.00
Rhode Island, RI1, 2 & 3 _____ 7.00
Riders of the Desert, 771A, B & C ____ 60.00
Rin Tin Tin, 930A, B & C _____ 10.00
Robin Hood, 972A, B & C _____ 8.00
Rock City Caverns and Lookout Moun-
tain, 327A, B & C _____ 3.00
Rocky Mountain National Park, 101, 102,
SP9042 _____ 10.00
Rome, Italy, 1601, 1602 & 1604 _____ 11.00
Roy Rogers, King of the Cowboys, 948A,
B & C _____ 20.00
Royal Canadian Mounted Police, 705A,
B & C _____ 12.00
Royal Gorge, Colo., 236, 238 & SP9043 ____ 3.00
Rudolph Shines Again, FT26, FT27 &
FT28 _____ 12.00
Russia Today, 2800A, B & C _____ 25.00
Sainte Anne De Beaupre, 390A & B
(2-reel packet) _____ 35.00
Salt Lake City, 121A, B & C _____ 11.00
Sam Sawyer Adventures #1, SAM1,
2 & 3 _____ 8.00
Sam Sawyer Adventures #2, SAM4,
5 & 6 _____ 15.00
San Diego Zoo, 214A, B & C _____ 9.00
San Francisco, 198A, B & C _____ 4.00
Santa's Workshop, North Pole, N.Y., 89A,
B & C _____ 20.00
Sequoia and Kings Canyon National
Parks, 115, 116 & 118 _____ 5.00
Sequoia National Park, 115, 116 & 117 ____ 9.00
Shiloh, 324A, B & C _____ 14.00
Silver Springs, Fla., 161A, B & C _____ 3.00
Snow White and the Seven Dwarfs, FT4A,
B & C _____ 5.00
South Carolina, SC1, 2 & 3 _____ 5.00
South Dakota, SDAK1, 2 & 3 _____ 6.00
South Pole, Conquest by Air, 6500 A,
B & C _____ 20.00
Southern Africa, 3000, 3001 & 3029 ____ 25.00
Spain, 1700, 1701 & 1705 _____ 21.00
Spanish Monastery, North Miami Beach,
171A, B & C _____ 30.00
Sun Valley, Idaho, 206A, B & C _____ 3.00
Sweden, 2125A, B & C _____ 11.00
Switzerland, 2000A, B & C _____ 15.00
Tarzan of the Apes, 976A, B & C _____ 20.00
Tennessee, TENN1, 2 & 3 _____ 5.00
Texas, TEXAS1, 2 & 3 _____ 5.00
Three Little Pigs (See Fairy Tales III)
Tom Corbett, Space Cadet, 970A, B & C ____ 25.00
Tulip Time, Holland, 1920, 1920A & B ____ 12.00
TV Stars, 745, 746 & 747 _____ 60.00
20,000 Leagues under the Sea, 974A,
B & C _____ 3.00
Two Mouseketeers, The, 812A, B & C ____ 11.00
United Nations, Your, 420A, B & C _____ 10.00

View-Master, three-reel packet, "Williamsburg, Colonial Restoration," in type S3 variant packet with the line drawings on the cover rather than a color photo. Such early variants command approximately a 25 percent higher value than the regular packet designs. (Gordon D. Hoffman Collection)

Most of the single reels were discontinued and remaining stock was placed in three-reel packets. All of the packets were renumbered and many were updated. The remaining stock was rubber stamped with the new numbering system on the reverse side of the packet envelopes. Remaining stocks of S3 packets with rubber-stamped numbered were still being sold in the early 1960s.

Prices are for complete packets with a story booklet (BK) as noted in near-new condition with no tears to the packet envelope. Booklets were not included in every packet; contents of the packets are noted on the reverse of the packet envelopes. Reels must be clean and show little or no use; deduct 50 percent for torn packets or reels showing use. Add 25 percent for mint, never open packets (MNO) with original cellophane wrap. Incomplete or badly damaged packets or reels have little or no collector value.

Utah, UTAH1, 2 & 3	5.00
Vancouver, B.C., 311A, B & C	12.00
Vermont, VT1, 2 & 3	6.00
Victoria and Butchart Gardens, 313A, B & C	7.00
Virginia, VA1, 2 & 3	5.00
Washington, WASH1, 2 & 3	5.00
Washington, D.C., 136A, B & C	5.00
Weeki Wachee "Springs of the Mermaids," Fla., 393A, B & C	30.00
West Indies, 564, 595 & 597	35.00
West Virginia, WVA1, 2 & 3	5.00
White Mountains of New Hampshire, 259, 260 & 270	20.00
Wild Birds in Natural Habitat, 895A, B & C	7.00
Williamsburg Colonial Restoration, 181A, B & C	6.00
Wisconsin, WISC1, 2 & 3	5.00
Wisconsin Dells, 124A, B & C	3.00
Wizard of Oz, The Wonderful, FT45A, B & C	5.00
Wonders of the Deep, 990A, B & C	6.00
Woody Woodpecker, Andy Panda, Chilly Willy, 821, 822 & 823	5.00
Wyoming, WYO1, 2 & 3	14.00
Yellowstone National Park, 126, 127 & 128	10.00
Yosemite National Park, 131, 132 & 133	5.00
Zion National Park, 141A, B & C	9.00

Prefix-Numbered Three-Reel Packets (1958–1982)

Beginning in 1958, Sawyer's completely revamped the marketing of the View-Master reels.

A001, Prairie Provinces	8.00
A002, Trans-Canada Highway	8.00
A004, Banff, Canadian Rockies	3.00
A005, Banff, Canadian Rockies	12.00
A006, Lake Louise, Jasper, Canadian Rockies	9.00
A007, Lake Louise, Canadian Rockies	6.00
A008, Jasper, Canadian Rockies	4.00
A009, Alberta	7.00
A012, Vancouver, B.C.	7.00
A013, Victoria and Butchart Gardens	7.00
A014, Beautiful British Columbia	7.00
A015, Victoria, B.C.	7.00
A016, Butchart Gardens	7.00
A020, Inside Passage to Alaska	7.00
A021, Vancouver, B.C.	7.00
A030, Maritime Provinces	7.00
A033, Upper Canada Village and Fort Henry	7.00
A035, Ontario Vacationlands	7.00
A035, Toronto	7.00
A036, Ottawa, Canada's Capital City and Eastern Ontario	7.00
A037, Niagara Peninsula and Southwestern Ontario	7.00
A038, Ontario Vacationlands	7.00
A039, This is Ontario	3.00
A042, African Lion Safari, Rockton	20.00
A043, Parc Safari, African	20.00
A050, Quebec City	9.00
A051, Montreal	6.00
A058, Detroit Zoo (may not have been issued)	
A059, St. Anne De Beaupre (two-reel packet)	30.00
A060, The Historical at Ste. Anne De Beaupre	30.00

A071, Expo '67, General Tour _____ 25.00
A073, Expo '67, Pavilions _____ 25.00
A074, Expo '67, Night Scenes _____ 25.00
A085, Iceland _____ 18.00
A090, Canada _____ 8.00
A094, Wonders of Our National Parks
(may not have been issued)
A101, Alaska, the 49th State _____ 6.00
A101, Alaska, The Last Frontier (State
Tour Series) _____ 14.00
A102, Eskimos of Alaska _____ 8.00
A103, Anchorage, Wilderness Beauty
(Eskimos) _____ 25.00
A104, Fairbanks, Yukon Trails and
Eskimos _____ 25.00
A104, Fairbanks, Mt. McKinley, Yukon
Trails _____ 20.00
A105, Juneau, Ketchikan and Sitka,
Alaska _____ 20.00
A106, Anchorage, Alaska _____ 20.00
A107, Mount McKinley National Park and
Fairbanks _____ 15.00
A108, Juneau, Sitka and Ketchikan,
Alaska _____ 20.00
A116, Flowers of Hawaii _____ 15.00
A120, Hawaii, the 50th State _____ 4.00
A120, Hawaii (map on cover) _____ 4.00
A121, Hawaiian Fruits and Flowers _____ 11.00
A122, Hawaiian Hula Dancers _____ 7.00
A122, Kodak Hula Show _____ 10.00
A123, Honolulu and Waikiki, Oahu _____ 6.00
A124, Islands of Hawaii, Maui and Kauai ___ 6.00
A126, Island of Oahu _____ 5.00
A127, Hawaii, the Orchid State _____ 5.00
A127, Islands of Hawaii _____ 11.00
A128, Hawaiian Islands _____ 4.00
A128, Islands of Kauai and Maui _____ 5.00
A129, Polynesian Cultural Center _____ 9.00
A130, Sea Life Park _____ 9.00
A135, Santa's Village _____ 15.00
A136, Mountain States _____ 5.00
A155, Nevada State _____ 4.00
A156, Las Vegas _____ 6.00
A157, Reno, Lake Tahoe, Virginia City,
Nev. _____ 6.00
A158, Hoover Dam _____ 4.00
A159, Las Vegas _____ 9.00
A160, Las Vegas #2 _____ 9.00
A160, Fabulous Las Vegas Strip _____ 5.00
A161, Lake Tahoe _____ 8.00
A163, Yosemite #2 _____ 9.00
A164, Muir Woods National Monument ___ 4.00
A165, Steinhart Aquarium _____ 6.00
A166, San Francisco _____ 3.00
A167, San Francisco Sightseeing Tour _____ 3.00
A168, Northern California _____ 8.00
A169, Southern California _____ 14.00
A170, California State _____ 6.00
A171, Yosemite National Park _____ 6.00
A172, San Francisco _____ 6.00
A173, San Diego Zoo, Calif. _____ 6.00
A174, Sequoia and Kings Canyon Na-
tional Park _____ 4.00
A175, Disneyland I—Main Street _____ 6.00
A176, Disneyland II—Frontierland _____ 6.00

A177, Disneyland III—Adventureland _____ 4.00
A178, Disneyland IV—Fantasyland _____ 6.00
A179, Disneyland V—Tomorrowland _____ 5.00
A180, Mickey Mouse Club Circus visits
Disneyland _____ 11.00
A181, Los Angeles _____ 6.00
A182, Redwood Highway, Calif. _____ 6.00
A183, California Missions _____ 10.00
A184, Lake Arrowhead and Santa's
Workshop _____ 25.00
A185, Pacific Coast, La Jolla, San Diego,
Tijuana _____ 15.00
A186, Pacific Coast—Monterey to Santa
Barbara _____ 5.00
A187, Mount Lassen and Mount Shasta ___ 10.00
A188, Marineland of the Pacific _____ 12.00
A189, University of Southern California ___ 12.00
A190, Hearst Castle _____ 7.00
A191, Trees of Mystery, Calif. _____ 8.00
A192, Sea World, San Diego, Calif. _____ 6.00
A193, Sea World, San Diego, Calif.,
Packet No. 2 _____ 14.00
A194, Hollywood _____ 8.00
A195, Palm Springs, Calif. _____ 7.00
A196, Lake Arrowhead and Big Bear
Lake, Calif. _____ 10.00
A197, San Diego Zoo II _____ 10.00
A198, San Diego _____ 10.00
A199, Marineland of the Pacific, Calif.,
Packet No. 2 _____ 10.00
A201, Los Angeles Zoo, Los Angeles,
Calif. _____ 10.00
A203, Death Valley National Monument ___ 10.00
A204, Magic Mountain, Valencia, Calif. ___ 10.00
A205, Monterey, Carmel and Big Sur
Coast _____ 10.00
A206, Historic Santa Barbara and
Solvang _____ 3.00
A207, San Diego Wild Animal Park _____ 8.00
A208, Sea World Shows and Animals,
Calif., Ohio, Fla. _____ 3.00
A209, Marine World, Africa, United
States, Redwood City, Calif. _____ 8.00
A210, Pacific Coast Vacationland _____ 8.00
A211, Balboa Park, San Diego _____ 8.00
A215, America on Parade (Disneyland) _____ 8.00
A219, San Francisco #3 _____ 5.00
A220, Winchester Mystery House, Calif. ___ 13.00
A231, Lion Country Safari _____ 13.00
A232, Japanese Village and Deer Park _____ 13.00
A233, Busch Gardens _____ 13.00
A234, Movieland Wax Museum _____ 8.00
A235, Knott's Berry Farm and Ghost
Town _____ 13.00
A236, Knott's Berry Farm II _____ 13.00
A237, Knott's Berry Farm III _____ 13.00
A238, Movieland Wax Museum and
Palace of Living Art #2 _____ 5.00
A241, Universal Studios I _____ 12.00
A242, Universal Studios II, Shows and
Special Effects _____ 12.00
A243, Busch Gardens, No. 2 _____ 12.00
A245, Oregon State _____ 6.00
A246, Crater Lake National Park _____ 11.00
A247, Oregon Coast _____ 12.00

A247, Sea Lion Caves and Oregon Coast __ 7.00
A247, Pacific Coast—Oregon Beaches _____ 5.00
A248, Oregon Caves _____ 4.00
A249, Columbia River Gorge, Oreg. and
Wash. _____ 3.00
A250, Oregon Centennial Exposition _____ 40.00
A251, Rose Festival, Portland, Oreg. _____ 35.00
A252, Portland Zoo _____ 8.00
A253, Portland, City of Roses _____ 8.00
A261, Petersen's Rock Garden _____ 8.00
A262, Sanctuary of Our Sorrowful
Mother _____ 8.00
A270, Washington State _____ 5.00
A271, Mount Rainier National Park _____ 8.00
A272, Century 21 Exposition, Seattle
World's Fair _____ 35.00
A273, Seattle World's Fair _____ 35.00
A274, Seattle, Washington _____ 12.00
A275, Seattle, Puget Sound and Olympic
National Park _____ 10.00
A276, Seattle Center, Seattle, Wash. _____ 15.00
A277, Grand Coulee Dam and Eastern
Washington _____ 10.00
A278, Olympic National Park and Puget
Sound, Wash. _____ 14.00
A285, Idaho State _____ 10.00
A286, Sun Valley _____ 5.00
A295, Montana State _____ 5.00
A296, Glacier National Park _____ 4.00
A305, Wyoming State _____ 9.00
A306, Yellowstone National Park, Wyo. __ 5.00
A307, Grand Teton National Park _____ 6.00
A309, Yellowstone National Park, North __ 4.00
A313, Victoria and Butchart Gardens _____ 7.00
A320, Colorado State _____ 5.00
A321, Pike's Peak _____ 5.00
A322, Rocky Mountain National Park _____ 5.00
A323, Royal Gorge _____ 6.00
A324, Denver and Mountain Parks _____ 4.00
A325, Mesa Verde National Park _____ 4.00
A326, Air Force Academy, Colorado
Springs _____ 8.00
A327, Durango-Silverton Railroad and
San Juan Loop _____ 25.00
A331, Colorado Ski Country _____ 6.00
A333, North Pole, Colo. _____ 8.00
A335, Broadmoor Hotel, Colo. _____ 4.00
A336, Garden of the Gods, Colo. _____ 8.00
A338, Denver Museum of Natural
History _____ 8.00
A345, Utah State _____ 5.00
A346, Bryce Canyon National Park _____ 4.00
A347, Zion National Park _____ 4.00
A348, Salt Lake City _____ 6.00
A354, Church of Jesus Christ of Latter
Day Saints _____ 9.00
A355, Glen Canyon Dam and Lake
Powell _____ 3.00
A356, Monument Valley, Ariz. and Utah __ 8.00
A360, Arizona State _____ 3.00
A361, Grand Canyon I _____ 4.00
A362, Grand Canyon II _____ 6.00
A363, Painted Desert and Petrified Forest __ 3.00
A364, Oak Creek Canyon _____ 6.00

A365, Petrified Forest National Park and
Painted Desert _____ 3.00
A366, Phoenix and Arizona's Valley of the
Sun _____ 14.00
A367, Tucson and Arizona Sonora Desert
Museum _____ 11.00
A370, Exploring the Grand Canyon _____ 4.00
A372, Grand Canyon River Expedition _____ 4.00
A375, New Mexico State _____ 4.00
A376, Carlsbad Caverns National Park,
N.Mex. _____ 5.00
A377, Carlsbad Caverns II, National Park __ 3.00
A379, Santa Fe and Albuquerque _____ 10.00
A390, Lincoln Heritage Trail _____ 7.00
A391, The Plains State _____ 13.00
A409, Lion Country Safari, Dallas/Grand
Prairie, Tex. _____ 6.00
A410, Texas, the Lone Star State _____ 5.00
A412, Six Flags over Texas, Dallas-Ft.
Worth _____ 11.00
A413, Six Flags over Texas, Packet No. 2 __ 11.00
A415, Dallas and Forth Worth, Tex. _____ 10.00
A416, Houston and Galveston, Tex. _____ 10.00
A417, San Antonio-Austin, Tex. _____ 6.00
A418, LBJ Country, The Historic Hill
Country of Texas _____ 20.00
A419, Big Bend National Park, Tex. _____ 5.00
A420, San Antonio, Tex. _____ 11.00
A421, El Paso, Tex., Juarez, Mexico _____ 6.00
A425, Manned Spacecraft Center,
Houston _____ 10.00
A425, NASA's Lyndon B. Johnson Space
Center, Houston, Tex. _____ 10.00
A430, Oklahoma _____ 5.00
A440, Arkansas _____ 4.00
A441, Hot Springs National Park _____ 8.00
A449, Ozark Mountains, Ark. and Mo. ___ 4.00
A450, Missouri _____ 5.00
A451, Meramec Caverns _____ 8.00
A452, Gay 90's Melody Museum, St.
Louis, Mo. _____ 30.00
A453, St. Louis _____ 10.00
A454, Kansas City, Mo. _____ 15.00
A455, The Shepherd of the Hills, Missouri
Ozarks _____ 8.00
A456, St. Louis Riverfront, Mo. _____ 4.00
A457, Silver Dollar City, Mo. _____ 8.00
A458, Six Flags over Mid-America, St.
Louis _____ 8.00
A459, St. Louis Zoo, St. Louis, Mo. _____ 15.00
A460, Busch-Clydesdale Horses, Mo. _____ 10.00
A461, Worlds of Fun, Mo. _____ 13.00
A465, Kansas _____ 3.00
A475, Nebraska _____ 5.00
A485, South Dakota _____ 6.00
A486, Black Hills, S.Dak. _____ 6.00
A487, Mount Rushmore, S.Dak. _____ 4.00
A488, Reptile Gardens _____ 10.00
A489, Badlands National Monument,
S.Dak. _____ 6.00
A491, Black Hills Passion Play _____ 10.00
A500, North Dakota _____ 16.00
A510, Minnesota _____ 6.00
A511, Minnesota State Parks _____ 15.00

View-Master, three-reel packet, A525, type S4, pastel envelope; 1958–1960 issue with booklet, "Wisconsin," from the "State Guide Series." $5.

A512, The Twin Cities, Minneapolis and St. Paul	15.00
A513, University of Minnesota, Bell Museum of Natural History	13.00
A525, Wisconsin	5.00
A526, Wisconsin Dells	6.00
A527, Milwaukee County Zoo, Wisc.	13.00
A530, Old-Time Circus: Train-Acts, Parade, Milwaukee	10.00
A532, Milwaukee County and Horticultural Conservatory	18.00
A534, Story Book Gardens, Wisconsin Dells, Wisc.	8.00
A540, Iowa	6.00
A541, Grotto of the Redemption	12.00
A550, Illinois, The Prairie State	6.00
A550, Illinois, Land of Lincoln	12.00
A551, Chicago, Ill.	6.00
A552, Museum of Science and Industry, Chicago, Ill.	16.00
A554, O'Hare International Airport, Chicago	35.00
A555, National Shrine of Our Lady of the Snows, Belleville, Ill.	30.00
A557, Lincolnland, Springfield-New Salem	15.00
A558, Shedd Aquarium, Chicago, Ill.	11.00
A559, Chicago at Night, Ill.	18.00
A565, Basilica of Our Lady of Sorrows, Chicago	18.00
A570, Indiana	15.00
A580, Michigan	7.00
A581, Detroit Zoo, Mich.	8.00
A583, Detroit	15.00
A584, Greenfield Village	6.00
A585, Mackinac Island	4.00
A586, Henry Ford Museum, Mich.	8.00
A595, Ohio	4.00
A597, Kings Island, Ohio	12.00
A598, Cedar Point #1, Ohio	8.00
A599, Sea World, Ohio	15.00
A600, Air Force Museum I, Ohio	7.00
A602, Air Force Museum, Packet No. 2	6.00
A603, Lion Country Safari, Kings Island, Kings Mills, Ohio	14.00
A604, Cedar Point #2, Ohio	8.00
A610, New England	6.00
A611, New England Covered Bridges and Fall Foliage	6.00
A630, Pennsylvania	7.00
A631, Philadelphia	4.00
A631, Modern Philadelphia	10.00
A632, Pittsburgh	10.00
A633, Pennsylvania Dutch and Amish Country	6.00
A634, Dutch Wonderland	6.00
A635, Independence National Historic Park	6.00
A635, Historical Philadelphia	12.00
A636, Gettysburg	6.00
A637, Hershey Estates	6.00
A637, Hershey Park	11.00
A638, National Wax Museum	11.00
A641, Phipps Conservatory	11.00
A644, New York City #1	10.00
A645, New York City #2	12.00
A647, New York City at Night	5.00
A648, Statue of Liberty	6.00

A649, New York City #1	6.00
A650, New York	7.00
A651, Your United Nations	4.00
A651, United Nations	6.00
A652, Rockefeller Center-New York City	8.00
A653, New York City	4.00
A653, New York City II	10.00
A653, New York City Manhattan Scenes	8.00
A654, Sight-Seeing in New York City	7.00
A654, New York City Sight-Seeing Tour	5.00
A655, Scenic Niagara Falls	6.00
A655, Niagara Falls (S5 & G1)	8.00
A655, Niagara Falls, New York (G3 & V1)	5.00
A656, Sight-Seeing at Niagara Falls	6.00
A656, Niagara Falls, Canadian Side	7.00
A657, Coney Island	21.00
A658, Brooklyn	30.00
A659, Long Island	35.00
A660, Santa's Workshop, North Pole, N.Y.	20.00
A661, Freedomland, USA (Amusement Park)	50.00
A664, Upper New York State	5.00
A664, Lake George-Adirondack Region	8.00
A665, West Point, United States Military Academy	10.00
A666, Corning Glass	10.00
A667, Bronx Zoo-New York City	8.00
A669, Operation Sail . . . The Tall Ships	15.00
A671, New York World's Fair—General Tour, 1964	25.00
A672, New York World's Fair—Amusement Area, 1964	25.00
A673, New York World's Fair—International Area, 1964	25.00
A674, New York World's Fair—Federal and State Area, 1964	25.00
A675, New York World's Fair—Industrial Area, 1964	25.00
A676, New York World's Fair—Transportation Area, 1964	25.00
A683, Old Fort Niagara	7.00
A690, Vermont	4.00
A700, New Hampshire	5.00
A701, Mountain Rides of New Hampshire	7.00
A702, White Mountains of New Hampshire	15.00
A715, Maine	8.00
A716, Maine Seacoast	15.00
A716, Coast of Maine	20.00
A725, Massachusetts	16.00
A726, Boston	12.00
A726, Modern Boston	15.00
A727, Cape Cod and Plymouth	6.00
A728, Old Sturbridge Village	6.00
A729, Freedom Trail—Boston	10.00
A730, Historic Boston	10.00
A731, Plymouth	4.00
A740, Rhode Island	9.00
A750, Connecticut	9.00
A751, Mystic Seaport	5.00
A760, New Jersey	8.00
A761, Atlantic City	35.00
A762, Duke Gardens	25.00
A763, Jungle Habitat	25.00
A764, Great Adventure—Enchanted Forest, Jackson, N.J.	8.00
A765, Great Adventure—Safari Park	6.00
A766, Historic Towne of Smithville, N.J.	11.00
A770, Delaware	11.00
A780, Maryland	5.00
A783, Annapolis—United States Naval Academy	12.00
A790, Washington, D.C.	7.00
A790, Washington, D.C., II (G5)	8.00
A791, National Gallery of Art	30.00
A792, Smithsonian Institution	8.00
A793, The White House	6.00
A794, National Capital-United States Capitol Buildings	4.00
A795, National Shrine of the Immaculate Conception	13.00
A796, Washington Cathedral	9.00
A797, Library of Congress and National Archives	8.00
A798, Lincoln Museum and Ford Theater	12.00
A799, Smithsonian Institution II	12.00
A800, Beautiful Washington, D.C.	4.00
A810, Virginia	5.00
A811, Shenandoah National Park, Va.	6.00
A812, Mount Vernon	5.00
A813, Colonial Williamsburg	4.00
A814, Historic Cities of Virginia	Extremely rare
A815, Jamestown Festival	18.00
A818, Arlington National Cemetery	6.00
A822, The Old Country, Busch Gardens	16.00
A825, Kings Dominion Park	10.00
A826, Kings Dominion Lion Country	16.00
A827, Monticello	6.00
A828, Natural Bridge, Va.	10.00
A829, Beautiful Caverns of Luray	4.00
A830, Car and Carriage Caravan	30.00
A831, Skyline Caverns	15.00
A835, West Virginia	5.00
A845, Kentucky	6.00
A846, Mammoth Cave	3.00
A847, Kentucky Cave	11.00
A848, Kentucky State Parks	8.00
A849, Mammoth Cave #2	8.00
A855, Blue Ridge Parkway	5.00
A856, The Old South	8.00
A875, Tennessee	6.00
A876, Lookout Mountain	3.00
A877, Shiloh National Military Park	9.00
A878, Opryland U.S.A.	6.00
A884, Rock City Gardens	3.00
A884, Rock City Gardens #1 (G3)	4.00
A885, Rock City Gardens	3.00
A885, Rock City Gardens #2 (G3)	4.00
A889, Great Smoky Mountains	6.00
A890, North Carolina	7.00
A891, Cherokee Indians	15.00
A892, Ghost Town and Maggie Valley	17.00
A894, Carowinds	10.00
A895, Santa's Land Park and Zoo	6.00
A905, South Carolina	5.00

A905, South Carolina (S6 & G1) _____ 6.00
A915, Georgia _____ 8.00
A916, Atlanta _____ 10.00
A917, Six Flags Over Georgia _____ 4.00
A918, Six Flags Over Georgia, Day and
Night Scenes _____ 9.00
A919 Ida Cason Callaway Gardens _____ 15.00
A920, Stone Mountain _____ 4.00
A921, Atlanta Cyclorama and Grant Park _ 10.00
A922, Underground Atlanta _____ 7.00
A923, Lion Country Safari _____ 11.00
A924, Savannah _____ 11.00
A925, Alabama _____ 5.00
A927, Battleship USS *Alabama* _____ 9.00
A930, Bellingrath Gardens _____ 4.00
A935, Mississippi _____ 6.00
A937, Sea World, Fla. _____ 10.00
A938, Authentic Old Jail _____ 4.00
A939, Everglades _____ 4.00
A940, Alligator Farm _____ 8.00
A945, Louisiana _____ 5.00
A946, New Orleans _____ 7.00
A947, Disney World—Main Street _____ 6.00
A948, Disney World—Fantasyland _____ 3.00
A949, Disney World—Adventureland _____ 4.00
A950, Disney World—Liberty Square _____ 6.00
A951, Disney World—Frontierland _____ 3.00
A952, Disney World—Tomorrowland _____ 3.00
A954, Disney World—America on
Parade _____ 3.00
A956, Lion Country Safari, Fla. _____ 6.00
A957, Busch Gardens _____ 7.00
A958, Florida East _____ 15.00
A959, Florida West _____ 9.00
A960, Florida _____ 7.00
A961, Cypress Gardens _____ 5.00
A962, Silver Springs _____ 6.00
A963, Greater Miami _____ 6.00
A963, Greater Miami and Miami Beach ____ 6.00
A964, Marineland of Florida _____ 5.00
A964, Marineland (S6, G1 & G3) _____ 7.00
A965, Parrot Jungle _____ 6.00
A966, Seaquarium _____ 6.00
A967, Water Ski Show, Cypress Gardens ___ 8.00
A968, Silver Springs Attractions _____ 11.00
A969, Cypress Gardens, Floral Paradise ____ 3.00
A970, Bird Performances, Parrot Jungle ____ 4.00
A971, Seaquarium #2 _____ 9.00
A972, Tropical Paradise _____ 14.00
A973, Homosassa Springs _____ 5.00
A974, Tiki Gardens _____ 15.00
A975, Cape Coral Gardens _____ 10.00
A976, Floridaland—Sarasota, Venice,
Fla. _____ 20.00
A977, Six Gun Territory _____ 15.00
A978, Sarasota Jungle Gardens _____ 5.00
A979, Busch Gardens, Wild Animal
Kingdom _____ 3.00
A980, Miami and Florida _____ 9.00
A981, Historic St. Augustine _____ 6.00
A982, The Miracle Strip _____ 8.00
A983, Lion Country Safari _____ 12.00
A984, The Golden Triangle _____ 12.00
A985, Monkey Jungle _____ 4.00

A987, Weeki Wachee _____ 13.00
A988, Busch Gardens _____ 6.00
A989, Citrus Tower _____ 11.00
A990, Placid Tower and Lake Placid Area _ 11.00
A991, Weeki Wachee _____ 5.00
A992, Sunken Gardens _____ 15.00
A993, Spanish Monastery, North Miami
Beach _____ 25.00
A994, Ringling Museum _____ 10.00
A995, Circus Hall of Fame _____ 15.00
A996, Scenic U.S.A. _____ 9.00
A997, United States of America _____ 15.00
A999, Cypress Gardens—Gardens of the
World _____ 6.00
B001, Mexico _____ 5.00
B002, Mexico City _____ 8.00
B003, Acapulco _____ 3.00
B004, Mexican Bullfight _____ 15.00
B005, Tijuana _____ 9.00
B006, Old Mexico _____ 8.00
B007, Guadalajara and Lake Chapala ____ 14.00
B008, Archaeology—Lost Civilizations of
Mexico _____ 6.00
B012, Guatemala _____ 12.00
B017, El Salvador _____ 12.00
B020, Nicaragua _____ 12.00
B021, Grand Tour of Central and South
America _____ 12.00
B022, Costa Rica _____ 12.00
B025, Panama _____ 6.00
B026, Nassau _____ 12.00
B027, The Bahamas, Self-Governing
British Colony _____ 6.00
B028, The Out Islands of the Bahamas ____ 15.00
B029, Bermuda _____ 11.00
B031, Trinidad and Tobago _____ 15.00
B032, Jamaica _____ 15.00
B034, Havana _____ 20.00
B036, Virgin Islands _____ 15.00
B037, Curacao _____ 15.00
B039, Puerto Rico _____ 4.00
B039, Modern Puerto Rico _____ 5.00
B040, San Juan _____ 4.00
B041, Historic Puerto Rico _____ 12.00
B044, Colombia _____ 8.00
B049, Caracas _____ 15.00
B050, Venezuela _____ 8.00
B057, Brazil _____ 6.00
B058, Rio de Janeiro _____ 8.00
B069, Uruguay _____ 8.00
B071, Argentina _____ 15.00
B072, Buenos Aires _____ 15.00
B079, Chile _____ 8.00
B082, Bolivia _____ 8.00
B086, Peru _____ 13.00
B091, Ecuador _____ 8.00
B095, In Darkest Africa _____ 20.00
B096, Africa, Cairo to Capetown _____ 25.00
B098, Grand Tour of Africa _____ 20.00
B101, Casablanca _____ 20.00
B114, Queen Elizabeth Visits Nigeria ____ 45.00
B120, Native Life in Congo and Ruanda __ 20.00
B121, Ruanda and the Congo's Lake
Area _____ 20.00

B122, Towns of Congo and Ruanda _____ 20.00
B123, Kenya, East Africa _____ 20.00
B124, South Africa _____ 20.00
B125, Capetown, South Africa _____ 25.00
B140, Cairo and the Land of Egypt _____ 6.00
B141, Pyramids and Antiquities of Egypt __ 13.00
B145, Grand Tour of Europe _____ 7.00
B146, Castles of Europe _____ 10.00
B147, Cathedrals of Europe _____ 10.00
B149, Five Little Countries of Europe _____ 25.00
B151, Sweden _____ 6.00
B153, Norway _____ 20.00
B155, Denmark _____ 6.00
B156, England _____ 10.00
B157, London _____ 15.00
B158, London Pageantry _____ 20.00
B159, Shakespeare Country _____ 15.00
B160, Ireland _____ 10.00
B163, Bonnie Scotland _____ 15.00
B167, Majorca—The Balearic Islands _____ 20.00
B168, Portugal _____ 20.00
B169, Spain _____ 16.00
B170, Wedding of Prince Rainier III and
Grace Kelly _____ 95.00
B171, Spain _____ 6.00
B172, France _____ 6.00
B173, Carnival of Nice _____ 15.00
B174, The Chateau on the Loire _____ 15.00
B175, Corsica (I'lle de beaute) _____ 20.00
B176, Lourdes and the Pyrenees _____ 15.00
B177, Paris _____ 10.00
B178, Vatican City _____ 8.00
B180, Italy _____ 6.00
B181, Canonization of Blessed Pius X ____ 20.00
B182, Rome _____ 4.00
B183, Venice _____ 14.00
B185, Switzerland _____ 10.00
B188, Belgium _____ 8.00
B190, Holland _____ 8.00
B192, Berlin _____ 8.00
B193, Germany _____ 7.00
B194, Oberammergau, Passion Play _____ 8.00
B195, The Rhine, Rudesheim to
Konigswinter _____ 15.00
B198, Austria _____ 8.00
B205, Greece _____ 6.00
B206, Athens _____ 15.00
B207, Legendary Islands of Greece _____ 20.00
B208, Turkey _____ 15.00
B210, Inside Russia _____ 15.00
B211, People of Russia _____ 20.00
B212, Russia Today _____ 20.00
B213, Russia _____ 10.00
B215, Grand Tour of Asia _____ 15.00
B223, Lebanon _____ 15.00
B224, Modern Israel _____ 8.00
B226, The Holy Land, Israel and Jordan ___ 6.00
B228, Mecca _____ 10.00
B231, Iraq _____ 15.00
B233, Pakistan _____ 15.00
B235, India _____ 6.00
B244, Burma _____ 15.00
B245, Thailand _____ 15.00
B246, Bangkok _____ 20.00
B247, Federation of Malaya _____ 9.00

B247, Malaya _____ 10.00
B248, Singapore _____ 15.00
B249, Cambodia _____ 15.00
B250, South Viet Nam _____ 9.00
B251, Hong Kong _____ 6.00
B252, Bali _____ 15.00
B255, Inside China Today _____ 15.00
B256, Mysterious Peking and Shanghai ___ 9.00
B257, Taiwan (Formosa) _____ 20.00
B260, South Korea _____ 16.00
B262, Japan _____ 5.00
B263, Kyoto _____ 11.00
B264, Tokyo _____ 6.00
B267, Nikko, Japan _____ 10.00
B268, Expo '70, General Tour I, Osaka ___ 50.00
B269, Expo '70, General Tour II, Osaka ___ 50.00
B270, Expo '70, Night Scenes, Osaka _____ 50.00
B271, Ise-Shima, Japan _____ 20.00
B274, The Philippines _____ 9.00
B282, Papua, New Guinea _____ 15.00
B288, Australia _____ 4.00
B289, Alice Springs and Central
Australia _____ 4.00
B294, Tasmania _____ 10.00
B300, Snow White and the Seven
Dwarfs _____ 3.00
B301, Little Red Riding Hood _____ 11.00
B302, Cinderella _____ 11.00
B303, The Three Little Pigs, etc. (includes
Little Black Sambo) _____ 15.00
B304, Sleeping Beauty, The Pied Piper of
Hamelin, and Thumbelina _____ 11.00
B305, Andersen's Fairy Tates _____ 8.00
B308, Sleeping Beauty (Disney) _____ 4.00
B309, Aesop's Fables _____ 9.00
B310, Little Red Riding Hood, The Three
Little Pigs, Three Billy Goats Gruff _____ 5.00
B311, Carlo Collodi's Pinocchio _____ 3.00

View-Master, three-reel packet, B311 ''Carlo Collodi's Pinocchio,'' type S3, $3. (Gordon D. Hoffman Collection)

B312, Grimm's Fairy Tales _____ 8.00
B313, Cinderella _____ 10.00
B314, Jack and the Beanstalk _____ 5.00
B315, Pinocchio, Lady and the Tramp,
Snow White (Disney) _____ 4.00
B316, Walt Disney presents Sword in the
Stone _____ 5.00
B317, Goldilocks _____ 4.00
B318, Cinderella (Disney) _____ 4.00
B319, The Little Red Hen, Thumbelina,
The Pied Piper of Hamelin _____ 9.00
B320, Puss in Boots _____ 8.00
B321, Charlotte's Web _____ 3.00
B322, Pippi Longstockings _____ 15.00
B323, Frankenstein _____ 7.00
B324, Dracula _____ 6.00
B340, Tom Sawyer _____ 15.00
B342, Robin Hood (Disney) _____ 4.00
B344, Holly Hobbie _____ 4.00
B360, Alice in Wonderland _____ 4.00
B361, The Wizard of Oz _____ 4.00
B362, Winnie the Pooh (Disney) _____ 3.00
B363, Walt Disney presents Jungle Book
by Rudyard Kipling _____ 8.00
B364, Alice through Looking Glass _____ 3.00
B365, Walt Disney presents The
Aristocats _____ 3.00
B366, Bedknobs and Broomsticks
(Disney) _____ 10.00
B367, Island at the Top of the World (Disney) regular three-reel packet _____ 25.00
B367, Island at the Top of the World (Disney), four-reel promotion packet put out
by Mobil Chemical Co., 1974 _____ 50.00
B368, Shaggy D.A. (Disney) _____ 4.00
B369, Winnie and Tigger Too (Disney) ___ 4.00
B370, 20,000 Leagues under the Sea ___ 6.00
B371, Robin Hood _____ 10.00
B372, Peter Pan (Disney) _____ 8.00
B374, Gulliver's Travels _____ 4.00
B375, Babes in Toyland (Disney) _____ 6.00
B376, Mary Poppins (Disney) _____ 20.00
B377, One of Our Dinosaurs is Missing
(Disney) _____ 15.00
B380, A Christmas Carol _____ 4.00
B381, The Littlest Angel _____ 3.00
B382, The Night Before Christmas _____ 6.00
B383, Christmas Story _____ 5.00
B390, Fiddler on the Roof _____ 25.00
B391, Poseidon Adventure _____ 18.00
B392, King Kong _____ 8.00
B393, James Bond "Live and Let Die." ___ 30.00
B400, Walt Disney presents Bambi _____ 6.00
B405, The True Story of Smokey Bear ___ 4.00
B406, Raggedy Ann and Raggedy Andy ___ 4.00
B410, Mother Goose Rhymes _____ 4.00
B411, The ABC's with Andy the Alphabet
Clown _____ 8.00
B412, 1-2-3 Farm _____ 3.00
B417, UFO (1969 live-action TV show) ___ 25.00
B419, Babar _____ 16.00
B425, Heidi _____ 10.00
B426, The Three Musketeers _____ 15.00
B430, William Tell _____ 5.00
B432, Treasure Island _____ 6.00

B433, Joan of Arc _____ 12.00
B434, The Three Musketeers _____ 12.00
B435, The Three Musketeers Add a
Fourth _____ 12.00
B436, Ali-Baba and the Forty Thieves ___ 6.00
B437, Christopher Columbus _____ 14.00
B438, Robinson Crusoe _____ 8.00
B442, Poly in Portugal _____ 5.00
B444, Tarzan of the Apes _____ 30.00
B460, Cowboy Stars _____ 15.00
B461, Roy Rogers, Gene Autry, Hopalong
Cassidy (cowboy stars) _____ 15.00
B462, Roy Rogers "King of the
Cowboys." _____ 20.00
B463, Dale Evens "Queen of the West." ___ 25.00
B464, Buffalo Bill, Jr. _____ 25.00
B465, Lone Ranger in "Mystery Rustler." ___ 25.00
B466, Brave Eagle _____ 25.00
B467, Rin-Tin-Tin _____ 10.00
B468, Jody McCrea in Johnny Moccasin ___ 20.00
B469, Zorro (Disney) _____ 25.00
B470, Annie Oakley in "Indian
Waterhole." _____ 25.00
B471, Bonanza (reel #1, position #1
shows the Cartrights showing their
middle fingers) _____ 25.00
B474, Lassie and Timmy _____ 10.00
B475, Roy Rogers Adventure Roundup ___ 14.00
B476, Walt Disney's Toby Tyler, or Ten
Weeks with the Circus _____ 30.00
B477, Television Shows at Universal City ___ 25.00
B478, The Mod Squad _____ 12.00
B479, Daniel Boone _____ 15.00
B480, Lassie, Look Homeward _____ 10.00
B482, Lost in Space _____ 75.00
B483, Voyage to the Bottom of the Sea ___ 15.00
B484, The Man from U.N.C.L.E. _____ 20.00
B485, Flipper _____ 8.00
B487, Bonanza, 1971 (without Pernell
Roberts) _____ 35.00
B488, Green Hornet _____ 50.00
B489, Lassie Rides the Log Flume _____ 15.00
B490, The Smith Family _____ 45.00
B491, Time Tunnel _____ 25.00
B492, Batman _____ 15.00
B493, The Monkees _____ 25.00
B494, Land of the Giants _____ 30.00
B495, The Flying Nun _____ 50.00
B496, City Beneath the Sea _____ 50.00
B497, Rowan and Martin's Laugh-in ___ 20.00
B498, Daktari _____ 15.00
B499, Star Trek (TV series) _____ 15.00
B500, Barbie's around the World Trip ___ 11.00
B501, Love Bug _____ 3.00
B502, Banana Splits _____ 8.00
B503, Dark Shadows _____ 20.00
B504, Lancelot Link-Secret Chimp _____ 20.00
B505, Mission Impossible _____ 10.00
B506, $1,000,000 Duck _____ 15.00
B507, Planet of the Apes _____ 18.00
B508, Woody Woodpecker Show _____ 3.00
B509, Space Mouse, Knothead and
Splinter, Gabby Gator _____ 6.00
B510, Woody Woodpecker, Andy Panda,
Chilly Willy _____ 15.00

B511, Two Mouseketeers/Tom & Jerry,
Spike & Tyke, Droopy _____ 11.00
B512, Huckleberry Hound _____ 4.00
B513, Top Cat _____ 8.00
B514, Flintstones _____ 5.00
B515, Bullwinkle _____ 9.00
B516, Popeye _____ 4.00
B517, Disney on Parade _____ 4.00
B518, Beetle Bailey _____ 14.00
B519, Deputy Dawg _____ 10.00
B520, Pebbles and Bamm-Bamm _____ 3.00
B521, Cartoon Carnival _____ 10.00
B522, Woody Woodpecker _____ 10.00
B523, Walt Disney Characters _____ 12.00
B524, Mickey Mouse Club Mouseketeers _ 10.00
B525, Donald Duck _____ 5.00
B526, Mighty Mouse _____ 4.00
B527, Popeye _____ 4.00
B528, Mickey Mouse _____ 4.00
B529, Pluto _____ 4.00
B530, Goofy _____ 7.00
B531, Bugs Bunny _____ 12.00
B532, 101 Dalmations _____ 5.00
B533, Casper, The Friendly Ghost _____ 4.00
B534, Quick Draw McGraw _____ 8.00
B535, Secret Squirrel and Atom Ant _____ 8.00
B536, Peanuts _____ 3.00
B537, Blondie and Dagwood _____ 11.00
B538, Beep, Beep, The Road Runner _____ 4.00
B539, Dennis the Menace _____ 4.00
B540, Bobby the Bunny _____ 9.00
B541, Max and Moritz _____ 10.00
B542, Tin Tin and The Temple of the
Sun _____ 15.00
B543, Tin Tin and The Expedition to the
Moon _____ 20.00
B544, Snoopy and The Red Baron _____ 3.00
B545, Casper's Ghostland _____ 4.00
B546, Fantastic Voyage _____ 10.00
B547, Hardy Boys _____ 4.00
B548, Charlie Brown's Summer Fun _____ 4.00
B549, Bugs Bunny—Big Top Bunny _____ 3.00
B550, Shazam _____ 4.00
B551, Mickey Mouse in Clock Cleaners
with Donald Duck and Goofy _____ 5.00
B552, Hair Bear Bunch _____ 9.00
B553, Scooby Doo—That Snow Ghost _____ 4.00
B554, Fat Albert and Cosby Kids _____ 4.00
B555, Star Trek—Mr. Spock's Time Trek _ 3.00
B556, It's a Bird Charlie Brown _____ 9.00
B557, Kong _____ 6.00
B558, Apple's Way _____ 15.00
B559, 6 Million Dollar Man _____ 8.00
B560, Captain Kangaroo _____ 11.00
B563, Bazooka Joe _____ 15.00
B564, Curiosity Shop _____ 10.00
B565, Captain Kangaroo Show _____ 10.00
B566, New Zoo Revue _____ 10.00
B567, New Zoo Revue Two _____ 10.00
B568, Brady Bunch _____ 15.00
B569, Partridge Family _____ 10.00
B570, Beverly Hillbillies _____ 25.00
B571, Family Affair _____ 25.00
B572, Julia _____ 10.00

B573, Nanny and the Professor _____ 25.00
B574, Sam Sawyer I _____ 8.00
B574, Archie _____ 4.00
B575, Sam Sawyer II _____ 15.00
B576, Barbie's Great American Photo
Race _____ 10.00
B577, World of Little Kiddles _____ 10.00
B578, Herbie Rides Again _____ 5.00
B579, Land of the Lost _____ 8.00
B580, Tarzan of the Apes _____ 20.00
B581, Tom Corbett Space Cadet _____ 25.00
B581, Tom Corbett and the Secret from
Space (S5) _____ 20.00
B582, Steve Canyon and Crisis at Big
Thunder _____ 20.00
B583, Flash Gordon _____ 4.00
B583, Flash Gordon in the Planet Mongo
(G5) _____ 8.00
B584, Superman _____ 4.00
B585, Adventures of G.I. Joe _____ 10.00
B586, Happy Days _____ 4.00
B587, Big Blue Marble _____ 10.00
B588, Here's Lucy—Lucy and the
Astronauts _____ 25.00
B589, Gunsmoke _____ 25.00
B590, Hawaii Five-O _____ 10.00
B591, SEARCH _____ 13.00
B592, Partridge Family #2 _____ 40.00
B593, Adam-12 _____ 6.00
B594, Run Joe Run _____ 6.00
B595, Sigmond and the Sea Monsters _____ 10.00
B596, Waltons _____ 8.00
B597, Emergency _____ 8.00
B598, Kung Fu _____ 10.00
B605, Little Yellow Dinosaur _____ 10.00
B610, Butterflies _____ 5.00
B611, Wild Birds of North America _____ 4.00
B612, Wonders of the Deep _____ 6.00
B613, Battle of the Monsters _____ 35.00
B614, Wild Animals of the World _____ 6.00
B615, Strange Animals of the World _____ 8.00
B616, Performing Animals—St. Louis
Zoo _____ 4.00
B617, Children's Zoo _____ 12.00
B618, Wild Animals of Africa _____ 7.00
B619, Prehistoric Animals _____ 8.00
B620, Dogs and Cats _____ 15.00
B621, Sharks _____ 3.00
B628, Garden Flowers _____ 12.00
B629, Desert Wildflowers _____ 9.00
B630, Alpine Wildflowers _____ 10.00
B656, Moon Rockets and Guided
Missles _____ 15.00
B657, America's Man in Space _____ 10.00
B658, Man on the Moon—NASA's Apollo
Project _____ 8.00
B660, Aircraft Carrier in Action at Sea _____ 15.00
B661, South Pole, Conquest by Air _____ 15.00
B662, U.S. Spaceport, Fla. _____ 7.00
B663, Apollo Moon Landing _____ 10.00
B664, A Step into the Universe (special
nine-reel set) _____ 90.00
B670, Judo and Karate _____ 30.00
B671, Automobile Racing _____ 20.00

B672, Modern Aircraft		20.00
B673, Eddy Mercky		45.00
B675, Our Planet Earth—Geology		10.00
B676, Prehistoric Life—Paleontology		6.00
B677, Rocks and Minerals—Mineralogy		10.00
B678, Birds of the World—Ornthology		4.00
B679, Fish Life—Ichthyology		6.00
B680, Plant Kingdom—Botany		15.00
B681, Conquest of Space—Astronautics		8.00
B682, Matter and Energy—Physics		9.00
B684, Probing the Past—Archaeology		15.00
B685, History of Flight		6.00
B686, Balance of Nature—Ecology		20.00
B687, Exploring the Universe—Astronomy		20.00
B688, Insect World—Entomology		28.00
B700, F.B.I. Agent		50.00
B720, Hunters of the Plains		25.00
B721, Riders of the Desert (number was assigned but may not have been issued)		
B721, Indians of the Southwest		10.00
B722, Hunters of the Forests		25.00
B725, American Indian		6.00
B728, Winneotou Und Das Halbblut Apanatschi		40.00
B731, Winneotou		40.00
B747, Pan Am's 747		15.00
B750, Royal Canadian Mounted Police		12.00
B759, Eighth World Boy Scout Jamboree (number was assigned but may not have been issued)		
B760, World's Fair Brussels—1958		30.00
B761, World's Fairs of Yesteryear		35.00
B765, Movie Stars (number was assigned but may not have been issued)		
B766, TV Stars (number was assigned but may not have been issued)		
B767, Baseball Stars (number was assigned but may not have been issued)		
B770, Circus (number assigned but may not have been issued)		
B773, Airplanes of the World		15.00
B775, Ringling Bros. & Barnum & Bailey Circus		7.00
B776, Shipstads and Johnson's Ice Follies		25.00
B777, American Ballet Theater		30.00
B780, Coronation of Queen Elizabeth II		15.00
B785, World's Fair Brussels, 1958		35.00
B786, World's Fair Brussels—Pavilions of the Nations		35.00
B787, World's Fair Brussels—Gay Brussels		35.00
B788, World's Fair Brussels—General Sections		35.00
B789, World's Fair Brussels—International Sections		35.00
B790, War Between the States		20.00
B790, The Civil War		19.00
B792, World War I		20.00
B793, Famous People		15.00
B794, Old Time Trains		20.00
B795, Old Time Cars		10.00
B796, Old Time Ships		10.00
B797, Old Time Airplanes		24.00
B810, The Revolutionary War		7.00
B811, Forging a Nation 1787–1886		8.00
B812, Westward Expansion		13.00
B813, The 20th Century		5.00
B814, Landmarks of American History		Extremely rare
B840, Rare Coins		6.00
B841, Famous Stamps		10.00
B851, Noah's Ark		5.00
B852, Bible Heroes		3.00
B853, Moses and the Plagues of Egypt		3.00
B854, Moses and the Ten Commandments		5.00
B855, In the Beginning		5.00
B865, History of Flight (error, should be B685)		12.00
B870, Rudolph the Red Nosed Reindeer		10.00
B871, Little Drummer Boy		5.00
B875, Birth of Jesus		4.00
B876, Parables of Jesus		4.00
B877, Jesus Teaches Forgiveness		4.00
B878, Miracles of Jesus		4.00
B880, Easter Story		4.00
B882, Jesus Christ		4.00
B901, Seven Wonders of the World		5.00
B925, Queen Elizabeth visits Canada and the United States		50.00
B935, NCAA Track and Field Championships		35.00
B936, International Invitational Swimming and Diving Meet		35.00
B940, Little League World Series		27.00
B942, National Soap Box Derby		35.00
B943, Pendelton Round-up		15.00
B945, Hydroplane Races		25.00
B946, Moto-Cross Motorcycle Race		25.00
B947, Tournament of Thrills		25.00
B948, Automobile Racing, Phoenix 200		35.00
B949, World Bobsled Championships		35.00
B950, Ice Skating by Ron and Cindy Kauffman		35.00
B951, Football by Don Maynard		11.00
B952, Physical Fitness for Boys and Girls		15.00
B953, Baseball with the New York Mets		22.00
B954, Tennis with Dennis Ralston		30.00
B955, Surfing with Linda Benson		30.00
B956, Swimming with Don Schollander		40.00
B970, Speleogoy		30.00
B971, Alpinisme (Mountaineering)		35.00
B972, Skiing		30.00
BB432, Treasure Island		5.00
BB450, Mannix		20.00
BB451, Space 1999		15.00
BB452, Rookies		10.00
BB453, S.W.A.T.		8.00
BB454, Joe Forrester		10.00
C001, Greece		8.00
C003, Classical Greece		15.00
C004, Historical Island (Greece)		15.00
C005, Wedding of Don Juan Carlos and Princess Sophia, Athens, 1962		75.00
C025, The Amalfi Coast		14.00
C026, Sicily		14.00

C027, Dolomite Mountains, Italy _____ 14.00
C028, Florence _____ 14.00
C029, Rome _____ 6.00
C030, Venice _____ 10.00
C031, Naples and Mt. Vesuvius _____ 12.00
C035, Ancient Rome _____ 12.00
C036, Modern Rome _____ 12.00
C038, Verona-Vicenza-Como, The Adriatic Coast _____ 15.00
C039, South Tyrol _____ 15.00
C041, Ventimiglia to Genoa, the Riviera _____ 15.00
C042, Genoa to La Spezia, the Riviera _____ 15.00
C044, Lake Como _____ 15.00
C052, Cortina de Ampezzo _____ 15.00
C053, Sardinia _____ 15.00
C055, Sicily _____ 15.00
C057, Pompeii and Herculaneum _____ 15.00
C058, Island of Capri _____ 20.00
C059, The Coast of Amalfi _____ 15.00
C060, Milan _____ 15.00
C090, Malta _____ 15.00
C115, Principality of Monaco _____ 25.00
C125, The Bernese Oberland _____ 20.00
C126, Lugano, Switzerland _____ 12.00
C127, Swiss Alpine Passes _____ 12.00
C129, French Switzerland _____ 12.00
C130, St. Moritz-Davos-Klosters _____ 12.00
C133, Lausanne to Montreux _____ 12.00
C134, Lucerne _____ 12.00
C136, Zermatt and the Valais _____ 15.00
C139, Swissminiatur _____ 18.00
C141, Geneva _____ 12.00
C142, Locarno and Lake Maggiore _____ 12.00
C143, Lake Lugano (Switzerland) _____ 15.00
C165, Auverge (France) _____ 15.00
C166, Paris _____ 5.00
C167, Normandy _____ 10.00
C169, Brittany _____ 10.00
C170, The Chateau on the Loire _____ 15.00
C171, Alsace (France) _____ 15.00
C172, Basque Country (France) _____ 15.00
C173, Corsica, I'lle de Beaute _____ 20.00
C174, The Palace of Versailles _____ 10.00
C175, Marseille _____ 15.00
C177, The Louvre, Paris, Famous Paintings _____ 20.00
C178, The Louvre, Paris, Famous Sculpture _____ 20.00
C181, Chamonix and Mont Blanc (France) _____ 15.00
C184, Lourdes and Surroundings _____ 12.00
C185, Nice and the Riviera _____ 15.00
C186, Cannes and the Riviera _____ 15.00
C187, Coast Road of the Riviera _____ 15.00
C191, Brittany, The Atlantic Coast (France) _____ 12.00
C192, Lacs Alpins de France _____ 15.00
C197, Mont St. Michel _____ 15.00
C200, Orly Airport, Paris _____ 40.00
C202, An Evening in Paris _____ 20.00
C240, The Costa Brava (Spain) _____ 15.00
C241, Majorca and The Balearic Islands _____ 15.00
C242, Madrid _____ 10.00
C243, Seville _____ 12.00

C244, Granada, Costa del Sol (Spain) _____ 15.00
C245, Toledo and Old Castile _____ 15.00
C249, Galicia _____ 20.00
C251, Barcelona and Montserrat _____ 15.00
C252, Sitges Tarragone Poblet _____ 20.00
C253, de Valencia a Alicante _____ 20.00
C254, El Escorial—Valle de Los Caldos _____ 15.00
C255N, Spaans Stierengevecht (Spanish bullfight) _____ 25.00
C260, The Canary Islands _____ 20.00
C267, Estoril-Sintra (Portugal) _____ 15.00
C268, Porto-Minho _____ 20.00
C275, The Norfolk Broads _____ 15.00
C276, The River Thames (England) _____ 10.00
C277, London _____ 4.00
C278, The Isle of Man _____ 25.00
C279, Strolling in London _____ 20.00
C280, The Wedding of Princess Margaret _____ 35.00
C281, The Royal Navy and Royal Marines (England) _____ 25.00
C282, Madame Tussaud's Waxworks (England) _____ 20.00
C283, London Airport _____ 45.00
C284, Tower of London _____ 20.00
C285, Cornwall (England) _____ 15.00
C288, Canterbury and Kentish Coast (England) _____ 15.00
C289, Blackpool and the Illuminations _____ 20.00
C290, The Lake District _____ 20.00
C291, Coventry Cathedral (England) _____ 15.00
C292, Brighton to Hastings _____ 20.00
C293, Torquay _____ 20.00
C294, Devon _____ 20.00
C295, London Pageantry _____ 25.00
C296, Cathedrals of England _____ 15.00
C297, Cotswolds _____ 15.00
C298, Shakespeare Country _____ 15.00
C299, Dorset-Somerset-Wiltshire _____ 20.00
C301, Kent and Sussex _____ 20.00
C304, East Anglia _____ 20.00
C320, Great Britain _____ 10.00
C324, Channel Islands (England) _____ 15.00
C325, The Western Highlands (Scotland) _____ 15.00
C326, Edinburgh _____ 10.00
C327, Southern Scotland _____ 20.00
C329, Central Scotland _____ 20.00
C330F, Ecosse (Scotland) _____ 15.00
C335, South and Central Wales _____ 20.00
C336, Snowdonia and North Wales _____ 20.00
C338, North and Central Wales _____ 20.00
C340, Northern England _____ 15.00
C341, Southwest Countries-Erie (Ireland) _____ 20.00
C342, Donegal and West Coast, Ireland _____ 20.00
C344, Dublin & Surroundings _____ 20.00
C344, Dublin and East Coast _____ 25.00
C350, Castiles of Belgium _____ 25.00
C351, The Abbey of Orval _____ 25.00
C352, Semois Valley _____ 30.00
C353, The 1960 Ghent Flower Show _____ 35.00
C354, The Royal Wedding, Belgium (Civil Marriage) _____ 75.00
C355, The Royal Wedding, Belgium (Religious Marriage) _____ 75.00
C356, Royal Wedding of King Baudouin

and Queen Fabiola _____ 65.00
C357, Royal Family of Belgium _____ 65.00
C358, Brussels (Belgium) _____ 10.00
C361, Bruges (Belgium) _____ 12.00
C362N, Octoberfest
(Weze Oktoverfeestn) _____ 20.00
C364, Les Grottes De Remouchamps _____ 20.00
C364, Liege et Sa Province (Belgium) ____ 20.00
C365, Valley of the Meuse (Belgium) ____ 20.00
C366, Ghent _____ 25.00
C367, Antwerpen (Belgium) _____ 20.00
C368, The Ardennes _____ 25.00
C369N, Velgische Kust _____ 20.00
C373, Ronquieres Incline (Le Plan
Incline) _____ 25.00
C380, Chternach _____ 20.00
C381, Luxemburg _____ 15.00
C385, Tulip Time _____ 8.00
C387, North Sea Resorts _____ 20.00
C388, Amsterdam _____ 15.00
C389, The Zuiderzee _____ 15.00
C391, Den Haag and Scheveningen,
Holland _____ 15.00
C392, Madurodam, Miniature Town,
Holland _____ 15.00
C394, Windmills of Holland _____ 18.00
C400, Nederland (Netherlands) _____ 5.00
C405, The Moselle Valley (Germany) _____ 15.00
C406, The Main Valley (Germany) _____ 15.00
C407, The Rhine, Rudesheim to
Konigswinter _____ 15.00
C409, Bodensee, Germany _____ 20.00
C410, The Black Forest _____ 15.00
C411, Heidelberg and Neckar Valley _____ 15.00
C418, Berchtesgaden Country _____ 20.00
C419, Garmisch—Partenkirchen Country _ 15.00
C420, Munich _____ 10.00
C421, The Passion Play, Oberammergau _ 8.00
C422, Royal Castiles of Bavaria _____ 15.00
C424, Romantische Strasse _____ 15.00
C426, Bergstrasse and Odenwald _____ 15.00
C428, Helgoland and Nordfreisische
Bader _____ 15.00
C475, Jutland and Danish Isles _____ 18.00
C476, Copenhagen (Denmark) _____ 10.00
C477, Jutland (Denmark) _____ 15.00
C480, Denmark _____ 6.00
C490, Oslo _____ 10.00
C491, The Fjord Country _____ 12.00
C492, Bergen and Towns of Western
Norway _____ 15.00
C494, Land of the Midnight Sun _____ 20.00
C500, Norway _____ 20.00
C510, Stockholm _____ 25.00
C512, Norrland (Sweden) _____ 25.00
C516, Gothenburg to Svinesund, West
Coast (Sweden) _____ 20.00
C517, Skansen and Millesgarden
(Sweden) _____ 20.00
C518, Gotland (Sweden) _____ 20.00
C519, Varmland and Dalsland (Sweden) _ 20.00
C535, Laplanders and Their Reindeer _____ 30.00
C536, Turku and Its Castle (Finland) _____ 20.00
C537, Helsinki (Finland) _____ 20.00

C540, Finland _____ 20.00
C541, Hameenlinna to Aulanko
(Finland) _____ 25.00
C545, Inside Russia _____ 15.00
C635, Prague _____ 20.00
C635, Czechoslovakia _____ 20.00
C647, Salzburg (Austria) _____ 20.00
C648, Vienna (Austria) _____ 15.00
C649, Winter in Tyrol (Austria) _____ 20.00
C651, Grossglockner Tour (Austria) _____ 20.00
C652, Zillerthal, Tyrol (Austria) _____ 20.00
C654, Salzkammergut (Austria) _____ 20.00
C655, Tyrol (Austria) _____ 20.00
C665, Hungary _____ 25.00
C680, The Coast of Dalmatia _____ 20.00
C713, Tunisia _____ 25.00
C806, Istanbul _____ 15.00
C831, Jerusalem and the Holy Week _____ 12.00
D101F, *Sebastien et la Mary Morgane*
(French motion picture) _____ 20.00
D104N, Jetpiloot, 1971 _____ 25.00
D114N, Tachtuliegtuigen (Tactical Military
Jets) _____ 25.00
D118E, Secrets of the Sea _____ 25.00
D127, Safari _____ 25.00
F002, Mexico Tour _____ 20.00
F003, Mexico City _____ 15.00
F005, Acapulco _____ 4.00
F008, Lost Civilizations, Mexico _____ 10.00
F010, Mexico, the West Coast _____ 5.00
F018, Baja, California _____ 9.00
F019, Mexico _____ 4.00
FPX6, Fairy Tales (six-reel packet) _____ 22.00
G002, Rebus Game _____ 4.00
H1, Land of the Lost #2 _____ 5.00
H2, Dr. Shrinker _____ 6.00
H3, Elektra Woman _____ 8.00
H5, Horses _____ 12.00
H6, Animals of Our National Parks _____ 12.00
H7, Old Time San Francisco _____ 12.00
H8, Mr. Lincoln _____ 15.00
H9, New Mickey Mouse Club _____ 4.00
H11, Spiderman, The Amazing _____ 3.00
H13, Smithsonian Air and Space
Museum _____ 6.00
H14, Golden Book Favorites _____ 3.00
H15, Kings Island, Ohio _____ 7.00
H16, Sea World, San Diego #1 _____ 7.00
H18C, Montreal, Canada _____ 9.00
H19, Tomorrowland (Disney World) _____ 4.00
H20, Vacation Kingdom (Disney World) _ 4.00
H21, Main Street, USA (Disney World) _ 4.00
H22, Frontierland (Disney World) _____ 4.00
H23, Adventureland (Disney World) _____ 4.00
H24, Liberty Square (Disney World) _____ 5.00
H25, Fantasyland (Disney World) _____ 4.00
H26, The Rescuers (Disney) _____ 6.00
H29, Knott's Berry Farm #1, Calif. _____ 10.00
H30, Knott's Berry Farm #2, Calif. _____ 10.00
H38, Pete's Dragon (Disney) _____ 4.00
H39, Thor _____ 4.00
H43, Captain America _____ 4.00
H44, Iron Man _____ 4.00
H48, Seaquarium 1, Miami _____ 8.00

H49, Seaquarium 2, Miami _____ 8.00
H50, Silver Springs, Fla. _____ 3.00
H51, Smithsonian Museum of History and
Technology _____ 9.00
H52, Adventureland (Disneyland) _____ 9.00
H53, Circus World, Fla. _____ 6.00
H54, For the Love of Benji _____ 6.00
H56, Mister Magoo _____ 4.00
H57, New York City #1 _____ 4.00
H58, New York City #2 _____ 9.00
H59, San Diego Zoo #1 _____ 10.00
H60, San Diego Zoo #2 _____ 10.00
H61, San Diego Animal Park _____ 12.00
H62, Children's Zoo _____ 10.00
H63, Los Angeles, Calif. _____ 8.00
H64, Hollywood, Calif. _____ 8.00
H65, Yellowstone National Park #2 _____ 6.00
H66, Yellowstone National Park #1 _____ 6.00
H68, Smithsonian Museum of Natural
History _____ 8.00
H69, The Harlem Globetrotters _____ 5.00
H70, Badlands National Park, S.Dak. _____ 8.00
H73, Mount Rushmore, S.Dak. _____ 8.00
H74, Great Smoky Mountains, Tenn. and
N.C. _____ 6.00
H75, Sea World, Orlando, Fla. _____ 10.00
H76, Sea World, Ohio _____ 5.00
H77, The Bad News Bears, Breaking
Training _____ 4.00
H81, Universal Studios #2 _____ 8.00
H82, Sea World Shows _____ 4.00
H83, Grand Ole Opry, Nashville, Tenn. _____ 15.00
H92, Little Red Riding Hood _____ 5.00
J1, Buck Rogers _____ 4.00
J4, Busch Gardens, Dark Continent #1 _____ 4.00

View-Master, three-reel packet, H70 "Badlands National Park," type G5 without a logo at upper-left corner. Note the staple holes at the four corners where it was originally on a hanging card. This packet is MNO, with the original cellophane wrap. $8. (Gordon D. Hoffman Collection)

View-Master, three-reel packet, H83 "Grand Ole Opry, Nashville, Tennessee," type G5. $15. (Gordon D. Hoffman Collection)

J5, Busch Gardens, Dark Continent #2 _____ 5.00
J6, Busch Gardens, Animals and Birds,
Fla. _____ 10.00
J10, Grizzly Adams _____ 10.00
J11, M.A.S.H. _____ 10.00
J12, Pink Panther _____ 4.00
J13, Happy Days II _____ 4.00
J14, The Wiz _____ 6.00
J16, Las Vegas, The City, Nev. _____ 10.00
J17, Las Vegas, The Strip, Nev. _____ 10.00
J19, Welcome Back Kotter _____ 4.00
J20, Laverne and Shirley _____ 4.00
J21, Little Orphan Annie _____ 5.00
J22, Cat from Outer Space (Disney) _____ 4.00
J23, Godzilla _____ 4.00
J24, Guinness Book of Records _____ 10.00
J25, Return from Witch Mountain
(Disney) _____ 4.00
J26, Hulk, The Incredible _____ 4.00
J27, Sub Mariner _____ 4.00
J28, Tweety and Sylvester _____ 4.00
J29, Mickey Mouse Jubilee _____ 3.00
J30, Wolf Man _____ 5.00
J31, Queen Mary, Long Beach, Calif. _____ 10.00
J32, Thailand _____ 6.00
J33, Taiwan _____ 12.00
J34, Hong Kong _____ 12.00
J46, Rio de Janiero _____ 6.00
J47, Close Encounters of the Third Kind _____ 9.00
J50, Weeki Wache, Fla. _____ 5.00
J51, Benji's Very Own Christmas Story _____ 4.00
J53, Naval Aviation Museum, Fla. _____ 5.00
J60, Dumbo (Disney) _____ 10.00
J63, Monkeys _____ 5.00
J65, Snakes _____ 8.00
J70, Super Star Barbie _____ 15.00
J75, Tutankhamen, Boy King _____ 8.00
J76, Knights in Armor _____ 15.00

J78, Superman, the Movie _____ 9.00
J79, United States Spaceport, Kennedy Space Center, Fla. _____ 4.00
K1, Main Street (Disneyland) _____ 5.00
K2, Frontierland (Disneyland) _____ 5.00
K3, New Orleans Square (Disneyland) _____ 4.00
K4, Adventureland (Disneyland) _____ 4.00
K5, Fantasyland (Disneyland) _____ 4.00
K6, Disney Laugh 'N Learn #1 _____ 4.00
K7, Disney Laugh 'N Learn #2 _____ 4.00
K8, Disney Laugh 'N Learn #3 _____ 4.00
K9, Disney Laugh 'N Learn #4 _____ 4.00
K10, Disney Laugh 'N Learn #5 _____ 4.00
K11, Disney Laugh 'N Learn #6 _____ 4.00
K15, Ruby Falls Inside Lookout Mountain Caves _____ 10.00
K16, Tomorrowland (Disneyland) _____ 5.00
K18, Ghost Town and Maggie Valley, N.C. _____ 10.00
K19, San Diego/Balboa Park _____ 10.00
K20, Romper Room _____ 4.00
K22, Dr. Strange _____ 3.00
K23, Buenos Aires _____ 6.00
K24, Malaysia _____ 8.00
K25, Singapore _____ 6.00
K26, The Muppets _____ 4.00
K27, Scenes from Jim Henson's *The Muppet Movie* _____ 4.00
K29, Caracas _____ 8.00
K31, Spiderman #2 _____ 4.00
K35, The Black Hole (Disney) _____ 6.00
K36, Fantastic Four _____ 4.00
K37, Winnie the Pooh and the Blustery Day _____ 4.00
K38, Circus _____ 10.00
K39, Circus Animals _____ 10.00
K40, Argentina _____ 10.00
K41, Brazil _____ 6.00
K42, Las Vegas #1 _____ 10.00
K43, Las Vegas #2 _____ 10.00
K44, Yosemite #2 _____ 10.00
K46, Meteor (motion picture) _____ 4.00
K48C, Ontario Place, Toronto, Canada _____ 14.00
K49, Jakarta _____ 6.00
K50, Indonesia _____ 8.00
K57, Star Trek, The Motion Picture _____ 4.00
K66, Fangface _____ 3.00
K67, Mork and Mindy _____ 4.00
K68, Moonraker (James Bond) _____ 8.00
K69, Walt Disney's Snow White and the Seven Dwarfs _____ 4.00
K71, KISS _____ 10.00
K76, Eight Is Enough _____ 4.00
K77, Dragons and Other Creatures _____ 8.00
K79, John Travolta _____ 4.00
K88, Raggedy Ann and Andy _____ 4.00
K89, The Thorne Rooms, The Art Institute of Chicago _____ 20.00
K90, Pope John Paul II Visits the United States _____ 8.00
K91, Stars Hall of Fame, Orlando, Fla. _____ 10.00
K92, Monterey Peninsula, Carmel-Big Sur, Calif. _____ 10.00
K94, Marriott's Great America _____ 17.00

L1, *Can't Stop The Music* (motion picture) _____ 7.00
L2, Bon Voyage Charlie Brown _____ 4.00
L6, Flintstones _____ 4.00
L7, Spider-Woman _____ 4.00
L9, Muppets Audition Night _____ 4.00
L12, Guadalajara, Mexico _____ 12.00
L14, CHIPS _____ 8.00
L15, Buck Rogers _____ 8.00
L16, Battle Beyond the Stars _____ 12.00
L17, The Dukes of Hazzard _____ 4.00
L18, Houston Astros _____ 12.00
L19, Philadelphia Phillies _____ 30.00
L20, New York Yankees _____ 20.00
L22, Minnesota Twins _____ 20.00
L23, Los Angeles Dodgers _____ 15.00
L25, Muppets Go Hawaiian _____ 4.00
L26, Legend of the Lone Ranger _____ 9.00
L27, Jetsons _____ 5.00
L28, Garfield _____ 11.00
L29, Fox and the Hound _____ 11.00
L31, Batman _____ 11.00
L32, Vote-I Go Pogo _____ 6.00
L33, Cheap Trick _____ 15.00
L46, Superman II _____ 15.00
M1, Museum of Science and Industry, Chicago _____ 14.00
M2, Colleen Moore's Fairy Castle and the U-505 _____ 40.00
M3, Sea World, Mission Bay Park, San Diego, Calif. _____ 4.00
M4, Sea World Shows and Animals, Calif., Ohio, Fla. _____ 4.00
M7, Great Muppet Caper _____ 3.00
M8, Liberty Square, Disney World _____ 4.00
M10, Bugs Bunny and Road Runner Show _____ 7.00
M19, The Dukes of Hazzard, Packet No. 2 _____ 3.00
M36, Era of the Space Shuttle _____ 15.00
N5, Monkey Jungle, Miami, Fla. _____ 5.00
R851, Disneyland Main Street, USA _____ 12.00
R852, Disneyland—Frontierland _____ 12.00
S889, Great Smoky Mountains, Tenn. and N.C. _____ 10.00
T100, Isis _____ 8.00

GAF TALKING VIEW-MASTER THREE-REEL SETS

In the early 1970s, GAF View-Master introduced the GAF Talking View-Master. This was an attempt to regain growth in the toy market. Intended for children, the viewer was bulky and clumsy to use. Getting a reel started properly was a frustrating experience, and once started, the sound quality was poor and the translucent record attached to the back of the reels made light diffusion difficult. Even with these problems, GAF manufactured the viewer and three-reel sets until about 1981. Collector interest for the GAF Talking View-Master is mixed. Talking sets rarely sell for very much. Completeness and condition are the key elements. The sets came in a colorful slipcase box with a molded tray for the reels and a story booklet. Most complete sets in excellent condition sell for $3 to $6. Listed here are the known sets. These are not to be confused with the improved Talking View-Master introduced in the mid-1980s.

AVA202, Disneyland
AVA646, New York City
AVA791, National Gallery of Art
AVA801, Washington, D.C.
AVA955, Walt Disney World
AVA998, Scenic USA
AVB096, Africa
AVB145, Grand Tour of Europe
AVB178, Vatican City
AVB254, Inside China Today
AVB300, Snow White and the Seven Dwarfs
AVB308, Sleeping Beauty
AVB310, Little Red Riding Hood
AVB311, Pinocchio
AVB314, Jack and the Beanstalk
AVB316, Sword in the Stone
AVB317, Goldilocks
AVB318, Cinderella
AVB321, Charlotte's Web
AVB322, Pippi Longstockings
AVB323, Frankenstein
AVB340, Tom Sawyer
AVB342, Robin Hood
AVB343, Huckleberry Finn
AVB360, Alice in Wonderland
AVB361, Wizard of Oz
AVB362, Winnie the Pooh
AVB363, Jungle Book
AVB365, Aristocats
AVB369, Winnie the Pooh and Tigger Too
AVB372, Peter Pan
AVB374, Gulliver's Travels
AVB376, Mary Poppins
AVB380, Christmas Carol
AVB382, Night Before Christmas
AVB383, Christmas Story
AVB400, Bambi
AVB405, Smokey Bear
AVB406, Raggedy Ann
AVB410, Mother Goose Rhymes
AVB411, The ABC's
AVB425, Heidi
AVB480, Lassie
AVB485, Flipper
AVB500, Barbie's Around the World Trip
AVB501, Love Bug
AVB507, Planet of the Apes
AVB508, Woody Woodpecker
AVB511, Tom and Jerry
AVB514, Flintstones

AVB516, Popeye
AVB520, Flintstones/Pebbles and Bamm Bamm
AVB525, Donald Duck
AVB526, Mickey Mouse
AVB528, Mickey Mouse
AVB531, Bugs Bunny
AVB532, 101 Dalmations
AVB536, Peanuts
AVB538, Beep, Beep, The Road Runner
AVB544, Snoopy and Red Baron
AVB545, Casper's Ghostland
AVB548, Charlie Brown's Summer Fun
AVB549, Bugs Bunny, Circus Star
AVB551, Mickey Mouse in "Clock Cleaners"
AVB552, The Hair Bear Bunch
AVB553, Scooby Doo
AVB555, Star Trek
AVB556, It's a Bird, Charlie Brown
AVB558, Apple's Way
AVB559, Six Million Dollar Man
AVB563, Bazooka Joe
AVB567, New Zoo Revue II
AVB568, The Brady Bunch
AVB574, Archie
AVB576, Barbie's Great American Photo Race
AVB578, Herbie Rides Again
AVB584, Superman
AVB585, Adventures of G.I. Joe
AVB586, Happy Days
AVB589, Gunsmoke
AVB590, Hawaii Five-O
AVB593, Adam 12
AVB595, Sigmund and the Sea Monsters
AVB596, The Waltons
AVB598, Kung Fu
AVB605, The Little Yellow Dinosaur
AVB612, Wonders of the Deep
AVB616, Wild Animals of the World

Talking View-Master, three-reel set, AVB568 "The Brady Bunch," $5.

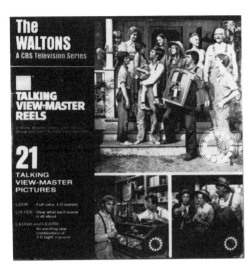

Talking View-Master, three-reel set, (AVB596), "The Waltons." $5.

AVB617, Children's Zoo
AVB658, Project Apollo
AVB676, Paleontology—Prehistoric Life
AVB678, Birds
AVB682, Physics
AVB687, Astronomy—Exploring the Universe
AVB853, Moses
AVB870, Rudolph, the Red-Nosed Reindeer
AVB871, Little Drummer Boy
AVB901, Seven Wonders of the World
TB324, Dracula
TB344, Holly Hobbie
TB392, King Kong
TB451, Space 1999
TB583, Flash Gordon
TH1, Land of the Lost
TH11, Spiderman
TH26, The Rescuers
TH56, Mr. Magoo
TJ19, Welcome Back, Kotter
TJ23, Godzilla
TVB452, Rookies
TVB453, S.W.A.T.

SPECIAL VIEW-MASTER SETS

The following are the most often encountered sets. Collectors prefer complete sets, but in some cases parts of sets were sold separately.

Cactus and Succulent Plants. Set includes twenty reels (C1 to C20), plus the book *Succulent Plants* by W. Taylor Marshall.

Complete set: $225.00
Individual reels: each 4–8.00
Book: 90.00

Mushrooms in Their Natural Habitats. Set includes thirty-three reels (MU1 to MU33), plus 626-page hard-bound book by Alexander H. Smith.

Complete set: 275.00
Individual reels: each 4–8.00
Book: 90.00

Alpine Wild Flowers. Set includes ten reels (WF1 to WF10), plus cloth-bound book *Alpine Wild Flowers of Western United States* by Howard R. Stagner.

Complete set: 75.00
Individual reels: each 3–5.00
Book: 45.00

Chinese Art. Set includes four hard-cover cloth-bound volumes with slip cases, each with forty to forty-four reels in pocket folios in front and back covers, by Sir Harry M. Garner and Margaret Medley, 1969. Stereo photography by William B. Gruber, the inventor of the View-Master System and Rupert P. Leach, senior photographer for View-Master. These sets were originally offered with the Model D Focusing Viewer on a stand plus a storage chest. Recently the remaining unsold stock of this set was purchased by Reel 3-D Enterprises and is still available minus the storage chests.

Complete set: 165.00
Books only: 95.00
Model D viewer: 85.00
Full color descriptive brochure
with special sample reel: 2.00

View-Master Theater Tour. Set includes fifteen reels (RP1001 to RP1015) plus booklet and a single-lens projector in a plastic canister.

Complete set: 20.00

Disneyland. Set includes seven reels (RP1016 to RP1022) plus a standard viewer in a plastic canister.

Complete set: 20.00

GAF View-Master Travel Theatre. Set includes ten reels (RP1030 to RP1039) plus a single-lens projector in a plastic canister.

Complete set: 20.00

Walt Disney Character Theatre (Disney Favorites). Stock #2425, set includes ten reels (RP1040 to RP1049) plus a single-lens projector in a plastic canister.

Complete set: 20.00

ABC Wide World of Sports. Set includes nine reels (RP1050 to RP1058) plus a standard viewer in a plastic canister.

Complete set: 100.00

Disney Theatre. Set includes ten reels (RP1060 to RP1069) plus a single-lens projector in a plastic canister.

Complete set: 20.00

'Round the World in 70 Pictures. Set includes ten reels (RP1100 to RP1109) plus a standard viewer in a plastic canister.

Complete set: 20.00

Charlie Brown Theatre. Set includes ten reels (RP1141 to RP1150) plus a single-lens projector in a plastic canister.

Complete set: 20.00

America's Bicentennial Celebration. Set includes ten reels (RP1157 to RP1166) plus a standard red/white/blue viewer in a plastic canister.

Complete set: 20.00

Sears World Library. Set includes eighteen reels (RP2002 to RP2019) plus a standard viewer in a plastic canister.

Complete set: 20.00

America's Scenic Wonders. Set includes ten reels (RP2101 to RP2110) plus a standard viewer in a plastic canister.

Complete set: 20.00

Animals of the World. Set includes seven reels (RP2111 to RP2117) plus a standard viewer in a plastic canister.

Complete set: 15.00

Disney Cartoon Favorites. Stock #2729, set includes seven reels (RP2151 to RP2157) plus a standard viewer in a plastic canister.

Complete set: 15.00

Disney Fairy Tales. Set includes nine reels (RP2161 to RP2169) plus a standard viewer in a plastic canister.

Complete set: 18.00

Children's Fables. Stock #2731, set includes eight reels (RP2171 to RP2178) plus a standard viewer in a plastic canister.

Complete set: 16.00

Disneyland, the Magic Kingdom. Set includes seven reels (RP2181 to RP2187) plus a standard viewer in a plastic canister.

Complete set: 20.00

Television Cartoon Favorites. Set includes seven reels (RP2191 to RP2197) plus a standard viewer in a plastic canister.

Complete set: 15.00

Instructional Sports. Set includes seven reels (RP2221 to RP2227) plus a standard viewer in a plastic canister.

Complete set: 60.00

The Magic Kingdom. Set includes seven reels (RP2231 to RP2237) plus a standard viewer in a plastic canister.

Complete set: 15.00

Fairy Tales. Set includes seven reels (RP3001 to RP3007) plus a standard viewer in a plastic canister.

Complete set: 15.00

Cartoon Favorites. Set includes seven reels (RP3011 to RP3017) plus a standard viewer in a plastic canister.

Complete set: 15.00

Disney Favorites. Set includes seven reels (RP3021 to RP3027) plus a standard viewer in a plastic canister.

Complete set: 15.00

It's Fun, Charlie Brown. Set includes eight reels (RP3071 to RP3078) plus a standard viewer in a plastic canister.

Complete set: 15.00

Old Time Disney Favorites. Set includes seven reels (RP3081 to RP3087) plus a standard viewer in a plastic canister.

Complete set: 15.00

Disney Fairy Tales. Set includes nine reels (RPB3161 to RPB3169) plus a standard viewer in a plastic canister.

Complete set: 15.00

Project-A-Show Canisters. From the early 1970s into the early 1980s, GAF View-Master offered a number of sets collectively called "Project-A-Show." These sets usually included a set or sets of reels usually with an RP prefix. Also included was a single-lens projector and the current standard viewer. Subjects included Hanna-Barbera characters (Huckleberry Hound, Flintstones, and so on), Disney characters, travel scenes and animals. Complete sets in special canisters have limited collector interest and usually are offered from $10 to $15 per set.

View-Master "Naval Aviation Training Division" reel with special United States Navy/Transfilm envelope. $20–25 each.

WORLD WAR II MILITARY TRAINING REELS

The following are the known military training sets. The reels are usually buff or light beige and are hand lettered. These are rarely found as single reels and only a few sets have had recorded sales.

"Stereoscopic Range Estimator." Naval Aviation Training Division, Bureau of Aeronautics, United States Navy. The set is known in three sizes.

50-reel boxed set, reels s1-s25 and t1-t25 in a blue box _____ 1000.00

100-reel boxed set, reels s1-s50 and t1-t50 in a blue box with two Model B viewers _____ 2000.00

150-reel boxed set, reels s1-s75 and t1-t75 in a blue box with two Model B viewers _____ 3000.00

"Fixed Gunnery Deflection." Specification 24900, Order No. 44-6482-AF, W33-038 AC-3010, twenty reels of German and Japanese planes (models) with sight rings. Photography by Transfilm Inc., New York City, 1944 in a khaki green box _____ 600.00

"Ship Identificiation." Twenty-seven reels of models of German and Japanese ships, "Study No. 1-21," "Test No. 1-3" and "Night Study No. 1-3." This set is known without a box, but it is assumed they were originally in a box _____ 500.00

Army Air Forces "Cones of Fire." At least nine reels without numbers, AAF Specification No. 24908, Order No. 44-6535-AF, W33-038-AC 3039. Photography and development by Three Dimension Co., Chicago, Ill., 1944. No known box _____ 450.00

OTHER 3-D COMMERCIAL PRODUCTS

From 1946 to about 1960, there were a number of products introduced using 3-D photography. View-Master and Tru-Vue were the primary makers. The following are some of those most often encountered by collectors.

Radex

This company issued a number of six-card sets with a plastic viewer. Most of the sets deal with children's subjects and overall the stereo photography is very good. Most sets examined were made in the mid-1950s. Complete sets in the box with the viewer in excellent condition sell for $40 to $50.

Realist

The David White Co. licensed the making of sets using their 35-mm system (Stereo Realist). Most of those examined are advertising or special promo sets. The most interesting is the fifty-view set made of President Eisenhower's Inauguration in 1952. This set comes in a red/white and blue presentation box with a plastic viewer. The set usually sells in the $200 to $300 range. The best advertising sets issued show the 1951 General Motors and Ford Motor Co. autos. Sets vary in quality.

Stori-Views

These sets usually feature children's stories and religious themes. They were sold in a number

Radex, set of color transparencies, "Paul Revere's Ride."
A set of six in the box with plastic viewer, ca. 1956. $45.
(Gordon D. Hoffman Collection)

of set sizes with a plastic viewer. Most twelve-card sets sell in the $10 to $15 range.

View-Master Look-Alikes

Meopta Reels

The Meopta Company of Czechoslovakia has never been fully investigated. They made View-Master format reels from the late 1950s into the early 1970s. The reels can be used in a View-Master viewer. Each reel is numbered, titled, and unlike View-Master there usually is a credit to the photographer. They used Gottwaldov color film and quality tends to vary. Most or all were issued with simple folder booklets and come in attractive pastel envelopes. They are uncommon in the United States. They are of interest because Meopta offered reel subjects of countries not found on the View-Master reels. Meopta made an extensive series on towns and resort areas in Eastern Europe including Czechoslovakia, Bulgaria, Yugoslavia and Russia. They also offered views of exotic countries like Senegal and Mongolia plus a series of Australia and Japan. Most reels sell in the $4 to $7 range. The viewers are scarce and usually bring from $25 to $30 each.

Stereo-Rama

Another View-Master look-alike, Stereo-Rama were made in Italy. They offered views of pinup

Pixie Views (Stori-Views), #SL-49, "Zoo Animals," in three-card hanging pack, sold by The Toy House. $10. (Gordon D. Hoffman Collection)

models and female nudes. The reels are usually orange and vary in quality. Most of the nude reels sell in the $10 to $15 range.

Other 3-D Visual Products

Since 1946, there have been hundreds of 3-D products offered. The most commonly encountered are anaglyphs. This is a printing process using filters to separate the stereo planes. Usually anaglyph filters are red and a bluish green. When a person reads the anaglyph with corresponding filtered glasses, he gets a 3-D effect. A number of magazines, dozens of comic books and many food and cereal premiums have used anaglyphs. *3D Movie Magazine* was published in at least two issues in 1953 and featured full-page anaglyphs of movie stars, including Marilyn Monroe.

More recently several anaglyphic products have been used in advertising promotions. In 1982, McDonald's restaurants used a "3-D Happy Meal" box with glasses and side panels reproducing antique views. There were at least five different boxes issued in selected cities. The glasses were in the shape of the famous "golden arches." Much scarcer is the 3-D anaglyphic promotion used by Burgerville USA late in 1986. It featured boxes, posters, tray liners and special 3-D glasses in their '3-D Meal

A Meopta reel, showing the envelope and single sheet folded "booklet." Made in Czechoslovakia, the Meopta reels can be viewed in View-Master viewers.

3D Movie Magazine, *vol. 1, no. 2, with glasses; featured full-page anaglyph of Marilyn Monroe, October 1953. $60.*

Asahi Trading Co., X-Graph, 3-D lenticular postcard featuring scene from Disney's ''Snow White and the Seven Dwarfs.'' Hundreds of different X-Graphs were imported by Asahi in a variety of subjects in sizes up to 12" by 16". These can be seen in 3-D without special glasses or viewers. (Gordon D. Hoffman Collection)

Deal' promotion. These were only available in Oregon and Washington states.

Also collectible are lenticular or X-Graphs, most commonly found in postcard size, but they were made up to 12" by 16" for framing. In recent years there have been several commercial ventures featuring holograms. These 3-D images can be viewed without special glasses or a stereoscope. All of these items are of recent vintage but are a collectible part of the 3-D heritage begun more than 150 years ago.

GLOSSARY

Albumen print: The primary type of photographic paper print used from the mid-1850s to the late 1890s had an emulsion of light-sensitive chemicals in a base of albumen (egg whites). These are recognized by yellow-brown to deep-brown tones.

Artistic mount: Ranging from 4″ by 7″ to as large as 5″ by 7″, this was a popular mount size from the mid-1870s to about 1890. They also are called cabinet or oversize mounts.

Backlist: The listing of views on the backs of mounts. This was a common practice of regional or local photographers from about 1860 to 1890.

Bent between prints: A condition of a stereo view mount where the mount has been creased vertically down the center between the pairs.

Blindstamp: An impression, usually at the edge of the mount, with a photographer's logo or name. Commonly encountered examples include E. and H. T. Anthony's *EA* in a circle, *D. Barnum, London Stereoscopic Co.* and *J. Elliott.* This was a common practice in the United States and Europe in the 1850s and 1860s.

Boudoir mount: Some dealers use this to identify cabinet or artistic mounts, but this type of mount is usually 5″ by 8″ and was not used in stereo view production.

Cabinet mount: (*See* artistic mount.) There is no preference, and the descriptions and usage are interchangeable.

Card: (*See also* Mount). This is the common word to describe all various stereo mounts, usually made of several thicknesses of laminated thick paper.

Copy view: From nearly the beginning of stereo view popularity in the late 1850s and up to about 1905, original stereo views were photographically copied and usually put onto cheap-quality card mounts. They usually appear without a photographer or publisher credit, and commonly are known as "American Series," "American Scenery," "Popular Series" and so forth. In most cases they are worth only a fraction of the value of the originals.

Curved mount (or warped mount): These first became popular in the mid-1880s. The mount (3½″ by 7″ thick card stock) was warped deliberately. It became common practice after 1890.

Domed print: Many stereo view publishers trimmed the pairs with curved or domed tops. This was the best method for trimming out flaws that appear at the edges of the negatives. It also gives the views an aesthetically pleasing appearance.

Fancy back: Many photographers and publishers embellished their stereo mounts with attractive graphic designs. Of special note are the backs of views by such photographers as A. F. Styles (Burlington, Vermont), Jackson Brothers (Omaha), A. A. Hart (Sacramento) and Charles Weitfle (Central City, Colorado). London Stereoscopic Company and D. Barnum had fancy designs in pre-1860 views, and E. and H. T. Anthony used a fancy back for their gelatin-bromide series. Although attractive, they rarely add to the current market value.

Flat mount: Any stereo view mount made prior to the late 1880s is flat (nonwarped). This term should not be confused with a view that is "flat" visually (without stereo effect). Mounts before 1860 are usually of a thinner stock than later mounts.

Flat view: Do not confuse flat view with "flat mount," as this refers to a view without

Untitled scenic study by Jackson Brothers, Omaha, Nebr., ca. 1867. Note the fancy back imprint. (John Weiler Collection)

stereo effect. Views without stereo effect usually are of less value than a view with the correct effect.

Folded mount: Damage done when the mount is bent or creased between the paired prints.

Foxing, foxed: Small brown spots or stains on the prints or mount caused by a mold, resulting from contamination of the adhesive (usually wheat paste) or the paper.

Gelatin print: The light-sensitive base chemical for photographic prints used from the mid-1880s to about 1910. The prints are characterized by a shiny finish and often appear yellowed.

Glue streaked, spotted: This is damage that appears as light or dark shadows on a print. It is believed to be caused by a mold in the adhesive, which was usually wheat paste. The streaks often detract from the viewing effect and thus reduce the value.

Instantaneous: Early attempts (1850s–1860s) to photograph moving objects without blurring. New emulsion formulations applied to glass plates allowed photographers to use faster exposure times and "freeze" the ac-

tion. Subjects no longer had to remain perfectly still for extended periods of time.

Litho, lithoprint, lithograph: A stereo view printed with lithographic stones. The views are printed directly to the mount and have tiny spots or dots. These were printed in large quantities from the mid-1890s until about 1915 as a low-cost alternative to the regular photo views. The lithos are usually in color. Although they often are attractive, they have very little collector value or interest.

Mount: The card stock used in stereo views.

Oversize mount: (*See* Artistic mount.)

Photographica: The word used to describe all types of photographic collectibles as a whole, including cameras, negatives and prints.

Pirated view: (*See* Copy view.)

Print: The photographic images in pairs for stereoscopic viewing.

Revenue stamp: To help finance the Civil War, an excise tax was levied on all photographic images from September 1, 1864, to August 1, 1866. The stamps were affixed at the time of purchase to the reverse of the card mounts.

The photographer or seller was required to cancel the stamp with ink, either by hand stamp or rubber stamp. This is a good way of dating a view.

Round-cornered mount: About 1870, the corners of the stereo mounts began to be rounded. Square-cornered mounts continued a little longer in Europe. Some collectors specialize in pre-1870 square-cornered flat-mount views. These are not necessarily more valuable than post-1870 views.

Silver print: These are images made using silver as the primary metallic base element, and were the type of print used in black-and-white photography from about 1910 to the present. Most Keystone views are silver prints and are characterized by deep black tones.

Square-cornered mount: (*See also* Round-cornered mount.) Stereo view card mounts had square corners from the 1850s to about 1870 in the United States. They continued in use in Europe into the early 1880s.

Standard-size mount: (*See also* Artistic mount.) In the 1850s the mounts were approximately $3\frac{1}{4}''$ by $6\frac{7}{8}''$. After 1860, 7'' became the standard width, and after 1870 the standard size was approximately $3\frac{1}{2}''$ by 7''.

Stereo view: This is the common name for a mounted pair of stereoscopic prints. Other usages include stereogram, stereograph and stereoscopic view.

Stereopticon, Stereopticon views: This is an incorrect word to describe stereoscopes or stereo views. A stereopticon is a double magic lantern used to bring two images one after the other onto a screen by light projection (dissolve). This word has nothing to do with stereoscopy or the 3-D effect. It is incorrect and should not be used when describing the topics in this book. Unfortunately, it is used by uninformed dealers and some collectors.

Stereoscopy: This is the science and study of 3-D imaging.

Stereoscope (stereoscopic viewer): This is an optical instrument designed for viewing stereo pairs (views). Hundreds of different designs have been manufactured since 1849. Most common is the Holmes-Bates ''skeleton'' stereoscope with a focusing slide and simple hood.

Toning (silvering): This is a condition often found on post-1890 views where the silver salts in the emulsion have begun to break down, resulting in a dark blotchy effect or a reflective metallic finish on the prints.

Vignetted, vignetting: This was a popular way to single out the main subject in a stereo view. When the view was printed, light was blocked out around the outside edges, thus giving a white border. This often was used by E. and H. T. Anthony and others when making portraits and scenes from the late 1850s into the 1880s. Vignetting is less common in post-1890 views. It often lessens the overall stereo effect because it eliminates the background.

View: (*See* Stereo view.)

Viewer: (*See* Stereoscope.) This is an interchangeable term.

Warped mount: (*See* Curved mount.)

INDEX